Pierre America (Ed.)

ECOOP '91
European Conference
on Object-Oriented
Programming

Geneva, Switzerland, July 15-19, 1991
Proceedings

Springer-Verlag
Berlin Heidelberg New York
London Paris Tokyo
Hong Kong Barcelona
Budapest

Series Editors

Gerhard Goos
GMD Forschungsstelle
Universität Karlsruhe
Vincenz-Priessnitz-Straße 1
W-7500 Karlsruhe, FRG

Juris Hartmanis
Department of Computer Science
Cornell University
Upson Hall
Ithaca, NY 14853, USA

Volume Editor

Pierre America
Philips Research Laboratories
P.O.Box 80.000, 5600 JA Eindhoven, The Netherlands

CR Subject Classification (1991): D.2.2, D.3.2, H.2.4

ISBN 3-540-54262-0 Springer-Verlag Berlin Heidelberg New York
ISBN 0-387-54262-0 Springer-Verlag New York Berlin Heidelberg

© Springer-Verlag Berlin Heidelberg 1991
Printed in Germany

Printing and binding: Druckhaus Beltz, Hemsbach/Bergstr.
2145/3140-543210 - Printed on acid-free paper

Lecture Notes in Computer Science 512

Edited by G. Goos and J. Hartmanis

Advisory Board: W. Brauer   D. Gries   J. Stoer

Preface

This volume constitutes the proceedings of the fifth European Conference on Object-Oriented Programming, ECOOP, held in Geneva, Switzerland, July 15–19, 1991. Previous ECOOP conferences were held in Paris (France), Oslo (Norway), Nottingham (England), and (jointly with OOPSLA) in Ottawa (Canada). Next year's ECOOP is planned to take place in the Netherlands.

From their beginning, the ECOOP conferences have been very successful as a forum of high scientific quality where the newest developments connected to object-oriented techniques could be discussed, and we are confident that this year's conference will continue this tradition. Over the last few years object-oriented technology has quickly gained widespread use and considerable popularity. In parallel with this, the field has matured scientifically. Fortunately, there is still a lot of room for new ideas and for hot debates over fundamental issues, as will become clear from these proceedings.

The 22 papers in this volume were selected by the programme committee from 129 submissions. The only selection criterion was the quality of the papers themselves; there was no desired distribution over subject fields or over countries. The paper selection was a hard task, and many good papers had to be rejected because of space limitations. The members of the programme committee and the other referees invested a large effort in this, and they more than deserve my sincere thanks. Of course, I also thank the authors of the submitted papers: without them there would be no proceedings.

Apart from the presentation of the selected papers, the conference also offers tutorials, workshops, invited lectures, and a panel. I thank the organizers and participants for their contributions. Further thanks are due to Eugene Fiume, who designed the ECOOP '91 graphic; to the organizers of the TOOLS conference and the conference co-sponsors for the help with mailing; to the organizers of previous ECOOP conferences (particularly Steve Cook and Gillian Lovegrove) for their help and advice; to Liliane Noël, the conference secretary; to the local organization team, Eduardo Casais, Laurent Dami, Betty Junod, Vicki de Mey, Xavier Pintado, Serge Renfer, and Marc Stadelmann; to the student helpers, Adriana Fernandez and Maria Marina Zouridis; and to Frank Stoots, who organized the programme committee meeting. All these people were essential in making ECOOP such a lively and stimulating conference.

May 1991

Pierre America
ECOOP '91 Programme Chair

Organization

Conference Chair:	Dennis Tsichritzis (Switzerland)
Programme Chair:	Pierre America (The Netherlands)
Organizing Chair:	Oscar Nierstrasz (Switzerland)
North American Coordinator:	Karl Lieberherr (USA)

Tutorial Organization

CHOOSE (Swiss Group for OO Systems and Environments)

Sponsor

The Centre Universitaire d'Informatique of the University of Geneva.

Co-sponsoring Organizations

SI (Swiss Informaticians Society)
GI (German Computer Society)
OCG (Austrian Computer Society)
AFCET (French Computer Society)
Hewlett-Packard, SA
IBM, Suisse
Georg Heeg Smalltalk-80-Systems

Programme Committee

Pierre America	Philips Research, The Netherlands
Bruce Anderson	University of Essex, United Kingdom
François Bancilhon	Altaïr, France
Jean Bézivin	Université de Nantes, France
Luca Cardelli	DEC SRC, USA
Joëlle Coutaz	LGI/IMAG, France
Brad Cox	Stepstone, USA
Simon Gibbs	University of Geneva, Switzerland
Joseph Goguen	Oxford University, England
Theo Härder	University of Kaiserslautern, Germany
Chris Horn	Trinity College, Ireland
Gerti Kappel	University of Vienna, Austria
Ole Lehrmann Madsen	Aarhus University, Denmark
Boris Magnusson	Lund University, Sweden
Luís Monteiro	Universidade Nova de Lisboa, Portugal
Barbara Pernici	Politecnico di Milano, Italy
Markku Sakkinen	University of Jyväskylä, Finland
Dave Thomas	Carleton University, Canada
Mario Tokoro	Keio University, Japan
Stanley Zdonik	Brown University, USA

List of Referees

Antonio J. Alencar
Birger Andersen
Valeria De Antonellis
Constantin Arapis
Lex Augusteijn
Lars Bak
Sean Baker
Joaquim M. Baptista
Brian M. Barry
Michel Beaudouin-Lafon
Mats Bengtsson
Paul Bergstein
Anders Björnerstedt
Franck Boissiere
Wim Bronnenberg
Marc H. Brown
Vinny Cahill
Eduardo Casais
José C. Cunha
Elspeth Cusack
Lars-Ove Dahlin
Laurent Dami
Stefan Deßloch
Razvan Diaconescu
Alexis Donnelly
Christophe Dony
John Duimovich
Johann Eder
Maria Grazia Fugini
Sanjay Ghemawat
José Félix Gomes da Costa
Sanjiv Gossain
Peter Grogono
Görel Hedin
Sandra Heiler
Leen Helmink
Alex Heung
Ian M. Holland

Kohei Honda
Yasuaki Honda
Jim J. Horning
Ben J. A. Hulshof
Walter Hürsch
Anette Hviid
Yutaka Ishikawa
Jan Martin Jansen
Kevin D. Jones
Eric Jul
Betty Junod
Niels Christian Juul
Bill Kalsow
Jørgen Lindskov Knudsen
Shinji Kono
Dimitri Konstantas
Kai Koskimies
Kevin Charles Lano
Jean-Marie Larchevêque
Doug Lea
Christophe Lecluse
Daniel Lesage
Theodore W. Leung
Karl Lieberherr
Roberto Maiocchi
Jean-Claude Mamou
Satoshi Matsuoka
Nelson Mattos
Brian Mayoh
James McGugan
Vicki W. de Mey
Scott Meyers
Mike Milinkovich
Sten Minör
Gail Mitchell
Roland Mittermeir
John P. Morrison
Thomas Mück

Jocelyne Nanard
Oscar Nierstrasz
Claus Nørgård
Chisato Numaoka
Dan Oscarsson
Jukka Paakki
Jens Palsberg
Michael Papathomas
Xavier Pintado
Gustav Pomberger
Vassilis Prevelakis
Joachim Reinert
Serge Renfer
Philippe Richard
Olivier Roux
Jean-Claude Royer
Pierangela Samarati
Elmer Sandvad
Michael Schrefl
Michael Schwartzbach
Etsuya Shibayama
Ignacio Silva-Lepe
Adolfo Socorro
J. Michael Spivey
Marc Stadelmann
Lynn Andrea Stein
Markus Stumptner
Hiroyasu Sugano
Ikuo Takeuchi
Brendan Tangney
Magnus Taube
Juha Vihavainen
Bridget Walsh
Takuo Watanabe
Mike Wilson
Cun Xiao
Yasuhiko Yokote

Contents

Modeling the C++ Object Model
An Application of an Abstract Object Model

Alan Snyder

Hewlett-Packard Laboratories

P.O. Box 10490, Palo Alto CA 94303-0969

Abstract

We are developing an abstract model to provide a framework for comparing the object models of various systems, ranging from object-oriented programming languages to distributed object architectures. Our purpose is to facilitate communication among researchers and developers, improve the general understanding of object systems, and suggest opportunities for technological convergence. This paper describes the application of the abstract object model to the C++ programming language. We give an overview of the abstract object model and illustrate its use in modeling C++ objects. Several modeling alternatives are discussed and evaluated, which reveal anomalies in the C++ language. We conclude by characterizing those aspects of the C++ object model that distinguish C++ from other object systems.

Introduction

Concepts originating in object-oriented programming languages are appearing in many variations in different technologies, ranging from distributed systems to user interfaces. In previous work [9], we identified what we believe are the essential concepts underlying these variations. Our current effort involves the creation of an abstract object model, which provides more precise definitions of the essential concepts. The purpose of the model is to serve as a framework for comparing the object models of different technologies to identify common properties, highlight differences, and suggest opportunities for technological convergence. The object model is being developed by applying it in turn to five major technologies of interest to Hewlett-Packard. This paper reports on the first such application, to the C++ programming language [5].

In this paper, we present an overview of the abstract object model and illustrate its use in modeling C++ objects. The presentation concentrates on aspects of the model where the application to C++ raises issues either about the model or about C++ itself. We begin by reviewing the relevant aspects of C++.

A Brief Overview of C++ Objects

In this section, we review the object-related aspects of C++. (Readers familiar with C++ should skim this section for terminology used in later sections.) For brevity, we omit certain features of C++ that do not significantly affect the presented material: access control, virtual base classes, and references.[1] In this section, all terms are C++ terms, not object model terms. For example, the term *object* means C++ object, which is a region of storage. Note that our description of C++ is abstract; it is not an implementation model.

---

1. For the purposes of this discussion, references are equivalent to pointers. They are called pointers herein.

The principal C++ construct related to object-oriented programming is the *class*. A class serves two roles, as a lexical scope and as a type. As a lexical scope, a class defines a set of immutable bindings (called *members*) between names and certain kinds of entities, which include data declarations and various kinds of literals (types, enumerations, and functions). The members of a class have distinct names, except for function members, which must be distinguishable by their names and their declared argument types (functions distinguished only by their declared argument types are called *overloaded functions*). A class provides lexical context for the definitions (bodies) of its function members and for nested class and function definitions; the enclosed definitions can reference the members of the class by name. Function members can be of several varieties: ordinary, static, virtual, and pure virtual. Data declarations can be of two varieties: ordinary and static.

A class also defines a type, which is a pattern for instantiating objects, called *class instances*. A class instance is a compound object: it consists of multiple subobjects, called *components*. (The C++ literature uses the term *member* for these subobjects; we introduce the term *component* to avoid confusion with class members.) The components of a class instance are determined by the class. For a simple class (not defined using derivation), there is one instance component for each data declaration, each ordinary function member, and each virtual function member. Function components can be viewed as closures unique to the instance: they have direct access to the components of that instance, and can refer to the instance itself using the variable *this*.

Class members are named directly (in their scope) or using the notation '*class::name*'. Instance components are accessed using the notation '*instance.member*', where *instance* is an expression denoting a class instance and *member* names a class member. A complex example is $a.A::B::x$, where x is a member of the class that is the B member of class A, and a is an instance of a class (such as $A::B$) containing a corresponding x component. Within a function component, components of *this* are accessed using the member name alone. There are many restrictions on the use of class members and instance components, but they are not important for this presentation.

For the purposes of the object model, we treat a pure virtual function as a virtual function with a distinguished definition (that cannot be referenced). We ignore the remaining kinds of class members (types, enumerations, static functions, and static data declarations) henceforth, as they do not impact the object model.

Figure 1 shows a class named A that defines two members: a data declaration (for an integer object) named x and an ordinary function named f. The second line provides the full definition of f. The third line creates an instance of A called a. It has two components, an integer object named x and a function named f. The following lines access the components of a. Note that the component function f of a accesses both the x and f components of a by name. The diagrams illustrate the class A and the instance a. We use shaded boxes to denote class members and unshaded boxes to denote instance components. We introduce the notation A/f to refer to the function member f of the class A and the corresponding function components. (Our examples will not involve overloaded functions.)

A class can be defined by deriving from one or more *base classes* (we use the term base class to mean *direct* base class, unless explicitly indicated otherwise). The effect of derivation on the derived class lexical scope is similar to nested scopes: the derived class lexical scope includes not only the members it defines directly, but also any member of a base class that is neither redefined in the derived class nor ambiguous in multiple base classes. The effect of derivation on instances of a derived class is composition: an instance of a derived class contains not only the components corresponding to the members defined directly in the derived class, but also one unnamed instance component of each base class. We call these unnamed components *base components*.

Figure 2 illustrates class derivation. The class D is derived from the class B. Class B's lexical scope has three members: x and y (both data declarations for integer objects), and f (an ordinary function). Class D defines two members: x (a data declaration) and f (an ordinary function). Class D's lexical scope includes x and f, but also includes y (which it inherits from B). An instance of class D contains three components: x (an integer object), f (a function component), and an unnamed instance of class B. The class B base component contains three components: x and y (integer objects) and f (a function component). The diagram illustrates the structure of an instance of class D.

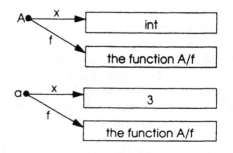

```
class A { public: int x; void f (int);};
void A::f (int g) {x = g; f (g+1);};
A a;
a.x = 3;
a.f (4);
```

Figure 1. A class and a class instance.

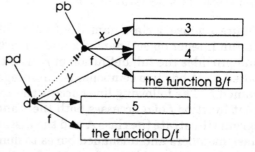

```
class B { public: int x, y; void f (int);};
void B::f (int g) {x = g; f (g+1);};
class D : public B { public: int x; void f (int);};
void D::f (int g) {x = g; f (g+2);};
D d;
D* pd = &d; // create a pointer to d
B* pb = pd; // type conversion
```

Figure 2. A class defined using derivation.

A function component can access only the components of the instance of its defining class. For example, the function B/f in Figure 2 can access only the components of the B base component; its variable *this* is equivalent to pb. In contrast, in the function D/f, *this* is equivalent to pd. Although redefined base class members are not part of the derived class lexical scope, they can be accessed from the derived class scope (and elsewhere) using explicit qualification. For example, the function D/f in Figure 2 can access the x component of the B base component using the name $B::x$.

An implicit type conversion is defined from type 'pointer to derived class' to type 'pointer to base class', for each base class. Its effect is to convert a pointer to the derived class instance to a pointer to the corresponding base component. Figure 2 illustrates this conversion: the pointer pd to the D instance is converted to the pointer pb to the B base component. This conversion achieves the *effect* of inclusion polymorphism [3]: a pointer to a D instance can be passed as an argument to a function expecting a pointer to a B instance.

A function member declared *virtual* produces a different instance structure. A virtual function component *overrides* (takes precedence over) any direct or indirect base class function components of the same name and type. (The actual rules are more complex.) Figure 3 shows the effect of declaring f to be virtual: in the lexical scope accessed from pb, f now denotes the component function D/f (instead of B/f). Virtual functions allow specialization to be effective with inclusion polymorphism: the derived class function component will be invoked even from a context where the object is known as an instance of the base class. For example, the function *test* in Figure 3 invokes D/f when its argument is pb (or pd), even though the variable p is of type 'pointer to B'.

Explicit qualification has the effect of suppressing virtuality: the expression $d.B::f$ refers to the B/f component of d, not the D/f component. Thus, the :: operation is *not* simply a scoping operator.

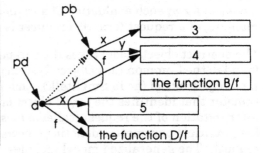

```
class B { public: int x, y; virtual void f (int);};
void B::f (int g) {x = g; f (g+1);};
class D : public B { public: int x; void f (int);};
void D::f (int g) {x = g; f (g+2);};
D d;
D* pd = &d; // create a pointer to d
B* pb = pd; // type conversion
void test (B* p) {p→f(0);}
```

Figure 3. Virtual functions.

The Abstract Object Model

In this section, we present an overview of the abstract object model. (A more complete presentation of an earlier version can be found in [8].) We concentrate on those aspects of the model that raise the most interesting issues when modeling C++. Terms, such as *object*, used in this section refer to model concepts, as distinct from C++ concepts.

The model is based on the following concepts we deem the essential concepts of objects (further information on these concepts can be found in [9]):

- An object explicitly embodies an abstraction that is characterized by services.
- Clients request services; a request identifies an operation and zero or more objects.
- Operations can be generic: an operation can be uniformly performed on a range of objects with visibly different behavior.
- Objects are distinguishable, and new objects can be created.
- Objects can be classified by their services, forming an interface hierarchy.
- Objects can share implementation, either in full (class instances) or in part (implementation inheritance).

The abstract object model is a partial description of the behavior of a computational system. To model a particular system (such as C++), one defines a *concrete object model* for that system. A concrete object model may differ from the abstract object model in several ways. It may *elaborate* the abstract object model by making it more specific, for example, by defining the form of request parameters or the language used to specify types. It may *populate* the model by introducing specific instances of entities defined by the model, for example, specific objects, specific operations, or specific types. It may also *restrict* the model by eliminating entities or placing additional restrictions on their use.

The abstract object model postulates a set of *clients* that issue requests for service and a set of *objects* that perform services. (An object can be a client, but clients need not be objects.) A request is an *event*: a unique occurrence during the execution of the computational system. A request has associated information, which consists of an *operation* and zero or more parameter *values*. A value may identify an object; such a value is called an *object name*. The operation identifies the service to be performed; the parameters provide the additional information needed to specify the intended behavior. A client issues a request by evaluating a *request form*; each evaluation of a request form results in a new *request*. The mapping of a request form to a request is called *spelling*.

The abstract object model takes the perspective of the *generalized* object models found in the Common Lisp Object System [1] and the Iris database [6]. In a *classical* object model (as in Smalltalk), each request contains a distinguished parameter that identifies the *target* object of the request, which then controls the interpretation of the request (called a *message*). A generalized object model allows multiple parameters denoting objects to influence the interpretation of the request. The generalized model includes classical models as a special case.

An operation is simply an identifiable entity. Its purpose is to characterize sets of requests with similar intended semantics. To allow operations to have associated semantics in a computational system, we believe it is necessary to allow developers to *create* operations (i.e., uniquely allocate an operation for a particular use). An operation is named in a request form using an *operation name*.

A *generic operation* is one that can be uniformly requested on objects with different implementations, producing observably different behavior. Intuitively, a generic operation is implemented by multiple programs, from which a single program is selected dynamically for each request.

A request is performed by transforming it into a *method invocation*. This transformation is called *binding*. A method invocation identifies a *method*, a collection of *method parameters*, and an *execution engine*. A method is a program. The method parameters are values, possibly from a different space than request parameters. The execution engine interprets the method in a dynamic context containing the method parameters; upon completion, a *result* is returned to the client. Execution of a method may alter the state of the computational system. The input to binding consists of a request (an operation and parameter values) and a request context. The request context supports the option of client-specific behavior.

To review, a client issues a request by evaluating a *request form*, which contains an *operation name*. The request form is mapped to a *request* by a process called *spelling*. The request identifies the *operation* and some parameter *values*, which may be *object names*. The request is mapped to a *method invocation* by a process called *binding*. This two-stage processing model is shown in Figure 4.

The intermediate stage of requests serves to capture the essential information provided by a client when requesting a service. Spelling and binding serve distinct purposes. Spelling is a convenience for clients: it provides flexibility in how things are written. Binding captures a fundamental property of object system: the provision of multiple implementations for a single semantic abstraction.

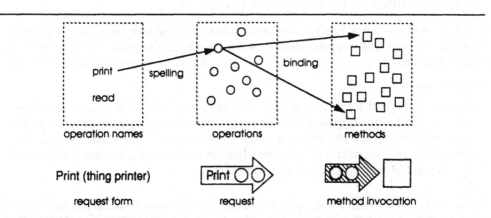

Figure 4. Spelling and binding.

The model defines the concept of a *meaningful request* to capture the notion that not all possible requests are sensible. (Many systems formalize this notion in a type system and verify type correctness using static or dynamic type checking.) *Meaningful* is a boolean predicate on requests that is defined in each model of a particular object system.

For convenience, several subsidiary concepts are defined: An *operation signature* is a description of the parameter values that are meaningful in requests that identify a particular operation. Effectively, operation signatures are a factoring of the *meaningful* predicate by operation. An operation signature may also constrain the results of the corresponding requests. A *type* is a boolean predicate on values that can be used in operation signatures. A relation called *subtype* is defined over types: a type *a* is a subtype of a type *b* if any value that satisfies type *a* necessarily satisfies type *b*. An *interface* is a (partial) description of an object that describes circumstances under which it is meaningful for an object to be named as a request parameter; in effect, an interface describes valid uses of an object, from a client perspective. An interface can be a type, called an *interface type*.

Examples: The signature of the *push* operation might specify that the first parameter must be a stack (an object name that satisfies a type *stack*) and the second parameter must be an integer (a value that satisfies a type *integer*). The stack interface (which describes stack objects) might specify that a stack can appear as the first parameter to the *push* and *pop* operations.

Using the Abstract Object Model

Using the abstract model to describe an existing system is a subjective process. The modeler makes choices that can be evaluated only using subjective criteria, such as simplicity, comprehensiveness, and utility. For example, consider a model in which there is exactly one operation, identified in every request. In this model, the operation conveys no information; the identification of the requested service would have to be communicated either as a parameter value or via the request context. We consider this model poor because it fails to use operations effectively to characterize sets of requests.

One aspect of our work has been to accumulate a set of more specific evaluation criteria. The criteria were developed as a way of justifying and explaining choices that were made intuitively. They are guidelines, not absolute requirements.

The criteria are:

- A typical request form should have the property that all evaluations of the request form issue requests that identify the same operation. In other words, most request forms statically identify an operation. This criterion reflects the intuition that each request form has an associated semantics that corresponds to the expectations of the client.[2]

---

2. We expect the primary exception to this criterion to be request forms that involve an *operation variable*. An operation variable is a distinct subform whose evaluation results in the identification of an operation and whose evaluation is independent of other parts of the request form.

- There should be generic operations (operations with multiple methods invocable from a single request form). Our intent is to exclude a model in which operations are identified with methods: such a model would incorporate binding into evaluation.

- Operation signatures should be useful (i.e., not too permissive); they should reflect inherent system structure. (The model with a single operation fails this criterion because the signature of the universal operation permits *any* collection of parameters.)

- Operations should distinguish request forms whose potential behaviors are disjoint. For example, two methods that can never be invoked from the same request form should be implementations of distinct operations.

- Operations should characterize objects, in terms of their legitimate use in requests. For example, in most object systems, an object supports a specific set of operations, meaning that it can appear as the target parameter in requests that identify those operations.

- The use of the request context in binding should be minimized.

Modeling C++ Objects

In this section, we present a model of C++ objects using the abstract object model. We concentrate on four aspects of modeling: identifying the objects, operations, values, and types. We discuss several issues that arose in developing the model, and their implications both on the abstract object model and on C++ itself. In this section we must refer to both abstract object model concepts and C++ concepts, some of which have the same terms. Where context is inadequate to avoid confusion, we will use terms like "C++ object" to refer to the C++ concept and "object" to refer to the abstract object model concept.

A fundamental modeling issue is tension between accuracy and expressiveness. Although C++ supports object-oriented programming, it is not a pure object-oriented language. It is not surprising, therefore, that we sometimes had to choose between a model that describes the full semantics of C++ and one that better captures the 'spirit' of objects, but fails to handle certain corner cases of the language. We have taken the latter option. We argue that this approach is better for the purpose of characterizing the C++ object model and comparing it to the object models of other systems. We would not take the same approach if our goal were to create a formal definition of C++.

What are the Objects?

The first issue: what are the objects? There are two independent choices. The first choice is whether all C++ objects are objects, or just class instances. We have chosen to model only class instances as objects, because (as we will describe) only class instances support generic operations.

The second choice is whether an instance of a derived class is modeled as a single object, or whether each base component is modeled as a separate object. This choice is more significant, and deserves a fuller explanation. (In both cases, a *named* instance component *is* modeled as a distinct object.)

The multi-object model (shown in Figure 5a) models each base component as a distinct object. The implication is that a pointer to a base component like *pb* is a *different value* than a pointer to the derived class instance like *pd*. These values have different types. Because they are different *values*, they can affect binding. For example, if class *B* and class *D* both define an ordinary function member *f*, then the fact that a request (*f pb*) invokes *B/f* and a request (*f pd*) invokes *D/f* can be understood as a consequence of the two requests identifying the same operation, but different parameter values.

The monolithic object model (shown in Figure 5b) models base components as lacking a separate identity. The implication is that a pointer to a base component like *pb* is modeled as *the same value* as a pointer to the derived class instance like *pd*. The fact that these pointers have different semantics cannot be explained based on values, but must be explained based on static types of expressions. Specifically, we use the static type of the target object expression to map the operation name *f* into *distinct operations*, which we will label as *B::f* and *D::f*. A request (*B::f pd*) invokes *B/f* and a request (*D::f pd*) invokes *D/f*.

The monolithic object model forces us to model *B/f* and *D/f* as distinct operations. We argue that this modeling is appropriate, because in C++ no single request form can invoke both of these functions (ignoring pointers to class members, which are *operation variables*). We prefer the monolithic object model, both because it is simpler, and because it is more consistent with the "mainstream" concept of object. (In most object systems, instances of classes defined using inheritance do not reveal themselves as consisting of distinguishable parts.) Furthermore, modeling *pb* and *pd* as the same value is consistent with C++ pointer comparison, which reports these pointers as being equal after an implicit type conversion.

The disadvantage of the monolithic object model is that it fails to handle a corner case of the language where an object visibly contains more than one base component of the same type. Clearly, multiple base components of the same type cannot be distinguished by type, but only by value. This situation involves a distinctive use of C++ multiple inheritance, illustrated in Figure 6. Class *D* is derived from classes *B* and *C*, each of which are derived from class *A*. A *D* in-

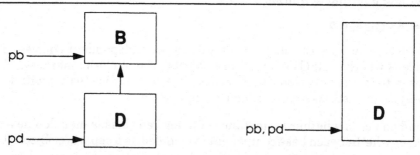

Figure 5a. Multi-object model.   **Figure 5b. Monolithic object model.**

stance contains two base components of class A. Using two levels of type conversion (one of which must be explicit), a client holding a pointer to the D instance (pd) can obtain pointers to either A instance ($pa1$ or $pa2$).

To reflect this case accurately, we must either model the A components as separate objects, or we must extend the abstract object model to include a concept of object port (where a single object can have multiple ports). Our position is that the extra complexity needed to handle this case is not justified. This position rests upon an assumption that the above situation is unusual, which we defend based on the fact that the client must use explicit type conversions to obtain access to the component instances.

To summarize, we model only C++ class instances as objects, and we model instances of derived classes as monolithic (base components are *not* separate objects).

What are the Operations?

The second modeling issue is to determine the space of operations. One possibility is to model only virtual function members as operations, because (as we will show) they correspond to generic operations. Alternatively, one could model all nonstatic function members as operations, or all function members. Our choice is to model *all* C++ functions as operations. This choice is consistent with the generalized object model approach. The abstract object model does not require that *all* operations be generic. Having made this choice, we model *all* C++ function invocations as request forms (one exception is introduced below); the various cases are shown in Figure 7.

How do C++ functions map to operations? The primary modeling issue is to define operations that are (potentially) generic. Recall the key characteristics of a generic operation: (1) it can have multiple methods selected based on request parameters, and (2) the methods of a generic operation can be invoked from a single request form. To model generic operations, multiple functions should map to the same operation: they are modeled as different methods for that operation. C++ provides two candidates for generic operations: overloaded functions and virtual function members.[3]

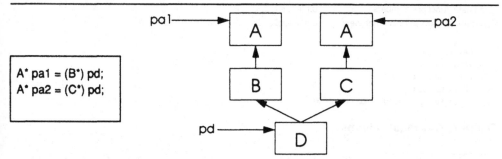

Figure 6. Repeated Inheritance example.

---

3. Other kinds of functions, such as non-virtual member functions, cannot be generic operations because they are statically identified in all request forms (ignoring pointers to functions).

C++ overloaded functions are functions that have the same name in the same lexical scope, but are distinguished by their formal argument types. For each invocation that names a set of overloaded functions, a specific function is selected from that set at compile-time based on the static types of the argument expressions. Therefore, a single request form *always* invokes the same function, which contradicts the key characteristics of generic operations. Thus, we do *not* model overloaded functions as generic operations. Specifically, we model each function in a set of overloaded functions as a *distinct* operation. We model overloaded function resolution as part of *spelling*: it is a convenience for programmers, not support for object-oriented programming.[4]

C++ virtual function members are appropriately modeled as generic operations because they satisfy the key characteristics of generic operations: a single request form naming a virtual function member can invoke function components that correspond to *different* function definitions. For example, as shown in Figure 3, an invocation of *f* using a pointer of type 'pointer to *B*' might invoke either *B/f* or *D/f*, depending upon whether the pointer points to an instance of *B* or an instance of *D*, respectively.

We model a generic operation as a single operation with multiple methods. In the simple case exemplified by Figure 3, the two functions *B/f* and *D/f* both correspond to a single operation ϕ; they are two methods for the same operation. A request form naming either function member issues a request for operation ϕ. The request $(\phi\ \alpha)$ is bound to the appropriate function based on the parameter value α, which is an object name that identifies an instance of *B* or a class directly or indirectly derived from *B*.

A more challenging example is shown in Figure 8a. Class *E* is a derived class with two base classes *B* and *D*, which are derived from classes *A* and *C*, respectively. Each of the five classes defines a virtual function member *f* with no arguments. There are five functions named *f*; how many operations are there?

---

ordinary functions	f (e1, e2, ...)
pointers to functions	e (e1, e2, ...)
static function members	C::f (e1, e2, ...)
nonstatic function members	o.f (e1, e2, ...)
pointers to class function members	o.e (e1, e2, ...)

f ∈ identifier
C ∈ class name
e ∈ expression – identifier
e1, e2 ∈ expression
o ∈ expression (denoting a class instance)

Figure 7. C++ request forms.

---

4. As an aside, if we wanted to model overloaded functions as generic operations, we would be forced to abandon the monolithic object model. Overloaded function resolution is based on static expression types. To model overloaded function resolution as part of *binding*, the parameter values must capture the static type information. The monolithic object model of values discards the static type information associated with pointers to base components.

Based on the previous example, it is clear that *A/f* and *B/f* are one operation (1) and that *C/f* and *D/f* are one operation (2). Furthermore, we argue that operations 1 and 2 are distinct: no single request form can invoke both *A/f* and *C/f* (ignoring pointers to class members). However, the logic of the previous example also argues that *E/f* is the same operation as both *A/f* and *C/f*: an invocation using a 'pointer to *A*' can invoke *E/f* (if the pointer denotes an *E* instance); an invocation using a 'pointer to *C*' also can invoke *E/f*.

Our solution to this problem is to model *E/f* as a method for *two* operations. (One can imagine that *E* actually defines two equivalent functions.) A potential problem with this solution is that an invocation of *f* using a 'pointer to *E*' is ambiguous: which operation does the request identify? Fortunately, the ambiguity is unimportant: either operation could be identified; the rules of C++ exclude as ambiguous any case where the choice would make a difference in the code that is executed (e.g., the following example).

A related example (shown in Figure 8b) illustrates an anomaly in C++ that was exposed during the creation of the model. We have changed the example by removing the definitions of *f* members in classes *B* and *E*. The name *f* is now ambiguous in class *E*, because it might refer to either *A/f* or *D/f*; an invocation of *f* using a 'pointer to *E*' is illegal in C++. The anomaly is that using the class scoping operator to disambiguate the two operations has undesirable effects, because explicit qualification suppresses virtuality. Although an invocation of *B::f* using a 'pointer to *E*' *will* invoke *A/f*, the client code is not resilient: if a definition of *f* is added to *E*, the invocation will still invoke *A/f*, not *E/f*. A better solution is to disambiguate using type conversion: converting a 'pointer to *E*' to a 'pointer to *B*' yields a value upon which the name *f* is unambiguous. This anomaly is not a problem for the object model; it is a shortcoming of C++ that in the lexical scope of class *E* there is no way to *spell* either operation.[5]

Modeling virtual function members as generic operations again fails to model the full semantics of C++. Specifically, it fails to model the ability of clients to use explicit qualification to name individual functions (such as *A/f*, *C/f*, and *D/f* in Figure 8b). For example, an invocation that names *C::f* cannot be modeled as a request form in this model: the operation corresponding to *C::f* is the same op-

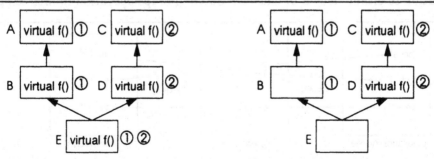

Figure 8a. Virtual function members.   **Figure 8b. An anomalous example.**

---

5. Proposals to correct this shortcoming were rejected by the ANSI C++ committee because a programmer can work around any problems by defining additional classes.

eration corresponding to D/f; the operation does not provide enough information to allow the client to invoke *either* function on the E instance (in distinct invocations). Although we could use the request context to provide the necessary information, we prefer to model such invocations as *direct method invocations*, rather than as request forms. We believe this choice is consistent with the spirit of the language, based on the recommendation of the language designer that such invocations be used *only* within methods, and not in client code [5, p. 210].

The modeling of C++ functions as operations is summarized as follows: Each C++ function (executable or pure) is a distinct operation, except for a virtual function member that overrides one or more base class virtual function members, which instead provides an additional method for each of the original operations. An operation in C++ is identified by a triple: a lexical scope (such as a file or a class definition), a function name, and the formal argument types (suitably canonicalized to reflect C++ overloaded function resolution). For an operation corresponding to a virtual function member, the identifying lexical scope is the "most base" class defining the virtual function member, i.e., the root of the class derivation tree where the virtual function member is introduced.

Operations are *values* in C++: they may be used as request parameters. Operations that correspond to ordinary functions and static function members are values whose types have the form 'pointer to function ...' (the elision describes the argument and result types); these operations have exactly one method each. Operations corresponding to nonstatic function members are values of type 'pointer to class ... function member ...' (the first elision names a class, the second describes argument and result types). Pointers to class function members identify a class member, *not* an instance component; an instance must be supplied when the function is invoked. (A pointer to a function *component* would be a *closure*, a concept not currently supported in C-like languages.) Pointers to class function members correspond exactly to operations in our model of C++: such pointers *cannot* distinguish between individual methods for the same operation (in the case of pointers to virtual function members).[6]

The operation model is summarized in Figure 9. The illustration assumes that class D is derived from class B, that f is virtual, and that class X is unrelated by derivation to either class B or class D. Spelling maps operation names to oper-

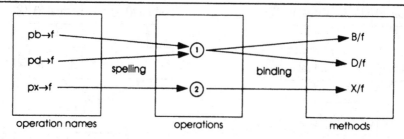

Figure 9. Operations in C++.

---

6. It is somewhat of an anomaly therefore that pointers to class function members are created using the syntax of explicit qualification, which in invocations is used precisely to make such distinctions!

ations; it involves lexical scoping and overloaded function resolution (both static), as well as evaluation (dynamic) in the case of operation variables (as discussed in the previous paragraph). Binding maps operations to methods, and involves a dynamic lookup based on request parameters (types) in the case of virtual operations (operations corresponding to virtual function members).

Using the access control feature, a C++ class can allow direct client access to a data component of its instances. We can model a client-accessible data component as an operation that returns a pointer to the component. This operation is like a non-virtual member function in having a single method. However, the method is defined by the implementation of C++, not by the class. Thus, use of this feature of C++ makes clients dependent on the implementation of objects.

What are the Values?

The abstract object model specifies that requests include parameters, called *values*. The values denote the information transmitted from the client to the service provider. The question of how C++ function invocations map onto this model of requests deserves some discussion. (Note that we need to be particularly careful in our use of terms in this discussion.)

C++ argument passing is based on these key concepts: A C++ *object* is a region of storage. The contents of a C++ object is an immutable data element called a C++ *value*. Both C++ objects and C++ values are *typed*: the types of a C++ object and its contents are identical. The formal argument of a function is bound upon the invocation of the function to a new local variable, which is a C++ object of the declared type. The initialization of this C++ object is based on information provided by the client in the function invocation. The modeling issue is how to denote this information as a value.

The initialization of a formal argument that is not a class instance is straightforward. (Note that this case includes the case of a formal argument that is a *pointer* to an instance, i.e., an *object name*.) The actual argument expression is evaluated to produce a C++ value of the designated type, which becomes the contents of the formal argument; the evaluation may include an implicit type conversion selected based on the static type of the expression. We model this C++ value as the request parameter; thus, any implicit type conversion is modeled as happening prior to issuing the request.

An alternative model is that the request parameter is the C++ value that is the *input* of the implicit type conversion. This model is viable, but has two disadvantages: (1) The signatures of operations can change over time as new classes with conversion functions are defined. For example, if a new class C is defined with a conversion function to *int*, then every operation with a formal argument of type *int* is extended to accept instances of class C. (2) Because conversion functions are selected based on static expression types, request parameters would have to encode the static type, which implies use of the multi-object model of derived class instances.

The initialization of a formal argument that is a class instance is more complex. The new class instance is created implicitly, then initialized by a *copy constructor* defined by the class. A constructor is a special kind of invocable entity, similar to a function; an implicit formal argument *this* allows the constructor to initialize the components of a new instance. The copy constructor takes a single argument of type 'pointer to C', where C is the declared class. (A class can define other constructors with different numbers or types of arguments.)

There is a special case, which we refer to below as the *optimized case*. A client can create a temporary object by explicitly invoking a constructor. If the actual argument expression is a constructor invocation, an implementation of C++ has the option of using that temporary object directly as the formal argument object (eliminating the use of the copy constructor), rather than passing a pointer to the object to the copy constructor. In all cases, however, the formal argument object is initialized by a constructor.

Three modeling possibilities come to mind for a formal argument of class type C:

1. The request parameter is a C++ value of type C, which becomes the contents of the formal argument instance. The value can be thought of as being the "output" of the copy constructor (or the explicitly invoked constructor in the optimized case). This choice is appealing because it is analogous to the model for non-instance formal arguments. However, the notion of copying the "output" of the constructor into a *new* instance is inconsistent with the semantics of C++, because the constructor can observe the *identity* of the formal argument instance (using *this*).

2. The request parameter is the pointer argument to the copy constructor, or the pointer to the temporary in the optimized case. This choice is closest to the actual language semantics. It is inconsistent with the model for non-instance formal arguments in that, in the optimized case, the formal argument is modeled as created by the *client* (i.e., prior to issuing the request). There is also a possible confusion between these implicit pointer parameters (for formals of a class type) and explicit pointer parameters (for formals of a pointer type), although this confusion is not important for binding, which examines only the request parameter corresponding to the target object.

3. The request parameter is a structured value that describes the information needed to select and invoke the appropriate constructor(s). The advantage of this choice is that the creation of the new C++ object is local to the service provider in all cases (this model might be the most appropriate for a distributed system based on the C++ object model). The disadvantage is the need to invent a kind of value that has no relation to any C++ type.

Although each choice has disadvantages, we prefer the second alternative (the request parameter is a pointer, i.e., an object name). One effect of this choice is that it conceals the fact that C++ passes instances "by value" when the formal argument is a class type. However, strictly speaking, the only guarantee is that the formal argument is a new instance. The copying of the contents is controlled by the copy constructor, whose behavior can be arbitrary; furthermore, in the optimized case, no copying is performed.

We model default arguments as a notational convenience: the client effectively calls an auxiliary function (associated with the *operation*) to compute the request parameter for an omitted argument. This choice is motivated by the fact that default arguments do not affect the type of a function in C++.

What are the Types?

In the abstract object model, types characterize values that are legitimate request parameters. Based on the previous discussion, a class instance can never be a request parameter, unlike a *pointer* to a class instance. Therefore, we model only C++ non-class types as types in the object model.

The only subtype relation defined over types in our model of C++ is between a type 'pointer to class D' and a type 'pointer to class B', where B is a direct or indirect base class of D. This relation is a consequence of the monolithic object model: a value of type 'pointer to class D' is legitimate as a parameter in a request that identifies an operation whose signature requires a value of type 'pointer to class B'. C++ implicit type conversions (such as the conversion from *char* to *int*) do not define subtype relations, because of our decision to model such conversions as taking place prior to issuing a request.

A C++ class whose members are all pure virtual functions is an *interface*. Such a class defines how certain objects can be used, without constraining how those objects are implemented. A pointer type to such a class is an *interface type*. A C++ function type is an *operation signature*: it can be used to define legitimate request parameter values that identify operations.

A Formal Model of Spelling and Binding

A formal model of spelling and binding in C++ is sketched in Figure 10. This model emphasizes the transformations performed by spelling and binding; it does not attempt to model the semantics of C++. For example, the model does not represent the state of the computational system. Also, the treatment of overloaded function resolution handles only invocations; C++ also resolves overloaded function names in expressions based on context.

The first two cases for spelling handle invocations of explicitly named functions. The second two cases handle invocations using pointers to functions and pointers to class member functions, respectively: we assume that such values are operations (i.e., spelling analogous to the first two cases is performed when pointer values are created). For convenience, we model the type of an argument list as a signature type, for overloaded function resolution. As described above, an expression of a class type evaluates to an object name. The binding model assumes that functions serve as methods, and that nonstatic function members have been transformed to take an explicit *this* argument.

Spelling:

request form   request

f(e1,e2,...)   (op[F[ε,f,Type[ε,(e1,e2,...)]]] E[ε,e1] E[ε,e2] ...)
o.f(e1,e2,...)   (op[MF[Type[ε,o],f,Type[ε,(e1,e2,...)]]] E[ε,o] E[ε,e1] E[ε,e2] ...)

e(e1,e2,...)   (E[ε,e] E[ε,e1] E[ε,e2] ...)
o.e(e1,e2,...)   (E[ε,e] E[ε,o] E[ε,e1] E[ε,e2] ...)

ε ∈ environment
f ∈ identifier
e ∈ expression − identifier
e1, e2 ∈ expression
o ∈ expression (denoting a class instance)
E: environment × expression → value   (evaluation)
F: environment × identifier × signature → function (lexical scoping and overloaded function resolution)
Type: environment × expression → type   (static type analysis)
MF: class × identifier × signature → function   (class scope lookup for overloaded functions)
op: function → operation
signature ⊂ type
class ⊂ type
function ⊂ value

Binding:

request   method invocation

non-virtual operation:
(φ v1 v2 ...)   (op⁻¹[φ] v1 v2 ...)

virtual operation:
(φ n v1 v2 ...)   (VF[φ,n] n v1 v2 ...)

φ ∈ operation
v1, v2 ∈ value
n ∈ object name
op⁻¹: operation → function
VF: operation × object name → function   (method lookup)
OType: object name → class   (dynamic typing)

VF[φ,n] = the most "specific" function f such that f.class ≥ OType[n] and op[f] = φ

Figure 10. Spelling and binding in C++.

Summary

Our model of C++ objects is summarized by the following points (object model terms are italicized):

- Class instances are *objects*.
- Pointers to class instances are *object names*.
- Pointers reveal *object identity* to clients.
- Base components of derived class instances are not *objects*.
- Public data members correspond to special *operations* that return pointers.
- All function invocations are *request forms*, except for invocations that suppress virtual function lookup, which are *direct method invocations*.
- Except for virtual functions, each function is a distinct *operation*.
- An overriding virtual function is a new *method* for one or more existing *operations*.
- Virtual functions are *generic operations*; overloaded functions are not.
- C++ values of non-class types are *values* (*request parameters*).
- C++ non-class types are *types*.
- *Subtyping* is defined between pointer types based on class derivation.
- A class whose members are pure virtual functions is an *interface*.
- A pointer type to an *interface* class is an *interface type*.
- *Operations* are *values*.
- A C++ function type is an *operation signature*.

Observations

In developing this model of C++ objects, we discovered (as have others) that C++ is a complex language that is difficult to master. Over a period of months, we repeatedly discovered new examples that forced us to reconsider our model. We cannot state with absolute confidence that we have found the last such example! Furthermore, we found several cases whose behavior did not appear to be defined by the existing language definition. We have advised the ANSI C++ committee that a more precise language definition is needed. A specific contribution of the abstract object model is the clear distinction between *operations* (which clients are expected to name) and *methods* (which should be hidden from clients); the existing C++ literature fails to clearly distinguish these concepts, using the term *virtual function* for both (the implementation term *vtable entry* is sometimes used for the *operation* corresponding to a virtual function).

The construction of the C++ object model helped us to identify several problems in the design of C++ itself: the inability of a class definer to prevent client access to overridden methods, the unfortunate inconsistent use of explicit qualification, and the inability to name ambiguous (virtual) operations in a class with multiple base classes.

The C++ object model helps to clarify the aspects of C++ that distinguish it from other object-oriented programming languages:

- Operations in C++ are lexically scoped; a common lexical scope (i.e., a common base class definition) is required for generic operations. (Many object-oriented programming languages, e.g. Smalltalk, define a global name space for operations. Lexically scoped operations are advantageous for programming in the large, as they reduce the probability of accidental name collisions. However, C++ provides inadequate flexibility in naming its lexical scopes to take full advantage of this feature: at the top level, class names share a single global name space. The disadvantage of lexically scoped operations is the need to share a common class definition to permit communication between modules, such as between a client module and an object implementation module; the typical *implementation* of C++ exacerbates this situation by requiring recompilation after most changes to a class definition.)

- An object in C++ defined using multiple inheritance can have inherited parts that are visible to clients as distinct entities. (In most object-oriented programming languages, instances of classes defined using inheritance do not reveal inherited substructure.)

- Using multiple inheritance, a derived class can "link together" operations so that individual methods implement multiple operations.

- Clients in C++ can directly invoke specific methods for an operation. (In many object-oriented programming languages, specific methods cannot even be named. Method combination in such languages is performed using special syntax, such as *super* in Smalltalk. The ability to invoke specific methods is less a concern than the inability to control such access.)

- C++ ordinary function members are operations associated with objects that have exactly one method each.

- In C++, a class instance can have state variables that are directly accessible to clients.

- C++ supports overloaded functions, based on static type analysis. Overloaded functions are a naming convenience.

- C++ request forms are transformed by the insertion of client-specific type conversions, based on static type analysis.

Related Work

Several researchers have developed formal models of objects. Cook [4] developed a model of inheritance for classical object systems using denotational semantics, which has been used to compare inheritance in several object-oriented languages [2]. Reddy independently developed a similar model [7]. In both models, objects are modeled as records indexed by message keys, which are equivalent to our operations. However, neither Cook nor Reddy discuss the mapping from programming language constructs to operations (spelling).

Wand [11] developed a formal model of objects that is closer in breadth to our work. Although there are similarities between the two models, there are significant differences. Wand's model of object includes client-visible state, called attributes. More significantly, Wand's model lacks the concepts of request, operation, and binding. Instead, objects change state in response to other state changes, as specified by constraints called laws. Wand excludes notions like binding and methods as implementation details. Our model intentionally includes these concepts to allow comparison of implementation features (which affect the ability of an object system to support reuse). Wand identifies messages and methods as a source of confusion; our definitions of operation and method resolve this confusion.

Conclusions

We found the process of modeling C++ objects challenging, in part because C++ has many differences from other object-oriented systems. Nevertheless, we conclude that the abstract object model is useful for identifying and explaining the distinctive characteristics of the C++ object model. During the modeling process, several problems in the design of C++ were identified. Although we developed several evaluation criteria during the modeling process, the modeling process remains a subjective one: the ultimate evaluation of a model is its usefulness. This paper has emphasized specific aspects of the abstract object model. Other aspects, such as the model of object implementations, are being developed as we apply the model to additional systems.

References

1. D. G. Bobrow, L. G. DeMichel, R. P. Gabriel, S. E. Keene, G. Kiczales, D. A. Moon. Common Lisp Object System Specification X3J13. *SIGPLAN Notices* 23, 9 (1988).

2. G. Bracha and W. Cook. Mixin-based Inheritance. *Proc. OOPSLA/ECOOP-90*, 303-311.

3. L. Cardelli and P. Wegner. On Understanding Types, Data Abstraction, and Polymorphism. *Computing Surveys* 17, 4 (Dec. 1985), 471-522.

4. W. Cook. *A Denotational Semantics of Inheritance*. Ph.D. Thesis, Brown University, 1989.

5. M. A. Ellis and B. Stroustrup. *The Annotated C++ Reference Manual*. Addison-Wesley, 1990.

6. D. H. Fishman, et al. Iris: An Object-Oriented Data Base System. *ACM Transactions on Office Information Systems* 5, 1 (1987), 48-69.

7. U. S. Reddy. Objects as Closures: Abstract Semantics of Object-Oriented Languages. *Proc. ACM Conference on Lisp and Functional Programming (1988)*, 289-297.

8. A. Snyder. *An Abstract Object Model for Object-Oriented Systems*. Report HPL-90-22, Hewlett-Packard Laboratories, Palo Alto, CA, April 1990.

9. A. Snyder. *The Essence of Objects: Common Concepts and Terminology*. Report HPL-91-50, Hewlett-Packard Laboratories, Palo Alto, CA, May 1991.

10. R. M. Soley, ed. *Object Management Architecture Guide*. Document 90.9.1, Object Management Group, Inc. Framingham, Ma., November 1990.

11. Y. Wand. A Proposal for a Formal Model of Objects. In *Object-Oriented Concepts, Databases, and Applications*. W. Kim, F. H. Lochovsky, eds. ACM Press, 1989, 537-559.

Optimizing
Dynamically-Typed Object-Oriented Languages
With Polymorphic Inline Caches

Urs Hölzle
Craig Chambers
David Ungar[†]

Computer Systems Laboratory, Stanford University, Stanford, CA 94305
{urs,craig,ungar}@self.stanford.edu

Abstract: *Polymorphic inline caches* (PICs) provide a new way to reduce the overhead of polymorphic message sends by extending inline caches to include more than one cached lookup result per call site. For a set of typical object-oriented SELF programs, PICs achieve a median speedup of 11%.

As an important side effect, PICs collect type information by recording all of the receiver types actually used at a given call site. The compiler can exploit this type information to generate better code when *recompiling* a method. An experimental version of such a system achieves a median speedup of 27% for our set of SELF programs, reducing the number of non-inlined message sends by a factor of two.

Implementations of dynamically-typed object-oriented languages have been limited by the paucity of type information available to the compiler. The abundance of the type information provided by PICs suggests a new compilation approach for these languages, *adaptive compilation*. Such compilers may succeed in generating very efficient code for the time-critical parts of a program without incurring distracting compilation pauses.

1. Introduction

Historically, dynamically-typed object-oriented languages have run much slower than statically-typed languages. This disparity in performance stemmed largely from the relatively slow speed and high frequency of message passing and from the lack of type information which could be used to reduce these costs. Recently, techniques such as type analysis, customization, and splitting have been shown to be very effective in reducing this disparity: for example, these techniques applied to the SELF language bring its performance to within a factor of two of optimized C for small C-like programs such as the Stanford integer benchmarks [CU90, CU91, Cha91]. However, larger, object-oriented SELF programs benefit less from these techniques.[‡] For example, the Richards operating system benchmark in SELF is four times slower than optimized C.

In addition, techniques like type analysis lengthen compile time. In an interactive environment based on dynamic compilation, compilations occur frequently, and a slow compiler may lead to distracting pauses. Thus, although techniques such as type analysis can improve code quality significantly, they may sometimes degrade overall system performance.

[†] Current address: David Ungar, Sun Labs, Sun Microsystems, Mail Stop MTV 10-21, 2500 Garcia St., Mountain View, CA 94043.

[‡] By "C-like" we mean programs that operate on relatively simple data structures like integers and arrays; but unlike in C, all primitive operations are safe, e.g. there are checks for out-of-bounds accesses and overflow. By "object-oriented" we mean programs which manipulate many user-defined data structures (types) and exploit polymorphism and dynamic typing.

This work has been supported in part by the Swiss National Science Foundation (Nationalfonds), an IBM graduate student fellowship, NSF Presidential Young Investigator Grant # CCR-8657631 and by Sun, IBM, Apple, Cray, Tandem, TI, and DEC.

We propose a new approach to the optimization of dynamically-typed object-oriented languages based on *polymorphic inline caches* (PICs). As an immediate benefit, PICs improve the efficiency of polymorphic message sends. More importantly, they collect type information which may be used by the compiler to produce more efficient code, especially for programs written in an object-oriented style where type analysis often fails to extract useful type information. In addition, the new wealth of type information enables design trade-offs which may lead to faster compilation.

The first part of the paper describes polymorphic inline caches, explains how they speed up polymorphic message sends, and evaluates their impact on the execution time of some medium-sized object-oriented programs. With PICs, the Richards benchmark in SELF runs 52% faster than without them.[†]

The second part explains how the type information accumulated in the PICs can be used to guide the compilation of programs and evaluates the impact of these techniques using an experimental version of the SELF compiler. For a set of typical object-oriented programs, the experimental system obtains a median speedup of 27% over the current SELF compiler and significantly reduces the number of non-inlined message sends.

The third part outlines a framework for efficient implementations of dynamically-typed object-oriented languages based on *adaptive compilation*. This framework offers a wide variety of trade-offs between compile time and execution efficiency and promises to produce systems which are simpler, more efficient, and less susceptible to performance variations than existing systems.

2. Background

To present PICs in context, we first review existing well-known techniques for improving the efficiency of dynamically-typed object-oriented languages. All of these techniques have been used by Smalltalk-80[‡] implementations.

2.1. Dynamic Compilation

Early implementations of Smalltalk interpreted the byte codes produced by the Smalltalk compiler [GR83]. The interpretation overhead was significant, so later implementations doubled performance by dynamically compiling and caching machine code [DS84]. This technique is known as *dynamic compilation* (called "dynamic translation" in [DS84]).

Translation to native code is the basis for efficient implementations; most of the techniques described here would not make sense in an interpreted system. We therefore assume for the rest of this paper that methods are always translated to machine code before they are executed, and that this translation can occur at any time, i.e. may be interleaved with normal program execution. This means that the entire source program must be accessible at all times so that any part of it can be compiled at any time.

2.2. Lookup Caches

Sending a dynamically-bound message takes longer than calling a statically-bound procedure because the program must find the correct target method according to the run-time type of the receiver and the inheritance rules of the language. Although early Smalltalk systems had simple inheritance rules and relatively slow interpreters, method lookup (also known as message lookup) was still responsible for a substantial portion of execution time.

Lookup caches reduce the overhead of dynamically-bound message passing. A lookup cache maps (receiver type, message name) pairs to methods and holds the most recently used lookup results. Message sends first consult the cache; if the cache probe fails, they call the normal (expensive) lookup routine and store the result in the cache, possibly replacing an older lookup result. Lookup caches are very effective in reducing the lookup overhead. Berkeley Smalltalk, for example, would have been 37% slower without a cache [UP83].

[†] In this paper, we will consistently use speedups when comparing performance; for instance, "X is 52% faster than Y" means that Y's execution time is 1.52 times X's execution time.
[‡] Smalltalk-80 is a trademark of ParcPlace Systems, Inc.

2.3. Inline Caches

Even with a lookup cache, sending a message still takes considerably longer than calling a simple procedure because the cache must be probed for every message sent. However, sends can be sped up further by observing that the type of the receiver at a given call site rarely varies; if a message is sent to an object of type X at a particular call site, it is very likely that the next time the send is executed it will also have a receiver of type X.

This locality of type usage can be exploited by caching the looked-up method address at the call site, e.g. by overwriting the call instruction. Subsequent executions of the send code jump directly to the cached method, completely avoiding any lookup. Of course, the type of the receiver could have changed, and so the prologue of the called method must verify that the receiver's type is correct and call the lookup code if the type test fails. This form of caching is called *inline caching* since the target address is stored at the send point, i.e. in the caller's code [DS84].

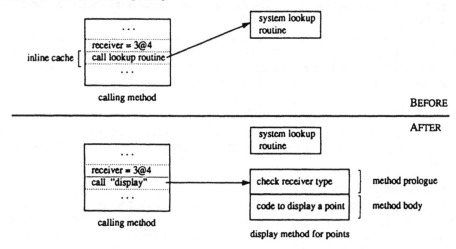

Figure 1. Inline Caching

Inline caching is surprisingly effective, with a hit ratio of 95% for Smalltalk code [DS84, Ung86, UP87]. SOAR (a Smalltalk implementation for a RISC processor) would be 33% slower without inline caching [Ung86]. All compiled implementations of Smalltalk that we know of incorporate inline caches, as does our SELF system [CUL89].

3. Handling Polymorphic Sends

Inline caches are effective only if the receiver type (and thus the call target) remains relatively constant at a call site. Although inline caching works very well for the majority of sends, it does not speed up a polymorphic call site with several equally likely receiver types because the call target switches back and forth between different methods.[†] Worse, inline caching may even slow down these sends because of the extra overhead associated with inline cache misses. The performance impact of inline cache misses becomes more severe in highly efficient systems, where it can no longer be ignored. For example, measurements for the SELF system show that the Richards benchmark spends about 25% of its time handling inline cache misses [CUL89].

An informal examination of polymorphic call sites in the SELF system showed that in most cases the degree of polymorphism is small, typically less than ten. The degree of polymorphism of sends seems to have a trimodal distribution: sends are either *monomorphic* (only one receiver type), *polymorphic* (a few

---

[†] We will use the term "polymorphic" for call sites where polymorphism is *actually* used. Consequently, we will use "monomorphic" for call sites which do not actually use polymorphism even though they might *potentially* be polymorphic.

receiver types), or *megamorphic* (very many receiver types). This observation suggests that the performance of polymorphic calls can be improved with a more flexible form of caching. This section describes
a new technique to optimize polymorphic sends and presents performance measurements to estimate the
benefits of this optimization.

3.1. Polymorphic Inline Caches

The *polymorphic inline cache* (PIC) extends inline caching to handle polymorphic call sites. Instead of
merely caching the last lookup result, PICs cache *all* lookup results for a given polymorphic call site in a
specially-generated stub routine. An example will illustrate this.

Suppose that a method is sending the display message to all elements in a list, and that so far, all list
elements have been rectangles. (In other words, the display message has been sent monomorphically.)
At this point, the situation is identical to normal inline caching:

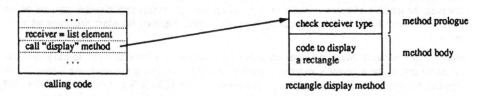

Figure 2. Inline cache after first send

Now suppose that the next list element is a circle. The inline cache calls the display method for rectangles which detects the cache miss and calls the lookup routine. With normal inline caching, this routine
would rebind the call to the display method for circles. This rebinding would happen every time the
receiver type changed.

With PICs, however, the miss handler constructs a short stub routine and rebinds the call to this stub
routine. The stub checks if the receiver is either a rectangle or a circle and branches to the corresponding
method. The stub can branch directly to the method's body (skipping the type test in the method prologue)
because the receiver type has already been verified. Methods still need a type test in their prologue because
they can also be called from monomorphic call sites which have a standard inline cache.

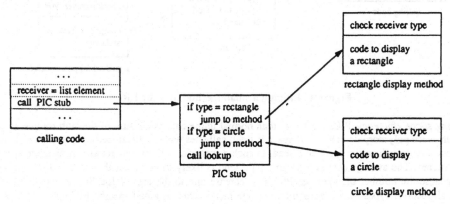

Figure 3. Polymorphic inline cache

If the cache misses again (i.e. the receiver is neither a rectangle nor a circle), the stub routine will simply
be extended to handle the new case. Eventually, the stub will contain all cases seen in practice, and there
will be no more cache misses or lookups. Thus, a PIC isn't a fixed-size cache similar to a hardware data
cache; rather, it should be viewed as an extensible cache in which no cache item is ever displaced by
another (newer) item.

3.2. Variations

The PIC scheme described above works well in most cases and reduces the cost of a polymorphic send to a few machine cycles. This section discusses some remaining problems and possible solutions.

Handling megamorphic sends. Some send sites may send a message to a very large number of types. For example, a method might send the `writeSnapshot` message to every object in the system. Building a large PIC for such a send wastes time and space. Therefore, the inline cache miss handler should not extend the PIC beyond a certain number of type cases; rather, it should mark the call site as being megamorphic and adopt a fall-back strategy, possibly just the traditional monomorphic inline cache mechanism.

Improving linear search. If the dynamic usage frequency of each type were available, PICs could be reordered periodically in order to move the most frequently occurring types to the beginning of the PIC, reducing the average number of type tests executed. If linear search is not efficient enough, more sophisticated algorithms like binary search or some form of hashing could be used for cases with many types. However, the number of types is likely to be small on average so this optimization may not be worth the effort: a PIC with linear search is probably faster than other methods for most situations which occur in practice.

Inlining short methods. Many methods are short: for example, it is very common to have methods which just return one of the receiver's instance variables. In SELF, many of these sends are inlined away by the compiler, but non-inlined access methods still represent about 10%-20% of total runtime (30%-50% of all non-inlined sends) in typical programs. At polymorphic call sites, short methods could be integrated into the PIC instead of being called by it. For example, suppose the lookup routine finds a method that just loads the receiver's x field. Instead of calling this method from the stub, its code could be copied into the stub, eliminating the call / return overhead.[†]

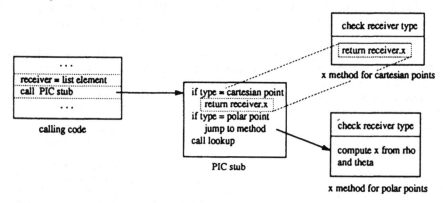

Figure 4. Inlining a small method into the PIC

Improving space efficiency. PICs are larger than normal inline caches because of the stub routine associated with every polymorphic call site. If space is tight, call sites with identical message names could share a common PIC to reduce the space overhead. In such a scenario, PICs would act as fast message-specific lookup caches. The average cost of a polymorphic send is likely to be higher than with call-site-specific PICs because the number of types per PIC will increase due to the loss of locality (a shared PIC will contain all receiver types for the particular message name, whereas a call-specific PIC only contains the types which actually occur at that call site). If the number of types is large, a shared PIC implemented with a hash table should be faster than the global lookup cache because the message name need not be verified and because the hit ratio will approach 100%.

[†] The CLOS implementation described in [KiRo89] uses a similar technique to speed up access methods (called "reader methods" in CLOS). The authors report that access methods represent 69% of the dynamically executed method calls for a set of large CLOS applications.

3.3. Implementation and Results

We implemented PICs for the SELF system, an efficient implementation of a dynamically-typed object-oriented language [CUL89, CU90, CU91]. All measurements were done on a lightly-loaded Sun-4/260 with 48 MB of memory. The base system used for comparison was the current SELF system as of September 1990. It uses inline caching; a send takes 8 instructions (9 cycles) until the method-specific code is reached (see Appendix B). An inline cache miss takes about 15 microseconds (250 cycles). This time could be reduced by some optimizations and by recoding critical parts in assembly. We estimate that such optimizations could reduce the miss overhead by about a factor of two. Thus, our measurements may overstate the direct performance advantage of PICs by about the same factor. On the other hand, measurements of the ParcPlace Smalltalk-80 system indicate that it also takes about 15 microseconds to handle a miss (see Appendix A), and thus our current implementation does not seem to be unreasonably slow.

Monomorphic sends in our experimental system use the same inline caching scheme as the base system. For polymorphic sends, a stub is constructed which tests the receiver type and branches to the corresponding method. The stub has a fixed overhead of 8 cycles (to load the receiver type and to jump to the target method), and every type test takes 4 cycles. The PICs are implemented as described in section 3.1. None of the optimizations mentioned in the previous section are implemented except that a call site is treated as megamorphic if it has more than ten receiver types (but such calls do not occur in our benchmarks). Appendix B contains an example of a PIC stub generated by our implementation.

In order to evaluate the effectiveness of polymorphic inline caches, we measured a suite of SELF programs. The programs (with the exception of PolyTest) can be considered fairly typical object-oriented programs and cover a variety of programming styles. More detailed data about the benchmarks is given in Appendix A.

Parser. A recursive-descent parser for an earlier version of the SELF syntax (550 lines).

PrimitiveMaker. A program generating C++ and SELF stub routines from a description of primitives (850 lines).

UI. The SELF user interface prototype (3000 lines) running a short interactive session. Since the Sun-4 used for our measurements has no special graphics hardware, runtime is dominated by graphics primitives (e.g. polygon filling and full-screen bitmap copies). For our tests, the three most expensive graphics primitives were turned into no-ops; the remaining primitives still account for about 30% of total execution time.

PathCache. A part of the SELF system which computes the names of all global objects and stores them in compressed form (150 lines). Most of the time is spent in a loop which iterates through a collection.

Richards. An operating system simulation benchmark (400 lines). The benchmark schedules the execution of four different kinds of tasks. It contains a frequently executed polymorphic send (the scheduler sends the runTask message to the next task).

PolyTest. An artificial benchmark (20 lines) designed to show the highest possible speedup with PICs. PolyTest consists of a loop containing a polymorphic send of degree 5; the send is executed a million times. Normal inline caches have a 100% miss rate in this benchmark (no two consecutive sends have the same receiver type). Since PolyTest is a short, artificial benchmark, we do not include it when computing averages for the entire set of benchmarks.

The benchmarks were run 10 times and the average CPU time was computed; this process was repeated 10 times, and the best average was chosen. A garbage collection was performed before every measurement in order to reduce inaccuracies. Figure 5 shows the benchmark results normalized to the base system's execution time (see Appendix A for raw execution times). For comparison, the execution times for ParcPlace Smalltalk-80 V2.4 are 262% for Richards and 93% for PolyTest (i.e. in Smalltalk, Richards runs slower and PolyTest slightly faster than the base SELF system).

With PICs, the median speedup for the benchmarks (without PolyTest) is 11%. The speedup observed for the individual benchmarks corresponds to the time required to handle inline cache misses in the base system. For example, in the base system PolyTest spends more than 80% of its execution time in the

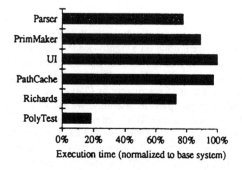

Figure 5. Impact of PICs on performance

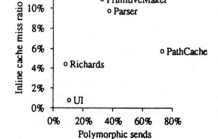

Figure 6. Inline cache miss ratios

miss handler, and thus it is more than five times faster with PICs. Overall, the performance impact of PICs is relatively small since the SELF compiler is able to inline many sends.

Interestingly, there is no direct correlation between cache misses and the number of polymorphic call sites (Figure 6). For example, more than 73% of the messages sent in PathCache are from polymorphic call sites, but the inline cache miss ratio is only 5.6%, much lower than Parser's miss ratio despite the higher percentage of polymorphic sends. This suggests that one receiver dominates at most call sites in PathCache, whereas the receiver type frequently changes in Parser's inline caches. Thus, ordering a PIC's type tests by frequency of occurrence (as suggested in section 3.2) might be a win for programs like PathCache.

The space overhead of PICs is very low, typically less than 2% of the compiled code (see Appendix A). This low overhead is also observed in our daily use of the SELF system, where the space used by PICs usually does not exceed 50Kbytes in a system which contains about 2 Mbytes of compiled code.

4. Background on Inlining and Type Information

The techniques described so far strive to reduce the cost of sending a message to that of calling a procedure. But even if these techniques were completely successful, the extremely high call frequency would still impose a severe limit on the performance of dynamically-typed object-oriented programs: even the fastest procedure call is too slow. For example, the Sun-4/260 on which our measurements were made executes about 10 million native instructions per second. The optimal calling sequence consists of two instructions per call. This would seem to limit SELF programs to significantly less than 5 million message sends per second (MiMS; see [CUL89]) even if every send was implemented optimally. However, many programs execute at 5 MiMS in our current system, and some benchmarks exceed 20 MiMS. How is this possible?

The best way to significantly speed up a call is by not executing it at all, i.e. by *inlining* the called method into the caller, thus eliminating the calling overhead entirely. In addition, inlining introduces opportunities for other optimizations like constant folding, common subexpression elimination, and better global register allocation. The benefits obtained through these optimizations often overshadow the savings from just removing the call/return overhead and are essential in order to optimize user-defined control structures.

Therefore, the SELF compiler tries to inline as many message sends as possible. However, inlining requires that the type of the target of a message send be known at compile time so that its definition can be looked up and inlined. Hence, many optimization techniques have focused on ways to obtain and exploit type information [Joh87]. The remainder of this section describes existing techniques to extract, preserve, and exploit this precious type information.

4.1. Type Prediction

Certain messages are almost exclusively sent to particular receiver types. For such messages, the compiler can *predict* the type of the receiver based on the message name and insert a run-time type test before the message send to test for the expected receiver type. Along the branch where the type test succeeds, the compiler has precise information about the type of the receiver and can statically bind and inline a copy of the message. For example, existing SELF and Smalltalk systems predict that '+' will be sent to an integer [UP82, GR83, DS84], since measurements indicate that this occurs 90% of the time [UP87]. Type prediction improves performance if the cost of the test is low and the likelihood of a successful outcome is high.

4.2. Customization

Customization is another technique for determining the types of many message receivers in a method [CUL89]. Customization extends dynamic compilation by exploiting the fact that many messages within a method are sent to self. The compiler creates a separate compiled version of a given source method for each receiver type. This duplication allows the compiler to *customize* each version to the specific receiver type. In particular, knowing the type of self at compile time allows all self sends to be inlined, without inserting type tests at every message send. Customization is especially important in SELF, since so many messages are sent to self, including instance variable accesses, global variable accesses, and many kinds of user-defined control structures.

4.3. Type Analysis and Splitting

Type analysis tries to get the most out of the available type information by propagating it through the control flow graph and by performing flow-sensitive analysis [CU90, CU91]. The compiler uses the type information obtained through the analysis to inline additional message sends and to reduce the cost of primitives (either by constant-folding the primitive or by avoiding run-time type checks of the primitive's arguments).

Often the compiler can infer only that the type of the receiver of a message is one of a small set of types (such as either an integer or a floating point number). This union type information does not enable the message to be inlined, since each possible receiver type could invoke a different method.

One approach to solving this problem is to insert type tests before the message send and create a separate branch for each of the possible types. This technique, *type casing*, is similar to type prediction and to the case analysis technique implemented as part of the Typed Smalltalk system [JGZ88].†

Splitting is another way to turn a polymorphic message into several separate monomorphic messages. It avoids type tests by copying parts of the control flow graph [CUL89, CU90, CU91]. For example, suppose that an object is known to be an integer in one branch of an if statement and a floating-point number in the other branch. If this object is the receiver of a message send following the if statement, the compiler can copy the send into the two branches. Since the exact receiver type is known in each branch, the compiler can then inline both copies of the send.

Type analysis and splitting provide a significant amount of additional type information that may be used to optimize object-oriented programs. These techniques work especially well for inferring the types of local variables and optimizing user-defined control structures. Nevertheless, there are classes of variables and expressions that type analysis cannot analyze well. One such class is the types of arguments to the method (our SELF system customizes on the type of the receiver, but not on the type of arguments). Another important class is the types of instance variables and array elements (actually, any assignable heap cell). These weaknesses of type analysis can be quite damaging to the overall performance of the system, especially for typical object-oriented programs.

5. PICs as Type Sources

PICs have a valuable property that can be used to inline many more message sends than with existing techniques. A PIC can be viewed as a *call-specific type database*: the PIC contains a list of all receiver types seen in practice at that call site. If the compiler can take advantage of this type information, it should be able to produce much more efficient code.

---

† The type information in Typed Smalltalk is provided by the programmer in the form of type declarations, while a dynamically-typed system would rely on type analysis to determine the set of possible receiver types.

Unfortunately, the information present in a method's PICs is not available when the method is first compiled, but only after it has been executing for a while. To take advantage of the information, the method must be *recompiled*. The rest of this section describes and evaluates the optimizations that may be performed when PIC-based type information from a previously compiled version of a method is available. Section 6 describes an extension to the recompilation scheme that leads to an adaptive system.

5.1. PIC-Based Type Casing

Type casing may be extended naturally in a system that recompiles methods based on PIC information. When the compiler encounters a send which it did not inline in the previous compiled version of a method, it can consult the corresponding PIC to obtain a list of likely receiver types for this send. The compiler then knows that the receiver type is the union of the types in the PIC, plus an unlikely unknown type (since a new receiver type might, but probably won't, be encountered in the future).

The compiler can then take advantage of the new type information by inserting run-time type tests and inlining the cases. For example, sending the x message to a receiver that was either a cartesian point or a polar point in the previous version's PIC would be compiled into the following code:

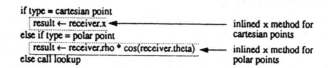

Figure 7. Inlining with type casing

5.2. Dynamic Type Prediction

PICs support better type prediction by replacing the *static* type prediction of existing systems with *dynamic* type prediction. Current systems hard-wire the set of predictions into the compiler and have no means to adapt if a particular application does not exhibit the predicted behavior. For example, if an application makes heavy use of floating point arithmetic, then predicting solely integer receivers for '+' messages penalizes the performance of floating point arithmetic.

Even worse, if an application makes heavy use of messages that are not recognized the compiler, these messages may run much slower than expected since the compiler is not using type prediction on them. For example, the initial SELF system defined a predecessor method for integers, and this message was type-predicted by the compiler. Later, programmers defined a pred method as a shorthand version of predecessor, but since this wasn't included in the compiler's static type prediction table, the performance of programs using pred was significantly worse than programs using predecessor.

These problems could be avoided by a system with PICs. The system would periodically examine all PICs, looking for messages with very skewed receiver type distributions. Those messages that clearly are only used with one or two receiver types should be type predicted. The compiler would augment or replace its built-in initial type prediction table with one derived from the actual usage patterns. As these usage patterns changed, type prediction would naturally adapt.

With PICs and recompilation, static type prediction theoretically could be eliminated, since the recompiled version will obtain the benefits of type prediction via type casing. However, since type prediction usually works very well for a few messages like '+' and ifTrue:, it is doubtful that the relatively minor simplification of the system is worth the expected loss of performance in the initial version of the compiled code.

5.3. PIC-Based Type Information and Type Analysis

The type information provided by PICs is neither strictly more nor strictly less precise than that computed using type analysis. It can be less precise because the analysis may be able to prove that an expression can have only a certain set of types at run-time. If this set is a singleton set, then the compiler can inline messages without needing a run-time type test to verify the type. On the other hand, type analysis may fail to infer anything about an expression's type (e.g. the type of an instance variable); in this case, the information provided by PICs is more precise because it includes specific types in addition to the unknown type.

The presence of PIC-based type information fundamentally alters the nature of optimization of dynamically-typed object-oriented languages. In "traditional" systems such as the current SELF compiler, type information is scarce, and consequently the compiler is designed to make the best possible use of the type information. This effort is expensive both in terms of compile time and compiled code space, since the heuristics in the compiler are tuned to spend time and space if it helps extract or preserve type information. In contrast, a PIC-based recompiling system has a veritable wealth of type information: *every* message has a set of likely receiver types associated with it derived from the previously compiled version's PICs. The compiler's heuristics and perhaps even its fundamental design should be reconsidered once the information in PICs becomes available; section 6 outlines such a system architecture designed with PICs in mind.

5.4. PIC-Based Type Information and Type Declarations

The type information present in PICs could be used in a programming environment. For every method which exists in compiled form, the system knows all receiver types that have occurred in practice. Thus, a browser could answer questions like "what kinds of objects does this parameter typically denote?" or "what kinds of objects is this message sent to?"[†] Such querying facilities could help a programmer to better understand programs written by other people and to verify her assumptions about the types of a parameter or local variable. Similarly, the system's type information could be used as a starting point for type checking in a system where type declarations are optional. Once an untyped program becomes stable, the system could automatically type-annotate all variables, and could quickly reject type declarations made by the user if they exclude types known to be used in practice.

In this scenario, type information would flow from the system to the user, in contrast to other approaches where type information flows from the user to the compiler [Suz81, BI82, JGZ88]. In our system, the programmer benefits from type information even for programs which do not contain any type declarations, and the declarations are not needed to obtain good performance. In fact, it is likely that our system can generate *better* code than existing systems based on user-specified type declarations since PICs contain only those types that are used in practice, whereas static type declarations must include types that theoretically might occur but rarely do so in practice. Thus PICs include useful information about the relative likelihood of the possible receiver types that is not present in traditional type declarations.

5.5. Implementation

We have built an experimental version of a recompiling system on top of the current SELF compiler in order to prove the feasibility of PIC-based adaptive recompilation and to estimate the quality of the code which could be produced using the type information contained in the PICs. In our experimental system, the current SELF compiler was augmented by a "type oracle" which provides the PICs' type information to the compiler. The compiler itself was not changed fundamentally, and it does not use dynamic type prediction. Each benchmark was run once to produce the first version of compiled methods and to fill the inline caches. Then a system flag was set and the benchmark was run again, which caused all methods to be recompiled using the type information contained in the inline caches. The second version was then measured to determine the improvement over the base system.

We measured the same benchmarks that were used in section 3. Figure 8 shows the performance of the experimental system and the system with PICs (described in section 3.3), normalized to the base system.

---

† Most of the mechanisms needed to find the appropriate compiled method(s) from the source method are already present in order to invalidate compiled code when a source method is changed.

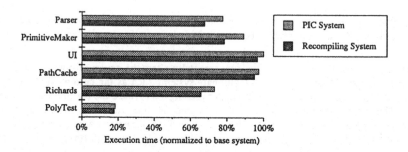

Figure 8. Performance of the Experimental System

With recompilation, the benchmarks show a median speedup of 27% over the base system and a median speedup of 11% over the system using PICs alone (excluding PolyTest). The experimental system is especially successful for Richards and Parser which are 52% and 48% faster than the base system, respectively. Because of several shortcomings of our experimental system, these numbers are conservative estimates of the performance achievable with our techniques. For example, the code for type cases generated by the experimental compiler is more than two times slower than an equivalent type case of a PIC because it reloads the receiver's type before every type test. The extra loads negate much of the savings achieved by inlining short methods; for example, PolyTest is only marginally faster even though recompilation has eliminated *all* message sends.

Figure 9 shows the impact of recompilation on the number of message sends. For each benchmark, three configurations are shown. The first bar represents the number of messages sent by the benchmark when compiled with the base system. The middle bar represents the number of message sends when using the experimental system with one recompilation. The third bar represents the steady state achieved after several recompilations; it can be viewed as the best possible case for the current compiler, i.e. what the compiler would produce if it had complete type information and inlined every message it wanted. Thus, the third scenario shows the minimum number of message sends given the inlining strategies used by the compiler.[†] The bars are normalized relative to the base system.

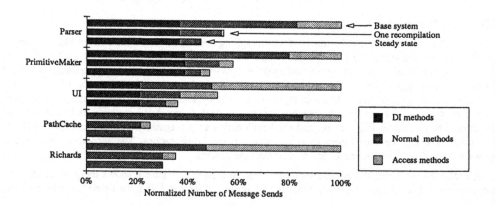

Figure 9. Impact of Recompilation on Number of Message Sends

[†] Some methods will not be inlined even when their receiver type is known, for example if they are too large. Because of limitations of the experimental system, the steady states for PrimitiveMaker and UI are not available; the data shown in the graph represent the best case which the experimental system currently can achieve.

The messages labelled "DI methods" invoke methods which use dynamic inheritance (DI), a feature of SELF which allows objects to change their parents on the fly. In the current SELF system, the use of DI prevents messages from being inlined even if their receiver type is known. Therefore, the experimental system cannot eliminate these sends. The messages labelled "normal methods" and "access methods" invoke ordinary methods and "wrapper" methods that only access an instance variable, respectively.

For our benchmarks, recompilation is extremely successful in reducing the number of dynamically executed message sends: recompiling once *halves* the total number of message sends. If DI methods are subtracted out, the median reduction of the number of message sends is a factor of 3.2. With several recompilations, a factor of 5.6 is achieved for PathCache. This surprising reduction provides strong evidence that a compiler using only static techniques such as type analysis, type prediction, and splitting cannot infer the receiver types of many message sends in object-oriented programs. PICs provide this missing information, and our experimental system is able to optimize away most eligible sends with just one recompilation.

6. Adaptive Compilation

Our experimental implementation demonstrates that code quality can be significantly improved by using the type information contained in PICs. However, it is built on top of a compiler which was designed with fundamentally different assumptions about what is important and cost-effective and therefore does not realize many of the potential benefits of a recompilation-based system. In this section we outline the benefits and problems of a new framework for efficient implementations of dynamically-typed object-oriented languages, based on the idea of incremental optimization of compiled code in an environment where type information is relatively abundant. In the tradition of Hansen [Han74] we will call this mode of compilation *adaptive compilation*.

One goal of such a system is to maximize overall system performance, i.e. to minimize the sum of compile time and execution time over the life of the system. Another somewhat conflicting goal is to minimize pauses caused by dynamic compilation so that applications always appear to the user to be making progress. These goals can be thought of as maximizing throughput (overall system performance) while minimizing latency (time to reach a certain point in an application), and as with other systems must be balanced against each other.

In our adaptive framework, methods are initially compiled with little or no optimization. As methods are used often, they are recompiled with more optimization. The recompilation can take advantage of the type information present in the previous version's PICs to generate reasonably good code without too much expensive analysis. Only those methods that are executed most frequently are eventually recompiled with full optimization, using relatively expensive techniques to generate the best possible code.

6.1. Faster Compilation

Adaptive compilation promises a number of important benefits. Perhaps the most important of these is that overall system performance should improve dramatically. We believe that a relatively simple and very fast compiler can generate good code using the type information provided by PICs because the greater amount of inlining should compensate for the optimization possibilities lost by not using expensive global techniques. The compiler could refrain from using expensive optimizations as long as possible and rely on the wealth of type information to generate good code quickly.

A fast compiler also means short compile pauses. Even for the critical methods which need to be optimized, compile pauses could be kept short by distributing the optimization effort over several recompilations or by compiling in the background. Also, recompilation could be performed in the background or during the user's "think pauses," similar to Wilson's opportunistic garbage collection [WM89].

Of course, recompilation has costs. Some time will be wasted by executing unoptimized code, and some time will be wasted because some work is repeated with every recompilation (e.g. code generation). However, we believe that the time saved by recompiling only the frequently-used methods will more than offset this additional overhead.

6.2. Trade-offs

To work well, an adaptive system needs to quickly adapt to the application to maximize overall performance. Specifically, the system must make three decisions:

- *What to recompile.* The system needs to identify the dominating parts of an application (the "hot spots") in order to optimize them. A simple approach is to count the number of times a method is executed. This should work well for relatively unoptimized programs which contain message sends in the body of every loop. The counters of the leaf methods called by the innermost loop will overflow first, and the system can then search up the call stack to find the loop. Once the methods become more optimized and contain inlined loops, standard profiling methods such as interrupt-driven PC-sampling can be used to find the methods responsible for significant amounts of execution time.

- *When to recompile.* When a method exceeds a certain threshold in the number of invocations, it will be recompiled. Thus the value of this threshold is one of the primary points of control of the adaptive system, and the system needs to do a good job in setting this value. The threshold could be determined empirically by estimating the cost and gains of recompilation. A more dynamic approach could estimate the recompilation time based on the size (and maybe previous compilation time) of a method, and adjust the recompilation threshold accordingly.

- *How much to optimize.* Spending more effort during recompilation can result in bigger savings in execution time and reduce the need for or number of future recompilations, but it will also lead to longer compile pauses. In some situations (e.g. when starting up a new application), latency is more important than absolute speed, and too much optimization would impair the responsiveness of the system.

One approach to managing the optimization strategy would be to have the system monitor the ratio of compile time to program execution time. When this ratio is high (when compilation time dominates execution time), the compiler would optimize less aggressively and recompile less frequently. Thus, the compiler would compile a new application's working set as quickly as possible. Once execution time returned to the forefront, the compiler could adopt a more aggressive recompilation stance to increase the performance of the hot spots of the application.

6.3. Preserving Information Across Code Cache Flushes

Recompilation may interact poorly with dynamic compilation and caching. If the cache for compiled code is too small to hold all of the system's code (especially with a system whose programming environment shares the address space with user applications), an optimized method might be flushed from the cache because it had not been used recently. However, the fact that the method was optimized indicates that when it is used again, it is likely to be used intensively. If the compiled code (and all the information it contains) is simply discarded when being flushed from the cache, the system will forget that the method is a "hot spot." When the code is needed again, time will be wasted by first compiling an unoptimized version, only to discover later that the method needs optimization.

To solve this problem, the system could keep some information about optimized methods even after they have been flushed from the code cache. For example, the system could keep a compressed form of the method's type information so that an efficient compiled version could be regenerated immediately without going through several recompilations. If there is not enough space to keep such compressed methods, the preserved information could be the mere fact that the method is important (time-critical); when the method has to be regenerated the system could recompile it more aggressively than it would do normally and thus could produce optimized code more quickly.

7. Related Work

Statically-typed languages can handle polymorphic sends in constant time by indexing into a type-specific function table, thus reducing the lookup to an indirect procedure call. In C++, for example, a dynamically-bound call takes between 5 and 9 cycles on a SPARC [Ros88, DMSV89, ES90, PW90]. This is possible because static type checking can guarantee the success of the lookup, i.e. the result of the table lookup need not be verified. Inline caching techniques are less attractive in this context because a direct call plus a type test take about the same time (6 cycles) as a full "lookup". However, statically-typed object-oriented languages could benefit from customization, type casing, and inlining [Lea90].

Kiczales and Rodriguez [KiRo89] describe a mechanism similar to PICs for a CLOS implementation. Their implementation of message dispatch does not use inline caching per se but it does use special dispatch handlers for some cases, e.g. when a call site uses only one or two distinct classes. In the general case, the lookup uses specific hash tables specific to the message names.

The concept of adaptive systems is not new. For example, Hansen describes an adaptive compiler in [Han74]. His compiler optimized the inner loops of Fortran programs at run-time. The main goal of his work was to minimize the total cost of running a program which presumably was executed only once. All optimizations could be applied statically, but Hansen's system tried to allocate compile time wisely in order to minimize total execution time, i.e. the sum of compile and run-time.

Some modern compilers for conventional languages use profiling information to perform branch scheduling and to reduce cache conflicts [MIPS86]. The optimizations enabled by this form of feedback are typically very low-level and machine-dependent.

Mitchell [Mit70] converted parts of dynamically-typed interpreted programs into compiled form, assuming that the types of variables remained constant. Whenever the type of a variable changed, all compiled code which depended on its type was discarded. Since the language did not support polymorphism and was not object-oriented, the main motivation for this scheme was to reduce interpretation overhead and to replace generic built-in operators by simpler, specialized code sequences (e.g. to replace generic addition by integer addition).

Suzuki [Suz81] reports that a type accumulation phase for Smalltalk-80 was suggested to him by Alan Perlis as an alternative to type analysis. In this approach, a program would be run in interpreted form against some examples and then compiled into more efficient code. However, the information would only be used to avoid lookups by inserting a type test for a likely receiver type and branching to the corresponding method (inline caching was not yet known at that time). As far as we know, Suzuki never implemented such a system. Furthermore, he maintained that the information obtained by a training run could never give useful information on polymorphic types, which is contradicted by our results.

8. Conclusion

Polymorphic inline caches (PICs) significantly speed up polymorphic sends: some programs making frequent use of polymorphism run up to 37% faster with PICs. More importantly, polymorphic inline caches are an important source of type information since they record the set of likely receiver types for every send; such type information is essential for optimizing compilers to generate efficient code. By taking advantage of this information, our experimental implementation of the SELF language executes some fairly typical object-oriented programs up to 52% faster than the base system and reduces the number of dynamically executed message sends by a factor of two to four.

The presence of PIC-based type information may fundamentally alter the problem of optimizing dynamically-typed object-oriented languages. In current systems, type information is *scarce*, and consequently the compiler needs to work hard in order to preserve and exploit the scarce information it has. Unfortunately, such techniques are expensive both in terms of compile time and compiled code space. In contrast, type information is *abundant* in a system using adaptive compilation. Such a system may reduce compilation times significantly by eliminating most of the computationally expensive type analysis phase and by only optimizing the most-used parts of programs. In addition, adaptive compilation could overcome some drawbacks of existing optimization techniques such as static type prediction. We are currently implementing such a system for the SELF language in order to validate our ideas.

Acknowledgments. We would like to thank Bay-Wei Chang and Ole Agesen for their helpful comments on earlier drafts of this paper.

9. References

[BI82] A. H. Borning and D. H. H. Ingalls, "A Type Declaration and Inference System for Smalltalk." In *Conference Record of the Ninth Annual Symposium on Foundations of Computer Science*, pp. 133-139, 1982.

[Cha91] Craig Chambers, *The Design and Implementation of the SELF Compiler, an Optimizing Compiler for Object-Oriented Programming Languages*. Ph.D. Thesis, Stanford University. In preparation.

[CPL83] Thomas J. Conroy and Eduardo Pelegri-Llopart, "An Assessment of Method-Lookup Caches for Smalltalk-80 Implementations." In [Kra83].

[CU89] Craig Chambers and David Ungar, "Customization: Optimizing Compiler Technology for SELF, a Dynamically-Typed Object-Oriented Programming Language." In *Proceedings of the SIGPLAN '89 Conference on Programming Language Design and Implementation*, Portland, OR, June 1989. Published as *SIGPLAN Notices 24(7)*, July, 1989.

[CUL89] Craig Chambers, David Ungar, and Elgin Lee, "An Efficient Implementation of SELF, a Dynamically-Typed Object-Oriented Language Based on Prototypes." In *OOPSLA '89 Conference Proceedings*, pp. 49-70, New Orleans, LA, 1989. Published as *SIGPLAN Notices 24(10)*, October, 1989.

[CU90] Craig Chambers and David Ungar, "Iterative Type Analysis and Extended Message Splitting: Optimizing Dynamically-Typed Object-Oriented Programs." In *Proceedings of the SIGPLAN '90 Conference on Programming Language Design and Implementation*, White Plains, NY, June, 1990. Published as *SIGPLAN Notices 25(6)*, June, 1990.

[CU91] Craig Chambers and David Ungar, "Making Pure Object-Oriented Languages Practical." To be presented at OOPSLA '91, Phoenix, AZ, October, 1991.

[Deu83] L. Peter Deutsch, "The Dorado Smalltalk-80 Implementation: Hardware Architecture's Impact on Software Architecture." In [Kra83].

[DMSV89] R. Dixon, T. McKee, P. Schweitzer, and M. Vaughan, "A Fast Method Dispatcher for Compiled Languages with Multiple Inheritance." In *OOPSLA '89 Conference Proceedings*, pp. 211-214, New Orleans, LA, October, 1989. Published as *SIGPLAN Notices 24(10)*, October, 1989.

[DS84] L. Peter Deutsch and Alan Schiffman, "Efficient Implementation of the Smalltalk-80 System." *Proceedings of the 11th Symposium on the Principles of Programming Languages*, Salt Lake City, UT, 1984.

[ES90] Margaret A. Ellis and Bjarne Stroustrup, *The Annotated C++ Reference Manual*. Addison-Wesley, Reading, MA, 1990.

[GJ90] Justin Graver and Ralph Johnson, "A Type System for Smalltalk." In *Conference Record of the 17th Annual ACM Symposium on Principles of Programming Languages*, San Francisco, CA, January, 1990.

[GR83] Adele Goldberg and David Robson, *Smalltalk-80: The Language and Its Implementation*. Addison-Wesley, Reading, MA, 1983.

[Han74] Gilbert J. Hansen, *Adaptive Systems for the Dynamic Run-Time Optimization of Programs*. Ph.D. Thesis, Carnegie-Mellon University, 1974.

[Hei90] Richard L. Heintz, Jr., *Low Level Optimizations for an Object-Oriented Programming Language*. Master's Thesis, University of Illinois at Urbana-Champaign, 1990.

[Ing86] Daniel H. Ingalls, "A Simple Technique for Handling Multiple Polymorphism." In *OOPSLA '86 Conference Proceedings*, Portland, OR, 1986. Published as *SIGPLAN Notices 21(11)*, November, 1986.

[JGZ88] Ralph E. Johnson, Justin O. Graver, and Lawrence W. Zurawski, "TS: An Optimizing Compiler for Smalltalk." In *OOPSLA '88 Conference Proceedings*, pp. 18-26, San Diego, CA, October, 1988. Published as *SIGPLAN Notices 23(11)*, November, 1988.

[Joh87] Ralph Johnson, ed., "Workshop on Compiling and Optimizing Object-Oriented Programming Languages." In *Addendum to the OOPSLA '87 Conference Proceedings*, pp. 59-65, Orlando, FL, October, 1987. Published as *SIGPLAN Notices 23(5)*, May, 1988.

[KiRo89] Gregor Kiczales and Luis Rodriguez, "Efficient Method Dispatch in PCL." Technical Report SSL-89-95, Xerox PARC, 1989.

[Kra83] Glenn Krasner, ed., *Smalltalk-80: Bits of History and Words of Advice*. Addison-Wesley, Reading, MA, 1983.

[Lea90] Douglas Lea, "Customization in C++." In *Proceedings of the 1990 Usenix C++ Conference*, pp. 301-314, San Francisco, CA, April, 1990.

[MIPS86]   MIPS Computer Systems, *MIPS Language Programmer's Guide*. MIPS Computer Systems, Sunny-
            vale, CA, 1986.

[Mit70]   J. G. Mitchell, *Design and Construction of Flexible and Efficient Interactive Programming Systems*.
            Ph.D. Thesis, Carnegie-Mellon University, 1970.

[PW90]   William Pugh and Grant Weddell, "Two-Directional Record Layout for Multiple Inheritance." In
            Proceedings of the SIGPLAN '90 Conference on Programming Language Design and Implementation,
            pp. 85-91, White Plains, NY, June, 1990. Published as *SIGPLAN Notices 25(6)*, June, 1990.

[Ros88]   John R. Rose, "Fast Dispatch Mechanisms for Stock Hardware." In *OOPSLA '88 Conference Proceed-
            ings*, pp. 27-35, San Diego, CA, October, 1988. Published as *SIGPLAN Notices 23(11)*, November,
            1988.

[ST84]   Norihisa Suzuki and Minoru Terada, "Creating Efficient Systems for Object-Oriented Languages." In
            Proceedings of the 11th Symposium on the Principles of Programming Languages, Salt Lake City,
            January, 1984.

[Suz81]   Norihisa Suzuki, "Inferring Types in Smalltalk." In *Proceedings of the 8th Symposium on the Princi-
            ples of Programming Languages*, 1981.

[UBF+84]   D. Ungar, R. Blau, P. Foley, D. Samples, and D. Patterson, "Architecture of SOAR: Smalltalk on a
            RISC." In *Eleventh Annual International Symposium on Computer Architecture*, Ann Arbor, MI, June,
            1984.

[Ung86]   David Ungar, *The Design and Evaluation of a High Performance Smalltalk System*. MIT Press,
            Cambridge, MA, 1986.

[UP83]   David Ungar and David Patterson, "Berkeley Smalltalk: Who Knows Where the Time Goes?" In
            [Kra83].

[UP87]   David Ungar and David Patterson, "What Price Smalltalk?" In *IEEE Computer 20(1)*, January, 1987.

[WM89]   Paul R. Wilson and Thomas G. Mohler, "Design of the Opportunistic Garbage Collector." In
            OOPSLA '89 Conference Proceedings, pp. 23-35, New Orleans, LA, October, 1989. Published as
            SIGPLAN Notices 24(10), October, 1989.

Appendix A. Raw Benchmark Data

The following table gives the execution times (in seconds) of all benchmarks. We estimate that inaccuracies due to hardware caching and context switching effects are below 5%.

	base	PIC	recompiled	Smalltalk-80
Richards	2.95	2.16	1.94	7.74
Parser	3.32	2.58	2.25	
PrimMaker	3.13	2.79	2.46	
UI	5.97	5.97	5.77	
PathCache	1.62	1.58	1.54	
PolyTest	20.48	3.76	3.68	19.14[†]

A variation of the PolyTest benchmark which performs 1,000,000 monomorphic sends instead of the polymorphic sends runs in 4.2 seconds in ParcPlace Smalltalk-80. Thus, we estimate that a cache miss takes about 15 microseconds in this system, or about the same time as a SELF inline cache miss.

The space overhead of PICs is given in the next table. The first column lists the size in bytes of the compiled code (without PICs) for each benchmark; this includes the code for all parts of the system which are used by the benchmark (e.g. strings, collections, etc.). The code sizes given below include method headers and relocation tables but not debugging information. The second column contains the size in bytes of the PICs (including headers and relocation tables), and the third column shows the space overhead relative to the base version.

	code size	PIC size	overhead
Richards	30,000	240	0.8%
Parser	269,000	4,000	1.5%
PrimMaker	973,000	16,500	1.7%
PathCache	64,000	4,400	6.9%
UI		not available	

The next table describes the number of sends that the benchmarks execute when compiled with the base system (see Figure 9). The column labelled "polymorphic" lists the number of messages sent from polymorphic call sites; "misses" is the number of inline cache misses in the base system.

	normal	access	DI	total	polymorphic	misses
Richards	380,600	421,600	0	802,200	65,800	35,500
Parser	176,200	66,300	139,600	382,100	90,900	23,600
PrimMaker	129,500	64,400	123,000	316,900	63,400	21,100
UI	119,900	212,300	88,600	420,800	35,500	2,600
PathCache	60,700	10,500	0	71,200	52,000	4,100
PolyTest	1,000,000	0	0	1,000,000	1,000,000	1,000,000

For the experimental system, the number of sends are as follows (the DI numbers remain unchanged):

	after one recompilation		steady state	
	normal	access	normal	access
Richards	241,400	41,800	241,400	0
Parser	63,500	3,300	32,800	0
PrimMaker	42,700	17,500	19,600	11,600[‡]
UI	67,400	61,800	43,100	20,000[‡]
PathCache	15,300	2,600	12,800	0
PolyTest	0	0	0	0

[†] The main loop of the benchmark was hand-inlined so that the Smalltalk compiler could produce better code; otherwise, the time would be 36.7 seconds.

[‡] Our experimental system cannot recompile this benchmark often enough to reach the steady state.

Appendix B. Example Code

The following code was produced by our system for a PIC containing two different receiver types; the code is given in SPARC assembler syntax. Branches have one delay slot on the SPARC; instructions in annulled delay slots (indicated by , a) are only executed if the branch is taken, except for branch always where the instruction in the delay slot is never executed. sethi/add combinations are needed to load 32-bit constants.

```
        andcc  %i0, 1                      tag test for immediate (integer, float)
        bnz,a  _mapTest                    branch to _mapTest if not an immediate
        load   [%i0+7], %g5                load receiver map (annulled delay slot)
        bra,a  _miss                       immediate: branch to _miss
_mapTest:
        sethi  %hi(type1), %g4             load first part of type 1 (32-bit literal)
        add    %g4, %lo(type1), %g4        load second part of type 1
        cmp    %g4, %g5                     compare with receiver type
        bne,a  _next                       try next case if not equal
        sethi  %hi(type2), %g4             load first part of type 2 (annulled delay slot)
        sethi  %hi(method1), %g4           success: load first part of first method's address
        jmp    %g4 + %lo(method1)          and branch to the method
_next:
        add    %g4, %lo(type2), %g4        complete the load of type 2
        cmp    %g4, %g5                     compare with receiver type
        bne,a  _miss                       no more types to check; goto _miss if not equal
        nop                                empty delay slot (could be eliminated)
        sethi  %hi(method2), %g4           success: load first part of second method's address
        jmp    %g4 + %lo(method2)          and branch to the method
_miss:
        sethi  %hi(Lookup), %g4            miss: load first part of lookup routine
        jmp    %g4 + %lo(Lookup)           and branch to the lookup routine
        nop                                empty delay slot
```

An Object-Oriented Logic Language for Modular System Specification °

Angelo Morzenti and Pierluigi San Pietro

Politecnico di Milano, Dipartimento di Elettronica, Piazza Leonardo da Vinci 32, Milano, Italy.

Abstract

We define TRIO+, an Object Oriented logic language for modular system specification. TRIO+ is based on TRIO, a first order modal language that is well suited to the specification of embedded and real-time systems, and provides an effective support to a variety of validation activities, like specification testing, simulation, and property proof. Unfortunately, TRIO lacks the possibility to construct specifications of complex systems in a systematic and modular way. TRIO+ combines the use of constructs for hierarchical system decomposition, and object oriented concepts like inheritance and genericity, with an expressive and intuitive graphic notation, yielding a specification language that is formal and rigorous, and still flexible, readable, general, and easily adaptable to the user's needs.

1 Introduction

The importance of the requirement specification phase for the development process of any system, and of software and hardware systems in particular, has been greatly emphasized in recent years. In fact, incorrect, incomplete, or poorly structured specifications can cause significant organizational and economical problems in all successive phases of system development. This justifies the great attention devoted in the research community to the study of specification languages and methods.

Formal specification methods proved to be well suited to the production of rigorous and unambiguous specifications. Formality in specifications also allows one to perform systematically or even automatically validation activities like testing and simulation, and to prove that the modelled systems possess desired properties. The use of formal methods is particularly valuable in the most "difficult" areas, such as embedded and real-time systems: these systems are required to perform critical or dangerous tasks, interacting with an environment which evolves independently at a speed that cannot be controlled. Typical examples in this category are weapon systems, patient control systems, plant control systems, flight control systems, etc: a failure of the system to react to certain input data signals within some specified time bounds can cause severe damages or even fatal disasters.

As [Wir 77] points out, "time" plays a fundamental role in real–time systems; in particular, correctness of such systems does depend on time. This constitutes a sharp departure from sequential and concurrent systems. In the case of sequential systems, time simply affects performance, not correctness. In the case of concurrency, systems can always be designed in a way that their behavior (and thus, correctness) does not depend on the speed of activities. Unfortunately, this is not true in the case of real–time systems, since ac-

° This work was partially supported by CNR-Progetto Finalizzato Sistemi Informativi e Calcolo Parallelo and by ENEL-CRA.

tivities occurring in the environment are not entirely under control. They evolve according to their own logic: they cannot be delayed and resumed "ad libitum" to meet the desired correctness criteria.

In the past years we developed TRIO [GMM 90], a logic language for the formal specification of real-time systems. TRIO is based on classical temporal logic, but it deals with time in a quantitative way by providing a metric to indicate distance in time between events and length of time intervals. Another extremely important aspect is that TRIO's formal semantics can accommodate a variety of time structures: from dense to discrete and finite. In particular, finite time structures are those that will be used to execute TRIO specifications. TRIO is provided with a formal semantics which permits validation activities such as testing specifications against a history of the system evolution, simulation of the system behavior in response to a sequence of stimuli coming from the environment, and formal proof of system properties. In [MRR 89] it was shown how the TRIO language can become the core of a specification environment where suitable tools can provide an automatic support to the specifications activity.

TRIO has proved to be a useful specification tool, since it combines the rigor and precision of formal methods with the expressiveness and naturalness of first order and modal logics. However, the use of TRIO for the specification of large and complex systems has shown its major flaw: as originally defined, the language does not support directly and effectively the activity of structuring a large and complex specification into a set of smaller modules, each one corresponding to a well identified, autonomous subpart of the system that is being specified. This is because TRIO specifications are very finely structured: the language does not provide powerful abstraction and classification mechanisms, and lacks an intuitive and expressive graphic notation. In summary, TRIO is best suited to the specification "in the small", that is, to the description of relatively simple systems via formulas of the length of a few lines.

However in the description of large and complex systems [CHJ 86], one often needs to structure the specification into modular, independent and reusable parts. In such a case, beyond formality, executability, rigor and absence of ambiguity, other language features become important, such as the ability to structure the specifications into modules, to define naming scopes, to produce specifications by an incremental, top-down process, to attribute a separate level of formality and detail to each portion of the specification [MBM 89]. These issues are similar to those arising in the production of large programs, an activity that is usually called programming-in-the-large [D&K 76]. Hence we may refer to the process of producing specifications of complex systems as specifying-in-the-large.

To support specification in the large, we enriched TRIO with concepts and constructs from object oriented methodology, yielding a language called TRIO+. Among the most important features of TRIO+ are the ability to partition the universe of objects into classes, inheritance relations among classes, and mechanisms such as genericity to support reuse of specification modules and their top-down, incremental development. Structuring the specification into modules supports an incremental, top-down approach to the specification activity through successive refinements, but also allows one to build independent and reusable subsystem specifications, that could be composed in a systematic way in different contexts. Also desirable is the possibility of describing the specified system at different levels of abstraction, and of focusing with greater attention and detail on some more relevant aspects, leaving unspecified other parts that are considered less important or are already well understood.

TRIO⁺ is also endowed with an expressive graphic representation of classes in terms of boxes, arrows, and connections to depict class instances and their components, information exchanges and logical equivalences among (parts of) objects. In principle, the use of a graphic notation for the representation of formal specifications does not improve the expressiveness of the language, since it provides just an alternative syntax for some of the language constructs. In practice, however, the ability to visualize constructs of the language and use their graphic representation to construct, update or browse specifications can make a great difference in the productivity of the specification process and in the final quality of the resulting product, expecially when the graphic view is consistently supported by means of suitable tools, such as structure-directed editors, consistency checkers, and report generators.

In our opinion this is the reason of the popularity of the so-called CASE tools, many of which are based on Data Flow Diagrams or their extension [DeM 78, Y&C 79, War 86]. These tools comprise informal or semi-formal languages as their principle descriptional notation, and exhibit problems such as ambiguity, lack of rigor, and difficulty in executing specs, but nevertheless they can be very helpful in organizing the specifier's job. On the other hand TRIO⁺ aims at providing a formal and rigorous notation for system specification, which includes effective features and constructs to support modularization, reuse, incrementality and flexibility in the specification activity.

The paper is organized as follows. Section 2 summarizes TRIO's main features, provides a simple model-theoretic semantics, and describes how the language can be used to perform validation activities on the specifications. Section 3 introduces TRIO⁺, the object oriented extension of TRIO; in particular, it illustrates the constructs for inheritance and genericity. The concepts are mostly presented through examples, and whenever possible a graphic representation of the specifications is constructed in parallel with the textual one. The semantics of TRIO⁺ is not provided in full detail: only an informal and sketchy description is given of how TRIO⁺ specifications can be translated into suitable TRIO formulas. Section 4 draws conclusions and indicates some directions of future research.

2 Definition of the TRIO language

TRIO is a first order logical language, augmented with temporal operators which permit to talk about the truth and falsity of propositions at time instants different from the current one, which is left implicit in the formula. We now briefly sketch the syntax of TRIO and give an informal and intuitive account of its semantics; detailed and formal definitions can be found in [GMM 90].

Like in most first order languages, the alphabet of TRIO is composed of variable, function and predicate names, plus the usual primitive propositional connectors '¬' and '∧', the derived ones '→', '∨', '↔', ..., and the quantifiers '∃' and '∀'. In order to permit the representation of change in time, variables, functions and predicates are divided into *time dependent* and *time independent* ones. Time dependent variables represent physical quantities or configurations that are subject to change in time, and time independent ones represent values unrelated with time. Time dependent functions and predicates denote relations, properties or events that may or may not hold at a given time instant, while time independent functions and predicates represent facts and properties which can be assumed not to change with time. TRIO is a typed language, since we associate a domain of legal values to each variable, a domain/range pair to every function, and a domain to all arguments of every predicate. Among variable domains there is a distinguished one, called the

Temporal Domain, which is numerical in nature: it can be the set of integer, rational or real numbers, or a subset thereof. Functions representing the usual arithmetic operations, like '+' and '-', and time independent predicates for the common relational operators, like '=', '≠', '<', '≤', are assumed to be predefined at least for values in the temporal domain.

TRIO formulas are constructed in the classical inductive way. A term is defined as a variable, or a function applied to a suitable number of terms of the correct type; an atomic formula is a predicate applied to terms of the proper type. Besides the usual propositional operators and the quantifiers, one may compose TRIO formulas by using primitive and derived temporal operators. There are two temporal operators, *Futr* and *Past*, which allow the specifier to refer, respectively, to events occurring in the future or in the past with respect to to the current, implicit time instant. They can be applied to both terms and formulas, as shown in the following. If *s* is any TRIO term and *t* is a term of the temporal type, then

$$\text{Futr}(s, t) \quad \text{and} \quad \text{Past}(s, t)$$

are also TRIO terms. The intended meaning is that, if *v* is the numerical value of term *t*, then the value of *Futr (s, t)* (resp. *Past (s, t)*) is the value of term *s* at an instant lying *v* time units in the future (resp. in the past) with respect to the current time instant. Similarly, if *A* is a TRIO formula and *t* is a term of the temporal type, then

$$\text{Futr}(A, t) \quad \text{and} \quad \text{Past}(A, t)$$

are TRIO formulas too that are satisfied at the current time instant if and only if property *A* holds at the instant lying *v* time units ahead (resp. behind) the current one. Based on the primitive temporal operators *Futr* and *Past*, numerous derived operators can be defined for formulas. We mention, among the many possible ones, the following:

AlwF(A)	$\overset{def}{=}$	$\forall t\,(t > 0 \rightarrow \text{Futr}(A, t))$
AlwP(A)	$\overset{def}{=}$	$\forall t\,(t > 0 \rightarrow \text{Past}(A, t))$
Lasts (A, t)	$\overset{def}{=}$	$\forall t'\,(0 < t' < t \rightarrow \text{Futr}(A, t'))$
Always (A)	$\overset{def}{=}$	$\text{AlwP}(A) \wedge A \wedge \text{AlwF}(A)$
NextTime (A, t)	$\overset{def}{=}$	$\text{Futr}(A, t) \wedge \text{Lasts}(\neg A, t)$
Becomes (A)	$\overset{def}{=}$	$A \wedge \exists \delta\,(\delta > 0 \wedge \text{Past}(\neg A, \delta) \wedge \text{Lasted}(\neg A, \delta))$

AlwF(A) means that *A* will hold in all future time instants; *Lasts(A, t)* means that *A* will hold for the next *t* time units; *NextTime(A,t)* means that *A* will take place for the first time in the future at a time instant lying *t* time units from now; *AlwP* has, for the past, the same meaning than the corresponding operator for the future. *Always(A)* means that *A* holds in every time instant of the temporal domain.

As an example, we consider a pondage power station, where the quantity of water held in the basin is controlled by means of a sluice gate. The gate is controlled via two commands, *up* and *down* which respectively open and close it, and are represented as a TRIO time dependent predicate named *go* with an argument in the range {*up, down*}. The current state of the gate can have one of the four values: *up* and *down* (with the obvious meaning), and *mvup, mvdown* (meaning respectively that the gate is being opened or closed). The state of the gate is modelled in TRIO by a time dependent variable, called *position*. The following formula describes the fact that it takes the sluice gate Δ time units to go from the *down* to the *up* position, after receiving a go (up) command.

$$(\text{position} = \text{down}) \wedge \text{go (up)} \rightarrow \text{Lasts (position} = \text{mvup}, \Delta) \wedge \text{Futr (position} = \text{up}, \Delta)$$

When a *go (up)* command arrives while the gate is not still in the *down* position, but is moving down because of a preceding *go (down)* command, then the direction of motion of the gate is not reversed immediately, but the downward movement proceeds until the *down* position has been reached. Only then the gate will start opening according to the received command.

$(\text{position} = \text{mvdown}) \wedge \text{go (up)} \rightarrow$
$\exists t \ (\text{NextTime (position} = \text{down}, t) \wedge \text{Futr ((Lasts (position} = \text{mvup}, \Delta) \wedge \text{Futr (position} = \text{up}, \Delta), t \ )$

If the behavior of the sluice gate is symmetrical with respect to its direction of motion, two similar TRIO formulas will describe the commands and their effects in the opposite direction.

In a way similar to what is done in classical first order logic, one can define the concepts of satisfiability and validity of a TRIO formula, with respect to suitable interpretations. For the sake of simplicity, in the following, we provide a straightforward model theoretic semantics, that can assign meaning to TRIO formulas with reference to unbounded temporal domains, like the set of integer, rational or real numbers. In [MMG 90] a truly model-parametric semantics for the language is defined, which may refer to any finite or infinite temporal domain. An interpretation for a TRIO formula is composed of two parts: a time dependent part L and a time independent one, G. The time independent part, $G = (\xi, \Pi, \Phi)$ consists of a variable evaluation function, ξ, that assigns values to time independent variable names, of a time independent predicate evaluation function, Π, that assigns a relation to every time independent predicate name, and of a function evaluation Φ that assigns a function to every function name. The time dependent part $L = \{(\xi_i, \Pi_i, \Phi_i) \ / \ i \in T\}$ contains, for each instant in the temporal domain T, one evaluation function ξ_i for time dependent variables, one evaluation function Π_i that assigns a relation to every time dependent predicate name, and one evaluation function Φ_i that assigns a function to every time dependent function name. Based on such interpretation, it is possible to define an evaluation function assigning a value to all TRIO terms and formulas in a generic time instant $i \in T$. For a complete definition of the model-theoretic semantics of TRIO, the interested reader can refer to [M&S 90b] which contains an extended version of the present paper.

A TRIO formula is said to be temporally *satisfiable* in an interpretation if it evaluates to true in at least one instant of the temporal domain. In such a case we say that the interpretation constitutes a *model* for the formula. A formula is said to be temporally *valid* if it is true in every instant of the temporal domain. Finally, a TRIO formula is said to be *time invariant* if it is either valid or it cannot be satisfied in any interpretation.

A TRIO formula is *classically closed* if all of its (time independent) variables are quantified; it is *temporally closed* if it does not contain time dependent variables or predicates, or if it has either *Sometimes* or *Always* as the outermost operator, or finally if it results from the propositional composition or classical closure of temporally closed formulas. It can be proved (see [Mor 89]) that any temporally closed formula is time invariant; this can be understood intuitively by considering that the operators *Sometimes* and *Always* provide a way to quantify existentially and universally the current time which is implicit in TRIO formulas.

For these reasons we define a *specification* of a real time system as a TRIO formula that is closed, both classically and temporally.

Since TRIO is an extension of the first order predicate calculus, it is evident that the problem of the satisfiability of a TRIO formula is undecidable, in its full generality. The problem is however decidable if we consider only interpretations with finite domains. In this hypothesis, we defined an algorithm that proves the satisfiability of a TRIO formula on a finite interpretation in a constructive way, that is, by constructing an interpretation where the formula is verified. This algorithm was inspired by the tableaux proof methods, that were first defined in [Smu 68] and have been widely used in different branches of temporal logic, like in [R&U 71, Wol 83, BPM 83]; the interested reader may refer to [GMM 90] for its detailed definition. The algorithm for the proof of the satisfiability of a formula can be used to prove its validity, by showing that its negation is unsatisfiable; also we can show that a specification ensures some given property of the described system, by just proving as valid the implication $\Sigma \rightarrow \Pi$, where Σ is the specification, and Π is the desired property. Thus, the specification can then be said to be executable, since we can perform proofs of properties in a mechanical way.

We point out that the tableaux-based algorithms, that permit the execution of TRIO specifications by constructing interpretations for closed formulas, assume as given the time independent part of the interpretation which assigns values to time independent predicate and functions. This because such logic entities represent static and general facts or invariant properties of the modelled system that are well known to the specifier. By contrast, when executing the specification, one is more interested in constructing the time dependent part of the interpretation, since it represents the events taking place in one possible dynamic evolution of the system.

Furthermore, executability of TRIO formulas is also provided at lower levels of generality, by giving the possibility to verify that one given temporal evolution of the system is compatible with the specification, and to simulate the specified system, starting from an initial, possibly incompletely specified, configuration. See [GMM 90, F&M 91] for more details about simulation and verification with TRIO.

3 Definition of the TRIO+ language

As we showed in section 2, the TRIO specification of a system is built by writing logical axioms. The TRIO$^+$ specification of the same system is expressed defining suitable *classes*. A class is again a set of axioms describing the system, but this set is built up in a modular, independent way, following information hiding principles and object oriented techniques. Classes may be *simple* or *structured*, and can be part of an *inheritance* lattice.

3.1 Simple classes

A simple class is very similar to an ordinary TRIO specification: it is a group of axioms, in which occurring predicates, variables, and functions must be explicitly declared, in order to have typed formulas. An example of simple class is the specification of the sluice-gate already treated in the example of section 2.

class sluice_gate
    Visible go, position
    Items   go: TD × {up, down} → boolean
                   position: TD → {up, down, mvup, mvdown}

Δ: → integer
Vars t: integer
Axioms

go_down: position=up ∧ go(down) → Lasts (position=mvdown, Δ) ∧ Futr (position=down , Δ)

go_up: position=down ∧ go(up) → Lasts (position=mvup, Δ) ∧ Futr (position=up, Δ)

move_up: position=mvup ∧ go(down) →

∃t NextTime (position=up, t) ∧ Futr (Lasts (position=mvdown, Δ) ∧ Futr (position=down,Δ), t)

move_down: position=mvdown ∧ go(up) →

∃t NextTime (position=down, t) ∧ Futr (Lasts (position=mvup, Δ) ∧ Futr (position=up, Δ), t)

end sluice_gate

The class header is followed by the **Visible** clause, which defines the class interface. In the example, *go* and *position* are the only available symbols when referring to modules of the class sluice_gate in the axioms of another class. The keyword **Items** is followed by the declarations of the local functions, predicates and variables which can be used in the axioms. The declarations are based on predefined scalar types, such as integer, real, boolean, finite sets, subranges. In the example *Δ* is an integer constant (constants are declared as zero-ary functions), *go* is a unary time dependent predicate on the set {up, down} (predicates are declared as boolean functions), *position* is a time dependent variable whose values may range on {up, down, mvup, mvdown} (time dependent variables are declared as a function of Temporal Domain, TD). Items are time dependent if they have TD as the type of their first argument; however, no corresponding argument appears in the use of the identifier in the formula, since time is implicit in TRIO. The **Vars** clause is followed by the declaration of the time independent variables which occur in the axioms. The **Axioms** are TRIO formulas, prefixed with an implicit universal temporal quantification, i.e. an *Always* temporal operator. For instance the first axiom in the sluice_gate class is to be understood as:

Always(position = down ∧ go (up) → Lasts (position = mvup, Δ) ∧ Futr (position = up, Δ))

Every axiom can be preceded by a name, which can be used as a reference for axiom redefinition in inheritance: see section 3.5. The name must be different from the names of the items of the class. The items of a class (including the inherited ones) are the only symbols of variables predicates and functions which can occur in class axioms. This rule will be relaxed in section 3.2.

An **instance** of the class is a **model** for the axioms of the class, i.e. an interpretation for all entities declared in the *Items* clause, such that all the axioms are true. So a class declaration is the intensional representation of the set of its models. As in the execution of TRIO specifications, we are mainly interested in the generation of the dynamic (i.e. time dependent) part of the interpretation, and assume that the static (i.e. time independent) part is given. A class instance of sluice_gate is then the following table (for the sake of brevity only four instants of the temporal domain are considered here):

field name	value
position	⟨ down, mvup, mvup, up, ... ⟩
go	⟨ {up}, {} ,{} ,{}, ... ⟩
Δ	3

Table 1. An instance of the class sluice_gate

Intuitively, the time dependent Items of an instance represent one complete possible evolution of the specified system. The value for *go* is a sequence of unary relations, one for every instant of the temporal domain. In the example go(up) is true in the first instant, and from the following moment the sluice_gate is moving (position=mvup) and go(.) is false (empty relation); Δ instants after the command, the gate is up (position=up).

TRIO+ is a pure logic language: no surprise there are *no* primitives like Create or New to explicitly control instance creation.

A class may have a meaningful graphic representation as a box, with its name written at the left top; the name of the items are written on lines internal to the box; if an item is visible, then the corresponding line is continued outside the box. Class *sluice_gate* is represented in Figure 1.

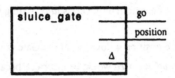

Figure 1. Graphic representation of the class sluice_gate

3.2 Structured classes

The fundamental technique for programming in the large is modularization, using the information hiding principle. In object-oriented languages modularization is obtained by declaring *classes*, that describe sets of objects. A class may have components of other classes, i.e. every instance of the class may contain parts which are instances of those classes. For example, a tank may contain two sluice gates, one for water input and the other for output: an object oriented description of this simple system consists of a class which has two components of type sluice_gate, to represent distinct and separately evolving objects. Classes which have components–called modules–of other classes are called *structured classes*. They permit the construction of TRIO+ modular specifications, expecially suited to describe systems in which *parts*, i.e. *modules*, can be easily recognized. The tank of the above example may be defined as having two modules of the class sluice_gate. This is achieved by the following class declaration (for the sake of simplicity, the example has no items and no axioms):

> **class** tank -- first partial version --
>> **Visible** inputGate.go, outputGate.go
>> **Modules** inputGate, outputGate: sluice_gate
> **end** tank

Recursive definitions of classes are not allowed: so a class (and its subclasses: see section 3.5) can not be used to declare its own modules. Structured classes have a meaningful graphic representation: the modules of the class are just boxes, with a name and a line for every visible item. The picture for the tank example is in Figure 2.

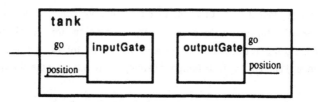

Figure 2. The graphic representation of class tank (draft version)

Modules cannot be used directly in axioms, because they are not logical symbols such as predicate or function names: they represent a set of items and modules definitions, with related axioms. For the same reason the visible interface can not list entire modules, but only their visible items, such as *inputGate.go*. The visible items of a module can be accessed in the axioms of an enclosing class by using a dot notation. For example, the following is a possible axiom of the class *tank*, stating that outputGate cannot be up when inputGate is down:

$$\text{inputGate.position} = \text{down} \rightarrow \text{outputGate.position} \neq \text{up}.$$

Instead, an axiom containing *outputGate.area* would be incorrect, because *area* is not a visible item of the class *sluice_gate*.

3.3 Specifying complex systems

TRIO+ supports some more facilities to specify complex real world systems. One facility tries to extend the expressiveness of the graphic notation. We illustrate it by enlarging the previous example. A more realistic tank may have two actuators, one to control each sluice gate, and a transducer which measures the level of the tank. The external plant is able to send four commands to control the tank, to open or close each sluice gate. This can be described by defining the class *tank*, depicted in Figure 3.

class tank

        Visible transducer.level, openInput, closeInput, openOutput, closeOutput

        Modules   inputGate, outputGate: sluice_gate
                        transducer: cl_transducer
                        actuator1, actuator2: actuator

        Items openInput, closeInput, openOutput, closeOutput: TD → Boolean

        Connections   { (openInput actuator1.open)
                           (closeInput actuator1.close)
                           (openOutput actuator2.open)
                           (closeOutput actuator2.close)
                           (actuator1.go inputGate.go)
                           (actuator1.position inputGate.position)
                           (actuator2.go outputGate.go)
                           (actuator2.position outputGate.position) }

end tank

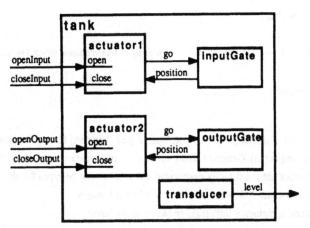

Figure 3. The graphic representation of the class *tank* (final version).

Every instance of this class contains two instances of sluice_gates, one instance of *cl_transducer* and two of *cl_actuator*. We assume classes *cl_transducer* and *cl_actuator* as already defined. The interface of *cl_transducer* includes a time dependent variable *level*, and the interface of *cl_actuator* contains the propositional time dependent variables *open* and *close*, plus *go* and *position* with the same meaning as in *sluice_gate*.

Connections is a list of pairs, denoting equivalence or identity between two items which are in the current scope. A connection is pictorially represented by a line joining the two items. If the two items have the same name, then this is repeated only once, near the linking line. Connections can often be interpreted as information flows between parts; it is then possible to use an arrow to represent the direction of the flow. However, the direction of arrows has no associated semantics, since there is no real distinction between the two items connected: it is only an expressive, although informal, notation.

In the example, we state that the commands openInput, closeInput, openOutput, closeOutput and the instantaneous value of tank level are all what the external world is allowed to know of a tank. The connections say the commands are not sent directly to the gates, but to the actuators, which control the gates and decide when moving them up and down.

Connections can be a useful method for the specification of a complex system: one describes system components separately and then identifies information flows between them. Using connections this can be made in a systematic way, with an expressive and convenient graphic meaning. A structured class can be thought as a complex system, composed of interacting subsystems; interactions are shown by the connections between modules.

Another TRIO+ facility is a tool to describe those real world systems which may contain groups of identical parts: for instance, a shift register is composed of a certain number of DT flip-flop's, a power generation station may have a group of generators working in parallel, and so on. These situations are easily described in TRIO+, because it is possible to define *arrays* of modules. For example, a class for a four-bit shift register may be declared as in the following, using a separately defined class DT_flip_flop:

class 4_places_shift_register

. . . .

    Modules DT: 1..4 → DT_flip_flop   -- an array of four modules, which are accessed as DT(.) --

. . . .

end 4_places_shift_register

3.4 Genericity

TRIO[+] is provided with a simple genericity mechanism (see [Mey 86] for a good introduction to genericity in object oriented languages). Generic classes have one or more parameters, which must be instantiated before use: generic classes are not directly executable. Parameters can be types for the items or classes for the modules, but also constants which can be used to declare subranges.

For example, a generic n-elements shift-register can be so declared:

    class N_places_shift_register [NumEl]   -- NumEl is a constant parameter --

    . . . .

        Modules DT: 1..NumEl → DT_flip_flop

    . . . .

    end N_places_shift_register

To declare an eight-place shift-register one can write:

        class 8_places_shift_register **is** N_places_shift_register [8]

The same syntax can be used to declare a class is generic with respect to classes or types.

3.5 Inheritance

Inheritance provides the possibility for a class–which in this case is also called a *subclass*–to receive attributes from other classes–called its *superclasses*. The reader is referred to [Weg 88] for thorough treatment of inheritance, its many advantages and a classification of the various sorts of inheritance.

The inheritance mechanisms are far to be well settled and universally accepted, but their definition is guided by two opposite concepts: monotonicity and freedom. The monotone approach is characterized by a strict semantic compatibility between superclasses and subclasses: every instance of a class must then be an instance of its superclasses, since it must satisfy all their axioms. This is very difficult to achieve in practice with reasonable and flexible constraints. The other approach, which is much more common, is to consider inheritance only a syntactic method to organize classes. This can be achieved in many different ways and degrees, from quasi-monotony to total freedom. For example inherited attributes might be redefined only as subtypes, or alternatively the user could be allowed to cancel or redefine them in a completely free way.

In TRIO[+] inheritance follows the liberal approach, because monotonicity is considered too severe for a specification language, which must provide a good degree of flexibility. Our definition tries to avoid incorrect uses of inheritance, which can lead to the definition of inconsistent classes, imposing some constraints. TRIO[+] inheritance allows the specifier to add and redefine items, modules, and axioms. The axioms can be redefined in a totally free way, while the redefinition of items and modules has some restrictions. Connections are inherited without changes. Redefinition of items is free, but users cannot change their arity, e.g. a two-place predicate must remain two-place, or else all formulas where it occurs would become syntactically incorrect. Instead, the declaration of the domains of items can change freely.

An example of axioms redefinition and item addition is the following: define a sluice_gate with an emergency command to open ten times faster than in normal conditions.

class sluice_gate_with_emergency_control
    Inherit sluice_gate [redefine go, go_up]
    Items go: TD $\times$ {up, down, fast_up} $\to$ boolean
    Axioms
    go_up: position = down $\wedge$ go(up) $\wedge$ Lasts ($\neg$ go(fast_up), Δ) $\to$
                           Lasts (position=mvup, Δ) $\wedge$ Futr (position=up, Δ)
    fastup: position = down $\wedge$ go (fast_up) $\to$ Lasts (position=mvup, $\Delta/10$) $\wedge$ Futr (position=up, $\Delta/10$)
end sluice_gate_with_emergency_control

In order to change an inherited axiom, item or module, its name must be listed in a redefine clause following the corresponding class (see [Mey 88] for the advantages of a similar syntax). In the example, we redefine the item *go,* adding the new command value *fast_up,* and the axiom *go_up,* and we add the axiom *fastup* to describe the new semantics. For the sake of clarity we have deliberately simplified the axioms: they state that the fast_up command has effect only when the sluice is down, and that a go(up) has no effect if a go(fast_up) will follow within Δ instants. A more realistic behavior would impose to redefine some more inherited formulas.

Notice that the simple addition of one more command imposes the redefinition of some axioms: if such a redefinition was not possible, as in a monotone approach, we should define from scratch a completely new class to describe the new sluice, losing the advantages of inheritance. Redefinition of modules must be achieved by specifying a subclass of the class used in the original declaration: for example a tank with the new sluice gate for the output is obtained as follows:

    class tank_2ndversion
        Inherit tank [redefine outputGate, actuator2]
        Modules   outputGate: sluice_gate_with_emergeny_control
                           actuator2: actuator_with_emergency_control
    end tank_2ndversion

The actuator2 must change to control the new sluice. For the sake of brevity we do not define its new class. A good solution to minimize redefinitions is to use multiple inheritance.

The constraint of using only subclasses to redefine modules is imposed in order to avoid that visible items of the component modules vanish, because the new module class used for redefinition does not possess them: this could make axioms incorrect, because they would refer to items that do not exist in the scope of the heir class. For the same reason we forbid to make invisible the inherited visible items: to this end, it would be equivalent to a cancellation.

The definition of **multiple inheritance** brings no additional difficulties, since it only requires to solve name clashes of inherited attributes that are homonymous. Using the technique adopted in the programming language Eiffel [Mey 88], name clashes are avoided by the use of a *rename* primitive, to differentiate inherited attributes. Note that there is no name clash if the two attributes are inherited from a common superclass, and they have not been redefined in an intermediate ancestor. An example of this situation and of the use of inheritance to classify and incrementally specify systems is the following description of S-R and J-K flip-flop's, starting from more elementary devices, according to the inheritance lattice shown in Figure 4.

All flip-flop's have an output and a delay of propagation between the commands and their effect. Thus a general definition of flip-flop's would be:

class flip_flop
    Visible Q
    Items $Q: TD \rightarrow$ Boolean   -- the state of the flip-flop, which can be True or False --
                $\tau: \rightarrow$ Real   -- maximum time of propagation of flip_flop --
end flip_flop

This class is so simple and general it has no axioms. A first specializations is adding a Set command:

class Set_ff
    Inherit flip_flop
    Items $S: TD \rightarrow$ Boolean
    Axioms *Set* $: S \rightarrow \text{Futr}(Q,\tau)$ -- a set command makes Q true after τ instants --
end Set_ff

Another possible specializations is adding a Reset (or *Clear*) command:

class Reset_ff
    Inherit flip_flop
    Items $R: TD \rightarrow$ Boolean -- R stands for Reset --
    Axioms *Reset:* $R \rightarrow \text{Futr}(\neg Q,\tau)$ -- a Reset command makes Q false after τ instants --
end Reset_ff

Now we want to describe a S-R flip-flop: it has both Set and Reset, and the output persists in its value when there is no command; it is not contemplated the possibility of Set and Reset true at the same time.

class SR_ff
    Inherit Set_ff, Reset_ff
        -- there is not a name conflict for τ, because it is inherited from a unique superclass: *flip_flop* --
    Axioms *Persistency*: $\neg S \wedge \neg R \rightarrow ((Q \rightarrow \text{Lasts}(Q,\tau)) \wedge (\neg Q \rightarrow \text{Lasts}(\neg Q,\tau)))$
end SR_ff

The *Persistency* axiom assures that in absence of any command the value of the output remains unchanged. A JK flip-flop (see Figure 5) is like SR but allows simultaneous Set and Reset (called J and K), which has the effect to change the state, whatever it is. A class describing JK's is easily obtained by specialization of SR_ff. Now the two axioms of set and reset must change:

class JK_ff

    Inherit SR_ff [**rename** S **as** J, R **as** K] [**redefine** Set, Reset]

      -- the renaming is not for a name clash, but only because J and K are more frequent names for S and R --

    Axioms   *Set*: $J \wedge \neg K \rightarrow \text{Futr}(Q, \tau)$

            Reset: $K \wedge \neg J \rightarrow \text{Futr}(\neg Q, \tau)$

            Commutation: $J \wedge K \rightarrow (Q \leftrightarrow \text{Futr}(\neg Q, \tau))$

end JK_ff

Note that J and K are visible even if this is not stated explicitly in the class JK_ff: they were visible in the superclasses S_ff and R_ff.

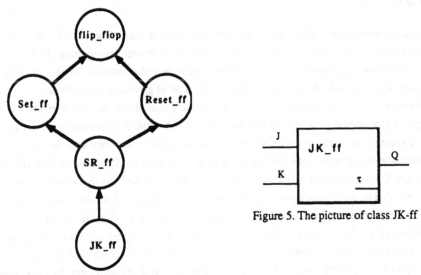

Figure 5. The picture of class JK-ff

Figure 4. The inheritance lattice for the flip-flop's

The example shows once more that even for simple objects the specification of a subclass may need retracting superclasses' axioms. When defining the set and reset commands one thinks there is no exception: a *set* command will always make the output true, and similarly for a *reset*. This is still true for SR flip-flop's. But when specifying JK flip-flop's one discovers that sometimes *set* is not sufficient to guarantee the output to be true: if at the same time a *reset* happens, then the output can become true or false, depending upon its past value. So one needs to change the set and reset axioms.

3.6 Semantics of TRIO⁺

The semantics of TRIO⁺ is provided via translation of a set of class declarations into a simple closed TRIO formula. Such formula is to be intended as a semantically equivalent (although poorly structured!) TRIO specification of the system originally described in TRIO⁺. A formal and thorough treatment of the semantics of TRIO⁺ is beyond the scope of the present paper; for this reason, and for the sake of brevity, in the following we will just provide an informal and descriptive account of the translation process, giving an intuitive explanation of its main steps and leaving to the reader's intuition the burden to fill in the missing details.

Since the axioms in TRIO⁺ specifications are ultimately expressed in terms of the *items*, which are the elementary, indivisible parts, the translation can be performed quite easily, by rephrasing the axioms in terms of the smallest components of the system, which can be uniquely identified by means of a suitable naming convention. In case the system contains arrays of homogeneous modules, the naming convention will take this fact into account by adding a suitable number of arguments to the corresponding TRIO entities: constants will be translated into functions, and functions and predicates will acquire additional arguments. The translation of a TRIO⁺ specifications into a TRIO formula is described by the following sequence of five steps.

1. Substitute textually the actual parameters (constant values or class names) in place of the formal parameters of generic classes. Include (again by means of textual substitutions) the parts (i.e. both items and modules) inherited and not redefined in all descendant classes. The result of these substitutions is a set of class declarations deprived of any form of genericity or inheritance.

2. Translate all *connections* clauses into the corresponding equivalence (for connected boolean parts) or equality (for other kinds of connected parts) axioms. We recall that connection clauses are allowed only among items (local, inherited or imported) visible in the current class declaration.

3. Determine the alphabet of the TRIO formula to be obtained as translation of the class specifying the system. Starting from the set of class declarations, consider the class that represents the specified system, that is, the highest class in the compositional hierarchy, and construct the *tree of parts* of its instances. The root of the tree corresponds to the class instance itself, the leaves are the *item* components of all involved classes, and each intermediate node corresponds to the module components of the structured classes. A node corresponding to a component of a given class has one leaf child for every item component, and one non-leaf child for every module component. By associating to the root node the empty string "", and to every other node the name of the part it represents[1], each leaf of the tree can be uniquely identified by the concatenation of the strings associated to the path from the root to the leaf itself.

The type of each element of the alphabet is the type of the corresponding item, if none of the components of which the item is a (sub)part are functions with a TRIO⁺ class as range, i.e. if the item is not included in any array of homogeneous parts. Otherwise, in presence of a declaration of an array of parts, the element of the alphabet acquires as arguments those of the function used to define the array. Thus, if the item was defined in TRIO⁺ as an n-ary function or predicate, then the addition of new arguments augments its arity; otherwise, if the item is a constant, then it becomes a function whose arguments are the indices in the array of components.

Any element of the resulting TRIO alphabet will be a time dependent entity if and only if this was the case for the TRIO⁺ item it represents.

---

[1] Recall that all parts have distinct names, and that parts of a class are *not* classes.

4. Translate every axiom in the class definitions into a TRIO formula, proceeding top-down from the system specification to its components, subcomponents and so on. In the axioms, substitute the names of the items with the names of the corresponding leaves in the tree of parts, with possible additional arguments as determined at step 3. The added variables corresponding to indices of vectors of components must be universally quantified, since the axioms of the corresponding class must be satisfied by every component. The axioms will be nested according to the structure of the tree of parts, and the scope of each added variable will be the set of axioms of the descending parts.

5. Conjunct all axioms and close temporally with an *Always* operator the resulting formula, thus obtaining the desired translation of TRIO$^+$ into TRIO.

Any model of the TRIO formula represents an object, or instance, of the class defined intensionally by the TRIO$^+$ declarations. As stated in section 3.2, the components of a TRIO$^+$ instance are instances of the respective classes. In logical terms, their models are constituted by the parts, in the overall TRIO structure, which assign a value to the corresponding elements of the TRIO alphabet, generated as in step 3. Let us consider on a toy example the result of the translation process of TRIO$^+$ specifications into TRIO formulas. We define a system like the tank of sec. 3.2, but with an array of level sensors. Every sensor is placed at a suitable depth in the tank and has a two-value output, which we represent with a time dependent propositional variable *above*, to indicate whether the water is or is not above the sensor. We assume that the value of *above* can be altered only after at least three seconds from the last change.

```
class sensor
     Visible above
     Items        above: TD → Boolean
     Axioms
             min-period: Becomes(above) → Lasts(above,3) ∧ Lasted(¬above,3)
end sensor
```

The sluice gates of the tank are of the class *sluice_gate* defined in Section 3.1, but for the sake of simplicity in the following we will only one of its axioms, *go_down*:

go_down: position=up ∧ go(down) → Lasts (position=mvdown, Δ) ∧ Futr (position=down , Δ)

The tank includes three sensors, which are placed respectively at low, middle, high levels, indicating thus four possible situations for the level of the water: below all sensors, between low and middle, between middle and high, above all sensors. All other situations are incorrect and must be signalled. The array of sensors can be represented as a function from the enumerated type *(low, middle, high)* to the class *sensor*.

```
class tank
     Visible      SensorFault, InputGo, OutputGo
     Items        SensorFault: TD → Boolean
                  InputGo, OutputGo: TD × {up, down} → Boolean
     Modules      inputGate, outputGate: sluice-gate
                  SensorSet: (low, middle, high) → sensor
     Connections      {(InputGo InputGate.go)
                        (OutputGo OutputGate.Go)}
     Vars s1,s2: (low, middle, high)
     Axioms
```

-- a fault occurs whenever the sensors give conflicting outputs --

Fault: SensorFault ↔ (∃s1 SensorSet(s1).above ∧ ∃s2 s2<s1 ∧ ¬SensorSet(s2).above)

end tank

The graphic representation of the class tank is depicted in fig. 6, while its tree of parts is in fig. 7.

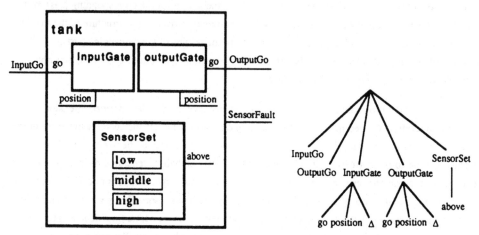

Figure 6. The picture of class tank.　　Figure 7. The tree of parts of class tank.

The following closed formula is obtained as result of the translation of the above TRIO+ specification into TRIO:

Always((InputGo ↔ InputGate_go) ∧

(OutputGo ↔ OutputGate_go) ∧

(SensorFault ↔ (∃s1 SensorSet(s1).above ∧ ∃s2 s2<s1 ∧ ¬SensorSet(s2).above)) ∧

(OutputGate_position=up ∧ OutputGate_go(down) →

　　Lasts (OutputGate_position=mvdown, OutputGate_Δ) ∧

　　Futr (OutputGate_position=down , OutputGate_Δ)) ∧

(InputGate_position=up ∧ InputGate_go(down) →

　　Lasts (InputGate_position=mvdown, InputGate_Δ) ∧

　　Futr (InputGate_position=down , InputGate_Δ)) ∧

∀s1(Becomes(SensorSet_above(s1)) → Lasts(SensorSet_above(s1),3) ∧

　　　　　　Lasted(¬SensorSet_above(s1),3)))

Notice that, in the TRIO names deriving from the concatenation of names of TRIO+ class parts, an underscore character "_" separates the components of the identifier; any possible dot notation is cleared: InputGate.go becomes InputGate_go. It can also be noted how, for the presence of the array SensorSet of components of class sensor, the zero-ary predicate *above* becomes a unary predicate on the domain (low, middle, high); a universal quantification on this domain is added to all the axioms of class Sensor.

4 Conclusions and future work

We presented TRIO+, an object oriented logic language for modular system specification, which allows the specifier to structure the description of the system in distinct, separate and reusable modules. TRIO+

was used successfully in the specification of hardware and software systems of significant architectural complexity, like pondage power stations of ENEL, the Italian electric energy board. Systems of this kind are highly structured and exhibit quite a complex behavior: they are governed by management programs whose validity lasts several days or weeks, respond with flexible and adaptable actions to a large variety of events coming from the surrounding environment, and include components with intrinsic time constants ranging from several hours (for a water basin) to microseconds (for the electronic circuitry that controls the power distribution).

The experience gained in this activity confirmed that for a specification language the possibility of structuring specifications, that is to divide them into parts and to define suitable abstraction levels to hide unessential details, is as crucial as for a design language. In particular, for a logical language, as the number and length of formulas increases beyond a certain threshold (which for humans is unfortunately quite low) then a significant or even prevalent part of the specifier time and effort is spent just in purely syntactical activities, like checking the name and type of entities, or the consistency between use and definition of an object.

In such a framework it was noted that a graphic notation, with its ability to convey a great deal of information in a compact, structured and intuitively appealing form, can be of great help. Also, the availability of language-dependent tools, such as syntax-directed editors, graphic editors, automatic consistency checkers, provides a support to exactly those parts that are not conceptually relevant nor difficult, but become painfully intricate and time-consuming when the specification increases in size. The use of such automatic tools allows the specifier to concentrate his efforts on the conceptually relevant and challenging aspects of the modelled system. We also point out that, unlike most informal specification languages and methods, which provide a graphic notation without an associated formal and rigorous semantics, TRIO+ combines in a suitable linguistic frame the possibility to structure the specification into modules and the description of semantic aspects, expecially those regarding the temporal behavior.

The support to semantic activities on the specification, like temporal analysis by means of testing, simulation, and property proof, is made possible by the fact that TRIO+ can be readily translated into TRIO, a formal language for which methods and tools to support executability are available. The execution of the TRIO+ specification of a system is certainly possible with the same computational effort necessary to execute the TRIO specification of the same system. In fact, the formulas obtained from the translation of TRIO+ are not longer than those one would write when constructing the TRIO specification from scratch. Thus, the use of TRIO+ as a methodology to structure TRIO specifications does not impose any overhead for what regards the size of the specification or its execution. In practice, there should even be an advantage in executing TRIO+ specifications instead of semantically equivalent TRIO+ formulas, since structuring the system into modules allows one to partition it into independent parts that can be executed separately, at a substantially lower cost than the execution of the system in its entirety.

Future work will thus be devoted to the construction of tools that provide a syntactic support to the construction and manipulation of large specifications, and a semantic support to the validation activities, taking advantage of the structure of the specification to increase the algorithms efficiency and to improve the quality of the visualization and presentation of the system during the simulation phases.

As noted above, such activities are possible because TRIO+ can be easily translated into TRIO. This is a clear symptom of the fact that TRIO+ is not substantially more expressive than TRIO. We can note that this happens because TRIO+ classes define macro constructs that can be used in the description of complex system, but do not define truly new mathematical entities. The main reason for this resides in the fact that TRIO+ axioms, which ultimately convey the meaning to TRIO+ specifications, are written in term of the *items* only, which are the elementary parts of a first order logic. Thus, the axioms can be expressed in terms of TRIO. It is not possible, in the language presented here, to declare variables representing values (i.e. objects) of a TRIO+ class, define on them higher-order operators or perform quantifications. This might seem a limit of the language, but was a deliberate choice intended to preserve the pleasant features of TRIO regarding execution of specifications.

A complementary approach is however possible, whereby one denotes explicitly sets of objects of a class and defines their properties using a higher order logic, thus augmenting considerably the expressiveness of the notation. On the other hand, the adoption of a higher-order logic would make any form of execution of the specifications virtually unfeasible, although still possible in principle, by means of translation of higher-order formulas into first order form, through well known techniques [End 72]. In this case the complexity of the tableaux-based algorithms would increase of several orders of magnitude.

The definition and use of a language of this kind would involve typical considerations of trade-offs among expressiveness, generality, and flexibility on one hand, simplicity and efficiency of representation and execution on the other. A draft version of TRIO+ that includes such features has been defined in [M&S 90], but its complete formal semantic is still to be provided. Such a semantics cannot be "transformational", i.e. obtained by syntactic translation as in section 3.5, because the language is much more powerful than TRIO; thus, the semantics of a class must be directly assigned via suitable, more complex interpretation structures.

The same direct approach can also be used to give an alternative, but equivalent, version for the semantics of section 3.5 for the language presented in this paper. For a simple class, this can be done in a very straightforward way by an usual TRIO structure adequate for the logical conjunction of the axioms of the class. For a complex class, a compositional definition is possible, which combines in a suitable way the structures of its components to build one structure for the class. Such a definition has not yet been developed, because our interests were mainly devoted to maintain compatibility with TRIO, in order to reuse existing tools, algorithms and results, but it will be part of our future work.

References

[BPM 83] M. Ben-Ari, A. Pnueli, and Z. Manna, "The Temporal Logic of Branching Time", Acta Informatica 20, 1983.

[CHJ 86] B. Cohen, W.T. Harwood, M.I. Jackson, "The Specification of Complex Systems", Addison Wesley Publ. Comp., Reading MA, 1986.

[D&K 76] F. DeRemer, H. Kron, "Programmaing-in-the-Large Versus Programming-in-the-Small", IEEE Transactions on Software Engineering, SE-2, (June 1976):80-86.

[DeM 78] Tom De Marco, "Structured analysis and system design", Yourdon Press, New York, NY, 1978.

[End 72] H.B. Enderton, "A mathematical introduction to logic", Academic Press, London, 1972.

[F&M 91] M.Felder, A.Morzenti, "Real-Time System Validation by Model-Checking in TRIO", 1991 Euromicro Workshop on Real-Time, Paris, 1991.

[GMM 90] C. Ghezzi, D. Mandrioli, and A. Morzenti, "TRIO, a logic language for executable specifications of real-time systems", The Journal of Systems and Software, Vol. 12, No. 2, May 1990.

[M&S 90a] A. Morzenti, P. San Pietro, "TRIO+ an Object Oriented Logic Specification Language", ENEL-CRA Research Report, January 1990 (in Italian).

[M&S 90b] A. Morzenti, P. San Pietro, "An Object-Oriented Logic Language for Modular System Specification", Int. Report no. 90.027, Politecnico di Milano, Dipartimento di Elettronica, 1990.

[MBM 89] A. Mili, N. Boudriga, F. Mili, "Towards structured specifying: theory, practice, applications", Ellis Horwood Ltd., Chichester, England, 1989.

[Mey 86] B. Meyer, Genericity versus Inheritance, OOPSLA, Portland, Oregon, 1986

[Mey 88] B. Meyer, "Object-oriented Software Construction", Prentice-Hall, 1988

[MMG 90] A. Morzenti, D. Mandrioli, C. Ghezzi, "A Model Parametric Real-Time Logic", Int. Report no. 90.010, Politecnico di Milano, Dipartimento di Elettronica, 1990.

[Mor 89] Angelo Morzenti, The specification of real–time systems: proposal of a logical formalism, PhD Thesis, Dipartimento di Elettronica, Politecnico di Milano, 1989.

[MRR 89] A. Morzenti, E. Ratto, M. Roncato, L. Zoccolante, "TRIO, a Logic Formalism for the Specification of Real-Time Systems", IEEE Euromicro Wirkshop on Real-Time, Como, Italy, 1989.

[R&U 71] N. Rescher and A. Urquhart, "Temporal Logic", Springer Verlag, Vienna-New York, 1971

[Smu 68] Raymond M. Smullian, "First order Logic", Springer Verlag, 1968.

[War 86] Paul T. Ward, The Transformation Schema: An Extension of the Data Flow Diagram to Represent Control and Timing, IEEE TSE, Vol. SE–12, no. 2, Feb. 1986.

[Weg 88] P. Wegner, Object-oriented concept hierarchies, Brown University, Technical Report, 1988

[Wir 77] N. Wirth, Towards a Discipline in Real-Time Programming, Comm. ACM 20-8, 577-583, Aug. 1977.

[Wol 83] P. Wolper, "Temporal logic can be more expressive", Information and Control 56, 1983.

[Y&C 79] E. Yourdon e L. L. Constantine, Structured design, Prentice Hall, Englewood Cliffs, NJ, 1979.

Capsules and types in Fresco

Program verification in Smalltalk

Alan Wills
University of Manchester
alan@cs.man.ac.uk

Fresco is a Smalltalk-based interactive environment supporting the specification and proven development of re-usable software components. These 'capsules' are deltas to the inheritance hierarchy, and form a more useful unit of designer-effort than class subhierarchies. Systems are built by composing capsules, which carry both specifications and code. The semantics of capsule composition is elucidated by examining the relationship between 'type' and 'class'. Type-descriptions take the form of model-oriented specifications.

The principles discussed here can be applied to other object-oriented languages.

Keywords: Smalltalk, module, capsule, Fresco, Mural, subtype, inheritance, specification, program proof.

1   Fresco

Fresco is an interactive environment supporting the evolutionary development of re-usable specified, proven software components. The prototype Fresco is based on Smalltalk: firstly, to preserve the evolutionary nature of Smalltalk programming, and to demonstrate that this is not incompatible with formal methods; and secondly, because of the availability of Mural, an interactive theorem prover's assistant, written in Smalltalk, which can readily be integrated with the development environment.

Although Fresco in its current form extends Smalltalk, the principles should apply equally well to other object-oriented languages such as C++; and some investigation has been done in this direction. However, this paper concentrates on two aspects of the Smalltalk manifestation: namely, the type/proof system, and its support for Fresco's novel 'capsule' system.

Fresco extends Smalltalk in two principal ways:

- Fresco systems are composed of re-usable units of software called 'capsules'; Fresco attempts to guarantee that no mutual interference will occur between them.

- Fresco extends the Smalltalk language with a notation for describing behaviour, and provides tools for verifying the code of capsules.

The next section introduces the idea of capsules and explains their utility; following that, the type and proof system is described; and then we return to see how the semantics of composing systems from capsules is formulated in terms of the type system.

2 The formalised goodie

2.1 Formal Methods and OOP

Object-oriented programming makes possible a culture in which systems are rapidly built from widely-distributed and adapted components. Developers can build and sell or exchange components as well as complete systems; and can treat their software libraries as capital resources which they augment every time they write a new component. There are three good reasons why behavioural specifications are more necessary in this software engineering paradigm than in a more traditional one:

- With parts acquired from everywhere, the designer must be especially careful to have an unambiguous understanding of what each part is supposed to do, and some guarantee that it will indeed do that. If you have to test each part just as carefully as if you'd built it yourself, much of the advantage of re-usability is lost.

- Furthermore, if updated versions of a component are to be distributed and incorporated into systems which use it, the systems' designers must be able to distinguish those features of the component's behaviour which are incidental, from those which will be retained in future versions. (A sorting routine example: is it a guaranteed feature that items with equal keys retain their original order, or just an artifact of this version?)

- Lastly, polymorphic code generally requires the types with which it deals (or is instantiated) to conform to some restriction. It is insufficient to check that objects passed to a sorting routine all accept the binary operator '<': additionally, '<' must work like a proper ordering on them. In a closed system which is all written by one designer, it may be acceptable to document these restrictions informally or not at all; but where polymorphic code is to be distributed widely for use in conjunction with classes its designers have never conceived of, it is important both that the precise constraints on client-classes are documented, and that the code is guaranteed to work with any client class which conforms to those constraints. Otherwise, again, the client designers might as well build and test the distributed code for themselves.

These considerations argue for the desirability of stating the required behavioural characteristics of a software component in unambiguous language, and (better still) of checking each component against its requirements.

Full formal verification is difficult to achieve, and there are a number of alternative strategies such as symbolic execution and axiom-directed testing; but this paper proceeds under the assumption of the author's opinion that there a sensible mixture of formal verification (where easy or crucial) and informal justification — annotated with remarks like 'obvious' or 'Alan thinks this is OK' — (where hard and inessential); and that this style (dignified with the term 'rigorous proof' [Jones90]) is achievable with suitably friendly and well-integrated mechanical assistance. Proofs can be checked mechanically once generated, and so the re-use of any software implies the re-use of the associated proofs.

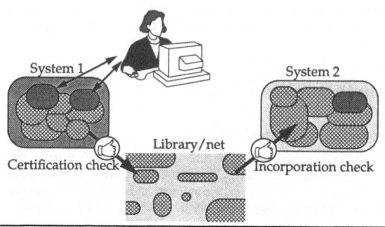

Figure 1.   Fresco systems are compositions of re-usable capsules

Such support is available in the form of the Mural interactive theorem-prover's environment, in which hierarchies of theory can be developed and proofs generated in the natural deduction system (as described in [Lindsay87]).   Mural was written in Smalltalk as part of an earlier Manchester project[JJLM91]. It provides a generic proof system which can be adapted to a wide range of formal systems, and has manifestations as a stand-alone theory database, as a VDM tool, and most recently as part of the Fresco software development environment.

2.2 Capsules

The units of distribution in the successful Smalltalk re-use culture are not classes, nor even groups of classes. A look at any 'goodies' library shows them to be mixtures of new classes, new methods for existing classes, and new implementations of existing classes and methods. (In Smalltalk, classes and methods are updated and compiled dynamically into the running system.) In goodies-lib@cs.man.ac.uk, 73% of the files modify existing classes, and 44% define no new classes. Each programmer's efforts build upon those of one or more predecessors by improvement and extension. Fresco formalises this mechanism.

If this notion of deltas as units of designer-effort seems a little strange, consider this scenario. Class A uses class B extensively, and sometimes passes B-instances back to its own clients. I design class C, which uses A; but C needs B to perform some extra function, used whenever B-instances are passed back from A. Ideally, I should design a B′ which inherits from B. But then I have to design an A′ which is all the same as A, except that it calls upon B′ instead of B. If A has been designed with sufficient foresight, then this will be easy; but more likely, it will be a pain! What I really want to do is just to add the extra function to B — more economical and less error-prone. More generally, many of the real-life examples of redefinition are connected in some way with improving the inheritability of a class, or broadening its functionality. Others are concerned with improving the performance (so that all clients get the benefit, not just those who know about the subclass); and most of the rest, with enhancing user-interaction without altering the procedural interface.

Functional units and their hierarchies are good for integrating into one structure all the diverse functions which can be created by a single designer [team] while the hierarchy remains under that designer's control; additional requirements may trigger a restructuring. But when we consider design effectively undertaken by many designers between which there is only a one-way flow of information, then the transmissible units of design-effort must be not functional units, but changes to their definitions. But it is important that when a system imports such deltas from diverse sources, they shouldn't invalidate each other: each should be able to change the implementation of what went before, and should be able to enrich any part of the system's behaviour, but not to alter (or delete!) the functional specification of existing behaviour, which other parts might depend on.

Fresco supports the specification and rigorous development of software capsules. A capsule contains code, specifications, and proofs, and systems are built by composing capsules. The mechanism has the potential to guarantee that each capsule functions as its author intended, without interference from others: although the functions a capsule provides can subsequently be extended or improved, the properties its clients rely upon will never be invalidated.

Part of the system's operation depends on restricting the ability of a capsule to override existing definitions, to those belonging to capsules on which it has a documented dependence: this by itself can help to reduce the likelihood of clashes. Whilst the full benefit depends on the (admittedly theoretical) employment of fully formal proofs, greater reliability is nevertheless obtained by using specifications with more or less 'rigorous' proofs. Even where proofs are completely informal, the system highlights correspondences between specification and code which should be rechecked whenever anything is altered.

A capsule may be created in any order: code first or specifications first. Fresco generates appropriate proof obligations wherever the consistency of the code and specifications cannot be verified automatically. Before the capsule may be exported for distribution to other designers, Fresco performs a 'certification check', that all the proofs have been completed, and are consistent with the definitions (see Figure 1). A complementary 'incorporation check' ensures that imported capsules (i) only alter the code of capsules they claim to know about and (ii) have internally consistent proofs (even if partly informal ones) and hence, hopefully, code that conforms to their specifications.

These mechanical features are not the main topic of this paper: rather, we concentrate on the notions of class, type, and conformance, and on the semantics of composing capsules into systems.

The next section introduces Fresco's type system and outlines how it fits into the proof system. We will ultimately return to capsules and explain their composition into systems, in the light of the type system.

3 Classes and types

3.1 Type/Class Definitions

'Class' and 'type' are distinct ideas in Fresco. Classes prescribe implementations of types. Types describe behaviour, visible as the object's response to messages and the constraints which apply to messages it may be sent. An object is an instance of only one class, but may

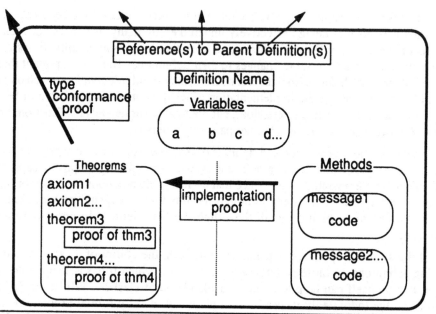

Figure 2. Components of a Fresco combined type/class definition (TCD)

belong to many types: any class implements many types.

Types are used to document constraints on variables or parameters. It's important to notice that a Fresco type can constrain more strongly than the machine-checkable types of conventional languages, since it requires that a member-object conform to a particular model of behaviour in response to a particular set of messages (procedure calls); compare this with C++ for example, where type membership imposes the requirement that an object should be able to respond to a given set of messages, but doesn't stipulate how.

Despite the distinction between class and type, type and class definitions are nevertheless interwoven, for convenience, into a single all-purpose piece of syntax, the type/class definition (TCD). Fresco has TCDs instead of classes, and they are realised by adding extra information to Smalltalk's classes. Smalltalk's interpreter treats a TCD exactly as a class, ignoring the type information; whilst typing assertions and type-building expressions ignore the class aspects of a TCD.

The following headings summarise classes, types and their relationships. Figure 2 illustrates the components of a Fresco TCD, and its relationships to other TCDs. The relationships of inheritance and conformance are the most significant.

The composite definitions are perhaps more easily explained by considering the two roles separately.

Class definitions

The essential components of a class definition in Fresco are unchanged from Smalltalk:

- Name of class
- Identity of parent class definition(s)
- Instance variables

- Mapping from selectors (operation signatures) to methods (operation code bodies)

Type definitions

Types are used to characterise the properties of objects which may be assigned to variables or parameters; and to characterise the properties of classes which may be used in conjunction with polymorphic code.

Fresco type definitions take the form of axiomatic specifications, with these components:

- Name of type
- Identity of parent type definition(s) (**not** supertype, necessarily)
- Model variables
- Theorems (axioms and derived theorems)

The type encompasses all those objects which behave according to the theorems. (Axioms are those which define the type; other theorems may be proven from the axioms, for the convenience of clients.) The theorems state invariant properties of the model, and describe the effects of messages (operation calls) on the model, using pre- and post-conditions. A model need not be used — it is possible for the theorems just to interrelate operations visible at the client interface — but experience in the formal methods culture suggests that model-based specifications are easier to read and write for all but the most fundamental types.

We write $c \in T$ iff c behaves according to T's theory: that is, the visible behaviour of c (how it responds to operations) satisfies T's axioms. If c's own internal components are invisible or different from T's, then you can still decide whether c behaves according to T's theory: generate (in the abstract!) all the theorems derivable from T's axioms; discard all those which mention the internal variables, leaving those which just mention external operations (like an algebraic spec); checking that all possible sequences of operations on c conform to those. In practice, there is an easier and (mostly) equivalent way, described below under 'reification'.

3.2 Theorems

Theorems are the basis of all the behavioural description in Fresco. The general form (which is developed from Cline and Lea's work on Annotated C++ [CL90]) is:

$$\{ \; |vars| \; \text{theorems} \vdash \text{precondition} :- \text{postcondition} \; \} \; [\text{code}] \; .$$

All parts may be omitted except postcondition.

vars are metavariables, with scope throughout the theorem, including the code. When the theorem is applied in a given context, each metavariable may be instantiated to match a particular expression. Unmatched metavariables effectively work like universally quantified variables.

Initial theorems preceding $\vdash$ are hypotheses: the rest of the theorem is valid iff the hypotheses can be proved. This kind of theorem can function as a proof rule.

The theorem states that if precondition is true before the execution of code, then postcondition will be true after it.

If 'precondition :-' is missing, the theorem is an invariant, true after the code if it is true before it; if code is missing, it is a universal invariant, true all the time.

precondition and postcondition are expressions. In postcondition, an overlined variable represents a copy of the same variable as it was before execution. (The copy is guaranteed not to be subject to any side effects of the code! The problems of interpretation and aliasing this presents are not the topic of this paper, but are the subject of ongoing work.)

code may be an expression or a sequence of statements. (In Smalltalk, conditionals and loops are expressions.) It may also be another theorem.

If code is omitted but ':-' is present, then the theorem represents any code which satisfies the theorem. This form may be used as a stand-in for as-yet-undeveloped code.

The syntax of the predicate parts of the theorems is adapted from that of the programming language. It may include inexecutable constructs such as quantifiers (unless the intention of the user is to employ the theorems as a debugging aid: which is not the assumption here). (Readers unfamiliar with Smalltalk should be aware of the postfix and mixfix syntax of its operators.)

A theorem may appear in any of four principal roles:

- As a 'specification statement', within the code of a method as an annotation and possibly a debugging aid. A theorem is executed by executing its code-part. It asserts that the code satisfies the pre/postcondition part. (Hypotheses are not used in this context.) A theorem can be proven by the use of rules which analyse its code, so that the code of a method can be proven stepwise — as fully explored in [Morgan90]. An outermost theorem of a method can be used to prove axioms of its class's home type. E.g.:

  $$\{ \, x \in \text{Real} \vdash \; :- (y{>}0) \wedge (y \in \text{Real}) \, \} \qquad [\, y := x \text{ abs} \,].$$
  $$\{ \, y \in \text{Real} \vdash x > 0 \; :- \; z{*}z = x \, \} \qquad [\, z := y \text{ sqrt} \,].$$

- As a step in a proof, following the style of [JJLM91]. Theorems may be used as proof rules; and are themselves proven by proving the conclusion of the theorem (that is, the parts left when hypotheses are removed) in a local context in which the hypotheses are assumed. Such proofs typically look like this (though regrettably, on a much larger and commensurately tedious scale):

  h $\quad x \in \text{Real}$
  1 $\quad \{x > 0 :- \uparrow{*}\uparrow = x\} \, [x \text{ sqrt}] \, . \qquad$ **by** defn-sqrt(x) **from** h
  c $\quad \{x > 0 :- y{*}y = x\} \, [y := x \text{ sqrt}] \, . \,$ **by** assign-$\uparrow$(y) **from** 1

  ($\uparrow$ refers, in a theorem, to the value yielded by the code.)

- As a proof obligation to justify claims of correct implementation, conformance, etc. For example, if we wish to claim that members of Colour can be sorted using the polymorphic class SortedCollection, then we must satisfy the latter's requirement that objects it deals with should be members of Ordered, whose axioms are (say) OA_i:

  $$\{ \, \{x \in \text{Colour} \vdash \text{OA\_1}\}. \, \{x \in \text{Colour} \vdash \text{OA\_2}\} \, ... \vdash \; \text{Colour} \le \text{Ordered}\}.$$

- As an axiom or derived theorem of a type. If we want to prove the assertion $x \in T$ where T is some type, then we must prove that all of T's axioms are satisfied by x. Conversely, if we know that $x \in T$, then we can use T's theorems as rules to prove things about x.

A body of axioms, together with all the theorems that can be derived from them, and usually some locally-declared variables, is called a theory. A theorem is always stated in the context of some theory. A type is defined by its theory (and hence each class with a home type is specified by a theory); and there is also a background theory, inherited by every other, which includes the usual rules of predicate calculus, together with the behaviour of the Smalltalk kernel; its theorems include, as examples:

{ |P R b S1 S2 | b∈ Bool, {P :- R } [b ifTrue: S1 ifFalse: S2]
                   ⊢ P :- R } [b ifFalse: S2 ifTrue: S1] . "ifTrue:ifFalse: reversal"

{|P M R S1 S2| {P:-M} [S1]. {M:-R} [S2] ⊢ P :- R} [S1. S2] .

{|P M R S1 S2| P :- R} [{P:-M}[S1]. {M :-R}[S2]]. "corollary of previous"

The operation specialisation axiom is especially important:

{ | P P1 R R1 S |

            {P ⊢ P1}. {R1 ⊢ R}.

            {P1 :- R1} [S]

   ⊢   P :- R } [S].

In the theory of a type, there are some implicit variables and axioms. '∈' is the type membership relation, and in the context of any one type T, it is automatically axiomatic that self∈ T. If a theory is extracted from the context in which it is stated, the theorems it depends on must be taken with it as extra hypotheses. In particular, when some theorem of T is used in a proof of a client, self∈ T must be added as a hypothesis (and then self must be substituted by some other metavariable, to avoid naming conflicts).

Stack
{size>0:–size=size-1}[self pop].

{s∈ Stack ⊢ s size>0 :– s size = s̄ size-1}[s pop].

3.3 Relationships between types and classes

Classes implement types

Class and type definitions may be mixed into one Type/Class Definition. The implication is that the class is intended to implement its 'home' type. This can be verified by proving that each axiom is satisfied by the code of the methods – an 'implementation proof'. For axioms whose code part is in the form self message, the code of the appropriate method is unfolded, and a proof by decomposition is done in a style after [Jones90] or [Morgan90]. Additionally, any invariant (axiom without precondition or code parts) may be assumed in conjunction with the precondition, and must be proven as a postcondition of each method.

This arrangement is similar to the way in which Eiffel [Meyer88] classes possess invariants and pre/postconditions: in Fresco, these functions are performed by the axioms.

(Since the technique is to prove the axioms true of the code, 'axiom' might seem a misnomer. However, it is appropriate in the sense that clients of the class assume the axioms to be valid, whilst it is an internal affair of the class's to get its code to fulfil the axioms.)

Whilst it seems good practice in general to restrict each axiom to determining the behaviour of one operation, there may be several axioms applying to one operation. This may arise through inheritance or capsule composition, or just because it's convenient. In that case, the axioms must each be proven against the code of the operation; or it might help to invent a lemma from which the 'axioms' follow, and prove the lemma against the operation.

It is possible for the axioms of a type to contradict each other — in which case, there can be no implementation. The only protection against this is the unprovability of any code which might be written for such a type.

Since theorems work as proof rules, new rules may be introduced with each class; so that its messages have the same status as basic linguistic constructs. Contrast this with the conventional proof system, in which there is a fixed set of rules for the language, some of which deal with procedure calls in a general and rather clumsy manner.

Example

A TCD SymbolTable is intended for use by compilers of block-structured languages, and maps identifiers to some form of reference. Identifiers may be declared within nested blocks of the language, so SymbolTable is modelled as a stack of dictionaries, the range elements of which are References:

SymbolTable

$\{s \in (\text{Stack of: (Dictionary from: Symbol to: Ref))}\}$.

(Every member of SymbolTable has a component s. $x \in (\text{Stack of: T})$ is defined elsewhere to be equivalent to $(x \in \text{Stack}) \wedge ((xi \text{ in: } x) \Rightarrow (xi \in T))$; and similarly for Dictionary.)

There are four operations, for entering and leaving nesting levels, for adding an identifier at the current level of nesting, and for finding the most deeply-nested current declaration of an identifier. Each of these 'advertised' operations is mentioned in the code part of one or more axioms (as opposed to model-components like s, which only occur within the braces). To give two axioms, as examples:

$\{ id \in \text{Symbol} :- (s \text{ top at: } id) = ref \}$ [self declare: id with: ref].
$\{ (s \text{ size} > 0) :- s = \bar{s} \text{ tail}\}$ [self leave].

(The operation declare:with: is not guaranteed to work unless its first argument is a Symbol; its result is that the Dictionary at the top of the Stack is now such that interrogating it about id yields ref. The operation leave works only if the stack is not empty, and its result is to reduce the stack to its former tail.)

(In this paper we ignore questions of framing — how to stipulate that the other members of the structure remain unaltered.)

Inheritance

Inheritance is a relationship which a designer may prescribe between definitions; it doesn't imply conformance between the behaviours described, nor vice versa. Variables and theorems are inherited from parent definitions; and methods are inherited, but (as in Smalltalk) may be overridden in child definitions. Theorems cannot be overridden in children.

There is multiple inheritance in Fresco. Synonymous variables inherited from different parents are identified; label-clashes amongst theorems are resolved by qualifying them with the names of the parents from which they come; synonymous methods are disallowed unless the child definition provides an overriding method.

The terms 'parent' and 'ancestor' will be used instead of 'superclass' here, to minimise traditional confusion between inheritance (the carrying of features from one definition to another) and conformance (where one behavioural definition satisfies another) [CHC90].

Conformance

Type C conforms to type A, written C≤A, iff $\forall c \cdot c \in C \Rightarrow c \in A$.

The conformance relation between types is used to determine whether member-objects of C may be supplied wherever A is expected. In turn, it can therefore be used to determine: whether one type (or class) correctly implements another; whether a type fulfills the requirements of a polymorphic piece of software; and whether a proposed modification to a class will produce a substitutable variant.

There is a component of each TCD, in which intended conformance to other type(s) may be recorded. An appropriate proof should also be recorded there; Fresco highlights the absence of one: literally so, in any screen display of the type, and also in the sense that a certification check will fail on an absent proof. Any change to the type at either end of the conformance relation will cause a similar behaviour until the proof is at least re-affirmed. These checks are beneficial even if the proof is completely informal, since the designer is forced to reconsider any assumption or justification which may no longer be valid.

To prove C≤A, we only have to prove that all the theorems of A hold in C: that is, that A's axioms can be derived as theorems from C's axioms. This means of course that C must provide for at least the same set of messages as A; beyond that, there are three interesting cases:

- C's model is different from A's. Some translation has to be done, in the form of a *retrieve axiom*, which interlinks the two models: the proof is made feasible by adding this extra axiom to C. The operation specialisation axiom above is crucial to such proofs, since most of the axioms specify the effects of messages. We also need to prove 'adequacy' – that there are sufficiently many states of C to represent A.

- A is an ancestor of C. In the case, the retrieval is trivial, since it just involves dropping the extra variables from the model. To ensure adequacy, C must avoid constraining variables inherited from A.

- A is not defined with the aid of a model. Fresco uses a loose interpretation in which there is no adequacy proof in this case. This is appropriate for specifications of individual properties.

Conformance and inheritance

A TCD's complement of axioms includes those inherited from others; and any methods it possesses must be proven against the inherited axioms as well as its own. There may be more than one axiom relating to each operation. Conversely, inherited methods must in general be proven against the class's own axioms, even if they have been proven against axioms in their own TCD.

In practice, Fresco allows only certain combinations of conformance and inheritance — the others seem unuseful or confusing. They are:

- *Reification*—conformance claimed between TCDs otherwise unrelated.

- *Nonconformant inheritance*—in which the variables and methods of a TCD may be inherited without at the same time inheriting its theory.

- *Conformant inheritance*—in which a TCD is claimed to conform to a parent, which will have axioms and may or may not have methods.

(The last two correspond to the two kinds of inheritance in C++: private and public.)

In conformant inheritance from a TCD which has both theory and methods, any inherited axiom need not be re-proven unless it relates to a method which is overridden or newly-defined in the child.

3.4   Encapsulation and Reification

'Encapsulation' is the idea that the clients of a unit of software design should depend only on its published interface, not on its innards: the knock-on effects of a change of implementation stop at the unit's boundaries, provided the interface description remains true. In OOP terms, this means that it is none of a client's business to use a class's internal functions, or to see internal data structures. This has sometimes been seen as prohibiting a model-oriented approach to specification, since such specifications describe externally visible behaviour in terms of their effects on an internal state.

This is true if the model data are constrained to be the same as the implementation variables: but no such restriction is necessary or desirable. For example, a dictionary may be modelled in TCD Dictionary as a set of key-value pairs with a uniqueness constraint on the keys; but it could be implemented as a tree in TCD TreeDict. The latter would carry a claim and proof that TreeDict≤Dictionary. Dictionary is advertised as the interface specification of TreeDict; and though Dictionary has its own model, it gives no insight to TreeDict's internal workings. Dictionary might have no executable code of its own; or it might, after the conventional style of Smalltalk abstract superclasses, offer additional operations built onto the specified interface. Thus TreeDict preserves its encapsulation by making its public interface the claim to implement another TCD.

'Data reification' — implementing one model with a different one — is a valuable technique, with considerable respectability in the literature of formal methods[Jones90]. The most appropriate model for human readers is by no means often the most appropriate for implementation, and performance cannot always be improved merely by adding fields (as in conventional inheritance).

An alternative approach is a purely algebraic style, in which the axioms interrelate only the externally visible operations. This works well for the most fundamental types (and indeed is the only way to specify them), but is difficult to use for more complex specifications.

It is common for a design to contain several stages of reification, each stage being a re-modelling of the preceding one.

Reification example

TableDict
       {(dict ∈ (Dictionary from: Symbol to: (Dictionary from: BlockId to: Ref)))
       ∧ (blockCount ∈ BlockId)
       ∧ (currentBlocks ∈ (Stack of: BlockId)) }.

This improves the efficiency of SymbolTable. There is one dictionary, in which all the current identifiers can be rapidly looked up; each of them has a stack of current (and some past) references, each associated with a block number so that outdated entries can be distinguished from current ones. enter and leave number the blocks, and keep track of which are current. The retrieval to SymbolTable is:

{ | i name |
     (0 < i) ∧ (i ≤ currentBlocks size) ⊢
     ((name in: (s at: i) dom) ⇔ ((currentBlocks at: i) in: (dict at: name) dom)) ∧
     (((s at: i) at: name) = ((dict at: n) at: (currentBlocks at: i))) }.

(For any index i to the stacks s (in SymbolTable) and currentBlocks (in TableDict), every name is found in the domain of the ith dictionary of s iff the current nesting block's id is in the domain of the subdictionary of dict at name; ....)

This structure is:

- obviously more difficult to understand than SymbolTable
- not just an extension of the SymbolTable
- unsuitable as an interface specification for the symbol table, since there are many other ways in which SymbolTable could be implemented
- not the final stage of reification, since we still have to decide which of many possible implementations of Dictionary to choose for its two occurrences
- clearly more appropriate for implementation than any extension of SymbolTable.

TCD conjunction

When two axioms {P1:–R1}[s], {P2:–R2}[s] apply to one code fragment, the effect is to weaken the precondition and strengthen the postcondition. It follows from the specialisation axiom that

$$\{(P1 \lor P2) :- (\overline{P1} \Rightarrow R1) \land (\overline{P2} \Rightarrow R2)\}[s] \vdash \{P1:-R1\}[s]$$

and the same for P2:–R2. If the preconditions are disjoint, the effect is to stipulate independent domains in which s should work; if they overlap, then {P1∧P2 :– R1∧R2}[s] will apply. Any object conforming to the conjunction {(P1∨P2) :– (P̄1⇒R1)∧(`P̄2⇒R2)}[s] thus conforms to the two originals. However, it is normally only necessary to consider the original axioms, rather than dealing with this conjunction explicitly.

This axiom conjunction occurs when axioms from an inheriting TCD and its parent(s) apply to the same method; or when the designer chooses to separate different concerns.

This can be extended to work for whole TCDs. The conjunction T1&T2 of two TCDs is formed by merging the axiom-sets and variable-sets; and by overriding any methods in T1 with those of the same name in T2. So if a TCD is a tuple <vars, axioms, methods>, where methods is a map from message selectors to method bodies and $\ominus$ is symmetric set difference,

$$\langle vars1, axioms1, m1\rangle \& \langle vars2, axioms2, m2\rangle =$$
$$\langle vars1 \cup vars2, axioms1 \cup axioms2,$$
$$\{sel \rightarrow (m1 \cup m2)(sel) \mid sel \in (dom(m1) \ominus dom(m2))\}$$
$$\cup \quad \{sel \rightarrow m2 \mid sel \in (dom(m1) \cap dom(m2))\}\rangle$$

The conjunction is valid if the proof obligations can be satisfied of

- conservative extension

$$\forall a \in A \; b \in B \cdot \exists ab \in (A\&B) \cdot ab\mid_A = a \; \wedge \; ab\mid_B = b$$

(where $ab\mid_A$ means removing the components which don't belong to A).

- correct implementation – satisfaction of the axioms by any methods in the result.

We claim that a valid composition A&B satisfies

$$\forall ab \in (A\&B) \cdot ab \in A \; \wedge \; ab \in B$$

Notice that TCD conjunction is symmetrical in its type components, and asymmetrical in the code — B's methods override A's.

The type defined by a conformant inheritor C of A is A&C.

Another interesting use of & is to split up specifications of operations for descriptive purposes: for example, the main and exceptional behaviour of an operation can be written separately.

Type constructors

Fresco has a few built-in type constructors, listed here with examples:

- union: List = Cons | EmptyList
- product:ListPair = List × List
- functions:ListDyadicInjection = ListPair → List
  cons ∈ ListDyadicInjection
- filter: ShortList = List ! [x | x length ≤ 5]
  (all members x of List such that ...)

Generic types, written as functions over types:

- T set = (Set ! [s | $\forall$ i∈s · i ∈ T])
- s∈ Set $\wedge$ ($\forall$ i∈s · i ∈ T) $\vdash$ s ∈ (Set of: T)
- (Map from: T1 to: T2) = (Map ! [m | $\forall$ (d,r)∈m · d∈T1 $\wedge$ r∈T2])
- T ≤ Ordered
  $\vdash$ sc∈ SortedCollection $\wedge$ ($\forall$ i∈ (1.. sc length) · (sc at: i) ∈ T)
  $\vdash$ sc∈ (SortedCollection of: T)

The user may define these arbitrarily.

The principles of conformance proof may readily be extended to cover these constructions.

Type checking

Although there is no typechecking in Smalltalk, nor at present in Fresco, types are neverthe-less a useful tool: $c \in T$ abbreviates the restatement of all T's axioms. There are no type constraints on parameters or variables, but we can nevertheless state that an axiom's conclu-sion depends on the assumption that $c \in T$: if the axiom is used as an invariant and c is an instance or model variable, then that is equivalent to stating the variable's type; all we lack is an automatic means to check this – the typing proposition just has to be proved like any other. (It could be argued that, since program development with Fresco is an interactive process, we no longer suffer such a strong imperative to separate the automatically-verifiable constraints (like type-checking) from the proofs which need the human touch.)

Typechecking has been added to Smalltalk [JGZ88] but there as in most languages, the idea of conformance is limited. Whilst the compiler can check that T' provides all the operations of T, it cannot check that they behave substitutably. Moreover, most OO typing schemes overlook the important 'reification' case in which one type conforms to another without inheriting its definition. The typechecker of POOL [AvdL90] is a step in that direction: it takes the names of informally-defined properties as clues to what is required in a conforming type.

In Fresco, conformance means substitutability, with or without inheritance. Of course, a solid guarantee of conformance would require a watertight proof, whereas informal justifi-cations are allowed in Fresco. Nevertheless, the experience of the formal methods tradition is that the obligation to supply even informal proofs brings about a measurable increase in reliability.

4   Capsules

All Fresco software development work — specification, coding, proof, documentation — is done within the context of some capsule. A designer may develop several at once within the same system, but has to switch consciously between them: each corresponds to a separate 'desktop'. Once developed, the designer can ask Fresco to certify the capsule: that is, to check that the proof obligations are all up-to-date and have complete proofs. A certified capsule can then be incorporated into another system.

Each capsule has a name which is unique worldwide: the full identification includes date and hostid of origin, and author's name etc. are included in the 'header' documentation. Each builds on the work embodied in other capsules, and a capsule's attributes include the names of its prerequisite capsules. A capsule cannot be incorporated into a system unless its prereq-uisites are already there. The prerequisite graph is acyclic and directed; capsules are not functional modules, but modules of programmer effort: if two modules are interdependent, then they should be defined as separate TCDs within the same capsule; capsules' dependen-cies are unidirectional.

During development, Fresco ensures that the designer does not use (or inherit from) anything defined by another capsule which is not a prerequisite. As far as TCDs and global variables are concerned, this is just a question of tracing the definitions of names: every defi-nition in Fresco is associated with a particular capsule. But for messages, this can't be done with complete certainty until an attempt to construct a proof, which must refer to the definitions of operations in particular types.

On incorporation into another system, Fresco checks that the definitions given by the incoming capsule do not clash with those of other capsules which are not its prerequisites. A renaming scheme can be invented which circumvents some of the problems, where a new definition accidentally has the same name as something else. But in the case where two cousin capsules (with a common prerequisite, but neither prerequisite of the other) try to redefine the same item in different ways, then they can only be declared incompatible and cannot both become part of the same system.

A capsule may only define new TCDs and conformant augmentations of existing ones. The TCDs in a capsule are therefore composed using '&' with the ones already existing in the system (which should come from prerequisites); so that the new code implements the old specification as well as the extension. (Figure 4.)

Once certified and published, a capsule cannot in general be modified (without renaming it); but a new version may be issued if it conforms to the old one. An extension to the naming scheme encodes the version history (branches are allowed, of course: improvements may be made by diverse authors), and prerequisites must be quoted with name and version. Then any later version will be a satisfactory substitute.

4.1 Capsule contents and composition

A capsule is a tuple ⟨name, version, prerequisites, definitions⟩.

Name, version and **prerequisites** have been covered above.

Definitions includes all TCDs, together with global-variable definitions.
TCDs include variables, methods, theorems, proofs, conformance claims.

A Fresco system is a tuple ⟨capsules, definitions, run-time-stuff⟩.

Capsules is a list of the capsules the system has incorporated. All definitions can be attributed to a particular capsule. Every system has a Kernel capsule, which contains all the standard-issue classes and globals.

Run-time-stuff is the heap, stack, interpreter state, and so on, which depends on the

Figure 4. Capsule composition conjoins specs and overrides implementations

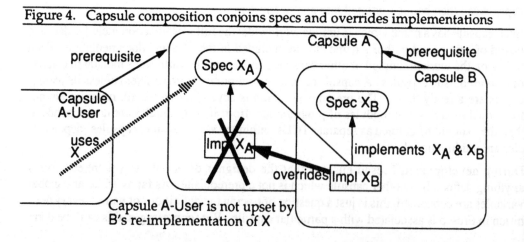

Capsule A-User is not upset by B's re-implementation of X

code in just the same way as it does in ordinary Smalltalk.

So the definitions in a system are determined by its capsules, and by the order in which they were incorporated, which in turn is determined by the prerequisite graph. Each capsule's incorporation produces a resultant system which is the & of the old system and the capsule.

For a system s and capsule c (where $\frown$ is concatenation),

$$\text{c.prerequisites} \in \text{s.capsules} \vdash \text{s \& c} =$$
$$\langle \quad \text{s.capsules} \frown \text{c, s.defs \& c.defs} \quad \rangle$$

which adds the new capsule to the list, conservatively extends the types, overwrites method definitions and adds fields to classes, replaces reification claims by new ones (by target), and unifies theories such that all the theorems of the old system are still true in the new.

The term of principal interest is s.defs & c.defs, which is defined thus, if defs is a mapping: Name $\rightarrow$ TCD:

$$\text{s.defs \& c.defs} \triangleq$$
$$\{n\rightarrow(\text{s.defs}\cup\text{c.defs})(n) \mid n\in (\text{dom s.defs} \ominus \text{dom c.defs})\} \cup$$
$$\{n\rightarrow \text{s.defs}(n)\&\text{c.defs}(n) \mid n\in (\text{dom s.defs} \cap \text{dom c.defs}) \}$$

so that the new capsule may contain new TCDs or extend existing ones with &. Extended TCDs should only include those belonging to prerequisites: so the author of the capsule must already have proved the validity of the composition; and will also have proved that the resultant specifications are met by any code which is added to the capsule in the future.

5 Continuing work

5.1 Framing

The examples of theorems shown here omit 'framing': any statement of what parts of the system's state may be altered by the code. In most model-oriented specification systems, the frame may be simply a set of variables, or it is a well-defined subcomponent of the data represented in a variable. That would be inadequate for Fresco:

- The heavy aliasing in Smalltalk means that it isn't so easy to divide up the state into subcomponents, some of which are writable and some of which are not: two subcomponents you thought were different might turn out to be the same, accessed through different strings of pointers.

- In a modular system, what is changed by an operation is partly the responsibility of server modules, so it is insufficient just to name a given part of the whole state.

A way of tackling this is the effects system [LG88]. In the realisation planned for Fresco, each class has a *demesne*, which identifies the set of objects which help it represent the type it is intended to represent. Normally, the demesne would be self + the demesnes of the components — though 'knows-about' pointers and caches would be excluded. We introduce a special assertion which can be appended to a postcondition, effect(someDemesne), together with rules for reasoning about such effects. This system should be sufficient to separate out all those problems associated with the fact that we are dealing with pointers rather than pure values.

5.2 Using programming language for specification

It is desirable to integrate the programming and specification languages; but it is difficult to understand the meaning of a postcondition or a line in a proof which itself has a side-effect on the system state.

The effects system gives us a way of reasoning about the purity of an expression: if we can prove that its effect is the empty demesne, then we are allowed to use it inside a theorem. So for example, it should be possible to discover which operations confine their effects to the demesnes of the receiver objects to which they are applied; so that such an operation followed by a 'deep' copy would be pure.

6 Summary and current status

The notion of conformance (= 'subtyping', but with the caveat that we aren't just referring to signatures) is important in the determination of whether one definition implements another, particularly in these contexts:

- To facilitate clear description, disjoint from implementation concerns, for re-users.
- Polymorphic code must define the properties of objects it is capable of working with.
- Adding an upgrade or delta to any piece of software should leave it still able to serve previous clients as it did before: it should satisfy the same specifications.

The last point is perhaps less familiar, and applies to capsules, which are monotonic deltas to system definitions; and which this paper argues form better units of re-use than classes do.

Composition of specifications and software must be guaranteed conformant in certain cases:

- Where a type is defined as the child of another, the intention is often that its members should be substitutable for its parents' members. Its own definition and the parent's must therefore be composed conformantly. The same applies with multiple parents.
- Polymorphic code may have several constraints that objects it is applied to must satisfy. The notion of a conformant composition of types is therefore useful.
- Composing capsules to make systems should not result in mutual interference between the constituents, which must therefore be conformantly composed.

Fresco type-definitions are in general model-oriented, which makes them easier to write and read. Encapsulation is not compromised by this approach if the technique of reification — implementing one model with a completely different one — is adopted.

Type and class definitions are combined, in Fresco, into one syntactical unit, the TCD. This provides for:

- separate type and class definitions where required.
- a 'home' type for a class, in which its instance variables form the model: implementation is verified by checking that each method satisfies all the applicable theorems.
- the conventional 'abstract class' style, if preferred.

Type descriptions are made up of theorems about the effects of code fragments on data. Theorems function as proof rules: as more TCDs are added, the body of rules increases.

Theorems can act as 'specification statements', and code is proven by decomposition. Theorems and proofs are written in an extensible pure subset of the Smalltalk language.

The conformant composition of capsules to build systems has been described in terms of conformant composition of the constituent TCDs.

Fresco supports conformant composition of capsules and TCDs, and code decomposition proofs, with a combination of mechanical checks and rigorous proof.

The current Fresco system is built on Smalltalk, whilst the principles may also be made to work in other languages. It currently supports capsules and specification annotations; but proof obligation generation and full linkage to mural are yet to be implemented. A mechanical typechecker would be beneficial. Current work includes the method of treating framing, aliasing, and the more reliable integration of the Smalltalk and specification notations.

Acknowledgments

Warmest thanks are due to Mary Brennan, John FitzGerald, Cliff Jones, the Nationwide Anglia Building Society, and the referees of this paper, for their diverse kinds of support.

7 References

[AvdL90] Pierre America and Frank van der Linden 'A Parallel Object Oriented Language with Inheritance and Subtyping' ECOOP 90

[CL90] Marshall Cline and Doug Lea: 'The Behaviour of C++ Classes'. Proceedings, Symp OOP Emphasizing Practical Applications, Marist Coll., Sept 90

[CHC90] William Cook, Walter Hill, Peter Canning 'Inheritance is not subtyping' ACM ToPLAS 1990 pp125–135

[JGZ88] Ralph Johnson, Justin Graver, Lawrence Zurawski 'TS: an optimizing compiler for Smalltalk' OOPSLA'88

[Jones90] Cliff Jones: 'Systematic software construction using VDM' (PHI, 2nd ed. 1990)

[JJLM91] C.B.Jones, K.D.Jones, P.A.Lindsay, R.C.Moore: 'Mural: a formal development support system' Springer Verlag, 1991

[Lindsay87] Peter Lindsay: Logical frames for interactive theorem proving. TR: UMCS 87-12-7, Dept of Computer Science, University of Manchester, UK 1987

[LG88] John M Lucassen and David K. Gifford: 'Polymorphic effect systems' Proc 15th ACM Symp Principles of Programming Languages Jan 88 pp47–57

[Meyer88] Bertrand Meyer: 'Object-oriented software construction' (PHI 88)

[Morgan90] Carroll Morgan: 'Programming from Specifications' (PHI 1990)

[Wegner90] Peter Wegner 'Concepts and paradigms of OOP' *OOPS Messenger* 1(1) Aug90 [ACM]

Schema Modifications in the LISPO$_2$ Persistent Object-Oriented Language

Gilles Barbedette

Altaïr

BP105

78153 Le Chesnay Cedex

email: gilles@bdblues.altair.fr

Abstract

This paper addresses the issue of schema evolution in LISPO$_2$, a persistent object-oriented language. It introduces the schema modifications supported by the LISPO$_2$ programming environment and presents the potential inconsistencies resulting from these modifications at the schema, method and object levels. Furthermore, it describes how the environment efficiently detects such inconsistencies using a database representing the schema definition. Moreover for correct modifications, it presents how this database is used to update the schema, to trigger method recompilations and to restructure objects using a semi-lazy evolution policy.

1 Introduction

Advanced application domains such as Computer-Aided Software Engineering or Office Automation require both modeling power to represent and manipulate complex objects (e.g. programs, documents or rules) and persistence facilities to store and share these objects between application executions. These new applications led to the development of object-oriented database systems (e.g. [Banc88], [Bane87a]) and persistent programming languages (e.g. [Agra89], [Atki81]). The former augment database systems with expressive power while the latter extend programming languages with persistence. Following this same trend, we developed LISPO$_2$ [Barb90], a language extending Lisp with the O$_2$ object-oriented data model [Lécl89a] and orthogonal persistence.

However, a language, alone, does not create a productive environment. The programmer needs tools which deal with the interactive design and implementation of applications. Recognizing the iterative nature of software development, as in [Booc90] and [Goss90], the LISPO$_2$ programming environment supports an "evolutionary prototyping" development process where design and implementation are not seen as sequential stages but as interleaved ones. In this process, the prototype iteratively evolves from its first version to the final product as the programmer gains experience with the application and refines its design and implementation. In order to support this mode of development, the programming environment has to facilitate the modification of the design in order to incorporate the results of previous experiments. To fulfill this requirement, the LISPO$_2$

programming environment provides a mechanism for class modification which enables the programmer to change class definitions on the fly, even though some objects have been previously created and some methods compiled. In such a situation, classical environments [Meye88], [Stro86] require exiting the environment, modifying class definitions, recompiling relevant classes and methods and reloading them. Moreover, the test database has to be regenerated. In contrast, the LISPO$_2$ environment checks the consistency of the modifications with respect to the static semantics of the language. Furthermore, it assists the developer in understanding the effects of his/her modification by pointing out the affected methods, and it triggers their recompilation. Finally, it updates objects automatically in order to meet their new class definitions.

The remainder of the paper is organized as follows. Section 2 introduces the features of the LISPO$_2$ language necessary for understanding the rest of the paper. Section 3 presents a taxonomy of the schema modifications supported by the programming environment. The next three sections address their repercussions respectively on schema definition, methods and existing objects. Moreover, they detail the implementation choices that we made to efficiently detect inconsistencies in the schema, to trigger method recompilations and to restructure objects after a schema modification. This is followed in Section 7 by a comparison with other related approaches. Finally, we conclude by summarizing the innovative features of the environment and by indicating future plans.

2 Overview of the LISPO$_2$ Language

This section briefly introduces the features of the LISPO$_2$ language relevant to the issue of schema evolution. For a more detailed presentation of LISPO$_2$, the reader is referred to [Barb90].

- **Classes, Types, Operations and Methods.**

  LISPO$_2$ is a class-based object-oriented language. A *class* defines the structure and the behavior of a set of objects called its instances. The structure of an object is defined by a *type*. A type in LISPO$_2$ is either an atomic type (e.g. integer or float) or a complex type built from other types and classes using the tuple, set and list type constructors. Tuple types are used to model aggregation. Set types represent homogeneous collections without duplicates while list types support indexable homogeneous collections. The behavior of an object is defined by a set of *operations*. A class definition introduces only the specification of operations, called *signatures*. A signature includes the name of the operation, the type/class of its arguments (if any) and the type/class of its result. The implementation of an operation is defined by a *method*. Separating the specification of an operation from its implementation allows the programmer to work with a partially implemented application (no method associated with an operation) or to explore alternative implementations of the same operation (several methods associated with an operation). Figure 1 shows the definition of the PERSON class. Its structure is described by a tuple structured type defining two *attributes*, and its operational interface contains two operations.

```
(defclass PERSON
      (OBJECT)
      (type (tupleof
                (name string)
                (spouse PERSON)))
      (operations
          (name () (return string))
          (set-spouse (PERSON) (return PERSON))))

(defclass CLUB-MEMBER
      (PERSON)
      (type (tupleof
                (entry-date DATE)
                (spouse CLUB-MEMBER)))
      (operations
          (set-spouse (CLUB-MEMBER) (return CLUB-MEMBER)))
      has-extension)
```

Figure 1: PERSON and CLUB-MEMBER classes

• **Inheritance.**

Classes are related to each other through inheritance links. A class inherits the structure and behavior of its superclasses. In Figure 1, the CLUB-MEMBER class is defined as a subclass of the PERSON class. Inheritance in LISPO$_2$ is based on subtyping and behavior refinement. The type of a subclass must be a subtype of that of its superclass. Figure 2 gives a syntactic definition of subtyping. For a formal description of the O$_2$ semantics of subtyping, the reader is referred to [Lécl89a]. In the example shown in Figure 1, the subtyping rules imply that the domain of the "spouse" attribute in the CLUB-MEMBER class (i.e. CLUB-MEMBER) must be a subclass of the one specified in the PERSON class (i.e. PERSON).

In addition, the subclass may extend or redefine the operations defined by its superclass. Operation redefinition occurs when the subclass defines an operation with the same name as one provided by the superclass. In that case, the operation defined in the subclass must have the same number of arguments as the one of its superclass. Moreover, the types of the arguments and result specified in the subclass must be subtypes of those specified in the superclass. This is illustrated in Figure 1 by the "set-spouse" operation in the CLUB-MEMBER class redefining the one defined in the PERSON class.

LISPO$_2$ supports multiple inheritance, i.e. a class can inherit from several direct superclasses. Multiple inheritance can lead to attribute or operation name conflicts. These conflicts are

. if T is an atomic type

then T' is an atomic type and T = T'.

. if T is set structured, i.e. of the form (**setof** E) (resp. list structured, i.e. (**listof** E)),

then T' is set structured, i.e. of the form (**setof** E') (resp. list structured, i.e. (**listof** E'))
and E' is a subtype of E.

. if T is tuple structured, i.e. of the form (**tupleof** $(a_1 \ TA_1) \ ... \ (a_n \ TA_n)$)

then T' is tuple structured, i.e. of the form (**tupleof** $(a_1 \ TA'_1) \ ... \ (a_m \ TA'_m)$)
$m \geq n$ and $\forall \ i \in [1, ..., n]$ TA'_i is a subtype of TA_i.

. if T is a class,

then T' is a class and T' is a subclass of T.

Figure 2: Subtyping rules asserting that T' is a subtype of T

solved explicitly by the programmer either by choosing which attribute/operation to inherit
or by defining a local attribute/operation in the subclass. This is further explained in Section
4.2.

- **Persistence by Reachability**.

In LISPO$_2$, persistence is orthogonal to the type system, i.e. all LISPO$_2$ data (either objects
or pure LISP data such as vectors or cons cells) have equal rights to persist. Moreover, to
eliminate the impedance mismatch problem, we introduce persistence in LISPO$_2$ by extension
of the usual LISP data lifetime. We allow data to remain alive between program executions
by defining a set of persistent roots. At the end of program execution, all data which
are directly or indirectly reachable from the persistent roots are made persistent without
any programming cost. These persistent roots are *database variables* and *class extensions*.
Database variables retain their associated data between application executions. They can be
seen as variables belonging to an everlasting scope. A class extension provides the automatic
grouping of all instances of a class (i.e. all objects generated by the class and its subclasses)
into a set. A class extension is generated by the **has-extension** option in a class definition
as for the CLUB-MEMBER class in Figure 1.

The *schema* of an application consists of the set of database variables and class definitions
appearing in its design.

3   Schema Modifications

In this section, we present the schema modifications supported by the LISPO$_2$ environment and
we outline how it processes them. These modifications reflect our intention to start with simple
but fundamental and useful modifications in order to understand their impacts on the schema,

its implementation and its associated database. These modifications can be roughly divided into three categories:

- **Modifications of the Persistent Roots.**

  This category contains the addition and deletion of database variables and class extensions. The programmer uses them, as needed, to modify the set of objects that could persist.

- **Modifications of the Class Content.**

  This concerns the addition/deletion of an attribute/operation and the modification of its specification (i.e. the domain of an attribute and the signature of an operation). These allow the programmer to complete a class definition as he/she gains experience with the application concept associated with the class.

- **Modifications of the Inheritance Graph.**

  This refers to adding and removing a leaf class as well as adding and removing an inheritance link between a class and a direct superclass. These are the most fundamental of all modifications since they cope with the general architecture of the application (i.e. the concepts introduced and their relationships).

When the programmer issues a schema modification, the environment processes it in several steps. First, it checks that the modification does not lead to a schema violating the static semantics of the language (e.g. subtyping rules). If it does, the modification is rejected. Otherwise, the environment points out to the programmer the set of methods which can be affected by the modification. Depending on the amount of induced change, the programmer can either confirm or cancel the modification. If he/she confirms it, every affected method is recompiled (if necessary) and marked as invalid if the compiler discovers new type errors. Finally, the relevant objects are restructured. The next three sections address in turn the impacts of schema modifications on the schema, methods and objects.

4 Repercussions of Schema Modifications on the Schema

In this section, we discuss the impacts of schema modifications on the schema. We first define the notion of a *valid schema*. A schema is valid if it satisfies the two following properties:

- The inheritance graph is a direct acyclic graph with one root (named the OBJECT class) and without disconnected classes. Moreover, the subtyping and operation redefinition constraints on inheritance are satisfied.

- There is no name conflict: classes and database variables are uniquely named as are operations and attributes in a class.

We now study each modification and point out how it can break the validity of a schema. Each major case of validity violation is illustrated by means of a simple example. Furthermore, we describe the logical updates to the schema induced by correct modifications. The data structures and algorithms used to efficiently detect the violations are then described.

4.1 Persistent Root Modifications

The addition of a database variable (resp. a class extension option) only implies checking name uniqueness (resp. option uniqueness). Removing a database variable (resp. a class extension option) does not affect the validity of the schema.

4.2 Class Content Modifications

Since the schema modifications concerning attributes and operations involve essentially the same checks, we present them in the same section. Moreover, throughout the rest of the paper, we follow the Eiffel [Meye88] terminology where a *feature* represents either an attribute or an operation. Thus, a *feature specification* represents either the domain of an attribute or the signature of an operation.

- **Add a Feature to a Class.**

First, the class should not already define a feature with the same name. If the class previously

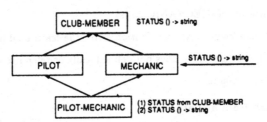

Figure 3: Name conflict in a feature addition

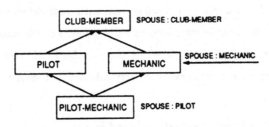

Figure 4: Redefinition error in a feature addition

inherited a feature with the same name, the validity of the induced *upward redefinition* is checked. Moreover, the new feature is propagated to any subclasses. This may lead to both name conflicts and redefinition errors. A name conflict occurs when a subclass already inherits a feature with the same name but coming from a different superclass. This is illustrated in Figure 3 by the addition of the "status" operation in the MECHANIC class. This addition induces a valid upward redefinition with the "status" operation defined in the CLUB-MEMBER class. However, it leads to a name conflict in the PILOT-MECHANIC class. Indeed, this class inherits both the status operation defined in the CLUB-MEMBER class and the one added to the MECHANIC class. Unlike systems like ORION [Bane87b], LISPO$_2$ does not provide a default rule based on the order of the superclasses to solve such name conflicts. The programmer has to solve them explicitly, either by choosing the operation to inherit using a "from" clause (e.g. the one from the CLUB-MEMBER class as in the first option) or by defining a local operation in the PILOT-MECHANIC class (in the second option). Choosing an operation through a "from" clause does not create a new operation in the PILOT-MECHANIC class. It only points to the operation defined in the CLUB-MEMBER class and thus implies sharing (in particular sharing of the implementation).

Redefinition errors arise when the subclass locally defines a feature with the same name but with a specification that violates the subtyping rules. This is illustrated in Figure 4 where the programmer adds the "spouse" attribute whose domain is the MECHANIC class. This leads to a *downward redefinition* error in the PILOT-MECHANIC class (since the PILOT class is not a subclass of the MECHANIC class).

If there is neither name conflict nor redefinition error, the feature addition is accepted and propagated to every subclass which does not define locally or reference (via a "from" clause) a feature with the same name.

- **Remove a Feature from a Class.**
  Removal of a feature may be performed only on the class defining it. If the feature is referenced through "from" clauses, the modification is rejected. The "from" clauses must first be cancelled (for example by replacing them with local definitions). Otherwise, the only inconsistency that may be introduced is name conflicts in the class. This occurs when the removed feature was previously blocking these conflicts. If there is no such conflict, the deletion is accepted and propagated to every subclass that inherits the feature without redefining it.

- **Change the Specification of a Feature in a Class.**
  This update is only allowed in the class which defines it. The new specification is checked against upward and downward redefinitions of the feature in the class defining it and in every class referencing it by a "from" clause. For example, Figure 5 presents the case where the programmer wants to change the domain of the "spouse" attribute in the MECHANIC class,

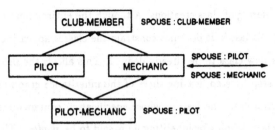

Figure 5: Conflict in feature replacement

stipulating that the spouse of a mechanic must be a mechanic. This modification fails because of the redefinition error occurring in the PILOT-MECHANIC class (i.e. the PILOT class is not a subclass of the MECHANIC class). If there is no redefinition error, the modification is propagated to every class inheriting or referencing the feature.

- **Rename a Feature in a Class.**

  A feature can be renamed only in the class defining it. If the feature is referenced through "from" clauses, the modification fails (since the "from" clause is used to solve name conflicts). The renaming can lead to name conflicts and redefinition errors in the class and its subclasses as for a feature addition. If there is none, the feature is renamed in the class and every subclass inheriting it.

4.3 Inheritance Graph Modification

- **Create a Class.**

  A new class can be created only as a leaf of the inheritance graph. Adding a class in

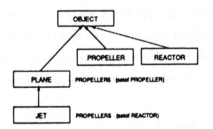

Figure 6: Class creation and the shadow mechanism

the middle of the inheritance graph can be achieved by a combination of class creation and superclass additions. The name of the class must not be used by an already defined class. The superclass(es) specified must have previously been defined. The subtyping and operation redefinition rules are checked. Moreover, if, due to multiple inheritance, a feature name conflict occurs, the programmer has to solve it explicitly.

The innovative facility offered by the LISPO$_2$ environment in this modification concerns the flexibility in the ordering of class creations. Although the environment requires a class to be created before its subclasses, it does not constrain the classes appearing in the specification of a feature of the new class to be already defined. This allows the programmer to develop and test a design step by step, leaving slices of the inheritance graph undefined while testing others. In such a case, the feature whose specification contains undefined classes (and consequently the class defining or inheriting it) is said to be *shadow*. The inheritance checks involving the undefined classes are presumed correct and memorized by the environment (as described in Section 4.4). However, when a previously undefined class is created by the programmer, the presumed correct checks are then really performed since the position of the class in the inheritance graph is known. If those checks fail, the definition of the previously undefined class is rejected. This is illustrated in Figure 6. In this example, the general PLANE class defines the "propellers" attribute whose domain is the type (**setof** PROPELLER). The JET subclass redefines this attribute with the domain (**setof** REACTOR). However, since the REACTOR class is not yet defined, the JET class and its "propellers" attribute are shadow. The subtyping check (i.e. (**setof** REACTOR) with respect to (**setof** PROPELLER)) leads to checking whether REACTOR is a subclass of PROPELLER, which cannot be performed. Thus, the check is memorized by the environment. When the REACTOR class is defined as a direct subclass of OBJECT, this check is performed completely and leads to a subtyping violation. Hence, the creation of the REACTOR class is rejected and the JET class remains shadow.

- **Delete a Class.**

  This modification can only be applied to the leaves of the inheritance graph. Class deletion in the middle of the inheritance graph can be achieved by a combination of inheritance link deletions and class deletion. The class can be referenced elsewhere in the schema through feature specification. Those features and the classes defining and inheriting them become shadow.

- **Add an Inheritance Link to a Class.**

  First, the environment checks that the new inheritance link does not induce a cycle in the inheritance graph. Then the features provided by the new superclass (either inherited or locally defined) are propagated along the new link and the same checks as for feature addition are performed.

- **Remove an Inheritance Link from a Class.**

  Removing a superclass from a class C can lead to inconsistencies in the schema due to the fact that a subclass relationship between a descendant of C (or C itself) and an ancestor

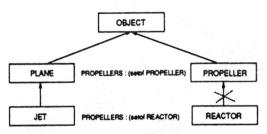

Figure 7: The "inheritance path break" problem

of C no longer holds. This kind of "inheritance path break" is illustrated in Figure 7. The inheritance link between the REACTOR class and the PROPELLER class is removed. This leads to a subtyping violation in the JET class since the redefinition of the "propellers" attribute is no longer valid.

Therefore, to accept the modification, everywhere in the inheritance graph that C or a subclass of C is used in a redefinition, the subclass check implied by the redefinition has to be performed again but without taking into account the removed inheritance link. If there still remains a path connecting the subclass of C to its presumed ancestor, there is no inconsistency. Moreover, the system also checks that the references to ancestors of C induced by "from" clauses in C and its subclasses are still valid. If the modification does not introduce inconsistencies, all the features inherited by the class and its subclasses via the removed link are deleted in them, except if they are still inherited through an alternative path. If the class is disconnected in the inheritance graph (i.e. with no superclasses), the OBJECT class is added as a default superclass.

4.4   Implementation

All information about the schema (classes, features, database variables) and its implementation (i.e. methods) is handled by a component of the LISPO₂ system, named the Schema Manager. The Schema Manager is implemented in the LISPO₂ language itself. The reason for this choice is twofold. First all information about the schema has to persist from one programming session to the other. Second, an object-oriented approach makes the implementation of the Schema Manager easier. It promotes a modular design (through information hiding) allowing the experimentation of different check algorithms. Moreover, inheritance allows code sharing and reusability. This is illustrated in Figure 8 which shows a portion of the "meta schema" used to represent class/feature definitions as objects. We can see the benefit of inheritance to gather the OPERATION class and the ATTRIBUTE class under the FEATURE class. This allows the sharing of all algorithms detecting the impact of feature modifications on the schema and methods. Moreover the late-binding mechanism, offering extensibility, allows us to easily add a new type constructor with its

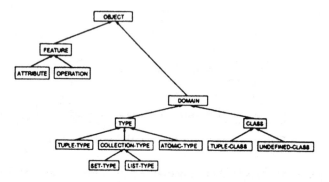

Figure 8: The meta schema

own subtyping rule. All we have to do is to define a class for this new type constructor, and to specify its local subtyping rule as an operation and its associated method. Thereafter, it will be immediately integrated into all of the schema modification framework.

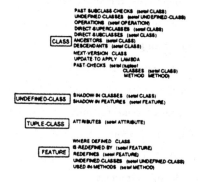

Figure 9: Some attributes defined by the meta schema

Figure 9 gives a subset of the definitions of the structures used to detect the inconsistencies in the schema induced by modifications. To handle fast name conflict detection, all features provided (i.e. defined or inherited) by a class are stored in the class (using the "operations" and "attributes" attributes defined respectively in the CLASS and TUPLE-CLASS classes). To detect name conflicts and distinguish locally defined features from inherited ones, the "where-defined" attribute (defined in the FEATURE class) stores the class where the feature is defined. To speed up redefinition checks (in the case of feature addition or feature replacement), each feature is linked to both its upward and downward redefinitions (through respectively the "redefines" and "is-redefined-by" attributes). This avoids walks in the inheritance graph to check for redefinition errors.

The inheritance graph is internally represented by the four "direct-superclasses", "direct-subclasses", "ancestors" and "descendants" attributes. The subclass check is then reduced to simply testing the membership of the presumed subclass in the descendants of the class.

The shadow mechanism is handled by several attributes and the UNDEFINED-CLASS class. Whenever an undefined class is used in a feature specification, an instance of the UNDEFINED-CLASS class is created. This instance acts as a stub recording all the checks that will have to be performed on the undefined class when it is defined. These checks are memorized by the operation implementing the subclass check when it is called on undefined classes. The shadow/deshadow detection is managed by the attributes "undefined-classes" defined in the FEATURE and CLASS classes. They record the undefined classes leading directly or indirectly (through a shadow class) to the shadow status of the feature/class. The pending cross-references are the "shadow-in-class" and "shadow-in-feature" attributes defined in the UNDEFINED-CLASS class. These attributes record respectively the classes and features which are shadow because of the undefined class. When a previously undefined class is introduced, the system sees if this new class is shadow or not. If the class is not shadow, it is removed from the cause of shadowness of its dependent features/classes. This removal can lead to their deshadowing. Otherwise, the set of undefined classes implying the shadow status of the new class replaces the class in the cause of shadowness of its dependent features/classes.

The detection of the inheritance path break problem (illustrated in Section 4.3) is handled by means of the "past-subclass-checks" attribute defined in the CLASS class. This attribute records all the superclasses which have been successfully tested as an ancestor of the class (due to feature redefinition for example). When a superclass is removed from a class, this attribute is scanned in the class and all its descendants, and the checks are performed again.

5 Repercussions of Schema Modifications on Methods

This section discusses the impacts of schema modifications on methods. Methods are coded in LISP extended with object manipulation expressions. Those expressions include creating objects, reading and writing attributes, and sending messages à la Smalltalk [Gold83]. Message sending involves the late-binding mechanism where the operation called depends on the class of the receiver. There also exists a "super" mechanism allowing the programmer to specify the starting class from which to look up the operation.

The LISPO$_2$ method compiler performs static type checking of the object expressions using type inferencing and user supplied type declarations (when needed). It catches any inconsistencies in the method with regard to the schema (e.g. detecting references to unknown attributes/operations). The type-checking algorithm allows each "variable" (i.e. formal argument of an operation, local variable or attribute) to be assigned an expression whose type is a subtype of the static (declared or inferred) type of the variable. Since the type-checking algorithm uses the schema at the moment of the method compilation (i.e. the defined classes with their features and the subclass relationships represented by the inheritance graph), a schema modification can affect the type validity of previously compiled methods. Indeed, schema modifications may have two kinds of impact on a method. They can lead to new type errors or they can imply a change in the behavior of the method due to the late-binding mechanism.

When a schema modification is issued, the induced actions on methods performed by the programming environment can be of three kinds:

- Directly mark a method as invalid. In this case, the environment knows, without having to recompile the method, that the modification introduces new type errors in the method.

- Recompile a method to detect type errors. In this case, the environment does not have enough information to directly assert the invalidity of the method but it knows that the change may induce a type error. So recompilation is necessary and the method is marked as invalid if the type-checker discovers errors.

- Warn the developer since the modification may change the behavior of the method.

5.1 Persistent Root Modifications

Only removal of a persistent root affects methods. All methods referring to the removed root are directly marked as invalid.

5.2 Class Content Modifications

- **Add a Feature to a Class.**

  If there was no previously inherited feature with the same name in the class, i.e. if there is no upward redefinition, there is no impact on methods. Otherwise, all methods referring to the inherited feature are pointed out because their behavior may change due to the late-binding mechanism.

- **Remove a Feature from a Class.**

  If there is no inherited feature replacing the removed one, all methods referencing the

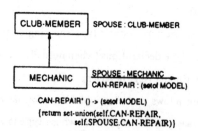

Figure 10: Type error induced by removing a feature

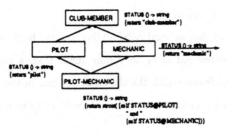

Figure 11: Change in behavior induced by removing a feature

removed feature are directly marked as invalid. Otherwise, there is a change analysis between the specification of the removed feature and the one of the newly inherited feature. If they are not the same, all methods referencing the removed feature are recompiled to discover new type errors. Figure 10 illustrates this case. In order to avoid disturbing the reader with syntactic details, the examples of methods use an abstract syntax where message sending is denoted by the "[]" brackets and attribute access by the dot notation. In this example, the programmer removes the "spouse" attribute defined in the MECHANIC class. The "spouse" attribute is then replaced in the MECHANIC class by the one defined in the CLUB-MEMBER class. However its domain is the CLUB-MEMBER class. This affects the "can-repair*" method computing all the plane models a mechanic can repair as the union of the plane models that the mechanic and his/her spouse can repair. Indeed, there is a loss of information (since the CLUB-MEMBER class does not provide the "can-repair" attribute), leading to a type error in the "can-repair*" method. In contrast, Figure 11 gives an example of a change behavior introduced by removing a feature. The "status" method is removed from the MECHANIC class. It is replaced by the one defined in the CLUB-MEMBER class which has the same signature but a different method. This leads to a changed behavior in the "status" method defined in the PILOT-MECHANIC class. This method calls the status operations provided by the MECHANIC and PILOT classes using the "super" mechanism (denoted by a @). So the result of this method is changed from "pilot and mechanic" to "pilot and club-member".

- **Change the Specification of a Feature in a Class.**
  There is a change analysis between the new and the old specification of the feature. If the new specification redefines the old one[1], all methods referencing the old feature are pointed out due to a potential changed behavior. Otherwise, these methods are recompiled in order to discover type errors.

---

[1]For an attribute, this means that the new domain is a subtype/subclass of the old one. For an operation, the definition rule holds between the new and the old signatures.

- **Rename a Feature in a Class.**

  If the renamed feature implies upward redefinitions, the methods referencing the newly redefined features are pointed out since they may suffer from a change in their behavior.
  Moreover, if an inherited feature with the old name appears in the class, a change analysis
  is performed between the specifications of the inherited and the renamed features as for a
  feature replacement.

5.3 Inheritance Graph Modifications

Creation of a class cannot induce type errors. The environment only points out the methods which
reference features redefined in the new class, since their behavior may be affected. Deletion of a
class leads to directly marking all methods referencing the class, either through one of its features
or through its name (e.g. in a variable declaration), as invalid. Addition of an inheritance link
can only induce potential redefinitions and thus a changed behavior in methods referencing the
newly redefined features. In contrast, removal of an inheritance link from a class C can lead to an
"inheritance path break" problem, i.e. C or one of its descendants is no longer a subclass of an
ancestor of C. All methods which might be type inconsistent due to this modification are directly
marked as invalid (as explained in Section 5.4). This is also the case for the methods referencing
a feature no longer provided by the class (or its subclasses) due to the removal. Renaming a class
has no impact on methods. This is due to the fact that methods, once compiled, refer directly to
the class without using its name.

5.4 Implementation

When the compiler is invoked on a method, it computes a compiling context. This context records
all properties of the schema which have been used to assert the type validity of the method. Such
properties include the classes used, the features which must be provided by these classes, and the
subclassing test performed. The cross-references implied by this context are represented by the
"used-in-method" attributes (defined in the FEATURE and CLASS classes as shown in Figure 9)
recording in which methods the feature/class is referenced. These attributes are used to find the
methods to be directly marked as invalid (e.g. when a class is removed) or to be recompiled (e.g.
when the specification of a feature is changed). Moreover, the "past-check" attribute (defined in
the CLASS class) stores all subclass checks performed by the compiler to assert the type validity
of the method. Therefore, when an inheritance link is removed from a class, all checks involving
the class (or its descendants) with respect to one of its ancestors are selected from this attribute
and are performed again.

```
(defun transform-mechanic ()
   (ifn (instance-of? old.spouse 'PILOT-MECHANIC)
        (setq new.spouse [old find-or-create-spouse])
        (setq new.spouse old.spouse)))
```

Figure 12: Transformation function example

6 Repercussions of Schema Modifications on Instances

6.1 Persistent Root Modifications

Persistent root modifications affect the set of references pointing to the instances and, thus, their deletion by the garbage collector. Adding a class extension makes persistent those instances of the class which were not referenced by the persistent roots, while removing a class extension (resp. a database variable) deletes objects if they are no longer referenced elsewhere in the database.

6.2 Class Content Modifications

Only modifications of attributes affect the structure of instances. Adding or renaming an attribute in a class leads to the logical addition of the attribute to all instances of the class and of the subclasses inheriting the attribute. Removing an attribute from a class implies its logical deletion from all instances of these classes if the attribute is not replaced by an inherited one.

Replacing the domain of an attribute (either directly by issuing a "replace" modification or indirectly by adding an attribute) does not affect instances if the new domain is a supertype/superclass of the old one. Otherwise, the object associated with the attribute in existing instances may not be of the new domain. For example, if we change the domain of the "spouse" attribute defined in the MECHANIC class from MECHANIC to PILOT, every instance having a mechanic as value of the "spouse" attribute violates the new class definition. In such cases, the default policy of the environment is to replace all values of the "spouse" attribute by a void reference. However, when the programmer issues the schema modification, he/she can specify a transformation function which will be applied to all affected instances. This function is in charge of computing a new value for the attributes which are affected by the schema modification. For example, the transformation function shown in Figure 12 does not change the value of the "spouse" attribute if it is an instance of the PILOT-MECHANIC class. Otherwise, it invokes the find-mechanic-spouse operation which retrieves or creates the mechanic spouse of the object. In a transformation function, two pseudo variables old and new are used. They represent respectively the old and new versions of the instance being transformed. The system ensures that a transformation function is performed only once for an object. This prevents infinite loops when cyclic objects are transformed.

6.3   Inheritance Graph Modifications

The impact of an inheritance link addition (resp. removal) on instances is reduced to a set of attribute additions (resp. removals). In contrast, removing a class raises the problem of what happens to the instances of the removed class. In LISPO$_2$, we delete them but this approach may lead to potential dangling references if those instances were referenced by objects of other classes. Therefore, all instances of the class are deleted and every object referring to a deleted instance through an attribute is updated with a void reference as the new value of the attribute (using a mechanism explained in Section 6.4).

6.4   Implementation

The restructuring of instances is based on a semi-lazy evolution policy. The modifications are immediately propagated to all instances which are in main memory. However, for the instances on disk, they are only performed when the instance is loaded in main memory (by an object fault mechanism). This policy results from a tradeoff between efficiency and interactivity. Immediate propagation of the modification on all instances would decrease the interactivity of the system if there is a great number of instances on disk. On the other hand, performing the propagation on demand would require checking, on every access to an object, if it has to be updated. This would decrease the performance of methods working on main memory objects. In order to perform the update check only once, a solution could be to flush all involved instances onto disk and to update them only at load-time (therefore the check has to be done once). Unfortunately, the current implementation of persistence in LISPO$_2$ uses a two address space model (i.e. an instance is identified by its RAM address in main memory and by a persistent identifier onto disk) as in PS-ALGOL [Atki81]. Therefore, the cost of the flushing step would be too high since we would have to convert main memory addresses into persistent identifiers when flushing instances on disk. This transformation would require the scan of the entire main memory.

The implementation of this semi-lazy policy requires two system facilities: the ability to enumerate all instances of a class in main memory and the capacity of storing instances of various versions of a class on disk. The first point is achieved by maintaining a class extension for each class (even if it has not been declared by the programmer). The extension in main memory chains all the direct instances of the class together and points to the extensions of its subclasses. The second point is handled by creating a version of the class after each modification. This is performed using the "next-version" and "update-to-apply" attributes defined in the CLASS class. The first attribute links the successive versions of a class. The second one stores the transformation to apply in order to make the instance evolve from the previous to the next version. Therefore, when an instance is loaded from disk, the version of its class is compared to the version which is in main memory. If they differ, the chain of versions is followed and each update is applied. Class versions are objects and, as objects, they are reclaimed automatically by the garbage collector when there are no references (here instances since an instance holds a reference to its class) to them.

This class versioning mechanism is also used to incrementally avoid the dangling references problem after a class removal. When a modification deleting a class is issued, a new class version is created for each class referencing the removed class as the specification of an attribute. The associated transformation function is automatically generated by the system. Its role is to replace the value of the attribute by a void reference eliminating the dangling reference.

7 Related Work

Two major systems, namely ORION[Bane87b] and GemStone[Penn86], address the problem of impacts of schema modifications on the schema and its instances. Only ORION supports multiple inheritance. In this system, the means of solving name conflicts is a default rule based on the order of the superclasses. In particular, this rule is used to block the propagation of modifications (such as adding, renaming or replacing a feature) when it implies a name conflict in subclasses. Thus, a modification can be partially applied. In contrast, the LISPO$_2$ philosophy of propagation is "all or nothing". That is, the modification is applied everywhere the feature is inherited if it is possible, otherwise it is not applied at all. This respects the natural view of inheritance where a feature is shared by all the subclasses inheriting it.

In order to preserve the structure of instances, these two systems reduce the power of schema modifications. For example, in ORION, the domain of an attribute can only be generalized. In the same vein, GemStone does not allow the addition of an attribute, if there is already an inherited attribute with the same name. Moreover GemStone allows class deletion only if the class has no instances. In contrast, ORION deletes all instances of the class leading to the problem of dangling references. In LISPO$_2$, there is no reduction of the power of schema modifications due to their impacts on the instances. Moreover, our restructuring policy avoids the problem of dangling references after a class deletion, as explained in Section 6.4.

GemStone does not support the addition and deletion of inheritance links while these modifications are provided by ORION. However, the potential "inheritance path break" induced by deletion of a superclass is not mentioned in [Bane87b] and does not seem to be handled. Concerning class creation, none of these systems allows the programmer to work with a partially defined schema (i.e. the shadow mechanism).

Neither GemStone nor ORION addresses the issue of the impacts of schema modification on methods. In contrast, Encore[Skarr86] promotes an interesting approach relying on a class versioning and error handling mechanism to make the change transparent to methods. In this approach, the programmer defines a set of routines attached to a class version. These routines handle errors due to the mismatch between methods and the class version, such as accessing an unknown attribute or violating a domain constraint. In LISPO$_2$, the aim is, first of all, the automatic detection by the environment of the components of the schema and its implementation affected by a modification. This provides the programmer with a global view of the impacts of a change before it is performed. The approach in Encore can be seen as complementary. When the change has been confirmed, this approach can be applied to all methods where new type errors are introduced. However, the burden on the programmer of the class versioning and error handling mechanisms has to be taken into account.

Concerning the transformation of affected instances, our approach is very similar to the one in [Lern90]. The transformation function ensures the mapping between the old and new versions of instances. However, [Lern90] only deals with the structural aspect of schema modification and does not address the issue of method recompilation.

8 Conclusion and Future Directions

This paper has presented the schema modifications supported by the LISPO$_2$ programming environment. They allow the programmer to quickly develop a first version (even incomplete) of the application and they enable him/her to easily incorporate changes suggested by previous experiments. We have illustrated the inconsistencies which may be introduced by these modifications at the schema, method and object levels. Furthermore, we have described the data structures used to detect such inconsistencies.

From the first uses of our schema modifications, we have identified two main drawbacks. The first one concerns the lack of a methodological tool asserting the quality of a resulting schema. Indeed, the use of schema modifications leads to a valid schema whose structure may present anomalies such as redundancies in the inheritance graph. These anomalies can be accepted in the first steps of the design but must be eliminated in the final one. To remedy this, a tool acting like a "lint" program is needed to point out the weakness of the final schema in quality domains such as maintainability or reusability. The second drawback concerns the hard-wired semantics and coarse granularity of the schema modifications. For example, when the programmer removes a superclass link, he might want to keep in the class some attributes which will disappear, or to explicitly indicate a new superclass when the class become disconnected. Therefore, we are working on a "toolkit" approach to address the schema evolution issue. It consists of schema modifications of finer granularity and

of a means of combining them in sequences. The validity of the compound schema modification
will be checked only at the end of the sequence based on analysis of the changes imposed on the
schema. Such an approach will provide a much more open-ended framework for schema evolution
allowing the customization and creation of new modifications.

References

[Agra89] R. Agrawal and N.H. Gehani, "ODE: The Language and the Data Model", *Proc.
SIGMOD Conf.*, Portland, 1989.

[Atki81] M. Atkinson, "PS-ALGOL: an Algol with a Persistent Heap", *Sigplan Notices*, 17(7),
July 1981.

[Banc88] F. Bancilhon, G. Barbedette, V. Benzaken, C. Delobel, S. Gamerman, C. Lécluse,
P. Pfeffer, P. Richard and F. Velez, "The Design and Implementation of O_2, an
Object-Oriented Database System", *in Advances in Object-Oriented Database Systems*, Springer-Verlag, 1988.

[Bane87a] J. Banerjee, H.T. Chou, J. Garza, W. Kim, D. Woelk, N. Ballou and H.J. Kim, "Data
Model Issues for Object Oriented Applications", *ACM Trans. Office Info. Syst.* 5(1),
January 1987.

[Bane87b] J. Banerjee, W. Kim, H.J. Kim and H.F. Korth, "Semantics and Implementation of
Schema Evolution in Object-Oriented Databases", *Proc. SIGMOD Conf.*, San Francisco, 1987.

[Barb90] G. Barbedette, "LISPO$_2$: A Persistent Object-Oriented Lisp", *Proc. 2nd EDBT Conf.*,
Venice 1990

[Booc90] G. Booch, *Object-Oriented Design*, Benjamin/Cummings, 1990.

[Gold83] A. Goldberg and D. Robson, *Smalltalk 80: The Language and its Implementation*,
Addison-Wesley, 1983.

[Cope84] G. Copeland and D. Maier, "Making Smalltalk a Database System", *Proc. SIGMOD
Conf.*, Boston 1984.

[Goss90] S. Gossain and B. Anderson, "An Iterative-Design Model for Reusable Object-Oriented
Software", *Proc. OOPSLA Conf.*, Ottawa 1990.

[Lécl89a] C. Lécluse and P. Richard, "Modeling Complex Structures in Object-Oriented
Databases", *Proc. PODS Conf.*, Philadelphia 1989.

[Lern90] B.S. Lerner and A.N. Habermann, "Beyond Schema Evolution to Database Reorganization", *Proc. OOPSLA Conf.*, Ottawa 1990.

[Meye88] B. Meyer, *Object Oriented Software Construction*, Prentice Hall, 1988.

[Penn86] D. J. Penney and J. Stein, "Class Modification in the GemStone Object-Oriented
DBMS", *Proc. 1st OOPSLA Conf.*, Portland 1986.

[Skarr86] A.H. Skarra and S.B. Zdonik, "The Management of Changing Types in an Object-
Oriented Database", *Proc. 1st OOPSLA Conf.*, Portland 1986.

[Stro86] B. Stroustrup, *The C++ Programming Language*, Addison-Wesley, 1986.

The Design of an Integrity Consistency Checker (ICC) for an Object Oriented Database System

Christine Delcourt(*), Roberto Zicari (**)

(*) Altaïr, France

(**) Politecnico di Milano, Italy

e-mail: relett15@imipoli.bitnet

Abstract

Schema evolution is an important facility in object-oriented databases. However, updates should not result in inconsistencies either in the schema or in the database. We show a tool called ICC, which ensures the structural consistency when updating an object-oriented database system.

1 Introduction

Schema evolution is a concern in object-oriented systems because the dynamic nature of typical OODB applications calls for frequent changes in the schema . However, updates should not result in inconsistencies either in the schema or in the database.

We present a tool which ensures the structural consistency of an object-oriented database system while performing schema updates. The tool has been implemented to evaluate the correctness of schema updates for the O_2 object-oriented database system [Ban91][LecRic89a].

1.1 Preliminary O_2 concepts

In this Section we briefly recall the fundamental concepts of O_2 which are relevant for our discussion. The reader is referred to [LecRi89a],and [LecRi89b] for a formal definition of the O_2 data model and to [Vel89] for the description of the system architecture. O_2 is an object-oriented database system and programming environment developed at Altaïr. Classically, in object-oriented data models, every piece of information is an object. In the O_2 data model, both *objects* and *values* are allowed. This means that, in the definition of an object, the component values of this object do not necessarily contain only objects, but also values. In O_2 we have two distinct notions: *classes* whose instances are objects and which encapsulate data and behavior, and *types* whose instances are values. To every class is associated a type, describing the structure of its instances. Classes are created using schema definition commands. Types are constructed recursively using *atomic types* (such as integer, string, etc.), *class names*, and the *set*, *list*, and *tuple* constructors. Therefore types can be complex. Objects have a unique internal identifier and a value which is an instance of the type associated with the class. Objects are encapsulated, their values are not directly accessible and they are manipulated by *methods*. Method definition is done in two steps: First the user declares the method by giving its *signature*, that is, its name , the type of its arguments and the type of the result (if any). Then the code of the method is given. In O_2, the schema is a set of classes related by inheritance links and/or composition links. The inheritance mechanism of O_2 is based on the subtyping relationship, which is defined by a set inclusion semantics.

Multiple inheritance is supported. O_2 offers a compile-time type-checker in an attempt to statically detect as many illegal manipulations as possible of objects and values. Objects are created using the "new" command. If a class is created "with extension" then a named set value is created which will contain every object of the class and will persist. O_2 allows object values to be manipulated by methods other than those associated with the corresponding class. This feature is obtained by making "public" the type associated with the class.

Methods in O_2 can call other methods of the same class, or "public" methods defined in other classes. They may access directly a type associated to a class (besides the class to which they are associated) if this type has been defined "public". The inheritance scope of a method can be changed by application of the "@" feature which allows a reference to a method from outside the scope of the method.

Example: Given two classes, C,C2 with C2 subclass of C, it is possible, in the body of method m2 defined in C2, to refer to a method m defined in C instead of method m redefined in class C2, as the scope rule would normally imply (see Figure 1).

```
C   m:(C->C')
|
C2  m:   (C2->C")
    m2:  (C2->C")
         body.m2 : [...m@C...]
```

Figure 1

When a class inherits methods or types from more than one class (multiple inheritance) conflicts with names for methods and attributes have to be explicitly solved by the designer. For example, two methods with the same name defined in different superclasses will not be inherited by the common subclass. The designer has two possible choices to solve the name conflict:

- either redefine the method in the subclass or

- specify which method he/she wants to inherit using a "*from class*" clause which specifies the chosen inheritance path.

1.2   Schema Updates: What is the problem?

Informally, the problem with updates can be stated as follows: We want to change the structural and behavioral part of a set of classes (schema updates) and/or of a set of named objects (object updates) without resulting in run-time errors, "anomalous" behavior and any other kinds of uncontrollable situation. In particular, we want to assure that the semantics of updates are such that when a schema (or a named object) is modified, it is still a consistent schema (object). Consistency can be classified as follows [Zic90a]:

a. *Structural consistency*. This refers to the static part of the database. Informally a schema is structurally consistent if the class structure is a direct acyclic graph (DAG), and if attribute and method name definitions, attribute and method scope rules, attribute types and method signatures are all compatible. An object is structurally consistent if its value is consistent with the type of the class it belongs to.

b. *Behavioral consistency*. This refers to the dynamic part of the database. Informally an object-oriented database is behaviorally consistent if each method respects its signature and its code does not result in run-time errors or unexpected results.

In this paper, we will only consider the issue of preserving structural consistency.

We will consider "acceptable" only those updates that do not introduce structural inconsistency, while we will allow behavioral inconsistencies that do not result in run-time errors. Any kind of behavioral inconsistency that has been caused by an update will be reported to the user (designer). We have implemented a tool, the ICC which guarantees such consistency.

1.3 Paper Organization

The paper is organized as follows: Section 2 defines more formally the notion of structural consistency for the O_2 object-oriented database system. Section 3 presents the list of updates we allow on the schema, and give a few definitions which will be used in the rest of the paper. Section 4 presents by means of a selected example, the algorithms performed by the ICC to ensure structural consistency. Section 5 gives some concluding remarks.

2 Ensuring Structural Consistency

In this Section, we discuss one basic type of consistency relevant to the O_2 system (but in general to every object-oriented database system) , namely *structural* consistency.

Structural consistency refers to the static characteristics of the database.

We recall here some of the basic definition of O_2 as defined in [LecRic89a] which will help us to define the notion of a consistent schema.

We denote $T(C)$ the set of all types defined over a class C. T(C) includes atomic types, class names, tuple, set and list types.

Inheritance between classes defines a class hierarchy: A class hierarchy is composed of class names with types associated to them, and a subclass relationship. The subclass relationship describes the inheritance properties between classes.

Definition 2.1 A *class hierarchy* is a triple (C, σ , $\prec$) where C is a finite set of class names, σ is a mapping from C to T(C), i.e. σ (C) is the structure of the class of name C, and $\prec$ is a strict partial ordering among C.

The semantics of inheritance is based on the notion of subtyping. The subtyping relationship $\leq$ is derived from the subclass relationship as follows:

Definition 2.2 Let (C, σ, $\prec$) be a class hierarchy, the subtyping relationship $\leq$ on $T(C)$ is the smallest partial ordering which satisfies the following axioms:

1. $\vdash c \leq c'$, for all c, c' in C such that $c \prec c'$. That is, a subclass is a subtype.

2. $\vdash : [\ a_1: t_1,...,a_n: t_n,...,a_{n+p} : t_{n+p}] \leq [a_1: s_1,...,a_n: s_n\ ]$, for all types t_i and s_i, i=1,...,n such that $t_i \leq s_i$. This is subtyping between tuple types. We can refine tuples by refining some attributes or by adding new ones.

3. $\vdash \{s\} \leq \{t\}$, for all types s and t such that $s \leq t$. This is subtyping between set types.

4. $\vdash < s > \leq < t >$, for all types s and t such that $s \leq t$. This is subtyping between list types.

5. $t \leq any$, for all types t. The symbol any is a type by definition.

As inheritance is user given, some class hierarchies can be meaningless.

In a class hierarchy an instance of a class is also an instance of its superclasses (if any). Therefore, if class c' is a superclass of class c, then we must have that the type of c is a subtype of the type of c'. More formally:

Definition 2.3 A class hierarchy $(C, \sigma, \prec)$ is *consistent* iff for all classes c and c', if $c \prec c'$ then σ (c) $\leq \sigma$ (c').

Example: This is a consistent class hierarchy. Class Employee is a subclass of Person, (i.e. Employee $\prec$ Person):

```
class Person
type tuple [name:string,
           age: integer,
           address: tuple [location: City,
                           street: string] ]

class Employee
type tuple [name:string,
           age: integer,
           address: tuple [location:City,
                           street: string],
           profession: string,
           company: string ]
```

A schema is also constituted of methods attached to classes. Methods have signatures.

Definition 2.4 A method *signature* in class C is an expression m: $c \times t_1 \times ... \times t_n \to t$, where m is the name of the method, and $c, t_1 ... t_n$ are types. The first type c must be a class name and is called the receiver class of the method.

We are ready to define a schema.

Definition 2.5 An O_2 *database schema* is a 5-tuple S=(C, σ, $\prec$,M,N), where:

- $(C, \sigma, \prec)$ is a consistent class hierarchy (see def.3)

- M is a set of method signatures in C

- N is a set of names with a type associated to each name

A schema is therefore composed of classes related by inheritance which follow the type compatibility rules of subtyping and a set of methods. Attributes and methods are identified by name. Within the schema, type attributes and method names have a *scope rule* (see def. 7). When we do not want to distinguish between a type attribute and a method name, we simply use the term *property*.

Now we are ready to define what we mean with structural consistency for a database schema.

Definition 2.6 A database schema S is *structurally consistent* iff it satisfies the following properties:

- if $c \prec c'$ and the method m is defined in c with signature m:c $\times t_2...t_n \to t$, and method m' is defined in c' , and m and m' have the same name, with signature m': c' $\times t'_2...t'_n \to t'$, then $t_i \leq t'_i$ and $t \leq t'$ (covariant condition)

- the class hierarchy is a DAG

- if there are classes c1 and c2 having a common subclass c4, with a property name p defined in both c1 and c2, but not in C4, then there is another subclass c3 of c1 and c2 in which the property p is also defined and c4 is a subclass of c3.

The first property assures that method *overloading* is done with *compatible* signatures, the second property constrains the structure of the class hierarchy, and finally the last property eliminates multiple inheritance conflicts (also denoted as *name conflicts*). Definition 2.6 is important, because we will always consider schemes which are structurally consistent. An update to a schema is a mapping which transforms a schema S into a (possibly) different schema S'. Schemes S and S' have to be structurally consistent. The semantics of the schema update primitives will have to ensure *at least* that structurally consistent schemes are produced as a result of an update. In our approach name or type conflicts occurring as a consequence of an update will not be solved automatically by the system.

We also give an auxiliary definition which will be used in the rest of the paper.

Definition 2.7 Given a property name p and a class C, the *scope* for p in C, denoted *scope(p,C)* is the set of C and all subclasses of C (recursively obtained) where p is not locally redefined plus all classes where p is referred to with the "*p from C*" clause. (The algorithm to construct a scope is given in Def.3.5)

An existing method or attribute in a class C can be

- locally defined in C or,

- inherited from a superclass or,

- specified with the "from C_p" clause, C_p being the class where p is locally defined.

When we do not want to distinguish between the above cases, we say that a property p "exists" in class C.

Figure 2 illustrates the three different cases of inheritance.

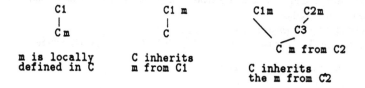

Figure 2

2.1 The ICC: A Basic Schema Update Tool

The way the designer updates the schema is a dialogue with an interactive tool called the Interactive Consistency Checker (ICC). The ICC is a basic update tool which, given a schema and a proposed update, detects whether structural inconsistencies may occur. It then refuses those updates which produce structural inconsistencies: the update is not performed. The reason for the refusal of the update is always given to the user.

3 Schema Updates

We present in this Section the complete list of basic updates one can perform on an O_2 schema.

Updates are classified in three categories: Updates to the type structure of a class, to methods of a class, and to the class as a whole. This classification is fairly similar to the one of [Ba87a,Ba87b]. However, the semantics of some updates is different. Updates have parameters and their semantics can be given in accordance to application's requirements. For details the reader is referred to [Zic90a] [Zic90b] where the syntax and semantics of the operators are defined.

SCHEMA UPDATES:

1. *Changes to the type structure of a class*

   Because in O_2 types can be arbitrarily complex, we have different ways to modify a class type. We can think of an update u which modifies the type structure T of a class C, as a mapping between types, $u : T \rightarrow T'$. Updates of this kind can be broadly classified in two categories: those for which $T' \leq T$ (we call them type-preserving), and those for which $T' \not\leq T$ (we call them non type-preserving). Of all possible type updates we list here only the most elementary ones:

   1.1 Add an attribute to a class type

   1.2 Drop an existing attribute from a class type

   1.3 Change the name of an attribute of a class type

   1.4 Change the type of an attribute of a class type

   Updates 1.1 and 1.3 are type-preserving. Update 1.2 is non type-preserving, while update 1.4 is type-preserving if new- type $\leq$ old-type.

2. *Changes to the methods of a class*

   2.1 Add a new method

   2.2 Drop an existing method

   2.3 Change the name of a method

   2.4 Change the signature of a method (this update may be also implied by a change to the class structure graph as defined below)

   2.5 Change the code of a method.

3. *Changes to the class structure graph*

   3.1 Add a new class

   3.2 Drop an existing class

   3.3 Change the name of a class

   3.4 Make a class S a superclass (subclass) of a class C

   3.5 Remove a class S from the superclass (subclass) list of C

The list of updates defined above can be reduced: There exists a basic set of updates which can be used to execute all other updates.

The basic set of updates is the following:

BASIC SCHEMA UPDATES:

1.1 Add an attribute to a class type	1.2 Drop an attribute from a class type
2.1 Add a method	2.2 Drop a method
3.1 Add a class	3.2 Drop a class
3.3 Change the name of a class	3.4 Make a class a superclass (subclass) of C
3.5 Remove a class from the superclass (subclass) list of C	

The other updates in the previous list can be executed using sequences of basic updates.

(e.g. 1.3 = <1.2 , 1.1>, this equivalence does not hold at
                         instance level
       1.4 = <1.2 , 1.1>, this equivalence does not hold at
                         instance level
       2.3 = <2.2 , 2.1>
       2.4 = <2.2 , 2.1>
       2.5 = <2.2 , 2.1)
       3.3 = <3.2, 3.1>, this equivalence does not hold at
                         instance level)

The sequence of basic updates corresponding to a non elementary update has to be atomic, to avoid inconsistency.

3.1 Additional Definitions

We give a few more definitions which we will use through out the paper.

3.1.1 DAG

A DAG is the formal representation of the class hierarchy. It is defined as follows:

Definition 3.1 : DAG
A direct acyclic graph (DAG) is defined as a pair $(E_c, \prec)$ where

- E_c is the set of *nodes*. Each node represents a class.

- $\prec$ is a partial order with class Object as root.
  $\forall\, C, C' \in E_c \times E_c, C' \prec C \Leftrightarrow C$ is a direct superclass of C'
  $\qquad\qquad\qquad\qquad\qquad\qquad \Leftrightarrow C'$ is a direct subclass of C.
  $C' \prec C$ represents an *edge* between C and C', C being higher than C' in the hierarchy. □

Definition 3.2 $\forall\, C, C' \in E_c \times E_c$, we can define a:

- **Path between two classes**
  $C' < C \Leftrightarrow (C' \prec C) \vee (\exists\, C_1, ..., C_n \in E_c \,/\, (C' \prec C_n), (C_n \prec C_{n-1}),..., (C_2 \prec C_1), (C_1 \prec C)).$
  $C' < C$ indicates that a path exists from C' to C going up: C and C' are related, C being higher than C' in the DAG. In this case, C is called a superclass of C' and C' a subclass of C. □

- **Set of all direct subclasses of a class**
  $direct\_subclasses(C) = \{C_i \,/\, C_i \in E_c \wedge (C_i \prec C)\}.$
  $direct\_subclasses(C)$ is the set of all direct subclasses of the class C. □

- **Set of all direct superclasses of a class**
  $direct\_superclasses(C) = \{\, C_i \,/\, C_i \in E_c \wedge (C \prec C_i)\}.$
  $direct\_superclasses(C)$ is the set of all direct superclasses of the class C. □

- **Set of all subclasses of a class**
  $subclasses(C) = direct\_subclasses(C) \cup (\cup_{(C_i \in direct\_subclasses(C))}\, subclasses(C_i)\,).$
  $subclasses(C)$ is the set of all subclasses of the class C. □

- **Set of all superclasses of a class**
  $superclasses(C) = direct\_superclasses(C) \cup (\,\cup_{(C_i \in direct\_superclasses(C))}\, superclasses(C_i)\,).$
  $superclasses(C)$ is the set of all superclasses of the class C. □

Example:

Given four classes C_0, C_1, C_2, C_3, with C_2, C_3 subclasses of C_1, C_1 subclass of C_0 as shown in figure 3, we have $C_2 < C_0$, $C_3 < C_0$, *direct_subclasses*$(C_0) = \{C_1\}$, *direct_superclasses*$(C_2) = \{C_1\}$, *subclasses*$(C_0) = \{C_1, C_2, C_3\}$ and *superclasses*$(C_2) = \{C_1, C_0, \text{Object}\}$.

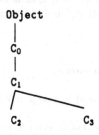

Figure 3

3.1.2   Virtual edge

We introduce the notion of *virtual edge* to represent a "from" clause in the DAG. All definitions here will be helpful in the detection of name conflicts and type incompatibility in the schema.

Definition 3.3 : A virtual edge represents a "from" clause

Given a property p and two classes C' and C*, if p in C' is defined using the "from C*" clause this requires that p is locally defined in C*. This reference is represented by a *virtual edge* in the DAG. This virtual edge is added between C* and C', it is labeled by the property with name p and it is denoted by: *virtual_edge(C*, C', p)*. □

Example: Consider three classes C, C', C* with C and C* superclasses of C and a property m in C1 defined using the from clause (see figure 4).

This corresponds to the virtual edge *virtual_edge(C*, C', p)* which is equivalent to p in C' from C*.

C p   C* p   C p   C* p

\   \   ⋰ P
 \   ≡   \   ⋰
  C' p from C*   C'

Figure 4

Note: A *virtual edge* is "stronger" than ordinary DAG edges. Given a *virtual_edge(C*, C', p)* to determine the inheritance of p in C' , only this virtual edge is considered and not the ordinary edges. In our example, C' inherits p from class C* and not p from class C or another class.

In fact, a "from" clause it is used to "force" the inheritance of properties to avoid name conflicts.

Note: In the actual implementation of O_2, the notion of virtual edge is constrained as follows:
A virtual edge $virtual\_edge(C^*, C', p)$ exists if and only if there exists a path $C'<C^*$.
Our definition of virtual edge is more general than this and allows a reference to a class C^* even if it is not connected to C'.

Definition 3.4 : Set_virtual_edge
Consider a property p existing in a class C, we have :
$set\_virtual\_edge(p, C) =$
> $\{V\ /\ virtual\_edge(C, V, p)\ exists\}$ in case p of V is locally defined in C.
> $\emptyset$ otherwise.

The set $set\_virtual\_edge(p, C)$ contains all classes of C which have a virtual edge going from the class C where p is locally defined. $\square$

3.1.3 Scope

Inheritance of properties is based upon the *scope* and *use* concepts which are defined in this section. These arising concepts will be helpful in the detection of possible name conflicts arising after a schema update.

Each property existing in a class has an associated scope. A scope is defined as follows.

Definition 3.5 : Scope of a property in a class
The *scope(p, C)* of a property p in a class C is the set of classes (including C) which inherit this property by inheritance or by a virtual edge. $\square$

We now show the algorithm to define the scope of a property p for a class C.
Scope constructive algorithm

Given a class C in which the property p exists, the algorithm is used to build the set *scope(p, C)*.
Begin
> $temp = \emptyset$.
> For each $C' \in direct\_subclasses(C)$
> > if p is inherited then $temp = temp \cup scope(p, C')$ endif
> endfor
> For each $C' \in set\_virtual\_edge(p, C)$
> > $temp = temp \cup scope(p, C')$
> endfor
> $scope(p, C) = \{C\} \cup temp$.
End

Example:
Consider the classes C_0, C_1, C_2, C_3, C_4 of figure 5 and the property p locally defined in C_0, C_1 and C_5. In C_2, p is defined with the "from C_0" clause.
We have $scope(p, C_0)=\{C_0, C_2, C_3, C_4\}$, $scope(p, C_5)=\{C_5\}$, $scope(p, C_1)=\{C_1\}$, $scope(p, C_2)=\{C_2, C_3\}$, $scope(p, C_4)=\{C_4\}$.

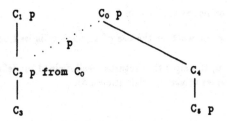

Figure 5

Definition 3.6 : A name conflict in a class

A name conflict occurs in a class C for a property p

⇔ there exist two classes C_1 and C_2 where p exists and is not locally defined in a common ancestor class and $C \in scope(p, C_1) \cap scope(p, C_2)$

Note: If a class inherits at least twice a property p locally defined in the same ancestor class then this property will exit in C only once.

Example: Consider the classes C_0, C_1, C_2, C of figure 6 and the property p locally defined in C_0. C inherits the property p locally defined in C_0 twice (by path C_0, C_1, C and by the path C_0, C_2, C) but p is considered in C only once. No name conflict occurs since those two p inherited are equal; they have the same local definition.

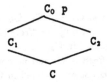

Figure 6

Definition 3.7 : A name conflict in a schema.

A *name conflict* in a schema occurs for a property p

⇔ there exist at least one class C in the schema where a name conflict occurs for p. □

To express how a property p is defined in a class, we introduce the notion of *use*.

Definition 3.8 : Use of a property in a class.

The *use* of a property p in a class C, denoted *use(p, C)* can be:

1. *well-defined*: if p exists in C and there is no name conflict in the class for p or,

2. *undefined*: if p does not exist in C or,

3. *not_well_defined*: a name conflict exists for p in C. □

We now give the algorithm to detect whether the use of a property is well defined, undefined or not well defined.

Given a class C and a property p, the algorithm returns: well_defined, undefined or not_well_defined. These correspond to the three values of *use* (see definition 3.8).

Algorithm
Begin
        Case 1: p is locally defined or is derived with the "p from" clause in C.
           if there exist at least
                - two local definitions for p in C, or
                - two "from" clauses for p in C, or
                - a local definition and a "from" clause for p in C
           then *use(p, C)* is not well defined, a name conflict appears. Return not_well_defined.
           else *use(p, C)* is well defined. Return well_defined.
           endif
        Case 2: otherwise
           Look at all superclasses of C (recursively) until p is locally defined in each path
           leading from C to Object. Note: going up from a class to its direct superclasses
           takes only the virtual edge for p if one exists.
           Case 2-1: If p is not encountered in at least one path then Return undefined.
           Case 2-2: If a unique local definition for p is encountered in those paths
                  then Return well_defined.
           Case 2-3: If at least two local definitions for p are encountered in two different classes
               for two different paths (and the definitions of p are not the same)
               then a name conflict appears, return not_well_defined.
End

Example:
Consider figure Figure 7. We have C_1, C_2, C_3, C_4, C_5, C_6, C_7, C_8 classes. A property p is locally defined in C_2, C_3 and in C_6 and p is defined using the "from C_3" clause in C_5.
We have *use(p, C_4)*=undefined, p is undefined in C_4,
        use(p, C_7)=well_defined, p is defined in C_7 and no conflict appears in C_7, and
        use(p, C_8)=not_well_defined, p is not well defined in C_8 because p of C_8 is defined in C_6
           and in C_3. A name conflict exists in C_8.

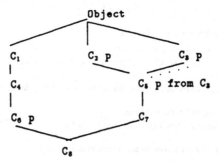

Figure 7

Definition 3.9 : Scope without conflict
In our system name conflicts are forbidden and all scopes need to be without name conflict. Given a class C and a property p, *scope(p, C)* is *"without conflict"* if and only if $\forall$ C' $\in$ *scope(p, C)*, *use(p, C')*$\neq$"not_well_defined".

Property 1 :
Given a class C and a property p locally defined in C, if *scope(p, C)* is *"without conflict"* then $\forall$C'$\in$*scope(p, C)*, *scope(p, C')* is *"without conflict"*

Property 2 :
Given two classes C and C' (C$\neq$C') and a property p existing in those two classes,
if C' $\in$ *scope(p, C)* then *scope(p, C')* $\subset$ *scope(p, C)*.

Property 3 : Name conflict detection
Given a property of name p, by property 1 and 2 we have:
No name conflict occurs in the schema for p $\leftrightarrow$ $\forall$ C' $\in$ E_c such that p is locally defined in C', *scope(p, C')* is *"without conflict"*.

3.1.4 Scope frontiers and type incompatibility

In this section, we introduce the notion of *frontiers* of a scope. We will see that this notion is of interest for the verification of type compatibility after a schema update is performed.
Let us first define the root of a scope.

Definition 3.10 : Root of a scope
Given a property p existing in a class C, *scope(p, C)* has an associated *root*. This root is denoted *root(p, C)* and it corresponds to the class where p is locally defined. $\square$

Given a property p existing in a class C, *scope(p, C)* has two kinds of *frontiers*, *top* and *lower adjacent limits*.

Definition 3.11 : Top of a scope
Given a property p existing in a class C,
the *top* of *scope (p, C)* corresponds to the set of classes belonging to this scope which contains, the class for which p is locally defined and the classes for which p is defined with the from clause. This set is denoted *top(p, C)* and is defined by:
$top(p, C)$ = {C} in case *virtual_edge*(S, C, p) exists
             = $\emptyset$ in case *root(p, C)*$\neq$C and $\not\exists$*virtual_edge*(S, C, p)
               in fact, p is inherited in C.
             = *set_virtual_edge(p, C)* $\cup$ {C} otherwise $\square$

We define here the *leaves* which allow the definition of the *lower adjacent limits* (see definition 3.13) for a given scope.

Definition 3.12 : Leaves of a scope
Given a property p existing in a class C,
the *leaves* of *scope (p, C)* correspond to the bottom classes of this scope. The set of those leaves is denoted *leaves(p, C)* and is defined by:
leaves(p, C) = {C_i / C_i $\in$ *scope(p, C)*, ($\not\exists$ C_j $\in$ *scope(p, C)* / C_j $\in$ *subclasses(C_i)*)}. $\square$

Definition 3.13 : Lower adjacent limits (lal) of a scope
Given a property p existing in a class C,
the *lower adjacent limits* (lal) of *scope (p, C)* correspond to the direct subclasses of its leaves. This set
is denoted *lal(p, C)* and is defined by: $lal(p, C) = \cup_{C' \in leaves(p,C)}\{C_i \ / \ C_i \in direct\_subclasses(C')\}$ □

Example:
Consider figure 8. We have C_1, C_2, C_3, C_4, C_5, C_6, C_7, C_8 C_9 classes. A property p is locally defined
in C_2, C_5 and in C_9 and p is defined using the "from C_2" clause in C_6 and C_7.
We have $top(p, C_2)=\{C_2, C_6, C_7\}$
$leaves(p, C_2)=\{C_3, C_6, C_8\}$
$lal(p, C_2)=\{C_5, C_9\}$

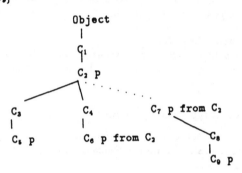

Figure 8

To have type compatibility between classes in the DAG, all properties in the DAG need to be type
compatible as defined below. Notation: *typing*(p, C) is the signature or the type of p, p being a method
or an attribute in a class C.

Definition 3.14 : Type compatibility for a property p in a class C:
A property p existing in a class C is *type compatible* $\Longleftrightarrow$
$(\ \forall\ C_i \in direct\_superclasses(C)$ such that p exists in C_i, $typing(p, C) \leq typing(p, C_i))$
$\wedge\ (\ \forall\ C_i \in direct\_subclasses(C), typing(p, C_i) \leq typing(p, C))$. □

As we will see, because a type modification will affect the scope of the entire DAG and not only of a
single class, it is interesting to define a type compatibility notion for a scope. Let us first define a well
typed scope.

Definition 3.15 : Well typed scope
Given a property p existing in a class C,
scope(p, C) is *well typed* if and only if $\forall$ C' $\in$ *scope(p, C)*, p in C' is *type compatible* (see definition 3.14).
□
We introduce the predicate *scope_compatibility(p, C)*=True to express that the *scope(p, C)* is well typed.
scope_compatibility(p, C) = true $\Longleftrightarrow$
(R1): $(\forall\ C_j \in top(p, C)$, $\forall\ C_i \in direct\_superclasses(C_j)$ with p existing in C_i, $typing(p, C) \leq typing(p, C_i))$
$\wedge$
(R2): $(\forall\ C_i \in lal(p, C)$, $typing(p, C_i) \leq typing(p, C))$.

Thus, the type compatibility problem for a property p is equivalent to the well typed scope problem.

Property 4 : **Type incompatibility detection for a property**

No type incompatibility occurs in a schema for a given property p $\iff$ $\forall$ C $\in$ E$_C$ such that p is locally defined in C, *scope(p, C)* is well typed.

This shows that using the definition of a well typed scope, the number of comparisons between signatures or types when a modification is done, can be limited to the frontiers of the modified scopes. In fact, for a given scope *scope(p, C)*, all classes have the same p, thus the same type; therefore only the frontiers are of interest.

Moreover, we have:

Property 5 *1. If the signature (type) of a property p is replaced by a superior signature (supertype) then the scope affected is well typed if (R1) is satisfied.*

2. If the signature (type) of a property p is replaced by an inferior signature (subtype) then the scope affected is well typed if (R2) is satisfied.

3.2 Basic and Parametrized Updates

The updates presented at the beginning of Section 3 are parametrized updates (see [Zic90a] for details). We can consider them still high level updates. In fact, among these updates, there exists a basic set of updates such that their corresponding structural check can be used to do the structural check of the other ones.

Therefore, we decided to define lower level schema updates. This level is composed of the following basic updates: (Note: The schema structural check is the same for the attributes and methods updates: we will in the following speak of property updates.) Thus we have defined a set of lower level updates

Changes to the properties of a class

- add a property local definition
- add a "from" clause for an existing property
- replace a local definition into a new local definition or a from clause for a property

- drop a property local definition
- drop a "from" clause for a property
- replace a from clause into a new local definition or a from clause for a property

Changes to the type structure of a graph

- add a node
- add an edge
- change the name of a node

- drop a node
- drop an edge

which can be used to implement all possible semantics of the updates (the ones of the high level) as indicated by the user.

In [DeZi91] it is shown the correspondence between user-parametrized updates and the basic updates.

When the user submits to the ICC a high level update u, this update is translated into a sequence of basic updates. For each of the basic updates the ICC performs a consistency check. If all basic updates composing the high level update are validated, then the high-level update is also validated. If one of the basic updates composing the high-level update induces structural inconsistency in the schema, the high-level update is refused and a warning is given to the user.

The ICC checks if a schema S after an update u is structurally consistent.

By definition, a schema S is structurally consistent iff the following invariants are satisfied:

Definition 3.16 : Invariants for a structural consistency

- Class lattice invariant:
  - All classes must be connected in the DAG
  - The root of the DAG is the class Object
  - The name of a class must be unique in the DAG
- Name conflict invariant: *use(p, C)* must be well-defined for all properties p existing in a class C.
- Type compatibility invariant: All classes in the schema have to be *compatible*.

□

The ICC is a *basic tool*; it only detects inconsistencies introduced by an update. It does not solve them automatically.

Given a schema and an update as an input, the ICC detects whether structural inconsistencies occurred or not. If a structural inconsistency arises the tool refused the update and provides all the detected inconsistencies to the user. If no structural problem occurs the update is done.

A study of a more sophisticated tool is considered in [De90a].

4 Schema structural consistency check

This section describes by means of a selected example some of the algorithms used by the ICC to verify schema structural consistency.

Notation:In the example, for each updates we consider an initial state and a final state. To represent those, each concept will be marked with the *after* or *before* marks. For example, given an update. $scope(..) = scope_{before}(..)$ before the update, and $scope(..) = scope_{after}(..)$ after the update.

While performing an update, the ICC check its effects on the schema to ensure structural consistency.

The structure of the checks is similar and include the following steps:

Algorithm:

1. C_check: A set of constraints are checked.

2. The DAG structure is checked.

3. NC_check: Name conflicts are detected.

4. TI_check: Type incompatibilities are detected.

5. CD_check: The dependency problem is studied.

If one problem occurs the update is refused otherwise it is performed.

end

4.1 An Example

We present in this section the algorithms to detect structural inconsistencies when performing a specific update: Adding a property in a class. The description of the algorithms for the other update primitives defined in Sect. 3.2 is reported in [DeZi91].

4.1.1 Property addition

Let us consider the addition of a property p in a class C. This addition consists of adding a local definition of p in C using the $add\_local\_property(p, C, \prec signature, type \succ)$ update.

Add_local_property: $add\_local\_property(p, C, \prec signature, type \succ)$

- <u>Semantics</u>:

  1. The DAG structure is not affected.
  2. We consider two cases :
     - <u>*Case 1*</u>: $use_{before}(p, C)=$"undefined" (p did not exist in C)
     - <u>*Case 2*</u>: $use_{before}(p, C)=$"well_defined" (p existed in C).

  If neither a name conflict nor a type incompatibility occurs then
     - case 1: $scope(p, C)$ is created.
     - case 2: $scope_{after}(p, R) = scope_{before}(p, R) - scope(p, C)$ with $R=root_{before}(p, C)$.

     A definition for p is locally added in class C. This property p is then propagated
     to the subclasses of C until a redefinition of p occurs.

     else the update is refused.

  We need to check name conflicts and type compatibilities. We first define the algorithm for name conflict detection then the one for type incompatibility detection.

- <u>Name conflict detection</u>:
  A conflict can occur only in classes of $scope_{after}(p, C)$.

  - case 1: $use_{before}(p, C)=$"undefined"
    $use_{after}(p, C')=$"not_well_defined" for $C' \in scope_{after}(p, C)$ $(C' \neq C)$
    $\Leftrightarrow$ p was inherited in C' before the update.

  - case 2: $use_{before}(p, C)=$"well_defined"
    * $use_{after}(p, C)=$"not_well_defined" $\Leftrightarrow C \in top_{before}(p, R)$ with $R=root_{before}(p, C)$
    * $use_{after}(p, C')=$"not_well_defined" for $C' \in scope_{after}(p, C)$ $(C' \neq C)$
      $\Leftrightarrow ((\exists X \in direct\_superclass(C')/$
      $(X \notin scope_{after}(p, C) \wedge$ p exits in X before the update)
      or $(X \in scope_{after}(p, C) \wedge use_{after}(p, X)=$"not_well_defined"))).

  Example: Let us look at figure 9 which gives two examples of name conflict after a property addition.

Algorithm: $NC\_add\_prop(DAG, p, C)$
Goal: This algorithm searches for the classes where a name conflict for p occurs after the addition of p in class C.
Input: the schema (DAG), the property p and the class C where p has to be added.
Output: the set of classes where a name conflict occurs for p.
Procedure:
  - if $use_{before}(p, C)=$"undefined"

Case 1:
We add a property p in class C
A conflict occurs in C_1

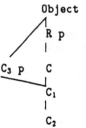

Case 2:
We add a property p in class C
A conflict occurs in C_1 and C_2

> then for each class C' ∈ $scope_{after}(p, C)$ (C'≠C) do
>
> > if $use_{after}(p, C')$="not_well_defined" (see name conflict detection: *case 1*)
> >
> > then **return CONFLICT** in C' endif
>
> endfor

endif

- if $use_{before}(p, C)$="well defined"

> then if $use_{after}(p, C)$="not_well_defined" (see name conflict detection: *case 2*)
>
> > then **return CONFLICT** in C **and exit**
>
> else for each class C' ∈ $scope_{after}(p, C)$ (C'≠C) do
>
> > if $use_{after}(p, C')$="not_well_defined" (see name conflict detection: *case 2*)
> >
> > then **return CONFLICT** in C' endif
>
> endfor

> endif

endif

Endprocedure.

Remark: To improve this algorithm, only the first conflict encountered for each path of $scope_{after}$(p, C) going down by width has to be given: the others are implied by the upper one. Thus, to be more efficient the best way is to order the classes of $scope_{after}$(p, C). The order should be the order of its building when the hierarchy is traversed by width from C going downward.

Example: Let us look at figure 10. We have classes C, R_1 R_2, C_1, C_2, C_3 and a property p is locally defined in R_1 and in R_2. The addition of a property p in class C results in a conflict in C_1, C_2 and C_3. The reason for the conflict in C_1 and C_3 is the same: it is the existence of p in R_1. Thus, the detection algorithm would have to warn of the conflict in C_1 and C_2 and that is all.

- **Type incompatibility detection:**

The classes which may be affected by type incompatibility are those of $scope(p, C)$; thus we have to verify that the scope frontiers are well defined after the update.

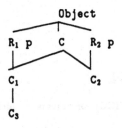

Type compatibility will be satisfied after the update if $scope\_compatibility(p, C) = true$ (see definition 3.15).

By hypothesis, after the update we have: $top_{after}(p, C) = \{C\}$. We have two cases:

- *case 1*: $use_{before}(p, C)=$"undefined"
  We just have to check type compatibility for the lower adjacent limits of $scope_{after}(p, C)$. That means to verify rule (R2) for the definition of $scope\_compatibility(p, C)$. The reason is because $top_{after}(p, C) = \{C\}$ and C has no superclasses where p exists.

- *case 2*: $use_{before}(p, C)=$"well_defined"
  Type compatibility for $scope_{after}(p, C)$ has to be verified for all its frontiers (see section 3.14). Rules (R1) and (R2) of $scope\_compatibility(p, C)$ needs to be verified.

Algorithm: TI_add_prop(DAG, p, t, C)
Goal: This algorithm searches for the type incompatibilities which occur in the schema after the addition of a property p in a class C.
Input: the schema (DAG) which is modified, a property name p with its signature or type t ($t=typing_{after}(p, C)$) and the class C where p has to be added.
Output: the classes where a type incompatibility occurs for the property of name p.
Procedure:

    if $use_{before}(p, C)=$"well_defined" with $R = root_{before}(p, C)$

    then we are in *case 2*:

            - if $t = typing(p, R)$ then **Return No_incompatibility, Exit** endif

            - if $t \nleq typing(p, R)$ (see definition 2.3)

        then **Return Incompatibility in C, Exit**

        else for each class $C' \in lal_{after}(p, C)$ do

            if $typing(p, C') \nleq t$ then **return Incompatibility in C'** endif

        endfor

        endif

    else we are in *case 1*

      for each class $C' \in lal_{after}(p, C)$ do

        if $typing(p, C') \nleq t$ then **return Incompatibility in C'** endif

      endfor

endif
Endprocedure.

5 Conclusions and future work

We have specified and implemented a tool (ICC) for schema evolution ensuring schema structural consistency.

This tool provides two levels of updates.

- The lower level is a set of basic updates. This level ensures the completeness of the tool since its provides all possible updates to obtain every consistent schemes.

- The higher level is composed of parametrized updates which are expressed using the lower level updates.

- The tool ensures the structural consistency of a schema while performing an update: the invariant properties for schema structural consistency are checked when an update is performed therefore only valid schemes are produced.

The ICC provides the basic mechanism for schema evolution. It has the advantage being flexible. The higher level updates can be redefined or completed by new parametrized updates. The ICC can be used to built on top a more sophisticated tool: an adviser helping the schema designer and providing the facility to define update transactions. So far, we have implemented two running prototypes of the ICC tool. The ICC prototypes are intended as experiments towards realizing a more powerful schema designer tool. The ICC tool has been developed independently from the O_2 product, and therefore, there is no direct relationships with the schema designer provided by the forthcoming O_2 product.

As future work, we plan to:

1. build a more sophisticate tool on top of the basic one described in this paper.

2. ensure behavioral consistency when updating the schema.A first proposal which uses a data-flow technique is reported in [CLZ91].

Acknowledgments
We thank the anonymous referees for valuable comments.
Luca Breveglieri provided invaluable support in consulting for LaTeX.

References

[CLZ91]   Coen A., Lavazza G., Zicari R.,"Updating the Schema of an Object-Oriented Database", IEEE Data Engineering bulletin,July 1991, to appear.

[Ng&Ri88] Gio-toan Nguyen and Dominique Rieux, "Schema Evolution for Object-Oriented Database Systems", INRIA Research report, 1988 December.
           ORION

[Ba&Al87a] J. Banerjee et al, "Semantics and Implementation of Schema Evolution in Object-Oriented Databases", ACM SIGMOD 1987.

[Ba&Al87b]   J. Banerjee et al., "Data Model Issues for Object-Oriented Applications", ACM TOOIS, vol.5,No.1, January 1987.

[Kim&Cho88]   W. Kim, and Hong-Tai Chou, "Versions of Schema for Object-Oriented Databases", Proc. 14th VLDB, 1988, Los Angeles.

[Ki&Al88]   W. Kim et al., "Integrating an Object-Oriented Programming System with a Database System, ACM OOPSLA , September 1988.

GEMSTONE

[Pen&Stei87] D.J. Penney, J. Stein, "Class Modification in the GemStone Object-Oriented DBMS", ACM OOPSLA October 1987.

ENCORE

[Ska&Zdo(a)] A.H. Skarra,S.B. Zdonik, "The Management of Changing Types in an Object-Oriented Database", ACM OOPSLA, September1986.

[Ska&Zdo(b)] A.H.Skarra,S.B.Zdonik, "Type Evolution in an Object-Oriented Database", in Research Directions in Object Oriented Systems, MIT press.

[Zdo87]   S.B. Zdonik, "Can Objects Change Types? Can Type Objects Change? (extended abstract)", Workshop Roscoff September 1987.

O2

[Ban91]   F. Bancilhon, C. Delobel, P. Kannelakis, (eds.) "The O$_2$ book", Morgan Kaufmann publisher 1991 to appear.

[Ben&Al88]   V. Benzaken et al.,"Detail Design of the Object Manager", Altair, October 1988.

[De90a]   C. Delcourt, "The schema update problem for the O$_2$ object oriented database system", July 1990.

[De90b]   C. Delcourt, "Schema updates: Integrity Consistency Checker for O$_2$ Object Oriented Database System", July 1990.

[DeZi91]   . DelCourt, Zicari R.,"The Design of an Integrity Consistency Checker (ICC) for an Object-Oriented Database System", Politecnico di Milano; Report 91-021, November 1990.

[Gam89]   S. Gamerman, "Detailed Specifications of the Type and Method Manager V04", Altair, January 1989.

[LecRic89a]   C. Lecluse,P. Richard, "The O2 Database Programming Language", Altair Report 26-89, January 1989. Also in Proc. VLDB , Amsterdam, 1989.

[LecRic89b]   C. Lecluse,P. Richard, "Modeling Complex Structures in Object-Oriented Databases", in proc of the PODS 89 Conference, Philadelphia, March 29,31, 1989.

[VelAl89]   F. Velez et al., "The O2 Object Manager: an Overview", Altair, February 1989.

[Wal89]   E. Waller, PhD Thesis in preparation.

[Zic90a]   R. Zicari, A Framework for Schema Updates in an Object-Oriented Database System, in the O2 book, (F. Bancilhon, C. Delobel, P. Kanellakis, eds.), Morgan Kaufmann publisher, 1991 to appear. A short version in Proc. IEEE 7th Data Engineering Conf., April 8-12, Kobe, Japan 1991.

[Zic90b]   R. Zicari, Primitives for Schema Updates in an Object-Oriented Database System, in Proc. OODBTG Workshop of the accredited standard committee, X3, SPARC,DBSSG,OODBTG, October 23, Ottawa, 1990.

Synchronizing Actions

Christian Neusius

Universität des Saarlandes

FB14 Informatik

W-6600 Saarbrücken, Germany

email: pool@cs.uni-sb.de

Abstract

A model of concurrency control, *synchronizing actions*, is presented specifically designed for concurrent object-oriented programming languages (COOPL). A current research problem in COOPL is the conflict arising from contradictory objectives related to concurrency and encapsulation. Synchronizing Actions presents a solution for this kind of problem. The model supports extension and reuse of a system, the major goals of object-oriented programming, i.e. it provides guidelines for the design of concrete synchronization mechanisms such that they do not interfere with inheritance. Synchronizing actions are a design frame rather than a specific realization. The model is not restricted to a specific model of concurrency, as for example serialization of method executions. We will show the suitability of the model by giving a specific synchronization mechanism based on this design frame.

1. Introduction

We will apply the term *object-oriented* in the sense of Wegner [Weg87], i.e. a language is object-oriented if it provides at least objects, classes and class-based inheritance. Our attention is focused on concurrent object-oriented programming languages (COOPL) that support the concurrency model of *active* objects as the concurrently executing entities. Note that some languages provide active and passive objects (passive objects are private to active objects); this approach allows balancing the degree of concurrency.

Nierstrasz and Papathomas state in [Nie90] that "none of the existing approaches (that combine inheritance and concurrency) has yet succeeded in resolving basic conflicts between concurrency mechanisms and encapsulation that is needed for the safe use and reuse of object-oriented code". Synchronizing Actions are a step towards the solution of this conflict; the model provides a clearer separation of concurrency control and implementation details than all existing approaches. Closely related to this problem are the interferences between concurrency control and inheritance discussed by Decouchant [Dec89] and Kafura and Lee [Kaf89]. Kafura and Lee state that decentralized interface control is a necessity when aiming at reusability and extensibility of object-oriented applications. In the model Synchronizing Actions a guideline is deferred from the

This work was supported by the Deutsche Forschungsgemeinschaft, SFB124, TP D3.

valuable approaches in ACT++ [Kaf89] and Rosette [Tom89]. This guideline alleviates the design of synchronization mechanisms that meet the requirements of the Object-Oriented Programming Paradigm.

In section 2 we evaluate synchronization mechanisms that are based on the decentralized interface control approach, and show how they interfere with encapsulation. The languages ACT++ [Kaf89] and Rosette [Tom89] provide synchronization mechanisms that do not interfere with inheritance. However, their synchronization mechanisms impose a restriction to the concurrency model, namely serialization of method executions per object. After shortly discussing the usefulness of internal concurrency, the model Synchronizing Actions is presented that refines the model of decentralized interface control from section 2. The model describes a design frame which allows different realizations of concurrency control. As an example we will show a concrete synchronization mechanism using this design frame. Finally some open problems and future research directions are mentioned.

2. Existing Synchronization Mechanisms

The design of COOPL providing active objects led to the development of several new synchronization mechanisms. The commonality of these mechanisms is the concept of *interface control* which will be explained below. First, we will briefly review these synchronization mechanisms and then discuss their strengths and shortcoming in combining inheritance and concurrency.

2.1 Language Classification

There are currently several languages combining Concurrency and Object-Oriented Programming. These emerged from two distinct motivations:

(a) Adding Concurrency to an OOPL

The extension is motivated by the claim that an OOPL should be good for modeling the real world [Mad88]. Thus an OOPL should support concurrency in a better way than it is in OOPLs as Simula-67 [Dah66] or Smalltalk [Gol83]. The new approach is thus to transform objects into active entities as in Beta [Kri87] or Concurrent Smalltalk [Yok86].

(b) Adding Object-Oriented paradigms to a Concurrent Object-based language.

Here the extension is motivated by the aim "Structured Programming" and support of code reuse and extensibility. Thus parallel programs become applicable to support the development of similar systems.

These different points of view influenced the language design, and particularly the design of synchronization mechanisms. Amongst the first COOPL was Concurrent Smalltalk (CST) [Yok86]. CST evolved from the object-oriented language Smalltalk [Gol83], and thus belongs to category (a). Like other languages of this category, CST provides *self reference* as an essential design criterion. The model of internal concurrency within an object was chosen since self reference interferes with the serialization of method executions. The consequences of this design decision will be discussed later.

Exponents of category (b) are ACT++ [Kaf89] and Rosette [Tom89]. They were developed on the basis of *actors* [Agh87]. The *actor* model emphasizes as model of concurrency the serialization of method executions within an actor (i.e. an active object). While adding classes and class-based inheritance, self reference was not considered in the language design. Some notes to the essence of self reference are given later.

2.2 Decentralized Interface Control

Interference of synchronization and inheritance was noted by Decouchant [Dec89], Kafura and Lee [Kaf89]. When synchronization is not properly separated from the specification of methods, the extension of code by adding a subclass may force the change of code within the superclass. This, however, contradicts the design rules of OOP. Note that a superclass may have several subclasses, and a change within a superclass will thus withdraw severe consequences. Kafura and Lee give a raw classification of synchronization mechanisms and state that only *decentralized interface control* can be combined with inheritance without restriction of reuse and extensibility.

The task of an object's *interface control* is to decide at a given moment if a message pending within the object's mail-queue may enter the object and thus may be processed or not. Once started, a method execution is no longer explicitly synchronized by the concurrency control. It may be involved in synchronization only when calling another method and waiting for the result. The decision of the concurrency control depends on the content of the mail-queue and on the state of the object's concurrency control. This state defines the set of messages that currently can enter the object; it is represented by a set of data. We will call this set of data the Interface Control Space (ICS) of the object.

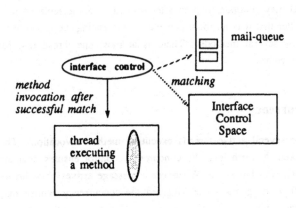

Figure 1. Execution Model *interface control*

When giving a detailed model of interface control we must consider the underlying model of concurrency. We compare in the following two models, *serialization* of method executions, and *internal concurrency* within an object.

2.2.1 Serialization of Method Executions

If an object has at most one active thread that has access to the ICS and data shared between methods, and this thread is involved in the execution of one method then method executions are serialized. During this execution the object is in the state **locked**, i.e. no further method can be invoked. As soon as the thread terminates, the object becomes unlocked. Then the concurrency control within the interface will be invoked. It matches the current state of the Interface Control Space with the mail-queue that contains the messages sent to the object. When a message matches with the ICS the corresponding method will be invoked, and the object becomes locked again. Otherwise the object remains delayed as long as no further message arrives and triggers the invocation of concurrency control.

Examples

ACT++ [Kaf89] provides *behavior abstractions* as the mechanism of concurrency control. Behavior abstractions are sets of method names. A method that returns control (i.e. unlocks the object) specifies by the choice of a behavior abstraction the set of methods that can be invoked next. A behavior abstraction represents an entity that can be redefined within subclasses. The matching process for *behavior abstractions* is a simple test, if there is a message in the mail-box such that the related method is in the state **open**.

Enabled-sets in **Rosette** [Tom89] have some similarities to the mechanism of *behavior abstractions* (as e.g. being redefinable entities of the ICS) but they provide a higher flexibility. The method name (and eventually some of the actual parameter values) contained in a queued message have to match an enabled-set in the Interface Control Space. Tomlinson and Singh call this mechanism matching by content, and compare it with the tuple space model in Linda [Car86].

Note that there may be more than one active thread within an actor in ACT++ and Rosette. This is because a thread may continue running after execution of the replacement behavior of the Concurrency Control. After that it is no more capable of influencing the Concurrency Control or to access data accessible by several methods. There is at most one thread that has the ability to change the Concurrency Control.

2.2.2 Internal Concurrency

An object may have several active threads executing method invocations. The object is thus always in a state unlocked. Nevertheless, the concurrency control ensures, that arriving messages will be delayed until their turn has come. Whenever a message arrives or a thread terminates, the concurrency control will be triggered. Once triggered the concurrency control may create several threads *at once* before terminating.

Examples

Guide [Dec89] provides boolean expressions attached to methods, the activation conditions. A method may be executed when its activation condition returns *true*. Activation conditions use amongst other parameters synchronization counters (introduced independently by Gerber [Ger77] and Robert and Verjus [Rob77]). For example, a counter *started*(m) is automatically increased by the system immediately before the creation of a thread executing method m, and *started*(m)-*completed*(m) delivers the number of threads currently executing method m. Since these counters are independent from method specification they are the key mechanism that supports the model of internal concurrency. Using only the counters, however, would not be flexible enough. Consequently, an activation condition uses instance variables that represent the internal state of the object. A programmer has to consider the consistent change and use of these variables within the method specification.

The synchronization mechanism of DCST [Nak89] is a combination of Method Relations and Method Guards. A Method Relation defines the constraint under which methods are not allowed to run concurrently. A Method Guard is a boolean expression attached to a method that evaluates instance variables. Obviously only the method relations are independent from method specification. This independency is necessary to support the model of internal concurrency since otherwise the consistent change of the instance variables used in Method Guards cannot be achieved.

2.3   Discussion

The source of trouble when combining concurrency control and inheritance is the dependency of the method specifications and the synchronization protocol of an object. The problems so far identified with this dependency concern (a) defining a new method in a subclass may interfere with the synchronization protocol of many superclass methods and (b) encapsulation is weakened. Below, we will discuss if and how the presented synchronization mechanisms solve these problems.

2.3.1 Interference of Concurrency Control and Inheritance

The languages ACT++ and Rosette support reuse and extension of systems in the way that changes of the concurrency control can be specified locally in a class without the need of changing code in other classes or rewriting inherited methods. The applied synchronization mechanisms separate the Interface Control Space from the normal set of data of the object (i.e. the instance variables), and build up the ICS by independent, **redefinable** units. The applied units are defined as sets that are easily changeable (in Rosette) or redefinable (in ACT++) by adding (subtracting) elements to (from) it. Each set represents a specific state of the object's Concurrency Control.

Guide and DCST do not sufficiently support reuse and extension of systems. In Guide, the main shortcoming is the strong attachment of method names and synchronization counters. Adding a method means also adding new synchronization counters. These synchronization counters unfortunately can only be reflected in the inherited activation conditions by redefining the attached inherited methods. Note also that a redefined method gets its own, new set of counters which additionally complicates the synchronization protocol.

In DCST changes of the synchronization protocol due to newly defined methods in a subclass cannot be reflected within the methods of the superclass or their related Method Guards . Thus one may have to redefine all inherited methods that are involved in the synchronization protocol.

2.3.2 Weak Encapsulation

All synchronization mechanisms mentioned above have one specific shortcoming in common, the conflict between the concurrency control and encapsulation. The data involved in the concurrency control (ICS) are accessible to the concurrency control of the subclasses. Since these data are used and even changed within methods encapsulation in the sense of Snyder [Sny87] is weakened. The impact of this weakness is shown below.

The interface control as defined in the above languages captures only a small part of the tasks of the concurrency control. These tasks consist of

(a) the decision of which methods may be executed or not and

(b) the change of concurrency constraints that are evaluated within this decision.

The task (a) may be characterized as the *matching phase*, and is equivalent to the definition of the interface control. The task (b) can be characterized as the *state transition phase* of the concurrency control. None of the synchronization mechanisms above has a clear separation of this *state transition phase* and the specification of implementation details. In Guide, the change of synchronization counters is separated from method specification, but the change of instance variables used in the activation conditions has to be specified within the methods. The same holds for DCST, where the Method Relations are separated from implementation details, but not the Method Guards. In Rosette and ACT++, the state transition phase is given by the computation of which set will override the old set in the ICS. This computation is specified within the methods.

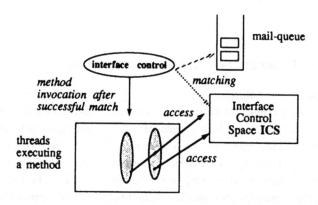

Figure 2. Weakening of Encapsulation.

Figure 2 outlines the violation of encapsulation. This *violation* complicates the understanding of the synchronization protocol since the changes of instance variables belonging to the ICS are hidden in the implementation. Additionally, the approach is particularly critical for the model of internal concurrency. Note that the change of the ICS itself requires mutual exclusion of methods that access the same data of the ICS. This can force the cautious programmer to introduce unnecessary serializations in an application.

Consider, for example, a bounded buffer providing put- and get-operations, where internal concurrency is supported. As soon as the thread executing a put is started, the ICS must switch from the acceptance of put requests to the delay of put requests. Another critical situation occurs when a variable counting the content of the buffer is used within the Interface Control, but changed within the put- and get-operations (as it would be the case in DCST). Then a put and a get operation running concurrently will both access this counter, thus violating mutual exclusion. The complexity of Concurrency Control dramatically increases when internal concurrency is supported.

3. Why Internal Concurrency ?

We will illuminate first the importance of self reference for object-oriented programming. Wegner and Zdonik [Weg88] emphasize self reference as an essential property of object-oriented programming.

> *"In a world without self-reference, inheritance reduces to invocation and inheritance hierarchies are simply tree-structured resource-sharing mechanisms."*

Self reference allows the definition of small sized redefinable units; the code to be rewritten when extending or reusing a system can be held minimal. The problem with *self* in COOPLs is the interference with the serialization of method executions [Yok86]. In the design of Concurrent Smalltalk [Yok86, Yok87] self is reduced to a local procedure call within the atomic, serializing objects. This is a severe restriction, and it is inapplicable when we apply decentralized interface control. While not entering the object by its interface, method invocations by self are excluded from concurrency control.

On the other hand, internal concurrency combined with self reference has the following advantage. A method may be invoked and then be executed up to that moment, where synchronization inevitably must take place. Here it will enter this synchronizing phase by calling self. Then it is delayed as long as the event occurs that allows the processing of the *synchronizing method*, and the calling thread regains control. An example will be shown in section 5.

Finally, a discussion at [WS89], p. 10 about the concurrency models in concurrent object-based languages may be cited. The supporters of the internal concurrency model argue that there should be concurrency within objects for reasons of performance and because there are objects in the real world that exhibit internal concurrency. The main argument against this model is the complexity of synchronization mechanisms (concurrent access of shared variables).

4. Synchronizing Actions

The dependency of the method specifications and the synchronization protocol of an object is the weak point that makes reuse and extensibility so difficult. In comparison to the traditional critical section approach the strength of the decentralized interface control lies in the (partial) separation of concurrency control and method specification. Nevertheless the model underlying the existing COOPLs still conflicts with the paradigm of encapsulation. The design frame *synchronizing actions* separates, besides the "matching phase", also the "state transition phase" of the concurrency control from the method specification. The data of the ICS are encapsulated by the concurrency control since only operations of the concurrency control have access to them. The instance variables are encapsulated by the methods accessing them. Synchronizing Actions can thus be seen as a necessary refinement of the idea "decentralized interface control". This refinement eases reuse and extension of code.

4.1 The Synchronization Model

The new synchronization model is characterized as follows. The synchronization of a method is defined by its *matching_rule*, a set of operations to be executed before the invocation of the method (*pre_action* specification), and a set of operations to be executed after termination of the method (*post_action* specification).

- The *matching-rule* is a boolean expression that evaluates the content of the mail-queue (messages and eventually parameters) and the state of Concurrency Control.

- The *pre_action* and the *post_action* specify the change of the concurrency control that becomes necessary by the invocation or termination of a method call, respectively. They consist of a sequence of operations working solely on the Interface control space. Pre_action and post_action are executed as atomic actions.

The set of matching-rules, pre_actions and post_actions of the methods are the only specifications that can access the ICS, i.e. they evaluate or change the state of the interface control. We will show how the mutual exclusion is guaranteed for the execution of them in the new execution model.

4.2 New Execution Model

The execution of the matching-rules, pre-actions and post-actions of the methods are serialized to achieve mutual exclusion. The Concurrency Control consists of one single thread, and calls synchronously the pre-actions and post-actions (see Figure 3). These may thus be seen as local procedures.

The Concurrency Control is triggered by an event "terminating method execution" or by an event "arrival of a new message". It works then as follows. When the concurrency control was started by the event "method execution terminated" it will execute the appropriate state transition defined within the *post_action* specification of the method. After that it will match if pending messages can be accepted for invocation. After a positive match for a method m the state transition - caused by the invocation of m - will be performed as defined in pre_action (m). Then a thread will be created for the execution of method m. The cycle "match, do pre_action(m), invoke(m)" is repeated until no more requests match for invocation.

By strengthening encapsulation, synchronizing actions also help in decreasing the conflict between concurrency control and inheritance. Nevertheless, the following guideline (learned from ACT++ and Rosette) must be considered in the design of a concrete synchronization mechanism.

Guideline.

When we add or redefine a method in a subclass - while extending the system - we must be able to reflect this within the concurrency control defined so far in the superclass(es). The amount of redefined code must be minimal. This can be achieved by defining the entities within the ICS as being independent and (eventually) redefinable.

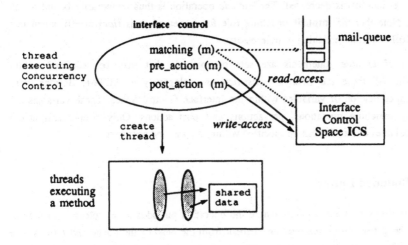

Figure 3. Separating Methods from ICS.

Independency of the entities of the ICS from the method specifications is one characteristic property of our model *synchronizing actions*. The second property of an entity in the ICS "to be redefinable" is sometimes necessary, for example when method names are used within the ICS. In the synchronization protocol of a bounded buffer, for example, all methods that try to get an element from an empty buffer should be delayed including those methods that may be added later within a subclass. Thus the entities in ACT++ and Rosette representing such a state "empty buffer" in the ICS are redefinable sets of method names.

As we will see in the next section an entity of the ICS does not necessarily have to be redefinable (see counter N in example *bounded buffer* where the condition N=0 represents the state "empty buffer").

5. An Exemplary Synchronization Mechanism

We will present the *bounded_buffer* example also given in [Kaf89] and in [Tom89], so a comparison with these contributions is possible. Nevertheless, the degree of internal concurrency for the example is small. The synchronization mechanism defined below should be seen as an exemplary *ad hoc* solution. Detailed investigations on flexible and easily usable synchronization mechanisms are one of our current research topics.

We define the synchronization mechanism as follows. Instead of a method's state **open** or closed as in ACT++ we introduce a *lock()* counter for each method that counts the number of lock- and unlock-operations on a method. A method **m** is locked by another method **m2** (to guarantee mutual exclusion) by an *exclude* statement within a pre_action specification; lock(**m**) is thus increased. When method **m2** terminates, the *exclude* statement is implicitly reversed by an unlock of the method **m**, i.e. lock(**m**) is decreased. The *exclude* operation is thus temporarily bound to the method execution. Note that the **implicit** matching rule for a method m is (*lock*(m)=0); when this condition is not fulfilled, further matching is unnecessary.

The arguments of *exclude* statements are sets of methods that may be redefined within subclasses. We will call these sets *behavior abstractions* analogously to ACT++. Besides these sets we allow the specification of variables within the Interface Control Space. These variables are accessible only by matching operations, pre_actions and post_actions. Only simple assignment operations to the variables of the ICS can be specified within the pre- and post-part.

5.1 Example "Bounded Buffer"

A bounded buffer acts as a FIFO queue where the operation put adds a new element to the tail of the queue, and the get operation removes an element from the head of the queue and returns it to the caller as result. To ensure mutual exclusion of operations on the same data, we define the sets op_on_head = { get } and op_on_tail = { put }. When a put is to be executed, an "exclude op_on_tail;" is called in the pre_action of put(). Thus, no other operations may act concurrently on this part of the shared data. As a further control mechanism we have to delay a put() operation when the buffer is full, and delay the get when the buffer is empty. The states full or empty of the buffer are captured by a counter N of the queue's content. It is evaluated in the matching rule, and changed within the post_actions of put() and get(). Note that the example is written in such a way that one put() and one get() may act concurrently because they access disjunct parts of the shared data. The example is shown in figure 4.

Extended Bounded Buffer

Now, we will show the extension of bounded_buffer by the method get_rear() as presented by [Kaf89] and [Tom89]. Note that put() and get_rear() act on the same position of the bounded_buffer and thus cannot act in parallel. The same will happen with get() and get_rear() if there is exactly one element queued in the bounded buffer. To give thus an easy solution, the execution of get_rear() requires the exclusion of another get_rear() as well as put() and get(). A more complex solution where get() and get_rear() may act concurrently (i.e. the content of the buffer is greater than 1) is not given. The redefined sets *op_on_head* and *op_on_tail* must be extended by adding get_rear(). The complete example is given in figure 5.

Note that the **exclude** mechanism used above could arbitrarily be replaced by simply using counters *op_on_head* and so on within the matching condition and the pre- and post-actions.

```
class bounded_buffer;

private:
    SIZE = 64;
    int in=0, out=0, buf[SIZE];
Concurrency_control:
    int N = 0;    // counts queued elements
    behavior abstraction
            op_on_head = { get }
            op_on_tail = { put }
public:
    method put (int elem);
        matching          (N<SIZE);
        pre       (      exclude op_on_tail; }
        action { increase in and add elem on tail of buf}
        post      {      N++; }
    method get ():int;
        matching          (N>0);
        pre       (      exclude op_on_head; }
        action { return element from head of buf and increase out }
        post      {      N--; }
end bounded_buffer;
```

Figure 4. *bounded_buffer*.

```
class extended_bounded_buffer inherits bounded_buffer;

Concurrency_control:
    behavior abstraction
        // redefinitions :
            op_on_head = { get, get_rear }
            op_on_tail = { put, get_rear }
        // new exclusion set for get_rear()
            op_on_head_or_tail = { put, get, get_rear };
public:
    method get_rear ():int;
        matching          (N>0);
        pre       {      exclude op_on_head_or_tail; }
        action { return element from tail and decrease in }
        post      {      N--; }
end extended_bounded_buffer;
```

Figure 5. *extended_bounded_buffer*.

5.2 Example "await_an_event"

In the following example a method *sync_on_event()* will execute up to that moment where it has to wait for the occurrence of a specific event. The occurrence of the event will be propagated to the object by calling a method *event_occurred()*. The occurrence of the event is represented in the ICS by a variable event_count. The example shows the use of self in the synchronization protocol. It also illustrates the separate execution of concurrency control issues (matching, pre- and post-part in the method specification) and the method operating on the instance variables of the object (action part in the method specification).

Note that the method event_occurred() does not provide an action part. The purpose of the "invocation" of method event_occurred() is to define a state transition of the concurrency control. The interface control does not have to create a thread executing the action part of the method. Other optimizations may be considered in a concrete language design as e.g. the efficient evaluation of the matching operations, or allowing a synchronous call of methods that provide no action part (see method await_event() in the example).

```
class Event_Example;
concurrency_control:
        int event_count = 0;
protected:    // i.e. visible only to subclasses
    method await_event() : bool;
        matching (event_count>0);
        pre { }
        action { return true }
        post { event_count-- }     // consume one event

public:
    method event_occurred();
        matching (true);
        // since action_part is empty, omitt pre- and action-part
        post { event_count ++ }
    method sync_on_event ();
        matching (true);
        pre { }
        action { ...
            // now synchronize on occurrence of event
            ok:= self!await_event();
            ... }
        post { };

end Event_Example;
```

Figure 6. *await_an_event* example.

6. Concluding Remarks

Kafura and Lee argue that the problem of synchronization mechanisms based on interface control is that defining a new method in a subclass may invalidate many superclass methods [Kaf89]. The approaches in ACT++ and Rosette solve this problem by defining a reflexive synchronization mechanism. The source of trouble of existing synchronization mechanisms in COOPL is the dependency of method specifications and the synchronization protocol of an object. This dependency makes reuse and extensibility so difficult. Changing the synchronization protocol automatically leads to changing the methods. Compared to the traditional *critical section* approach *interface control* as it is understood in the existing approaches is already one step towards a solution of this problem.

The synchronization concept *synchronizing actions* presents a further step towards better solutions by augmenting the independency between the method specifications and the synchronization protocol. Additionally, a basic conflict between encapsulation and concurrency control is solved by introducing two distinct sets of data. The concurrency control exclusively works on the interface control space, whereas the methods exclusively work on the traditional instance variables of the object. The new approach reduces substantially the complexity of the concurrency model supporting internal concurrency within an object compared to existing approaches.

Investigations on flexible synchronization mechanisms obeying the model of *synchronizing actions* are underway. Many fruitful ideas from the existing synchronization mechanisms can be adapted and combined.

In the future research on synchronization in COOPL the development of large applications programmed in COOPLs will be of significance. The experiences made in writing real applications are small compared to concurrent object-based languages as POOL-T [Ame87]. By this way, it must be inspected if the complex model of internal concurrency is appropriate for developing, understanding and maintaining systems. When rejecting this complex model one has to dispense with self reference, or at least this will lead to considerations about a new semantics of self reference.

Similar guidelines like those for the use of the Object-Oriented Programming Technique ([Mey88], [CACM90]) must be developed for COOPL in order to enforce the correct use of synchronization mechanisms. This depends on experience in programming and is thus closely related to writing real applications.

Acknowledgments

I am grateful to the anonymous referees, H. Scheidig, R. Spurk and R. Schäfer for their comments on earlier versions of the paper.

References

[Agh87]   Agha, G. and Hewitt, C. Actors : A Conceptual Foundation for Concurrent Object-Oriented Programming. In *Research Directions in Object-Oriented Programming*, ed. B.Shriver and P.Wegner, MIT-Press 1987, pages 49-74.

[Ame87]   America, P. POOL-T : A Parallel Object-Oriented Language. In *Object-Oriented Concurrent Programming*, ed. A.Yonezawa and M.Tokoro, MIT-Press 1987, pages 198-220.

[CACM90]   Special issue on Object-Oriented Design. *CACM* Vol.33, No.9 (Sept. 1990).

[Car86]   Carriero, N., Gelernter, D., and Leichter,J. Distributed Data Structures in Linda. In Proc. of *POPL 13*, ACM, 1986, pp.236-242.

[Dah66]   Dahl, O.-J. and Nygaard, K. Simula - An Algol-based Simulation Language. *CACM* 9:9 (Sept.66), pp. 671-678.

[Dec89]   Decouchant, D. et al.: A Synchronization Mechanism for Typed Objects in a Distributed System. In [WS89], pages 105-107.

[Gol83]   Goldberg, A. and Robson, D. *Smalltalk-80: The Language and its Implementation*. Addison-Wesley, 1983.

[Ger77]   Gerber, A.J.. Process Synchronization by Counter Variables. *ACM Operating Systems Review*, Vol.11 (4), Oct 1977, pp. 6-17.

[Kaf89]   Kafura, D.G. and Lee, K.H. Inheritance in Actor Based Concurrent Object-Oriented Languages. In Proc. of *ECOOP'89*. BCS Workshop Series, jul. 1989. Cambridge University Press, pp. 131-145.

[Kri87]   Kristensen,B.B., Madsen,O.L., Møller-Pedersen,B. and Nygaard,K. The BETA Programming Language. In *Research Directions in Object-Oriented Programming*, ed. B.Shriver and P.Wegner, MIT-Press 1987, pages 7-48.

[Mad88]   Madsen,O.L, and Møller-Pedersen,B. What object-oriented programming may be - and what it does not have to be. In Proc. of *ECOOP'88*, LNCS 322, Springer, 1988, pp. 1-20.

[Mey88]   Meyer, B. *Object-Oriented Software Construction*. Prentice Hall, 1988.

[Nak89]   Nakajima, T. et al.,: Distributed Concurrent Smalltalk. In [WS89], pp. 43-45.

[Nie90]   O.Nierstrasz, M.Papathomas. Viewing Objects as Patterns of Communicating Agents. In *OOPSLA ECOOP'90 Conference Proc.*, ed. N.Meyrowitz. Special issue of SIGPLAN Notices 25 (10), Oct. 1990.

[Rob77]   Robert, P., Verjus, J.-P. Toward Autonomous Descriptions of Synchronization Modules. *Information Processing 77*, North Holland, 1977, pp. 981-986.

[Sny87]   Snyder, A. Inheritance and the Development of Encapsulated Software Components. In *Research Directions in Object-Oriented Programming*, ed. B.Shriver and P.Wegner, MIT-Press 1987, pages 165-188.

[Tom89]   Tomlinson, C. and Singh, V. Inheritance and Synchronization with Enabled-Sets. In *OOPSLA'89 Conference Proceedings*, ed. N.Meyrowitz. Special issue of SIGPLAN Notices 24 (10), Oct. 1989.

[Weg87]   Wegner, P. Dimensions of Object-Based Language Design. In *OOPSLA'87 Conference Proceedings*, ed. N.Meyrowitz, Oct. 1987. Special issue of SIGPLAN Notices 22 (12), Dec. 1987.

[Weg88]   Wegner, P. and Zdonik, S.B. Inheritance as an Incremental Modification Mechanism. In Proc. of *ECOOP'88*, LNCS 322, Springer, 1988, pages 55-77.

[WS89]   *ACM SIGPLAN Workshop on Concurrent Object-Based Language Design*. Special issue of SIGPLAN Notices 24 (4), April 1989.

[Yok86]   Yokote, Y. and Tokoro, M. The Design and Implementation of Concurrent Smalltalk. In *OOPSLA '86 Conference Proc.*, ed. N.Meyrowitz, Portland, Oregon, Sept. 1986. Special issue of SIGPLAN Notices 21 (11), Nov. 1986.

[Yok87]   Yokote, Y. and Tokoro, M. Experience and Evolution of Concurrent Smalltalk. In *OOPSLA'87 Conference Proceedings*, ed. N.Meyrowitz, Oct. 1987. Special issue of SIGPLAN Notices 22 (12), Dec. 1987.

An Object Calculus for Asynchronous Communication

Kohei Honda and Mario Tokoro*

Department of Computer Science,
Keio University
3-14-1 Hiyoshi, Kohoku-ku, Yokohama, 223,
Japan

Abstract

This paper presents a formal system based on the notion of objects and asynchronous communication. Built on Milner's work on π-calculus, the communication primitive of the formal system is purely based on asynchronous communication, which makes it unique among various concurrency formalisms. Computationally this results in a consistent reduction of Milner's calculus, while retaining the same expressive power. Seen semantically asynchronous communication induces a surprisingly different framework where bisimulation is strictly more general than its synchronous counterpart. This paper shows basic construction of the formal system along with several illustrative examples.

1 Introduction

The formal system introduced in this paper is intended to accomplish two purposes. First, it provides a simple and rigorous formalism which encapsulates essential features of concurrent object-orientation [24, 23]. Being successful as a programming methodology for dynamic concurrent computing, its theoretical contents are far from well-understood,[1] leaving theorists and practitioners without a core theory on which they can reason and develop further ideas. Second, it offers a possible foundation for concurrency theory which is quite different from the usual one in the sense that the formalism is purely based on asynchronous communication, both computationally and semantically. The usual observation-based equivalence theory for processes is recaptured as asynchronous bisimulation for objects where asynchronous experiments induces a somewhat more general semantic framework.

The formalism is based on a series of studies on a port passing process calculus now called π-calculus, initiated by Nielsen and Engberg [17], reformulated by Milner and his colleagues [14], and developed in a crucial way by Milner [16]. Especially [16] has been essential in our construction due to its separation of *structural rules* from *transition rules*, and in its distinction between *computational transition* and *semantic transition*. One interesting thing is that the capability to generate and pass communication ports turns out to be essential not only for object-orientation (which is obvious) but also for control of causality chains in the face of pure asynchrony. This reminds us of the studies on the actor model of computation by Hewitt and his colleagues [8, 7, 5, 1]. Also readers may refer to the authors' work on conceptual framework for open distributed computing environments [21, 22] to understand their general orientation in a different context.

This paper only provides basic concepts and definitions for the formal system along with several illustrative examples, leaving the full presentation of our theoretical results to the coming exposition.

---

*Also with Sony Computer Science Laboratory Inc. 3-14-13 Higashi-Gotanda, Shinagawa-ku, Tokyo, 141, Japan
[1]Though recently several important works appeared in this context including [6, 11, 16].

Section 2 defines the basic syntax and other constructs of the formal system. Section 3 introduces reduction relation which defines the basic computational mechanism in combination with structural rules. Section 4 provides important primitive constructs for our system and shows that they can be used to encode a fragment of π-calculus [16] which is a superset of our formalism. Section 5 reviews the general semantic framework of asynchronous bisimulation, giving basic definitions and examples. Object-orientation in our semantic framework is also discussed. Finally Section 6 concludes the paper.

2   Syntax and Bindings

This section first briefly summarizes the basic idea of our formalism, then provides definitions for syntax and bindings.

Basic Framework

In the formalism presented hereafter, the notions of objects and communication are captured in the following way.

- **An object** is a collection of *receptors* and *pending messages*. A receptor has a *handle* (an input port) and a *carrier* (a formal parameter) at its *head*, and consumes a message to receive the value at its carrier which carries the value to its *body*. Then this body generates zero or more receptors and zero or more messages. The original receptor just disappears. Notationally, it is expressed as $ax.P$ (a is a handle, x is a carrier, and P is a body). All receptors within an object may operate concurrently and asynchronously.

- **A message** is a simple data structure which carries a piece of information to its target. It should have its *target* and *value*, each being supposed to be a *port name* (i.e. no value is considered except names of ports themselves). The notation for a message is $\leftarrow av$ (a is a target, v is a value). Some of generated messages may go out (becoming output messages), some may be consumed by receptors (causing internal configuration change), and some may be just pending within the object.

The computational implication of this framework is that a message will be consumed by a receptor if and only if its target is the same as the handle of the receptor, that is, $\leftarrow av$ will be consumed by $ax.P$, but not by $bx.P$. Existence of multiple receptors in an object implies an object may have multiple input ports, possibly with duplicate names. The port names are only values to be considered here, sent by messages and consumed by receptors. A configuration will generate new port names which extends the domain of computation.

Syntax

Syntactically our formal system *reduces*, not extends, constructs in process calculi[12, 13, 9, 15], to incorporate asynchronous communication. The key idea is to express asynchronous messages as output processes without subsequent behaviour. That is, $\bar{a}v.P$ (a process which outputs v through port a) is reduced to $\leftarrow av$ (a message to the target a with a value v). In Section 4 we will see that this reduction does not result in loss of expressive power. Below are syntactic definitions of port names, messages, receptors (including recursively defined ones), and general configurations called term expressions. Term variables are necessary for recursively defined receptors. In the right-hand side of each definition, we give formal designation for these syntactic constructs.

Definition 1 The sets of port names **N**, of sequences of port names $\widetilde{\mathbf{N}}$, of term variables **V**, and of term expressions **C**, are given by the following abstract syntax.

$$
\begin{array}{rll}
\mathbf{N} & = & x \mid \mathbf{N}' \qquad\qquad\qquad\qquad\qquad\qquad\qquad \text{(port names)} \\
\widetilde{\mathbf{N}} & = & \varepsilon \mid \mathbf{N}\widetilde{\mathbf{N}} \qquad\qquad\qquad\qquad\qquad\qquad \text{(sequences of names)} \\
\mathbf{V} & = & X \mid \mathbf{V}' \qquad\qquad\qquad\qquad\qquad\qquad \text{(term variables)} \\
\mathbf{C} & = & \leftarrow\!\mathbf{NN} \qquad\qquad\qquad\qquad\qquad\qquad \text{(a message)} \\
& \mid & \mathbf{NN}.\mathbf{C} \qquad\qquad\qquad\qquad\qquad\qquad \text{(a receptor)} \\
& \mid & \{\mathbf{V}(\widetilde{\mathbf{N}}) :: \mathbf{NN}.\mathbf{C}\}(\widetilde{\mathbf{N}}) \qquad \text{(a recursively defined receptor)} \\
& \mid & \mathbf{V}(\widetilde{\mathbf{N}}) \qquad\qquad \text{(a term variable with parameters))} \\
& \mid & |\mathbf{N}|\mathbf{C} \qquad\qquad\qquad\qquad\qquad\qquad \text{(scope restriction)} \\
& \mid & \mathbf{C},\mathbf{C} \qquad\qquad\qquad\qquad\qquad\qquad \text{(concurrent composition)} \\
& \mid & \Lambda \qquad\qquad\qquad\qquad\qquad\qquad\qquad \text{(the null term)} \quad\blacksquare
\end{array}
$$

There are several important conventions we will obey hereafter.

Conventions 1 *Conventions on notation and designation.*

(i) Non-capital alphabets $(a, b, c, ..)$ range over **N**, the set of port names. We will often call port names as simply *names*.

(ii) $\tilde{a}, \tilde{b}, \tilde{c} \ldots$ range over $\widetilde{\mathbf{N}}$.

(iii) $X, Y, Z, \ldots$ range over **V**.

(iv) $P, Q, R, \ldots$ (sometimes $A, B, C, \ldots$) range over **C**, which are sometimes called *configurations*. Specifically, $M, M', \ldots$ ranges over the subsort of **C** which are of the form $\leftarrow\!\mathbf{NN}$.

(v) $\mathcal{I}, \mathcal{J}, \mathcal{K}$ etc. denote incomplete expressions.

(vi) We will assume that the constructor "," is the weakest in association, others being of the same precedence.

(vii) In $\leftarrow av$, we call a a *target*, v a *value*. In $ax.P$, we call the portion ax a *head*, P a *body*. The body expression is *guarded* by the head part. In the head, a is called a *handle* (or more descriptively *input port*), x a *carrier*. In $\{V(\tilde{x}) :: yz.C\}(\tilde{v})$ and $X(\tilde{a})$, $\tilde{x}, \tilde{a}$ and $\tilde{v}$ are called *parameter parts*, and their preceding sections *main parts*. Then we say $\tilde{x}$ is a *parameter* of V etc. $\qquad\qquad\blacksquare$

Following these conventions, we will explain some of constructors and their intuitive meaning as follows.

Examples 1 *Meaning of constructors.*

(i) $\leftarrow av$. A message with a target a and a value v. (Note that both are port names.)

(ii) $ax.(\leftarrow ax)$. A receptor with a handle a which, when it consumes a message, creates the same one and dies. Note that the first occurrence of x binds the second x.

(iii) $\{X(x) :: xy.(\leftarrow xy, X(x))\}(a)$. A receptor with a handle a which, when it consumes a message, creates the same one and regenerates itself. Note that the first occurrence of x is *instantiated* to a at the end, and that the x binds the later occurrences of x.

(iv) $ax.P, \leftarrow av, by.Q$. Two receptors and one message. The left receptor may consume the message.

(v) $ax.(|v| \leftarrow cv), \leftarrow av$. The first two occurrences of v and the third one denote different port names, because the first one is declared as private (restricted) and the third one is not within the same scope. *Restricted names are meant to have different values from those which are outside of the scope, even syntactically they are the same.* $\qquad\blacksquare$

Free and Bound Names, and Substitution

The following gives definitions for bound and free names, and substitutions.

Definition 2 *Free and Bound names, substitution.*

(i) In $ax.P$, a is free, x is bound, and free occurrences of x in P are bound by the carrier x. In $\leftarrow av$, both a and v are free. In $|v|P$, v is bound, and free occurrences of v in P are bound by $|v|$. In $\{X(\tilde{x}) :: C\}(\tilde{a})$, names in $\tilde{a}$ are free, and names in $\tilde{x}$ binds their occurrences in C.

(ii) Similarly in $\{X(\tilde{x}) :: C\}(\tilde{a})$, we define free occurrences of X in C and say those occurrences are bound by X at the top. *Hereafter we will only deal with the cases where no term variables occur free at the top configuration. We also assume that the length (as a sequence) of the parameter of a bound term variable should correspond to the parameter of the term variable which binds it.*

(iii) $\mathcal{N}(P)$ is a set of names in P. $\mathcal{FN}(P)$ (resp. $\mathcal{BN}(P)$) is a set of free (resp. bound) names in P. $\mathcal{HN}(P)$ denotes a set of names used for handles of receptors in the subexpressions of P.

(iv) We assume that, in the expression $\{X(\tilde{x}) :: C\}(\tilde{a})$, $\mathcal{FN}(C) \subset \{\tilde{x}\}$, and also any pair of names in $\tilde{x}$ are pairwise distinct.

(v) $P[v/x]$ denotes the result of (inductively) substituting the free occurrences of x in P for v, following the standard convention for name collision (cf. [2]).

(vi) We inductively define α-convertibility among terms starting with $ax.P$ is α-convertible to $ay.(P[y/x])$ if y is not free in P, similarly $|x|P$ is α-convertible to $|y|(P[y/x])$ with the same condition. We will assume $[x/y]$ is stronger than any other constructor (i.e. $|x|P[v/x] \overset{\text{def}}{=} |x|(P[v/x])$ etc.). ∎

We will give some examples of substitutions.

Examples 2 *Examples of substitutions.*

(i) $(\leftarrow xv)[a/x] \equiv \leftarrow av$.

(ii) $(|v| \leftarrow xv)[v/x] \equiv |w| \leftarrow vw$. Here we first perform an α-conversion, then do the substitution. Remember restricted port names denote values *different* from those outside of the scope. ∎

Now we are ready to define syntactic equivalence relation called *structural equivalence* and *reduction* (computation) rule for our formal system.

3 Structural Equivalence and Reduction

Structural Equivalence

In port passing calculi, transition rules become quite complicated because of intricate interaction between the port passing concept and scoping rules. It was found by Milner in [16], however, the introduction of congruence relation for syntactic terms, *modulo* which transition rules are defined, results in a surprisingly compact and tractable formulation. The idea is to incorporate within the structural rules tacit yet basic semantics of various constructors, freeing transition rules from expressing those static features laboriously[2]. Thus we can concentrate on truly significant aspects of computational and semantic properties of the target system.

---

[2]Inspired by Chemical Abstract Machine [3]. It can also be likened to the separation of structural rules in Natural Deduction or to the treatment of α-conversion in [2].

Below is our formulation of such structural rules, which is generally based on that of [16], yet somewhat weakened to make computational aspects explicit. Notable facts are (a) the equation cannot be applied to guarded expressions (i.e. the body of receptors), so that ≡ is not a congruence relation, and (b) the relation induced by (ii), (iii), and (vi)-(ix) is finite for a given term.

Definition 3 *Structural equivalence*, denoted by ≡, is the smallest equivalence relation over terms defined by:

(i) $P \equiv Q$ if P is α-convertible to Q

(ii) $(P, Q), R \equiv P, (Q, R)$

(iii) $|x||y|P \equiv |y||x|P$

(iv) $P, \Lambda \equiv P$

(v) $|x|\Lambda \equiv \Lambda$

(vi) $|x|P, Q \equiv |x|(P, Q) \quad (x \notin \mathcal{FN}(Q))$

(vii) $P, Q \equiv Q, P$

(viii) $\{X(\tilde{x}) :: P\}(\tilde{a}) \equiv P[\tilde{a}/\tilde{x}][\{X(\tilde{x}) = P\}/X]$.

(ix) $P \equiv Q \implies (P, R \equiv Q, R \wedge |x|P \equiv |x|Q)$

where, in (viii), $[\{X(\tilde{x}) = P\}/X]$ denotes syntactic substitution of term variables with a recursive structure[3]. ∎

Note that by rule (ii), we can soundly write P, Q, R (i.e. without parentheses). Similarly we will write $|xyz|P$ etc. by rule (iii). Several examples of application of structural equivalence will be helpful in its understanding.

Examples 3 *Examples for structural equivalence.* Please note that all of the multiple equations below can be one step from transitivity.

(i) With the definition of $\mathcal{I} \overset{\text{def}}{=} \{X(x) :: xy.(\leftarrow xy, X(x))\}$ (this already appears in (iii) of Examples 1), we have, by rule (viii),

$$\mathcal{I}(a) \equiv ay.(\leftarrow ay, \mathcal{I}(a))$$

(ii) A message can freely *move around* (i.e. change its place in concurrent composition) due to rule (vii).

$$ax.P, Q, \leftarrow av \equiv ax.P, \leftarrow av, Q \equiv \leftarrow av, ax.P, Q.$$

(iii) The below abstractly states that a restricted name functions as a globally distinct name.

$$ax.(\leftarrow xv), |v| \leftarrow av \equiv ax.(\leftarrow xv), |z| \leftarrow az \equiv |z|(ax.(\leftarrow xv), \leftarrow az) ∎$$

Reduction

Below we define reduction (computation) of terms. The intuitive idea is a communication event occurs when a message and a receptor with a target and a corresponding handle somehow meet together, and this is the only way for computation in the configuration to proceed (as far as we do not consider its interaction with outside).

[3]Because of the condition stated in Definition 2 (v), the problem of name collision never occurs.

Definition 4 *Reduction of terms*, denoted by $\longrightarrow$, is the smallest relation between terms inferred by:

$$\text{COM}: \qquad \leftarrow av,\ ax.P \longrightarrow P[v/x]$$

$$\text{PAR}: \qquad \frac{P_1 \longrightarrow P_1'}{P_1,\ P_2 \longrightarrow P_1',\ P_2}$$

$$\text{RES}: \qquad \frac{P \longrightarrow P'}{|x|P \longrightarrow |x|P'}$$

$$\text{STRUCT}: \qquad \frac{P_1' \equiv P_1,\ P_1 \longrightarrow P_2,\ P_2 \equiv P_2'}{P_1' \longrightarrow P_2'} \qquad \blacksquare$$

The reduction rules, together with structural rules, state basic mechanism of computation in our formal system. We will give some descriptive examples of reduction of terms.

Examples 4 *Examples of Reductions.*

   (i) A simple reduction.

$$
\begin{aligned}
ax.(\leftarrow cx),\ cy.(\Lambda),\ \leftarrow av \ &\equiv\ \leftarrow av,\ ax.(\leftarrow cx),\ cy.(\Lambda) \\
&\longrightarrow\ \leftarrow cv,\ cy.(\Lambda) \\
&\longrightarrow\ \Lambda\ .
\end{aligned}
$$

  (ii) With $\mathcal{I}$ as defined in (iii) of Examples 3,

$$
\begin{aligned}
\leftarrow av,\ \mathcal{I}(a)\ &\equiv\ \leftarrow av,\ ax.(\leftarrow ax, \mathcal{I}(a)) \\
&\longrightarrow\ \leftarrow av,\ \mathcal{I}(a) \\
&\longrightarrow\ \leftarrow av,\ \mathcal{I}(a) \\
&\longrightarrow\ \ .....
\end{aligned}
$$

     and so on. $\mathcal{I}(a)$ *functions as if it were nothing.*

  (iii) By (vi) of Examples 3, we have:

$$
\begin{aligned}
|v| \leftarrow av,\ ax.(\leftarrow xv)\ &\equiv\ |z|(\leftarrow az,\ ax.(\leftarrow xv)) \\
&\longrightarrow\ |z| \leftarrow zv
\end{aligned}
$$

    This shows how scope opening, together with α-conversion, induces computation in the face of restriction and name collision. $\blacksquare$

In regard of functionality of the structural equivalence in its relationship to reduction relation, though the structural equivalence is somewhat weak in comparison with structural congruence in [16], it can nonetheless induce the same reduction relation. That is, if we denote the stronger equivalence by $\dot{\equiv}$ (to be formulated as $\equiv$ in [16]) and corresponding reduction rule by $\dot{\longrightarrow}$, then we have $(\dot{\longrightarrow}^\bullet) = (\longrightarrow^\bullet \dot{\equiv})$ where $\longrightarrow^\bullet$ etc. means reflexive and transitive closure of the relation. We can even omit rules (iv) and (v) to get the same result. Detailed study of formulation of structural rules in combination with reduction and other transition rules is required.

4   Expressing Causality

This section introduces two important concepts for constructing *causal chains* in our purely asynchronous formal system. They are sequentialization and selection. Along the way various primitive constructs for general computation are expressed in our formal system.

Sequentialization

Our formal system is characterized with its lack of sequential constructors except when inevitable (i.e. in value passing and resulting term generation). But as we see below, this can be realized by a chain of communication events, sequentialization of value passing in this case.

Definition 5 (a) *Notations for sequentialization.* Suppose E is a term expression. We define *sequential connectives* $\lhd$ (of type $N^2 \times \widetilde{N}$) and $\rhd$ (of type $N^2 \times \widetilde{N} \times C$) as follows.

$$\begin{cases} ax \lhd \varepsilon & \stackrel{\text{def}}{=} & \Lambda \\ ax \lhd v\tilde{w} & \stackrel{\text{def}}{=} & ax.(\leftarrow xv, \; ax \lhd \tilde{w}) \end{cases}$$

$$\begin{cases} \leftarrow ax \rhd \varepsilon.E & \stackrel{\text{def}}{=} & E \\ \leftarrow ax \rhd y\tilde{w}.E & \stackrel{\text{def}}{=} & \leftarrow ax, \; xy. \leftarrow ax \rhd \tilde{w}.E \end{cases} \quad \blacksquare$$

Based on these connectives, we define the following expressions.

Definition 5 (b) *Notations for communication of a series of names.* We define $\leftarrow a{:}\tilde{v}$ and $a{:}\tilde{x}.E$ as follows. We suppose that r, c are not free in E and $\tilde{v}$, respectively.

$$\leftarrow a{:}\tilde{v} \stackrel{\text{def}}{=} |c|(\leftarrow ac, \; cx \lhd \tilde{v})$$
$$a{:}\tilde{x}.E \stackrel{\text{def}}{=} az.|r|(\leftarrow zr \rhd \tilde{x}.E) \quad \blacksquare$$

Examples 5 *Sequentialization of communication.* With the condition that r, c, x are not free in P or $\tilde{v}$,

$$\begin{aligned}
\leftarrow a{:}v_1 v_2, \; a{:}x_1 x_2.P \;\; &\equiv\;\; |c|(\leftarrow ac, \; cx \lhd v_1 v_2), \; az.|r|(\leftarrow zr \rhd x_1 x_2.P) \\
&\longrightarrow\;\; |cr|(cx \lhd v_1 v_2, \; \leftarrow cr \rhd x_1 x_2.P) \\
&\longrightarrow\;\; |cr|(\leftarrow rv_1, \; cx \lhd x_2, \; ry_1. \leftarrow cr \rhd y_2.P) \\
&\longrightarrow\;\; |cr|(cx \lhd v_2, \; \leftarrow cr \rhd y_2.(P[v_1/y_1])) \\
&\longrightarrow\;\; |cr|(\leftarrow rv_2, \; ry_2.(E[v_1/y_1])) \\
&\longrightarrow\;\; |cr|P[v_1/y_1][v_2/y_2] \\
&\equiv\;\; P[v_1/y_1][v_2/y_2] \quad \blacksquare
\end{aligned}$$

Thus two values v_1 and v_2 are passed respectively to y_1 and y_2, preserving their order. Because communication is taking place solely using private ports, no interference from the third party is possible after the first reduction. In a sense, c and r are functioning as *private communication channels* between P and Q. For any $\tilde{v}$ and $\tilde{y}$ with the same length[4], it is easy to verify the below.

$$\leftarrow a{:}\tilde{v}, \; a{:}\tilde{y}.P \;\longrightarrow^* \; P[\tilde{v}/\tilde{y}] \;.$$

Another example uses these sequentialization features nontrivially, showing the mapping of our formal system to its superset calculus presented in [16].

---

[4]This constraint is not essential since a little change in Definition 5 (b) results in capability of coping with cases where two lengths can be different, by using new port generation.

Examples 6 *Encoding for the extended calculus.* We replace expressions $\leftarrow av$ and $\{X(\tilde{x}) :: C\}(\tilde{a})$ with $\bar{a}v.P$ and $!P$ respectively, and assume a structural rule

$$!P \equiv P, \, !P$$

and a reduction rule

$$\bar{a}v.P, \, a(x).Q \longrightarrow P, \, Q[v/x] \ .$$

Then a mapping from the expressions in the extended system to the reduced system, written as $[\cdot]$, is given as follows.

$$
\begin{aligned}
[\bar{a}v.P] &= |c|(\leftarrow a:vc, \, c:\varepsilon.[P]) \\
[ax.P] &= a:xy.(\leftarrow y:\varepsilon, \, [P]) \\
[!P] &= |c|(\leftarrow c:\varepsilon, \, \{X(x):: x:\varepsilon.([P], \, \leftarrow c:\varepsilon, \, X(x))\}(c)) \quad (c \notin \mathcal{FN}(P)) \\
[|x|P] &= |x|[P] \\
[P,Q] &= [P],[Q] \\
[\Lambda] &= \Lambda \ . \quad \blacksquare
\end{aligned}
$$

The key idea of the coding is to let the *receiver* of a message send the activation message as a reply to the sender, so that the subsequent behaviour of the sender (which is coded as another receptor, $l : \varepsilon.[P]$) can become active. We do not verify the correctness of this mapping in this paper, which can be done by saying that if there is a reduction in the world of superset expressions then the corresponding reduction does exist in our coding, and that if a term in our coding reduces to something then it has some further reduction which corresponds to some reduction in the domain of the superset.

Selections

A more advanced way of constructing a causal chain can be achieved through the use of *selections*. This is especially important for us because the formal system has no summation. We only deal with binary selection but it can be extended with ease.

Definition 6 *Notations for selection.* Suppose E, E_1, E_2 are term expressions and $i = 1$ or $i = 2$. We define *connectives for selection* of type $\mathbf{N}^4 \times \mathbf{C}$ and of type $\mathbf{N}^3 \times \mathbf{C}^2$ as follows.

$$
\begin{aligned}
x : y_1 y_2 \triangleleft_i v : E &\overset{\text{def}}{=} x : y_1 y_2.(\leftarrow y_i : v, \, E) \\
\leftarrow x : y_1 y_2 \triangleright_1 (E_1) \triangleright_2 (E_2) &\overset{\text{def}}{=} \leftarrow x : y_1 y_2, \, y_1 : \varepsilon.E_1, \, y_2 : \varepsilon.E_2 \quad \blacksquare
\end{aligned}
$$

The idea is for the first one to selectively send a message ($\leftarrow y_i v$) and generate a term (E), and the second one to send the options ($\leftarrow x : y_1 y_2$) and wait for activation ($y_1 : \varepsilon.E_1$, $y_2 : \varepsilon.E_2$). To safely use these connectives, we again rely on new port name generation. The encoding for natural numbers and the successor function are given below.

Examples 7 *Natural numbers and the successor function.*

$$
\begin{aligned}
0(n) &\overset{\text{def}}{=} \{X(x):: (x : y_1 y_2 \triangleleft_1 x : X(x))\}(n) \\
N'(n) &\overset{\text{def}}{=} |p|(\{X(xz):: (x : y_1 y_2 \triangleleft_2 z : X(xz))\}(np), \, N(p)) \\
S(s) &\overset{\text{def}}{=} s : nc.|z|(\{X(xn):: (x : y_1 y_2 \triangleleft_2 n : X(xp)\}(n), \leftarrow cz)) \quad \blacksquare
\end{aligned}
$$

Note that a natural number is expressed as an *object* which knows its predecessor (p in above), in contrast to the expression of a natural number as a *function* in λ-calculus. Thus even "0" is defined recursively, which is necessary because its handle will be passed around among its "users". c in the successor stands for a *customer* [1], the target of the reply. The predecessor and judgment of zero should *decode* these data structures.

Examples 8 *The predecessor and judge-if-zero functions.*

$$\mathcal{P}(p) \overset{\text{def}}{=} s:nc.|y_1y_2|(\leftarrow n:y_1y_2 \triangleright_1(\leftarrow c:p) \triangleright_2(\leftarrow c:p))$$

$$\mathcal{J}(jtf) \overset{\text{def}}{=} j:nc.|y_1y_2|(\leftarrow n:y_1y_2 \triangleright_1(\leftarrow c:t) \triangleright_2(\leftarrow c:f)), \; 0(t), \; 0'(f) \; \blacksquare$$

Here *true* and *false* are expressed as 0 and 1 respectively.

The next example shows more advanced branching structures.

Examples 9 *If and Parallel Or.*

$$\mathcal{C}(i) \overset{\text{def}}{=} i:bp_1p_2.|y_1y_2|(\leftarrow b:y_1y_2 \triangleright_1(\leftarrow p_1:\varepsilon) \triangleright_2(\leftarrow p_2:\varepsilon))$$

$$\mathcal{O}(o) \overset{\text{def}}{=} o:b_1b_2c.|s_1...s6|$$
$$(\leftarrow b_1:s_3s_4 \triangleright_1(\leftarrow s_1:b_1) \triangleright_2(\leftarrow s_2:b_1),$$
$$\leftarrow b_2:s_5s_6 \triangleright_1(\leftarrow s_1:b_2) \triangleright_2(\leftarrow s_2:b_2),$$
$$s_1:x.(\leftarrow c:x, \; s_1:\varepsilon.\Lambda),$$
$$s_2:x.s_2:x. \leftarrow c:x) \; \blacksquare$$

The combination of conditional expressions can easily construct "and", sequential "or", and "not", so we omit them here. The "parallel or" above uses the method similar to the one by Nierstrasz in [19], using a synchronizer to invoke only one action out of multiple candidates. This method is directly usable to realize the parallel case construct. Primitives for selection can also be used for *method invocation* in usual object-orientation. It cab be proved that we can construct any computable functions on natural numbers by combination of the constructs we have encoded and the use of recursively defined receptors.

Finally we show a very simple stateful entity called a *cell*. It is primitive yet indeed possesses typical properties of concurrent objects as we know. Its first option is "read", and the other option is "write". It contains some port name as its state. It gets o as its option (representing 0 or 1), and then decodes it to take an action accordingly. w is used as a value to write, but when the option is "read", w is just neglected. Note that how it regenerates itself, with or without change of its state according to the option.

Examples 10 *A cell.*

$$\mathcal{L}(lv) \overset{\text{def}}{=} \{X(xy):: x:owc.(|y_1y_2| \leftarrow o:y_1y_2 \triangleright_1(\leftarrow c:y, X(xy)) \triangleright_2(X(xw)))\}(lv)$$

This small concurrent object concludes this section, and we proceed to see a bit of the semantic framework of our formalism.

5 Semantics

This section gives several basic definitions for our semantic framework based on asynchronous interaction, and discusses its notable theoretical properties informally.

Asynchronous Interaction

Our semantic framework is based on the notion of observation by *asynchronous experiments*. This means that an experimenter just sends asynchronous messages to the concerned system, and (possibly continuing to send further messages) wait for output messages from the configuration. Thus it does not matter whether or not a message the experimenter sends is actually consumed by some receptors in the configuration. This notion of *asynchronous interaction* can be given its formal representation as a labeled transition system.

The below shows a set of labels we will use for our labeled transition system.

Definition 7 *Labels.* The sets of labels for interaction L and of their series $\tilde{L}$ are given by the following abstract syntax.

$$\mathbf{L} \;=\; \tau \mid \downarrow N|N \mid \uparrow N|N \mid \uparrow N|N|$$
$$\tilde{\mathbf{L}} \;=\; \epsilon \mid L\tilde{L} \qquad \blacksquare$$

The above labels have the following intuitive meanings.

(1) τ denotes the internal computation (unseen from the outside), that is, the same thing as *reduction* (Definition 4).

(2) $\downarrow av$ means that the configuration asynchronously gets a message $\leftarrow av$ from outside. Seen differently, this rule tells us that the experimenter sends a message to the configuration.

(3) $\uparrow av$ means the configuration asynchronously emits a message or the experimenter receives such a message.

(4) $\uparrow a|v|$ means sending a value of a name restricted inside the configuration, corresponding to scope opening in structural rules (Definition 3 (vi)). For an experimenter, this means that he acquires a piece of new information which he has not had until then.

Conventions 2 *Notation.*

(i) We will let $l, l',...$ range over $\mathbf{L}$, $\tilde{l}, \tilde{l}',...$ range over $\tilde{\mathbf{L}}$.

(ii) We denote $\mathcal{FN}(l)$ to be a set of port names in l except in the case $l = \uparrow a|v|$, then $\mathcal{FN}(l) = \{a\}$. Similarly $\mathcal{BN}(l) = \phi$ except $\mathcal{BN}(\uparrow a|v|) = \{v\}$. $\mathcal{N}(l)$ is the union of these two. This is extended to the case $\tilde{L}$. $\blacksquare$

Based on these definitions and conventions, we define the *interaction relation* as follows. It is a triple of (P, l, P'), which is written as $P \xrightarrow{l} P'$.

Definition 8 *Interaction of terms*, denoted by $\xrightarrow{\cdot}$, is the smallest relation inferred by:

IN : $\Lambda \xrightarrow{\downarrow av} \leftarrow av$

OUT : $\leftarrow av \xrightarrow{\uparrow av} \Lambda$

COM : $\leftarrow av, \, ax.P \longrightarrow P[v/x]$

PAR : $\dfrac{P_1 \xrightarrow{l} P_1'}{P_1, \, P_2 \xrightarrow{l} P_1', \, P_2}$ $(\mathcal{BN}(l) \notin \mathcal{FN}(P_2))$

RES : $\dfrac{P \xrightarrow{l} P'}{|x|P \xrightarrow{l} |x|P'}$ $(x \notin \mathcal{N}(l))$

OPEN : $\dfrac{P \xrightarrow{\uparrow ax} P'}{|x|P \xrightarrow{\uparrow a|x|} P'}$ $(a \neq x)$

STRUCT : $\dfrac{P_1' \equiv P_1, \; P_1 \xrightarrow{l} P_2, \; P_2 \equiv P_2'}{P_1' \xrightarrow{l} P_2'}$ $(\mathcal{BN}(l) \notin \mathcal{FN}(P_2))$ $\blacksquare$

Intuitively, these rules define behaviour of a configuration in terms of its interaction with the outside as asynchronous exchange of messages between them. In this regard the essential rule which is directly related with asynchronous character of the semantics, is the first IN rule. Indeed this is the only rule which differentiates this semantic definition from Milner's one in [16], yet which results in surprisingly different semantic properties. For the purpose of comparison, we stipulate the synchronous counterpart of our semantics, which is a reformulated version of Milner's one.

Definition 9 *Synchronous interaction of terms*, denoted by $\xrightarrow{l}_s$, is the smallest relation inferred by the same rules as Definition 8, with $\xrightarrow{l}$ replaced by $\xrightarrow{l}_s$ except IN rule which is reformulated as

$$\text{IN}_s: \quad ax.P \xrightarrow{av}_s P[v/x] \quad \blacksquare$$

A few remarks on Definition 8 are due here.

(1) The rule clearly shows that $\xrightarrow{\tau} = \longrightarrow$.

(2) Note the symmetry between IN and OUT rules in Definition 8. This is destroyed by introduction of IN_s rule. Also note that the corresponding forms of IN and OUT in π-calculus also enjoy a symmetry of their own [16]. This implies the naturalness of synchronous semantics for π-calculus and asynchronous one for our system.

(3) One interesting aspect of interaction rules lies in OPEN rule, which denotes that if one configuration emits a private label to outside, it is regarded as free (i.e. public) from then on. This reminds us of Agha's notion of "adding receptionists by communication to outside" in the context of the actor model [1].

(4) It may seem rather extraordinary that because of IN rule in Definition 8, *any* message can come into the configuration, regardless of the forms of inner receptors. But this is perfectly consistent with our intuitive notion of asynchronous experiments. As the experimenter is not synchronously interacting with the configuration (which means he should own corresponding input/output port names), such he may send any message as he likes. Moreover it does not result in difficulties in proving various semantic properties as far as we know.

Asynchronous Bisimulation

As we noted already, from the experimenter's point of view, IN rule states that the experimenter sends some message to the concerned configuration and OUT rule states he receives some message from the configuration. This recaptures Milner's notion of experiments (cf. [12]) in the setting of asynchronous communication. Below we define (weak) bisimulation, or observation equivalence, as a semantic representation of this new notion of experiments. While simulation preorder should be regarded as somewhat more fundamental than the equivalence, within this elementary exposition we confine ourselves to bisimulation.

Definition 10 *Asynchronous bisimulation.* Let us define $\xRightarrow{l}$ as $\xrightarrow{\tau}^* \xrightarrow{l} \xrightarrow{\tau}^*$ if $l \neq \tau$ and if else as $\xrightarrow{\tau}^*$. Then P and Q are asynchronously bisimilar, denoted by $P \approx_a Q$ if and only if

(i) Whenever $P \xrightarrow{l} P'$ then, for some Q', $Q \xRightarrow{l} Q'$ and $P' \approx_a Q'$.

(ii) $\approx_a$ is symmetric. $\blacksquare$

For comparison again, we define its synchronous counterpart.

Definition 11 *Synchronous bisimulation.* Let us define $\overset{l}{\Longrightarrow}_{\!\!*}$ as $\overset{\tau}{\longrightarrow}_{\!\!*}^{\;*} \cdot \overset{l}{\longrightarrow}_{\!\!*} \cdot \overset{\tau}{\longrightarrow}_{\!\!*}^{\;*}$ if $l \neq \tau$ and if else as $\overset{\tau}{\longrightarrow}_{\!\!*}^{\;*}$. Then P and Q are synchronously bisimilar, denoted as $P \approx_{\!*} Q$ if and only if

(i) Whenever $P \overset{l}{\longrightarrow}_{\!\!*} P'$ then, for some Q', $Q \overset{l}{\Longrightarrow}_{\!\!*} Q'$ and $P' \approx_{\!*} Q'$.

(ii) $\approx_{\!*}$ is symmetric. ■

Note that Definition 11 is simpler than the corresponding one in [14], which needs an additional condition for equivalence after substitution of names. This may come from the formulation of their IN rule as shown below.

$$ax.P \overset{bx}{\longrightarrow}_{\!\!*} P$$

The rule means that the received name should *not* be the same as any free names in P. We do not discuss this point further except pointing out that the following reduction (not interaction) is allowed both in our formal system and (in the corresponding form) in π-calculus. We hope that this will provide an argument for our formulation of IN rule.

$$\leftarrow av, \; ax.(\leftarrow xc, \; vy.P) \;\longrightarrow\; \leftarrow vc, \; vy.P \; .$$

A few examples will be helpful to understand how asynchronous bisimulation works.

Examples 11 *Asynchronous bisimulation (1).*

(i) *Replication.* Let us assume a new notation (cf. Examples 6).

$$!P \overset{\text{def}}{=} |c|(\leftarrow c{:}\varepsilon, \; \{X(x){::}\;x{:}\varepsilon.(P, \; \leftarrow c{:}\varepsilon, \; X(x))\}(c)) \qquad (c \notin \mathcal{FN}(P)) \;.$$

Then the following holds.

$$!P \approx_a P, \, !P \; .$$

To verify, take a relation $(\,(!P,\, R),\; (P,\, !P,\, R)\,)$ where R can be an arbitrary term expressions. This is an example where both $\approx_a$ and $\approx_{\!*}$ hold.

(ii) *The successor function.* Using notation in Examples 7,

$$|sz|(0(z),\; S(s),\; \leftarrow s{:}zc) \;\approx_a\; |x|(1(x), \leftarrow cx)$$

(to check, just compute). Again we see both $\approx_a$ and $\approx_{\!*}$ hold.

(iii) *Permutation in input.* P and Q are given as follows.

$$P \overset{\text{def}}{=} ax.(by.R) \qquad Q \overset{\text{def}}{=} by.(ax.R)$$

Then we have both $P \not\approx_{\!*} Q$ and $P \not\approx_a Q$. The former obviously holds and the latter can be differentiated by

$$P \overset{bav}{\longrightarrow} \leftarrow av, \; ax.(by.R) \overset{\tau}{\longrightarrow} by.R[v/x]$$

but

$$Q \overset{bav}{\longrightarrow} \leftarrow av, \; by.(ax.R) \overset{\varepsilon}{\Longrightarrow} \leftarrow av, \; by.(ax.R) \overset{bav}{\longrightarrow} by.ax.R \; .$$

Please note that the only difference comes from the message which comes in and just goes out, while it is possible for it to get consumed[5]. ■

---

[5] This shows that transition relation as formulated in Definition 8 lacks the notion of *locality*.

None of the above examples show any difference between two bisimulations. As the order of sending messages generally cannot matter in asynchronous communication, the next example may seem rather promising.

$$P \stackrel{\text{def}}{=} |l|(\leftarrow lz, \, lz.(\leftarrow av, \, |m|(\leftarrow mz, \, mz. \leftarrow bw)))$$

and

$$Q \stackrel{\text{def}}{=} |l|(\leftarrow lz, \, lz.(\leftarrow bw, \, |m|(\leftarrow mz, \, mz. \leftarrow av)))$$

Here we have $P \approx_a Q$ as expected, providing an interesting comparison with the expressions in π-calculus, $\bar{a}.\bar{b}.\Lambda$ and $\bar{b}.\bar{a}.\Lambda$. However the example does not distinguish $\approx_a$ and $\approx_s$, because $P \approx_s Q$ holds. Is there any case where one can differentiate between these two equivalence theories? The next example shows that such a case does exist.

Examples 12 *Asynchronous bisimulation (2).* Let us remember the expression $\mathcal{I}$ in Section 3 (Example 3 (iii) and Example 4 (ii)). For this special agent, the following holds for any a .

$$\mathcal{I}(a) \approx_a \Lambda$$

To verify, make a relation $\mathcal{R} = (\, (\mathcal{I}(a), P), \, P \,)$, where P is zero or more messages without bound names.

(i) Firstly, if

$$\mathcal{I}(a), P \xrightarrow{\text{bv}} \mathcal{I}(a), P, \leftarrow av \, .$$

then clearly

$$P \xrightarrow{\text{bv}} P, \leftarrow av \, .$$

where $(\, (\mathcal{I}(a), P, \leftarrow av), \, (P, \leftarrow av) \,) \in \mathcal{R}$. We can similarly verify in the case

$$\mathcal{I}(a), P \xrightarrow{\text{bv}} \mathcal{I}(a), P' \, .$$

(ii) Next if

$$\mathcal{I}(a), P \xrightarrow{\tau} Q \, .$$

then the only possibility is there is some P' such that

$$P \equiv P', \leftarrow av$$

but then

$$\mathcal{I}(a), \leftarrow av, P' \xrightarrow{\tau} \mathcal{I}(a), \leftarrow av, P' \equiv P$$

As obviously $P \stackrel{\epsilon}{\Rightarrow} P$, this case holds.

Thus the relation is bisimulation, and just by taking $P \stackrel{\text{def}}{=} \Lambda$, the argument holds. ∎

This example is notable in two respects.

(1) Because we have $\approx_s \subset \approx_a$ (the proof is not so difficult), the above example shows that this inclusion is strict.

(2) Another fact is that $\approx_a$ is a congruence relation (as well as $\approx_s$) in our system (both proofs are rather long). Thus the example shows that the term $\mathcal{I}(a)$ or any term which is bisimilar to it can be added or deleted from a configuration arbitrarily without changing its meaning. Based on this fact, there is a method to construct $\approx_s$ from $\approx_a$ by adding appropriate $\mathcal{I}(x)$'s to configurations. This suggests the exact range of difference between $\approx_a$ and $\approx_s$.

The difference between $\approx_a$ and $\approx_s$ is important in that it suggests asynchronous interaction (the relation $\overset{l}{\longrightarrow}$") is more *abstract* than synchronous one ($\overset{l}{\longrightarrow}_s$") in the sense that it does not care the order of consecutive inputs or consecutive outputs. Hence we will deal with *collections* (to be exact, multisets) of messages rather than their sequences. This gives rise to an elegant mathematical treatment of asynchronous interaction semantics, and the property can be directly reflected in our equivalence theory if we add a certain locality notion. Then we have $ax.by.P \approx'_a by.ax.P$ (cf. Example 11 (iii)). We leave the further details to the subsequent exposition to be published elsewhere in the near future.

6 Conclusion

We have seen so far that a formal system based on the notion of pure asynchronous communication can be constructed with full expressive power and important semantic properties. The investigation of the concurrency formalism based on asynchronous communication has just begun, and there are many problems to be solved. Other than the study on asynchronous interaction semantics and its relationship with objects notion, two important points should be pointed out.

(1) We should study whether the construction (or reduction) we performed in this exposition can be applied to CCS or other process calculi formalisms. Especially we should study what results one will obtain for higher-order process calculi which passes processes [20, 4].

(2) The most important possibility of our formal construction in the pragmatic context may exist in sound formulation of the notion of *types* for concurrent object-based computing. There is an interesting work in this direction by Nierstrasz [18]. We hope that the study of asynchronous semantics will provide us with suggestions for typed programming for concurrent objects.

Finally the authors would like to thank Carl Hewitt, who stayed in Keio University from Autumn 1989 to Summer 1990, for beneficial discussions with them, to Professor Joseph Goguen for his suggestions, to Vasco Vasconcelous for discussions and comments on the paper, to Chisato Numaoka for discussions on concurrency, to Kaoru Yoshida for her stimulating e-mails, and to all the labo members for their kind assistance and cheers.

References

[1] Agha, G., *Actors: A Model of Concurrent Computation in Distributed Systems*. MIT Press, 1986.

[2] Barendreght, H. *The Lambda Calculus: Its Syntax and Semantics*. North Holland, 1984.

[3] Berry, G. and Boudol, G., The Chemical Abstract Machine. In *Proc. 17 the Annual Symposium on Principles of Programming Languages*, 1990.

[4] Boudol, G., Towards a Lambda-Calculus for Concurrent and Communicating Systems. In *Proc. TAPSOFT 1989*, LNCS 351, Springer-Verlag, 1984.

[5] Clinger, W. *Foundations of Actor Semantics*. AI-TR-633, MIT Artificial Intelligence Laboratory.

[6] Goguen, J., *Sheaf semantics for concurrent interacting objects*. To appear in Proc. REX School on Foundations of Object-Oriented Programming, Noorwijkerhout, The Netherlands, May 28-June1, 1990.

[7] Hewitt, C., *Viewing Control Structures as Patterns of Passing Messages*. Artificial Intelligence, 1977.

[8] Hewitt, C., Bishop, P., and Steiger, R., A Universal Modular ACTOR Formalism for Artificial Intelligence. In *Proc. of the 3rd International Joint Conference on Artificial Intelligence*, August 1973.

[9] Hoare, C.A.R., *Communicatin Sequential Processes*. Prentice Hall, 1985.

[10] Honda, K., *A Short Note On Language PROTO*, a manuscript, August 1989.

[11] Meseguer J., *Conditional Rewriting Logic as a Unified Model of Concurrency*. SRI-CSL-91-05, Computer Science Laboratory, SRI International, 1991. Also to appear in *Theoretical Computer Science*.

[12] Milner, R., *Calculus of Communicating Systems*. LNCS 92, Springer-Verlag, 1980.

[13] Milner, R., Calculi for Synchrony and Asynchrony. *Theoretical Computer Science 25*, 1983.

[14] Milner, R., Parrow, J.G. and Walker, D.J., *A Calculus of Mobile Processes. Part I and II*. ECS-LFCS-89-85/86, Edinburgh University, 1989

[15] Milner, R., *Communication and Concurrency*. Prentice Hall, 1989.

[16] Milner, R., Functions as Processes. In *Automata, Language and Programming*, LNCS 443, 1990. The extended version under the same title as Rapports de Recherche No.1154, INRIA-Sophia Antipolis, February 1990.)

[17] Nielson and Engberg, *A Calculus of Communicating Systems with Label Passing*. Research Report DAIMI PB-208, Computer Science Department, University of Aarhus, 1986.

[18] Nierstrasz, O., *Towards a Type Theory for Active Objects*. in [23].

[19] Nierstrasz, O., *A Guide to Specifying Concurrent Behaviour with Abacus*. in [23].

[20] Thomsen, B., A calculus of higher order communicating systems. In *Proc. 16 the Annual Symposium on Principles of Programming Languages*, 1989.

[21] Tokoro, M., Computational Field Model: Toward a New Computing Model/Methodology for Open Distributed Environment. In *Proc. of The 2nd IEEE Workshop on Future Trends in Distributed Computing Systems*, Cairo, 1990.

[22] Tokoro, M. and Honda, K., Computational Field Model for Open Distributed Environment. To appear in Yonezawa, A., McColl, W., and Ito, T., ed., *Concurrency: Theory, Language, Architecture*, LNCS, Springer Verlag, 1991.

[23] Tsichritzis, D., ed. *Object Management*. Centre Universitaire D'informatique, Universite de Geneve, July 1990.

[24] Yonezawa, A., and Tokoro, M., ed., *Object-Oriented Concurrent Programming*. MIT Press, 1986.

DEFINITION OF REUSABLE CONCURRENT SOFTWARE COMPONENTS [1]

S.Crespi Reghizzi   G.Galli de Paratesi
Dipt. Elettronica - Politecnico di Milano, Piazza Leonardo, 32 - Milano, Italy 20133.
S.Genolini
TXT Ingegneria Informatica SpA
Via Socrate 41, Milano, Italy 20128

Abstract

In O.O. languages with active objects, a constraint (or behaviour) on method activations is needed to avoid inconsistencies and to meet performance requirements. If the constraint is part of a class definition, the class population grows with the product of the number of behaviours. As pointed out in [Goldsack and Atkinson 1990] this undesirable growth may be controlled by separating the specification of the functional characteristics and the behavioural characteristics of a class. This work extends the concept of behavioural inheritance (b-inheritance) which provides a behaviour to a sequential class. Furthermore, the interaction between b-inheritance and inheritance is discussed. Deontic logic notation for specifying behaviour is extended to deal with the definition of more complex constraints and to improve reusability characteristics of components. The proposal is formalized by extended Petri nets and the translation into a concurrent language is outlined. The project is under development within the O.O. ADA extension DRAGOON [Di Maio et al 1989].

1. Introduction

This work addresses the specification of software components, for concurrent systems in the specific perspective of software reuse. A first, more conservative, approach to concurrent component design assumes an existing collection of sequential components, which have to be used in a concurrent setting; this can cause inconsistencies in state variables, saturation of resources or other problems, unless suitable restrictions are imposed on concurrent activations.

A second, more organic approach, not investigated in this paper, assumes that components are designed from the beginning with concurrent use in mind. This approach is strongly recomandable in the design of highly parallel systems, since the very structure of algorithms differs from the sequential case.

A typical O.O. language with classes, multiple inheritance, and objects is taken into consideration; classes can be active, i.e. endowed with a control thread. Method invocation is the protocol for communication betweeen objects Because of the presence of many threads, methods of an object can be concurrently called causing unpredictable results: hence the

[1]This work was initially supported by ESPRIT Project DRAGON, and is continuing under project REBOOT. We also aknowledge support by Italian MURST 40% and CNR.

need to specify a constraint on their activations. Constraints are also motivated by the need to control computer resource usage (e.g. by limiting the number of concurrent activations of a reentrant method).

There are essentially two basic strategies for introducing concurrency features [America 1989]. The first approach is to encapsulate sequential and concurrent features within the same class specification. The second is to superimpose concurrency constructs as an extra layer, *orthogonal* to the object-oriented paradigm. Specifying sequential and concurrent features at the same time may raise two kinds of problems:

- *First*: there may be a conflict between the use of inheritance to support software adaptability, and the inclusion of synchronization constraints in the class, to ensure correctness. In fact, modification of a class functionality may involve adding new methods or removing existing ones, thereby making the synchronization constraints inconsistent w.r.t. the new class interface.

- *Second*: class population increases by a large factor. For instance a class SymbolTableManager can have a variety of behaviours, such as mutual exclusion on all methods, concurrent activation of methods performing a read operation but mutual exclusion of methods involving updates, concurrency limited by a constant k in order to avoid task proliferation, various priority constraints, etc. The definition of a separate class for each combination of functional and behavioural specifications besides being unpractical, moves in the opposite direction of software reuse.

As a consequence it was argued ([Goldsack and Atkinson 1990], [Di Maio et al 1989]) that synchronization constraints, called *behaviours*, should not be a part of class specification, but should be superimposed using an orthogonal construct. Class behaviour must be specified separately and independently of functionality: a *behavioural class* (b-class) is an abstract, generic, specification of behaviour. Multiple inheritance, called *behavioural inheritance*, is exploited to associate a synchronization constraint, specified by a behavioural class, with the methods of a sequential class.

This approach is consistent with the hypothesis that the design of concurrent behaviours and the reuse of existing classes are the concerns of two different kinds of persons dealing with a software component base. The *normal user* is not expected to design new abstract behaviours, but only to use library's b-classes, whereas the *expert user* can specify new behaviours to be added to the component base.

This research focuses on the notation for specifying concurrent behaviour, on the formalization of behavioural inheritance by extended Petri nets, and on the automatic generation of concurrent code for behavioured objects.

In Sect. 2 the notion of concurrent behaviour, behavioural inheritance and its relation to inheritance is discussed. Furthermore, a gamut of constructs for expressing generic synchronisation constraints is analyzed using the method of deontic predicates (a notation related to path expressions [Campbell and Habermann 1974]). For each construct. expressive power, degree of reusability and runtime efficiency are evaluated. In Sect.3 the formalization of the behavioural heir by means of Petri nets extended with firing predicates is presented together with an implementation in terms of Ada tasks, with optimization options.

The research is part of DRAGOON, an O.O. variant of Ada designed to support reuse, distribution and dynamic reconfiguration ([Di Maio et al 1989]), but the concepts, notation, formal definition, and implementation are applicable to O.O. languages, such as C++ or Eiffel. The implementation can be adapted to other multi-task environment, e.g. Unix.

2. Specification of concurrent behaviour

In our reference model objects can be active. An active object is an instance of an active class, that is of a class which has a *thread* in addition to methods. A thread is similar to a method, except that it cannot be invoked but is activated at object instanciation time. Here we need not be concerned with object instanciation, but we can assume that in the system there are several concurrent activities, which can simultaneously invoke the methods of an object. This raises the issue of specifying a synchronization rule, also called a *behaviour*, for the activation of methods. There are different scenarios in which the rule could constrain the order of activation of methods:

-methods of a single object;

-methods of different objects of the same class;

-methods of any object of any class.

For simplicity we restrict the scope to the first case: in other words, we do not address the issue of regulating the activations of methods belonging to different objects. The restriction causes no loss of generality, at least in principle: in fact a semaphore can be easily defined as an object with two methods *signal* and *wait*, and any concurrent system can be designed using semaphores.

We call *free* a class *(f-class)* without constraints on method activations: this means that its methods can be executed in parallel on behalf of different active calling objects. When no other concurrent behaviour is indicated, what should the default be? Without a default no class can be instanciated unless the designer provides a behavioural specification: a burden for him when the system to be designed is purely or predominant sequential. The following reasonable alternatives have been considered:

1 -default behaviour is free;

2 -default behaviour is mutually exclusive;

We assume that classes are free by default; this is sometimes a dangerous assumption, since concurrent activation of methods originally intended for serial execution could cause critical races or inconsistencies. But the opposite hypothesis 2 causes inacceptable penalty on run-time efficiency, because every object must be implemented as a task. We prefer to leave to the designer responsibility for the introduction of a mutex constraint when needed.

Concurrent behaviours are specified by special abstract classes, called *behavioural* (shortly *b-class*). A class which can be instanciated, because all of its methods have a body, is called *concrete (c-class);* otherwise it is an *abstract* class (*a-class*). In order to regulate the concurrent behaviour of a free class, we use multiple (actually double) inheritance: the first parent is a f-class (but see later for another possibility), the other is a b-class, and the heir is the result of the prescribed regulation for the methods of the f-class. This heir class is called *behavioured* or *regulated (r-class)*, and this special form of inheritance is called behavioural (*b-inheritance*).

For instance, consider (Ex.2 in Fig 2.) the concrete f-class *Buffer3* (with methods *put, get* and *size*), and the b-class *Mutex:* the result of b-inheritance is an r-class, *BufferMutex3*. An instanciation of *BufferMutex3* is an object interfaced by mutually exclusive methods *put, get* and *size*.

Combination of b-inheritance and inheritance

An important issue is the combination of concurrent and functional specifications within the class hierarchy. In a sequential component catalogue, multiple inheritance relations link a class to its parents and siblings (subclasses).

Moving down an inheritance chain, one usually finds an abstract class progressively made concrete by method bodies, enriched by new methods, and specialized by method redefinitions. Sometimes methods are canceled or hidden. Of course (partially) abstract classes cannot be instanciated. The question is where the concurrent behaviour should be specified, inside the inheritance graph (which is a DAG). The range of possibilities for b-inheritance is presented in Fig.1. We comment each possibility.

	Parent 1 (P1)	Parent 2 (P2)	Result (R)
1	f-class ∩ a-class	b-class	r-class ∩ a-class
2	f-class ∩ c-class	b-class	r-class ∩ c-class
3	r-class ∩ a-class	b-class	r-class ∩ a-class
4	r-class ∩ c-class	b-class	r-class ∩ c-class

Fig.1- Possible domains of parents in behavioural inheritance.

1 - b-inheritance can only be applied to a free class, i.e. at most once along a path in the DAG. This means that the behaviour to be attached to a class P1 must be specified in a single step. If P1 is abstract, the result R is not instanciatable.

2 - same as 1, but in addition P1 must be a concrete class, hence R is instanciatable.

3 - P1 is a behavioured class (abstract), resulting from a previous b-inheritance. Thus an r-class can be obtained by incrementally specifying its behaviour in several steps down the DAG path.

Cases 1 to 3 are illustrated by the examples in Fig.2.

4 - same as 3, but P1 must be concrete; R is thus instanciatable.

For simplicity and code efficiency we opted for 2, ruling out the possibilities of creating abstract behavioured classes and of superimposing onto a behavioured class another behaviour. Other reasons for this choice are presented later.

Actually, in order to complete the picture, we need to consider (Fig.3) the allowed domains

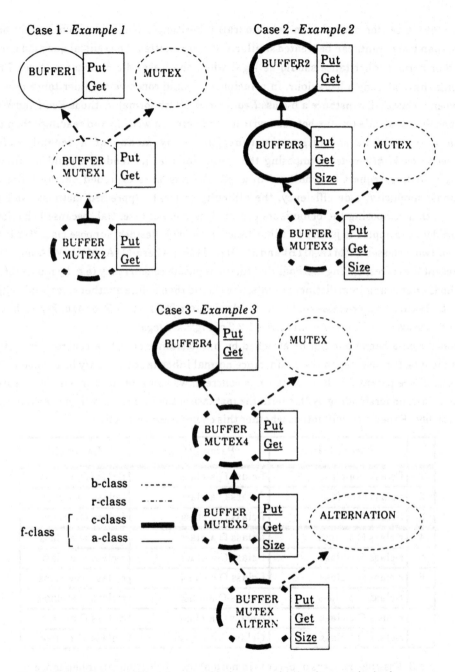

Fig.2 - Inheritance (solid arrows) and behavioural inheritance (dashed arrows)
Methods provided with a body are underscored.

of parent classes for normal (non behavioural) inheritance. The cases of one parent or of more than two parents can be treated similarly and are omitted. The central question here is whether normal inheritance should be legal when one (cases 4,5,6) or more (cases 7,8,9) parents have already a behaviour. In principle one could conceive an inheritance relation between b-classes: for instance a b-class *ReaderWriter* with formal methods *Read* and *Write* defines the usual rule (mutex between writing and between writing and reading); then this behaviour could be specialized by inheritance, by means of a second b-class *ReaderWriterWithPrecedence* imposing the constraint that no reading should be allowed when a writing request is pending. These possibilities were excluded on the following grounds: simplicity, code efficiency, the difficulty to treat suppressed methods, and the opinion that composing the behaviours of two classes is not essential, because behaviours are seldom so complex to justify an inheritance taxonomy. Besides, suppose class P12 is the heir of two r-classes P1(M1A,M1B) and P2(M2A,M2B), where M1A, M1B, M2A and M2B represent the corresponding methods. In order to regulate concurrency (e.g. by mutex) of the methods originating from distinct parents, one should then define another class b-inheriting from P12 (which is an r-class), and from a b-class *mutex*. This is case 3 (or 4) of Fig.1, that we intended to exclude. Therefore only cases 1,2,3 of Fig.3 are legal.

In conclusion a behaviour can be attached by b-inheritance only to a concrete, free class. This must be the last step in the chain, since normal inheritance can only be applied to free classes. Since parent 2 of b-inheritance is concrete, we can refer to it as an object, rather than a class, understanding by this term the instance of the P2 class to which behaviour is to be attached. Experience will tell us whether this choice is too restrictive.

	Parent 1 (P1)	Parent 2 (P2)	Result (R)
1	f-class ∩ a-class	f-class ∩ a-class	f-class ∩ a-class
2	f-class ∩ c-class	f-class ∩ a-class	f-class ∩ a-class
3	f-class ∩ c-class	f-class ∩ c-class	f-class ∩ c-class
4	r-class ∩ a-class	f-class ∩ a-class	r-class ∩ a-class
5	r-class ∩ c-class	f-class ∩ a-class	r-class ∩ a-class
6	r-class ∩ c-class	f-class ∩ c-class	r-class ∩ c-class
7	r-class ∩ a-class	r-class ∩ a-class	r-class ∩ a-class
8	r-class ∩ c-class	r-class ∩ a-class	r-class ∩ a-class
9	r-class ∩ c-class	r-class ∩ c-class	r-class ∩ c-class

Fig.3 -Possible domains of parents in normal (non-behavioural) inheritance

Specification of behavioural classes

A b-class abstractly specifies constraints to be imposed on certain events (method activations). It does so independently of the actual methods of any f-class, by referring to formal method names, that will be bound to actual method names at b-inheritance time.

Several possible styles of specification could be adopted: a concurrent programming language, Petri nets or path expressions [Campbell and Habermann 1974]. We chosed the *deontic logic,* a predicative notation [von Wright 1980], which is similar in power to path expressions and quite adequate for the job.

For each formal method parameter MF of a b-class there is a deontic axiom of the form: *permitted*(MF) ⇔ deontic predicate. Activation of the corresponding actual methods MA_1, ..., MA_n is permitted only when the predicate (right-hand side) is true. Notice that MF stands for a <u>set</u> of actual methods, to be ruled by the same constraint.

Deontic expressions use a few *historical* operators returning the activation history of methods. Fig.4 summarizes the basic and derived operators.

Operator	Meaning
Deontic predicate head	
per(MF)	Activation of MF is permitted iff predicate is true.
Historical operators	Historical operators count specific occurrences of events since system start time
req(MF)	No. of requests of method MF
act(MF)	No. of activations of method MF
fin(MF)	No. of terminations of method MF
State operators	State operators return the number of items currently present in run-time system queues
act_now(MF) --derived	No. of current activations of method: act_now(MF) = act(MF) - fin(MF)
req_now(MF) --derived	No. of pending requests of method: req_now(MF) = req(MF) - act(MF)

Fig.4 - Historical and state operators. When MF is a set of methods, the operators return the aggregate result for all methods MA in the set.

Historical and state operators can be extended in the natural way to a set of methods instead that to a single one.

Mutex, mutual exclusion of methods (MF_1, MF_2, ...), is a common deontic expression:

per(MF_i) ⇔ ∀ j : act_now(MF_j) = 0   -- i = j prevents multiple activations of same method

It is convenient to shorten this expression with the notation (> <).

Several possibilities of increasing complexity for the deontic predicate are shown in Fig.5 and discussed on later. We now explain the syntax referring to Ex.1 of Fig.5. Formal method parameters are introduced by the keyword "ruled", for each formal parameter there is exactly one deontic axiom. This specification clearly imposes that the first method to be activated is FOPS (i.e. one of the actual methods that will be bound to FOPS by b-inheritance), since per(FOPS) is true when and only when act(FOPS) = fin(SOPS) = 0 Once FOPS has been activated, act(FOPS) becomes 1, hence per(SOPS) becomes true, and per(FOPS) false, etc. Before discussing the other cases of Fig. 5 we present an explanation

Arguments	Examples
1 -*Historical and state operators (see Fig.4) applied to formal methods* *Example : alternation of activations of two sets of methods FOPS and SOPS*	**behavioural class ALTERNATION is** **ruled FOPS , SOPS;** -- formal methods are -- partitioned into two sets : F(irst)_OP_Set and -- S(econd)_OP_Set **where** per(FOPS) ⇔ act(FOPS) = fin(SOPS) --FOPS activation is permitted iff the no. of past --activations of FOPS and SOPS are equal; per(SOPS) ⇔ fin(FOPS) > act(SOPS) --SOPS activation is permitted iff the no. of --finished activations of FOPS exceeds the no. --of past activations of SOPS; **end ALTERNATION;**
2- *Generic b-class w.r.t. a parameter* *Example:*limits the max number of active methods	**generic** **NUM : POSITIVE;** **behavioural class LIMITER is** **ruled OPS;** **where** per(OPS) ⇔ act.now(OPS) < NUM; **end LIMITER;**
3 -*Generic b-class w.r.t the number of method groups* *Example:* methods are activated according to their priority	**generic** --a generic b-class **K : POSITIVE;** -- the no. of priority groups; **behavioural class PRIORITY is** **ruled OP enum;** --enumeration of sets of formal --methods in order of decreasing priority; **where** per(OP'FIRST) ⇔ (> <); -- > < is mutex; per(OP) ⇔ per(OP'PRED) **and** req-now(OP'PRED) = 0; --OP activation is permitted iff activation of the --preceding (in the enumeration) formal set of --methods is permitted, and there no pending --requests for it; **end PRIORITY;**

Fig.5 - Arguments of deontic predicates in behavioural classes.

of b-inheritance.

A b-class is used in b-inheritance to provide a behaviour to a c-class. Consider the examples of b-inheritance in Fig.6, which refer to the b-classes of Fig.5.

Case A (Fig.6): The f-class UNI.BUFFER has three methods PUT, PUTLONG and GET, the b-class is ALTERNATION (Fig.5), and the result is the r-class ALTERNATION.UNI. BUFFER. The syntax identifies the parent b-class by the keyword "ruled by". Two actual methods, PUT and PUTLONG, correspond to the formal FOPS, and GET corresponds to SOPS. Thus a possible activation sequence is: PUT, GET, PUT, GET, PUTLONG, GET, ...

Not all kinds of behaviour can be conveniently expressed by such b-classes: for instance the constraint that the number of active methods should be less than a constant, NUM . The generic parameter NUM is introduced in Ex.2 of Fig.5, in order to avoid the need of a separate b-class for each different value of NUM.

Arguments	Examples

4 *-Formal Boolean functions (guards) returning a truth value depending on the state of the formal object.*
 	
Example: activations of two sets of methods (PT and GT) are permitted in mutex, with additional constraints against underflow and overflow; size of buffer is unknown to the b-class, but a Boolean formal function FULL_GUARD is used to inspect the state of the buffer. This function is activated in mutex.
	generic
	with function FULL_GUARD return BOOLEAN;
	behavioural class GUARDED is
	ruled PT, GT;
	where
	  per(GT) $\Leftrightarrow$ (> <) **and** act(GT) < fin(PT);
	    -- no underflow
	  per(PT) $\Leftrightarrow$ (> <) **and not** FULL_GUARD;
	    --no overflow
	  per(FULL_GUARD) $\Leftrightarrow$ (> <) ;
	end GUARDED;

5 *-Formal functions returning the state of the formal object.*
 	
Example: the max number of activations of OP is determined at run-time. The number can be changed at run-time by calling the method SETUP
	generic
	 with function MAX return NATURAL;
	behavioural class GUARDED_LIMITER is
	 ruled OP,SETUP;
	 (MAX,SETUP);
	where
	per(OP) $\Leftrightarrow$ act.now(OP) < MAX **and**
	              act.now(SETUP) = 0 **and**
	              req.now(SETUP) > 0;
	per(SETUP) $\Leftrightarrow$ act.now(MAX) = 0 **and**
	              act.now(SETUP) = 0 ;
	per(MAX) $\Leftrightarrow$ act.now(SETUP) = 0 **and**
	              req.now(SETUP) > 0;
	end GUARDED_LIMITER;

6 *-Parameters of formal methods* *Example:*determining the priority level on the value of parameter I	**generic** **type OP_TYPE is** (< >) **behavioural class MULTI_QUEUE is** **ruled A(OP_TYPE);** **where** per(A(I)) $\Leftrightarrow$ act(A(I)) = fin(A(I)) -- I is in the range of OP_TYPE **end MULTI_QUEUE**

Fig.5 (continued) - Arguments of deontic predicates in behavioural classes.

Consider next the activation of methods according to their priorities. If the methods can be partitioned in a fixed number k of priority groups, the deontic specification is:

per(MF$_1$) $\Leftrightarrow$ (> <);
per(MF$_2$) $\Leftrightarrow$ (> <) **and** req.now(MF$_1$) = 0;
....
per(MF$_k$)) $\Leftrightarrow$ (> <) **and** req.now(MF$_{k-1}$) = 0 **and** ...... req.now(MF$_1$) = 0;

This is verbose and strictly dependent on k. A different b-class would be required for different numbers of priority groups. To solve the problem, *generic* b-classes have been introduced. The use of recursive deontic definitions (case 3 of Fig. 5), permits a single specification of priority behaviour, independently of the number of priority groups. In this case the number of formal methods is determined at inheritance time. Correctness

f class (1st parent)	b-class (2nd parent)	b-inheritance
A) **class** UNI_BUFFER **is** **procedure** PUT(ITEM : **in** ELEMENT); **procedure** PUTLONG (LONGITEM: **in** LONGELEMENT); **procedure** GET(ITEM : **out** ELEMENT); **end** UNI_BUFFER;	ALTERNATION	**class** ALTERNATION_UNI_BUFFER **is** **inherits** UNI_BUFFER; **ruled by** ALTERNATION; **where** PUT, PUTLONG $\Rightarrow$ FOP; GET $\Rightarrow$ SOP; **end** ALTERNATION_UNI_BUFFER;

B)
class SERVER **is**
  procedure FIRST;
  procedure SECOND;
  procedure THIRD;
end SERVER;
	PRIORITY	**class** PRIORITY.SERVER **is**
		inherits SERVER;
		ruled by PRIORITY;
		where
		  $K \Rightarrow 3$;
		  FIRST $\Rightarrow$ OP[1];
		  SECOND $\Rightarrow$ OP[2];
		  THIRD $\Rightarrow$ OP[3];
		end PRIORITY SERVER;

C)
class POLY_BUFFER **is**
procedure PUT(ITEM : **in**
ELEMENT);
procedure PUTLONG(ITEM :
in LONGELEMENT);
procedure GET(ITEM : **out**
ELEMENT);
function IS_FULL **return**
BOOLEAN ;
end POLY_BUFFER ;
	GUARDED	**class**
		GUARDED_POLY_BUFFER **is**
		inherits POLY_BUFFER;
		ruled by GUARDED;
		where
		  PUT, PUTLONG $\Rightarrow$ PT;
		  GET $\Rightarrow$ GT;
		  IS_FULL $\Rightarrow$ FULL_GUARD;
		end
		GUARDED_POLY_BUFFER;

D)
class MESSAGE_HANDLER
is
procedure
SEND(M:MESSAGE;
  C:PRIORIY)
end MESSAGE_HANDLER
	MULTI_
	QUEUE
		class Q_MESSAGE_HANDLER
		is
		inherits MESSAGE_HANDLER
		ruled by
		  MULTI_QUEUE(PRIORITY)
		where
		  $A(I) \Rightarrow$ SEND(M, C $\Rightarrow$ I);
		end Q_MESSAGE_HANDLER;

Fig.6 - Examples of b-inheritance.

conditions of recursive definitions are presented in [Galli 1991].

A second solution uses universal quantification instead of recursion:
generic
K : POSITIVE; -- the no. of priority groups;
behavioural class PRIORITY **is**
ruled MF enum; -- keyword "enum" indicates that there is an ordered set of method groups,
  per(MF_k)) $\Leftrightarrow$ ($><$) **and** $\forall 1 \leq i < k$: req.now(MF_i) $= 0$
end PRIORITY;

Going back to the priority problem, suppose now that priority does not depend on the method name M, but on the method caller, and that the caller priority is encoded by a parameter of the method: thus M(1) takes priority over M(2). The previous deontic specs are unsuitable since they do not have visibility of actual parameters. A solution to this problem [Goldsack and Atkinson 1990] is described in case 6 of Fig.5.

Next we consider the use of Boolean side-effect free methods (called *guards*) within deontic predicates. Guards are used to inspect part of the private state of an object. The f-class POLY__BUFFER (case C of Fig.6) provides two methods for writing data and one for reading. The behaviour is specified in Ex.4 of Fig.5: mutual exclusion, with the constraints that writers activation must be blocked when the buffer is full; this condition is checked by means of the guard FULL__GUARD. In Fig.6, a correspondence between the guard and the Boolean method IS__FULL is established. Note that, in the case of guards (or more generally state-inspecting functions), a formal method parameter cannot be bound to more than one actual method (Case C of Fig.6).

A further step is represented by the use of non-boolean functions in deontic expressions. Similar to guards, such functions could be used to inspect the state of the object.

Discussion

Fig.7 summarizes the pros and cons of each form of b-class specification. Case 1 suffers from two limitations: any constant in the deontic predicates is fixed at b-class definition time. If Ex.2 of Fig.5 were to be specified by a non generic b-class, different b-classes would have to be written for each value of NUM. The same problem occurs w.r.t. Ex.3 of Fig.5 which requires a varying number of method groups, one for each priority level. The advantages of case 1 are simplicity and reduced run-time overhead. Case 2 is perhaps the optimum w.r.t. expressivity, efficiency and reusability. Case 3 adds expressive power at the cost of increased abstraction and run-time overhead. Cases 4 and 5 permit to specify state variable dependent behaviour, (Ex.4 Fig.5) which cannot be simulated by previous cases. The use of state inspecting functions within the predicates makes somehow the b-class dependent on the signature of the f-class, thereby reducing reusability. The translation for this case is shown in section 3. Case 6 [Goldsack and Atkinson 1990] is also dynamic, since it allows to specify behaviours wich depend on actual values of methods parameters before they are stored into the object's state. Such message oriented specification is incomparable with cases 4 and 5. We have not developed the translation because we feel that this case is hard to understand in complex situations. In conclusion we recommend the use of genericity for b-classes, but we defer until feedbacks from experimentation will be available a judgement on the convenience of dynamic classes.

Notice that in b-classes guards, as other formal methods, are regulated by a deontic predicate. The safest solution is to activate a guard in mutual exclusion, but weaker conditions still ensuring consistency are proposed in [Galli 1991]. For instance in case 5 of Fig.5 the function MAX can be activated in parallel with any method of the set OP.

Since a guard is usually defined only for synchronization purposes and is not invoked by other objects, the question is when it should be evaluated. Conceptually a guard value

b-class	Limits	Pros/Cons
Non-Generic b-class *1 -Historical and state operators (see Fig.4) applied to formal methods*	Number of method groups: fixed at b-class definition time; Number of methods within a group fixed at b-inheritance time; Deontic predicates non-parametric;	Low reusability High run-time speed Simplicity
Generic b-class		
2- with respect to a parameter	Number of method groups: fixed at b-class definition time; Number of methods within a group fixed at b-inheritance time; Deontic predicates parametric w.r.t. a generic parameters	High reusability High run-time speed Simplicity
3- enumeration of method groups	Number of method groups: fixed at b-inheritance time; Number of methods within a group fixed at b-inheritance time; Deontic predicates parametric w.r.t. a generic parameters	Highest reusability Low run time speed High abstraction reduces readibility
Dynamic b-class *4,5- Formal functions (guards) returning the state of the formal object.*	Number of method groups: fixed at b-class definition time; Number of methods within a group fixed at b-inheritance time; Deontic predicates non-parametric	Lower reusability. The b-class is closely coupled to the features of the c-class. Some overhead introduced by the evaluation of the guards Possibility of run-time varying behaviour
Parametric b-class *6- Parameters of formal methods*	Number of method groups: fixed at b-class definition time; Number of methods within a group fixed at b-inheritance time Deontic predicates - parametric	Lower reusability High run-time speed The b-class is strictly coupled to the signature of the f-class.

Fig.7 - Analysis of features of b-classes. Combinations of cases are also possible.

should be continously monitored. In practice, evaluation is only required when the state of the object may change, that is each time a method activation terminates.

3. Translation of behavioural inheritance

Semantics of behavioural inheritance

The semantic of behavioural inheritance can be expressed using high level Petri Nets (E/R nets [Ghezzi et al 1991]). Tokens can have values associated to them. A transition is enabled depending on the value of a predicate associated to the input tokens. Thus we associate to each transition a predicate, and some actions that specify the value of the output tokens. If no actions are specified, a dummy (without a value) token is created.

In the initial configuration (Fig.8) there are several valued tokens denoted Y, but no dummy tokens. For instance we consider the b-class 4 of Fig.5, and b-inheritance with c-class (C of Fig.6) POLYBUFFER exporting the methods PUT, PUTLONG, GET and IS-FULL. The E/R net of b-inheritance is represented in Fig.8. The historical operators are translated into places containing a token with an associated value. The values are updated according to the actions when a transition fires. A bidirectional arrow stands for two simple ones. The places containing dummy tokens are used to represent the state of the graph and to enable the correspondent transitions. In Fig 9 we list the predicates and actions for the transitions in Fig.8. Notice that the resulting net has a behaviour which depends on the state of the sequential class, through the marking of the place STATE GUARD. For simpler, unguarded b-classes there is no such dependency. For further examples and discussion of E/R models of behaviour refer to [Galli 1991].

Translation into ADA

For Ada translation of a b-class, we examined the following options:

- Ada code is produced separately for b-classes, and for free c-classes and at b-inheritance time the two parts are linked together.

- at first only the Ada code for the free c-class is produced, and at b-inheritance time the code for the r-class is produced; no code is produced for the b-classes, which are not present in the library.

To compare the options, suppose that the c-classes C1 and C2 have to be regulated by the same b-class B, producing the r-classes R1 and R2. With the first option, there is one Ada component B•Ada for B (using tasks and possibly generics). There are no Ada components for R1 or R2, and each instance of R1 (or R2) is the link of C1•Ada (a purely sequential code) and B•Ada.

With the second option, there is no Ada component for B, but only a descriptor. After b-inheritance, two different Ada components for R1 and R2 are created.

Advantages of the first option are: consistency with the library organisation of DRAGOON: economy of components, since there is only one component per b-class; and reduced number of Ada compilations. The basic advantages of the second option is that code is more specific, hence more efficient. The decision is stil open, but we present an example of the first option, which has been analyzed in more detail. Notice that the hypotheses on domains of parents

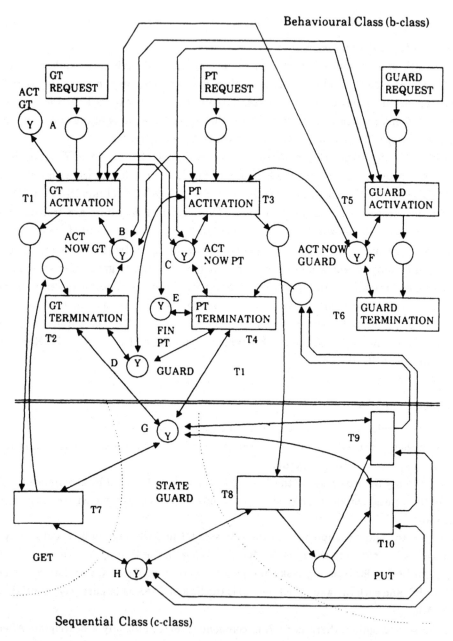

Fig.8 -Modeling a guarded behavioural class with Petri nets (see Ex.4 fig.5).

in behavioural inheritance (*vs* Fig.1 and 3 and previous discussion) are based on the first option.

A second choice that has been investigated concerns the assignment of a value to the formal parameters of a generic b-class; we examined the following options:

P T1:
    A.Y < E.Y and
    B.Y = 0 and
    C.Y = 0 and
    F.Y = 0
AC T1:
    A.Y: = A.Y + 1;
    B.Y: = B.Y + 1;
    C.Y: = C.Y;
    F.Y: = F.Y;
    E.Y: = E.Y + 1;
	P T3:
	    not D.Y = True
	    and
	    B.Y = 0 and
	    C.Y = 0 and
	    F.Y = 0
	AC T3:
	    D.Y = D.Y;
	    B.Y: = B.Y;
	    C.Y: = C.Y + 1;
	    F.Y: = F.Y;
		P T5:
		    B.Y = 0 and
		    C.Y = 0 and
		    F.Y = 0
		AC T5:
		    B.Y: = B.Y;
		    C.Y: = C.Y;
		    F.Y: = F.Y + 1;

AC T2:
    D.Y: = G.Y;
    B.Y: = B.Y - 1;
    G.Y: = G.Y;
	AC T4:
	    D.Y: = G.Y;
	    C.Y: = C.Y - 1;
	    G.Y: = G.Y;
	    E.Y: = E.Y + 1;
		AC T6:
		    F.Y: = F.Y - 1;

AC T7:
    G.Y: = False;
    H.Y: = H.Y - 1;
AC T8:
    H.Y: = H.Y + 1;
	P T9:
	    H.Y < Buffer.dim
	AC T9:
	    G.Y: = False;
	    H.Y: = H.Y;
		P T10:
		    H.Y = Buffer.dim
		AC T10:
		    G.Y: = True;
		    H.Y: = H.Y;

Fig.9 - Predicates (P) and actions (AC) in the E/R net of Fig.8.
Transition without predicates are assumed TRUE by default .

-Assignment of values at b-inheritance time.

-Assignment of values at creation time of an instance variable of the corresponding r-class.

The second solution is attractive because it permits to have, after b-inheritance, <u>one</u> library component (generic Ada package) for every r-class. This component is customized w.r.t. the values of the formal parameters of the b-class (e.g. NUM in Ex.2 Fig 5) at object creation time. On the other hand, this forces the normal user to consider the structure of the b-class at every object creation action. Consider b-class PRIORITY (Ex.3 Fig 5) and a c-class C with methods that must be grouped into three priority groups. When creating an instance of C regulated by PRIORITY, the user must correctly specify the value 3 for the number of groups. Due to this drawback, we chose the first alternative, which increases the number of library components, but not the size of object code.

Next we describe the structure of the code. First recall the translation of sequential classes. As usual in O.O. languages, the translation of a method call, say PUT, for a free concrete class must account for run-time selection of the method body. In DRAGOON this takes the following form (called a *shell*):

procedure SHELL.PUT(...) **is**
begin

```
   ...
PUT( ... );
      ...
end SHELL__PUT;
```

where SHELL__PUT is a runtime system procedure which takes care of dynamic binding (polymorphism). Next consider the translation of the r-class:

```
class ALTERNATION__UNI__BUFFER is
inherits UNI__BUFFER;
ruled by ALTERNATION;   --see Fig. 5 Ex.1
where
PUT, PUTLONG ⇒ FOP;
GET ⇒ SOP;
end ALTERNATION__UNI__BUFFER;
```

For r-classes, the previous scheme has to be modified, by enclosing a method call between two statements: the first is a call to a system procedure START__METHOD, the last one is a call to a system procedure END__METHOD.

```
procedure SHELL__PUT( ... ) is
 begin
 GUARDED.START__METHOD(PT, ... );
    ...
 PUT(... );
    ...
 GUARDED.END__METHOD (PT, ... );
 end SHELL__PUT;
```

The code is organized as a generic package (since the b-class ALTERNATION is generic) GUARDED, defining the following major entities:

A procedure START__METHOD that interfaces to the entry of each method, via evaluation of the deontic predicate.

A procedure END__METHOD which is invoked by a method upon termination.

A task type BEHAVIOUR; an instance of the task is created at object creation time, for each instance of the r-class. The task offers two kinds of entries. In order to achieve synchronisation, the entries belonging to the first group are invoked by START__METHOD and the entries belonging to the second group by END__METHOD.

```
 generic
 with FULL__GUARD return BOOLEAN;
 package GUARDED is
  type METHOD__SET is (PT, GT, FULL__GUARD);
  procedure START__METHOD(OP: METHOD__SET, REF: in DUMMY );
  procedure END__METHOD (OP: METHOD__SET, REF: in DUMMY );
  private
  task type BEHAVIOUR is
    ...............
    entry START__PT;
    entry START__GT;
    entry START__FULL__GUARD;
    entry END__PT;
    entry END__GT;
    entry END__FULL__GUARD;
  end BEHAVIOUR;
 end GUARDED
```

```
package body GUARDED is
 procedure START__METHOD(OP:METHOD__SET, ·......) is
  begin
   case OP is
    when PT      = > REF.START__PT;
    when GT      = > REF:START__GT;
    when FULL__GUARD = > REF.START__FULL__GUARD;
   end case;
  end ;
 procedure END__METHOD(OP:METHOD__SET, ....) is
  begin
   case OP is
    when PT      = > REF.END__PT;
    when GT      = > REF.END__GT;
    when FULL__GUARD = > REF.END__FULL__GUARD;
   end case;
  end;
 ................
 task body BEHAVIOUR is
    ACT__GT    : NATURAL := 0;    --the numbers correspond to the
    FIN__PT    : NATURAL := 0;    --historical functions
    ACT-NOW     : NATURAL := 0;
    FULL__GUARD__FLAG: BOOLEAN := FALSE;
  begin
  accept INIT(.......) do
    ............
  end;
  FULL__GUARD__FLAG := FULL__GUARD;
  loop
   select
    when ACT-NOW = 0 and ACT__GT < FIN__PT = > --translation of the first axiom
     accept START__GT do
       ACT-NOW := ACT-NOW + 1;        --update of the historical functions
       ACT__GT := ACT__GT + 1;
     end;
    or
    when ACT-NOW = 0 and not FULL__GUARD__FLAG = > --translation of the
     accept START__PT do                          --second axiom
       ACT-NOW := ACT-NOW + 1;        --update of the historical functions
     end;
    or
    when ACT-NOW = 0 = >                --translation of the third axiom
     accept START__FULL__GUARD do
       ACT-NOW := ACT-NOW + 1;        --update of the historical functions
     end;
    or
     accept END__GT do                --termination of the method GET
       ACT-NOW := ACT-NOW - 1;        --update of the historical functions
       FULL__GUARD__FLAG := FULL__GUARD;
     end;
    or       accept END__PT do        --termination of the method PUT
       ACT-NOW := ACT-NOW - 1;        --update of the historical functions
       FIN__PT := FIN__PT + 1;
       FULL__GUARD__FLAG := FULL__GUARD;
     end;
    or
     accept END__FULL__GUARD do       --termination of the evaluation of
       ACT-NOW := ACT-NOW - 1;        --the guard
     end;
   end select;
```

```
      end loop;
        end BEHAVIOUR;
    end GUARDED;
```

Historical operators (see Fig.4) are naturally mapped onto counters. For each method group in the b-class there is an entry for START and another for END. Each entry of kind START is guarded by a deontic predicate; upon acceptance, historical counters are updated. Entries of kind END are called when a method finishes; no predicate is needed, but only historical counters are updated and values returned by guards or state-inspecting functions (if any) are updated. Notice that the task accesses FULL_GUARD without going through the method selection shell.

The previous translation present a serious problem for run-time performance: the task is always busy waiting inside the loop containing the *select* statement. This causes much overhead for systems with many behavioured objects, since each one corresponds to an active task. To avoid the problem, the *select* statement is expanded with an *else* branch, which is entered when no other entry call is accepted. The *else* branch put the task to sleep. The task is awakened by the next incoming call to START or to END a method.

The translation of behaviours with a generic number of method groups (e.g. Ex. 3 in Fig.5) is more complex, and the reader should refer to [Galli 1991] for more details. Essentially, for each group there are two families of task entries in the task BEHAVIOUR. An analysis of the translation for the various b-classes (Fig.7) shows that generic b-classes with a varying number of formal method groups introduce the highest run-time overhead.

The above translation is not essentially dependent on the Ada tasking model, and a similar solution could be worked out for other multi-task systems (e.g. Unix).

4. Conclusion

In our opinion the separate specification of functional aspects and method synchronization constraints (behavioural aspects) is necessary for the orderly construction of large, reusable collections of components. Behavioural inheritance provides a coherent, "divide and conquer" approach. We have investigated a range of abstract notations for expressing behaviour which differ in genericity, degree of reuse, and run-time efficiency; they are all based on deontic logic, a rigorous yet not too cryptical notation which we found suitable for the representative cases we considered.

The proposal needs now to be validated by experience. In particular the cost effectiveness of the deontic notations incorporating guards or method parameters has to be assessed. In fact on one hand it certainly enlarges the range of expressible behaviours, but on the other hand it introduces a tighter coupling with the functional class interface. In the worst case this could defeat the very objective of having reusable abstract behaviours.

Another critical issue to be further investigated is performance of implementation. The generated code attempts to minimize tasking overhead, but this could prove insufficient for large, heavily constrained real-time systems.

Finally we mention a problem to be considered: specification of time constraints.

Aknowledgement

Most of the ideas presented have emerged from joint work on DRAGOON. In particular we thank C.Atkinson, R.Bayan, M.De Michele, C.Destombes, A.Di Maio, S.Goldsack; S.Morasca for the E/R net model, and M.Paci for helpfull suggestions.

5. References

America P. : "POOL-T: A parallel object oriented language", in *Object oriented concurrent programming*, MIT Press, pp. 199-220, 1989

Atkinson C. : "An object-oriented language for software reuse and distribution", *Ph.D. Thesis*, Imperial College, London, 1990.

Campbell, R.H. and Habermann A.N. : "The specification of process syncronisation by path expression," *ACM Computer Survey*,17(4), 1974.

Cardigno C. et al : "Object Oriented Concurrency and Behavioural Inheritance", *Proc. ECOOP'89 Workshop on Object-Based Concurrent Programming*, Nottingham, July,1989.

Di Maio A. et al. : "Dragoon: An Ada-Based Object Oriented Language for Concurrent, Real-Time, Distibuted Systems", *Proc. Ada-Europe Conference*, Madrid 1989.

Galli de' Paratesi G. : "Specifiche di concorrenza per ADA orientato ad oggetti", *Thesis* Dipartimento di Elettronica - Politecnico di Milano(Draft), 1991.

Ghezzi C. et al. : "A unified high level Petri net for time-critical system", *IEEE Transaction on Software Engineering*, February 1991.

Goldsack S.J.,Atkinson C.: "Separating concerns for synchronisation and functionality in an Object-Oriented Language", submitted for publication, 1990.

Von Wright G.H.: "Problems and Prospects of Deontic Logic: A Survey", in *Modern Logic - A Survey: Historical, Philosophical and Mathematical Aspects of Modern Logic and its Applications*, (Agazzi E. ed.), Reidel Publishing Company, 1980.

Inheritance In Object Oriented Z

Elspeth Cusack

British Telecom

St Vincent House

Ipswich IP1 1UX

United Kingdom

Abstract

The Z notation for the formal specification of software and systems is based on set-theory and first-order predicate calculus and is widely used and understood. Recent research has demonstrated that by extending the notation to include the idea of a *class schema* grouping together a state schema and the operation schemas referring to it, an object oriented specification style can be supported.

This paper introduces the concept of inheritance into object oriented Z in two ways. First of all, it defines *derivation*, an incremental inheritance technique for expressing new class schemas in terms of old ones. Secondly, it characterises *subtyping inheritance* as a technique for the hierarchical classification of objects. Thus derivation in Z is a basis for reusing existing specification modules. Subtyping inheritance is the basis for considering the substitutability of one class for another.

1 Introduction

There has been for some time considerable research interest in formalising the object oriented approach, using λ-calculus (for example [4, 6]) or the theory of abstract data types (for example [14]). Recently there have been various attempts to develop object-oriented styles of using pre-existing formal specification languages such as CSP [16, 7], LOTOS [21, 18, 8, 9] and Z [20, 5, 11, 12]. This latter work has been strongly motivated by the need for modelling and specification techniques capable of rigorously describing international standards for large scale open distributed systems [22, 23].

Objects, interpreted as locally-understandable communicating modules of specification, have a natural affinity with distributed systems. Object oriented specification has intuitive appeal, and offers the potential benefits of modularity, flexibility and reusability. (These attributes are as attractive to communication system designers as they are to programmers.) Formal specification in the language of choice provides a fixed notation with implementation-independent semantics, and involves the development of a mathematical model of the system about which we can reason. Formal specification and object orientation seem in short to have complementary strengths, and therefore to be suitable for combination.

This paper contributes to the development of object oriented Z by introducing two inheritance techniques representing different ways of strengthening the 'is-a' relation. The techniques are derivation(section 6), an incremental inheritance technique for expressing new classes in terms of existing ones, and subtyping inheritance (sections 7, 8), a technique for the hierarchical classification of objects according to the substitutability of one class for another. The introduction of inheritance to object oriented Z is made possible by an enrichment of usual typing in Z (sections 4 and 5). Sections 2 and 3 set the scene with background information on object oriented Z and inheritance.

The Z notation has been developed over the past twelve years for the specification of systems and software, and is widely understood and used [1, 15]. Z is based on set-theory and first order predicate logic. Familiarity with the concepts and notation of Z is assumed in this paper, and can be easily acquired from Spivey's book [20].

A style of program development from specifications in languages such as Z is presented in [17].

2 Object oriented Z

A Z specification consists of modules called schemas, which may be linked by an informal commentary. Each schema consist of a declaration part and a predicate (which may be empty) over the declared variables. Schemas describe static aspects such as the states the system can occupy, and the invariant relationships (if any) that are maintained as the system state changes. For example:

$$
\begin{array}{|l}
\hline
\_Invoice _____ \\
\hline
id : IDset;\ state : \{unpaid, paid\} \\
\hline
\end{array}
$$

A binding of a Z schema is an object (an abstraction of an implementation entity) with components named by identifiers corresponding to the variables declared in the schema. Thus a schema determines a set of bindings. In the example, the identifiers *id* and *state* are used to read the value of the corresponding component of each binding of the schema *Invoice*.

Different schemas describe dynamic aspects, such as the operations that can take place, in terms of the relationships between the inputs and outputs and the resultant changes of state. Here is the schema which explains what happens when an invoice is paid:

```
┌─ Pay ─────────────────────────────────────────────────────────────
│ Δ Invoice
│ ─────────────────────
│ id' = id ∧ state = unpaid ∧ state' = paid
└────────────────────────────────────────────────────────────────────
```

The Δ notation is a conventional shorthand which declares two copies of the schema referred to, one with unprimed variables (to express the system state before an operation) and the other with primed variables (to express the system state after an operation).

The central idea introduced in 'Object Z' [5] is a class schema, which groups together a schema describing a state space with the schemas which describe operations on the state space (including possible input and output variables). The data contained in an instance of a class in encapsulated in the sense that it can only be read by use of identifiers declared in the state schema, and can only be changed by the application of a defined operation.

A list of 'inherited classes' and an initial state schema may be included in a class schema. To simplify the presentation, this paper ignores initial state schemas (though they can be included without much extra work [10]). This means that the syntax for a class schema is reduced to:

```
┌─ Class Name ──────────────────────────────────────────────────────
│ inherited classes
│ state schema
│ operation schemas
└────────────────────────────────────────────────────────────────────
```

A precise interpretation of the class defined by a class schema will be given later on. For the moment, we note that the above syntax on its own fails to deal satisfactorily with operations - there is nothing to stop an operation schema being simultaneously inherited from a parent class and redefined. This observation motivates the work reported here, which provides a more expressive syntax together with a semantic interpretation.

The worked examples in [5, 12] show how objects can communicate using a parallel operator to specify the simultaneous occurrence of two operations, with inputs and outputs with the same base name being identified and hidden.

3 Inheritance

It is now clearly understood that the original object oriented concept of inheritance can be 'unbundled' into two separate concepts - *incremental inheritance* and *subtyping inheritance* (see for example [19, 2]). Incremental inheritance is the process of adding 'methods and variables' to an existing class definition to obtain a new class definition. The code for evaluating existing methods remains in the old (parent) class and is accessed by instances of the new (derived) class. This technique is exemplified in the Smalltalk-80 language [13]. It provides a basis for the reuse of the code of the parent class without any guarantee that the newly-derived class will be a specialisation of the parent class. A λ-calculus formalism for incremental inheritance is given in [6].

Subtyping inheritance, on the other hand, is a technique for arranging class definitions in a hierarchy, satisfying the condition that members of the subclass are also members of the superclass. The subclass is independently defined and can be reliably substituted for the superclass in a system description. Subtyping can therefore be regarded as a limited refinement of the superclass, subject to the substitutability condition being met.

A simple set-theoretic model of subtyping inheritance was developed in [7, 8, 9]. Each class (set of instances) C_t is associated with a class type t, an abstract specification of the common features (including behaviour) of the objects in C_t. The set of all class types is endowed with a pre-order $\geq$ (a reflexive and transitive relationship) satisfying $s \geq t$ only if $C_s \subseteq C_t$. In other words, if s is a more specialised or stronger class type than t, then instances of C_s are also instances of C_t. This means that a given object will in general be associated with more than one class type.

4 Comparing state schemas: extending Z typing

Before we can consider inheritance in object oriented Z, we need to enrich the existing typing in Z (see [20]).

Every mathematical expression in a Z specification has either a *basic type* t (that is, it is a member of a given set of the specification) or a *composite type*. There are three kinds of composite type - *set types* $\mathsf{P}\, t$ (describing sets), *cartesian product types* $t_1 \times ... \times t_k$ (describing tuples) and *schema types* $\langle\!\langle p_1 : t_1; ...; p_l : t_l \rangle\!\rangle$ describing bindings.

Sets, tuples and bindings are therefore the abstractions fundamental to Z. But object orientation in Z demands more subtle abstractions:

Definition 1 An *instance* of a state schema is a binding of the schema type which satisfies the schema predicate. □

It is easy to endow a collection of Z types with a pre-order. Let s and t be basic types. We change the Z convention by allowing given sets to intersect, so that an object may have more than one type. Write $s \geq t$ whenever $s \subseteq t$ (regarded as given sets). Write $\mathsf{P}\, s \geq \mathsf{P}\, t$ only if $s \geq t$ and $s \times v \geq t \times u$ only if $s \geq t$ and $v \geq u$. Define $\langle\!\langle q_1 : s_1; ...; q_k : s_k \rangle\!\rangle \geq \langle\!\langle p_1 : t_1; ...; p_l : t_l \rangle\!\rangle$ to mean that $k \geq l$ and $s_i \geq t_i$ for each i between 1 and l.

It follows that if s and t are schema types with $s \geq t$ then there exists a mapping f taking bindings of s to bindings of t. Simply, f discards the 'extra' components of the binding of s, and coerces values of type s to be values of type t. Furthermore, if A and B are state schemas satisfying

- schema type $(B) \geq$ schema type (A), using the pre-order above, where

  schema type $(B) = (\!| \ q_1 : s_1; \ ...; \ q_k : s_k \ |\!)$ and

  schema type $(A) = (\!| \ p_1 : t_1; \ ...; \ p_l : t_l \ |\!)$

- predicate(B)$(q_1, ... q_k) =$ predicate(A)$(q_1, ... q_l) \wedge$ new.predicate$(q_1, ... q_k)$

then f takes instances of B to instances of A. This motivates the next definition:

Definition 2 If A and B are state schemas satisfying

- schema type $(B) \geq$ schema type (A), where schema type $(B) =$

  $(\!| \ q_1 : s_1; \ ...; \ q_k : s_k \ |\!)$ and schema type $(A) = (\!| \ p_1 : t_1; \ ...; \ p_l : t_l \ |\!)$

- predicate(B)$(q_1, ... q_k) =$ predicate(A)$(q_1, ... q_l) \wedge$ new.predicate$(q_1, ... q_k)$

then each instance of B *is-an* instance of A. □

For example, instances of *Late Invoice* can be treated as instances of *Unpaid Invoice* (by embedding of the state space), and in turn instances of *Unpaid Invoice* can be treated as instances of *Invoice* by dropping the variable *days.o/s*:

```
┌─ Invoice ──────────────────────────────────────────────────────
│ id : IDset;  state : {unpaid, paid}
```

```
┌─ Unpaid Invoice ───────────────────────────────────────────────
│ Invoice;  days.o/s : N
├────────────────────────────────────────────────────────────────
│ state = unpaid
```

```
┌─ Late Invoice ─────────────────────────────────────────────────
│ Unpaid invoice
├────────────────────────────────────────────────────────────────
│ days.o/s ≥ 30
```

Note that although we now have a way of comparing state schemas, our expressive power is limited - there is no way of expressing state changes. For example, we cannot describe what happens when an unpaid invoice is paid.

5 Classes and operations

We now formulate a precise definition of the class schemas whose syntax was set out in section 2.

Definition 3 A *class schema* consists of a state schema A together with zero or more operation schemas $O_1, .. O_m$ each referring to ΔA with additional input and output variable declarations, as required. □

The instances described by a class schema are exactly the instances of the state schema A (see Definition 1). But in moving from the state schema on its own to the class schema, we have gained the expressive power to describe operations (corresponding to conventional object oriented 'methods').

From now on, we find it essential to distinguish the name of a class schema from its associated state schema - compare the naming of function-level and object-level modules in FOOPS [14]. Thus, in the following example, *INVOICE* is the name of the class schema whose associated state schema is *Invoice*:

```
┌─ INVOICE ──────────────────────────────────────────
│  ┌─ Invoice ──────────────────────────────────────
│  │ id : IDset; state : {unpaid, paid}
│  └─
│  ┌─ Pay ──────────────────────────────────────────
│  │ ΔInvoice
│  │ ────────────────────────────────────────────────
│  │ id' = id ∧ state = unpaid ∧ state' = paid
│  └─
└─────────────────────────────────────────────────────
```

Definition 4 An *instance* of a class schema is an instance of the associated state schema on which the operations set out in the class schema are defined. □

A class schema is therefore an abstraction of the instances it determines, encompassing both state and behavioural features, and so is a class type in the sense of section 3. This concept of class type completes the enrichment of typing in Z begun in section 4. Class types (that is, class schema names) should be available for use in defining *composite objects*, instances of class schemas whose state schema declarations refer to previously-defined class types, extending the idea of composite types defined in section 4. (See for example the definition of composite objects in FOOPS [14].) Further consideration of composite objects is beyond the scope of this paper.

6 New classes from old: incremental inheritance in Z

In order to discuss inheritance in Z, we need first to introduce some concepts and notation concerning operations. Let X_A denote the state space of a state schema A. Each operation O_j can be represented by a relation $R(O_j)$ between X_A and $X_A \times V_j$, where V_j is the (possibly empty) set in which the output variable takes its value. (Without loss of generality, we can ignore input variables, and assume at most one output variable per operation). Thus $R(O_j) \subseteq X_A \times X_A \times V_j$.

Our suggested notation for an incremental inheritance technique in Z is based on the observation that a class schema *TYPE* whose associated state schema is A, and a state schema B such that each instance of B is-an instance of A in the sense of Definition 2, together uniquely determine a new class schema *DERIVED TYPE*.

The state schema associated with *DERIVED TYPE* is B. As explained in section 4, there therefore exists a mapping $f : X_B \to X_A$ taking instances of state schema B to instances of state schema A. We can use the derived mapping $f \times f \times 1$ to map $X_B \times X_B \times V_j$ into $X_A \times X_A \times V_j$, where 1 denotes the identity mapping on each V_j.

Definition 5 Let *TYPE* be a class schema with associated state schema A and operations $O_1, ..., O_m$ and suppose that B is a state schema such that each instance of B is-an instance of A in the sense of Definition 2. Let f be the mapping taking instances of state schema B to instances of state schema A.

The class schema *DERIVED TYPE* with associated state schema B, and operations $P_1, .., P_m$ defined by $R(P_j)^{f \times f \times 1} = R(O_j) \cap (X_B^f \times X_B^f \times V_j)$ for each j between 1 and m, is said to define a *derived class* of the *parent class TYPE*. Alternatively, *DERIVED TYPE* is said to be *derived from TYPE* by the mapping f. If $R(P_j)^{f \times f \times 1}$ is empty, then the operation P_j is not defined in *DERIVED TYPE*. □

We can now introduce into the schema for *DERIVED TYPE* the notation

    derived from TYPE by $f : X_A \to X_B$

as a shorthand way of listing the derived operations $P_1, .., P_m$.

This description of derivation ensures that the schema associated with each P_j refers to ΔB, as Definition 3 requires. We can specify operations in *DERIVED TYPE* in addition to those inherited from *TYPE*, so long as we choose new names for the schemas.

```
┌─ TYPE ─────────────────────────────────────────────
│  ┌─ A ──────────────────────────────────────────────
│  │ declaration
│  ├──────────────────────────────────────────────────
│  │ predicate(A)
│  └──────────────────────────────────────────────────
│ O₁
│ .
│ .
│ Oₘ
└────────────────────────────────────────────────────
```

```
┌─ DERIVED TYPE ─────────────────────────────────────
│  ┌─ B ──────────────────────────────────────────────
│  │ declaration
│  ├──────────────────────────────────────────────────
│  │ predicate(B) = predicate(A) ∧ new.predicate
│  └──────────────────────────────────────────────────
│ inherits from TYPE by f : X_B → X_A
│ P_{m+1}
│ .
│ .
│ P_n
└────────────────────────────────────────────────────
```

The syntax for *DERIVED TYPE* is therefore essentially the same as the class schema syntax from [5] mentioned in section 2. But we now have a precise understanding of what the syntax means.

Each instance of *DERIVED TYPE* is-an instance of the state schema A (Definition 2) but need not be an instance of the class schema *PARENT TYPE* (Definition 4). Notice that there is nothing to prevent a class inheriting from more than one parent class so long as operations with the same name in each parent class are consistently defined.

In practice, the names used for operations O_j and P_j, for each j, will be the same. The instances defined by *DERIVED TYPE* may be *implemented* independently from those defined by *TYPE*. But the suggested notation makes it quite clear that the inherited operations are *specified* by reference to the parent class. Note that Definition 5 describes *strict* inheritance, since operations in *TYPE* cannot be redefined in *DERIVED TYPE*.

The next example shows how the class schema *UNPAID INVOICE* can be derived from *INVOICE*:

$$
\begin{array}{|l}
\hline
\text{\_\_ UNPAID INVOICE _____}\\
\quad\begin{array}{|l}
\hline
\text{\_\_ UnpaidInvoice _____}\\
\text{Invoice; } days.o/s : \mathsf{N}\\
\hline
state = unpaid\\
\hline
\end{array}\\
\quad \textit{derived from INVOICE by } f : (x, days.o/s) \rightarrow x \textit{ , for } x \in X_{UNPAID\ INVOICE}\\
\quad\begin{array}{|l}
\hline
\text{\_\_ Count _____}\\
\Delta\, Unpaid\ Invoice\\
\hline
id' = id \wedge days.o/s' = days.o/s + 1\\
\hline
\end{array}\\
\hline
\end{array}
$$

An instance of *UNPAID INVOICE* is-an instance of the state schema *Invoice* but not of the class schema *INVOICE*. However, the definition of derivation makes it clear that an unpaid invoice can be paid by severing its connection with the class schema *UNPAID INVOICE* and treating as an instance of the class schema *INVOICE*. 'Type change' of this nature is one of the topics considered further in [10].

7 Comparing operation schemas: extending operations

In order to investigate subtyping inheritance in object oriented Z we need to be able to compare class types. In section 4 we introduced a pre-order on schema types which enabled us to compare state schemas. Since a class schema consists of a state schema and a number of operation schemas, it is therefore necessary to find a corresponding way of comparing operation schemas.

Recall that an operation O on a state space X_A with output values in a set V can be represented by a relation $R(O) \subseteq X_A \times X_A \times V$. $(R(O)$ is a function from X_A to $X_A \times V$ exactly when O is deterministic.) Operations on a state space can therefore be compared by examining the corresponding relations, using the concept of the *domain restriction* of a relation R to a set D, written $D \lhd R$

Definition 6 Let P and Q be relations between sets X and Y. Then Q *extends* P if and only if

- $domP \lhd Q \subseteq P$

- $domP \subseteq domQ$

$\square$

This definition means that Q has weaker preconditions than P (that is, its domain is a superset of P's) and stronger postconditions than P on the domain of P. The definition does not constrain Q on elements of its domain *not* in $domP$. In other words, Q can be interpreted as behaving like a more deterministic version of P on $domP$, but being unconstrained elsewhere. [1]

For example, set $X = Y = \{1,2,3,4\}$, $P = \{(1,1), (2,3)\}$, $R = \{(1,1), (1,2), (2,3)\}$ and $Q = \{(1,1), (2,3), (3,4), (4,4)\}$. Then $domR = \{1,2\} \subseteq \{1,2,3,4\} = domQ$, and $domR \lhd Q = \{(1,1),(2,3)\} \subseteq R$. So Q extends R. On the other hand, $domP = domR$, but R is not a subset of P. So R does not extend P.

8 Specialisation and substitutability: subtyping inheritance in Z

Let T be a class schema with an associated state schema A, and let B be a state schema such that each instance of B is-an instance of A in the sense of Definition 2. As before, there exists a mapping $f : X_B \to X_A$ taking instances of state schema B to instances of state schema A. Let S be a class schema whose associated state schema is B.

Suppose that T has operations $O_1,..,O_m$. Recall from section 3 that we want instances of a subclass to be instances of the superclass. That means that for each j between 1 and m there is a corresponding operation P_j in S. In other words, instances of S can respond to any input value that might be sent to an instance of T, In order to compare P_j with O_j (to ensure that the reponse is correct) we need to be able to embed $R(P_j)$ in $X_A \times X_A \times V_j$.

---

[1] The term 'extension' is borrowed from the theory of testing implementations for conformance to process specifications written in LOTOS [3] or CSP [7]. Recall that the semantics of a CSP process A with alphabet αA is completely determined by its failure set $failures(A)$, a relation between $traces(A)$ and $P\alpha A$ assigning to each trace t of A the refusal sets of A after t. If A and B are CSP processes, then B extends A in the sense of [7] exactly when $failures(B)$ extends $failures(A)$ in the sense of Definition 6.

We know that $R(P_j) \subseteq X_B \times X_B \times W_j$, where the output variable of P_j takes values in a (possibly empty) set W_j. If V_j is empty, we can define a mapping h embedding $X_B \times X_B \times W_j$ in $X_A \times X_A$ by dropping the third component then applying $f \times f$. This corresponds to the assumption that if output is not expected from an instance of T then output produced by the substitute instance of S will be ignored by the rest of the system[2].

If V_j is not empty, we require that W_j is not empty, and that there exists a mapping $g : W_j \to V_j$. This corresponds to the fact that if output *is* expected from an instance of T then the output produced by the substitute instance of S should be something that could have been produced by the instance of T. We then define a mapping h embedding $X_B \times X_B \times W_j$ in $X_A \times X_A \times V_j$ by $h = f \times f \times g$.

Definition 7 Let $TYPE$ be a class schema with associated state schema A and operations $O_1, ..., O_m$ and suppose that B is a state schema such that each instance of B is-an instance of A in the sense of Definition 2. Let f be the mapping taking instances of state schema B to instances of state schema A.

The class schema $SUBTYPE$ with associated state schema B, and operations $P_1, .., P_m$ is a *subtype* of the *supertype* $TYPE$, or equivalently $SUBTYPE$ defines a *subclass* of the *superclass* defined by $TYPE$, if and only if (in the notation introduced above)

- for each j between 1 and m, if V_j is not empty then neither is W_j and there exists a mapping $g : W_j \to V_j$

- for each j, $R(P_j)^h$ extends $X_B^f \lhd R(O_j)$ in the sense of Definition 6, where f is the mapping taking instances of B to instances of A (which must exist) and h is the mapping defined above in terms of f and g

□

Notice that the definition permits additional operations $P_{m+1}, .., P_n$ to be included in class schema S.

Subtyping is easily shown to be a transitive relation on class types. Definition 7 together with Definitions 2 and 4 guarantees that each instance of a subtype is an instance of of each supertype. Thus the definitions presented in this paper realise in object oriented Z the set-theoretic model mentioned in section 3. There is nothing to prevent a class being a subclass of more than one superclass, so long as operations with the same name are consistently defined.

Subtyping can be used to arrange a number of class schemas in a specialisation hierarchy. Since a subclass is described without reference to any superclass, superclasses may be deleted. Subtyping inheritance can therefore be used as a technique for the limited refinement of class descriptions, subject to substitutability being maintained.

---

[2]If this assumption is not valid, then we can simply assume that W_j is empty if V_j is.

In the following example, the required mapping $f : X_{BETTER\ INVOICE} \rightarrow X_{INVOICE}$ simply drops the *goods.received* component of each possible state. Since $R(BetterPay)^k = R(Pay)$, *BETTER INVOICE* is a subtype of *INVOICE* in the sense of Definition 7.

```
┌─ BETTER INVOICE ─────────────────────────────────────────────────────
│  ┌─ Better Invoice ──────────────────────────────────────────────────
│  │ id : IDset;  state : {unpaid, paid};  goods.received : {yes, no}
│  └───────────────────────────────────────────────────────────────────
│  ┌─ Better Pay ──────────────────────────────────────────────────────
│  │ Δ Better Invoice
│  │ letter! : {confirmation, reminder}
│  │ ──────────────────────────────────────────────────────────────────
│  │ id' = id ∧ state = unpaid ∧ state' = paid∧
│  │ (goods.received = yes ∧ letter! = confirmation)
│  │ ∨
│  │ (goods.received = no ∧ letter! = reminder)
│  └───────────────────────────────────────────────────────────────────
└──────────────────────────────────────────────────────────────────────
```

BETTER INVOICE cannot be derived from *INVOICE*, since the operation *Better Pay* does not correspond to *Pay* in *INVOICE* in the required manner. It has an output variable *letter!* whose value cannot be determined by the state schema *INVOICE* and the embedding of the state space of *Better Invoice* in the state space of *Invoice*. Notice that *BETTER INVOICE* could satisfactorily replace *INVOICE* in the definition of *UNPAID INVOICE* in section 6. The consequences for derivation relationships of replacing a type with a subtype need further attention.

Derivation makes no guarantees about subtyping. For example, although it is derived from *INVOICE*, *UNPAID INVOICE* is *not* a subtype of *INVOICE* because the state space of *UNPAID INVOICE* is not closed under the operation *Pay* (and thus the conditions of Definition 7 are not met). These examples establish the independence of derivation and subtyping inheritance. A sequel to this paper extends the definition of subtyping and describes other incremental inheritance techniques for object oriented Z which (unlike derivation) guarantee subtyping subject to certain proof obligations being fulfilled [10].

9 Conclusions

Previous authors have described a natural way of adding a concept of class to the popular formal specification language Z, and demonstrated the usefulness of preparing object oriented Z specifications. This paper has shown that for the price of a simple enrichment to typing in Z, two well defined concepts of inheritance become available to the object oriented Z specifier. Derivation is an incremental inheritance technique by which a new class (the derived class) can be expressed in terms of an existing one (the parent class). Subtyping inheritance can be used for hierarchical classification of objects, or as a technique for the refinement of a class definition (a type) to a subclass definition (a subtype) in a way which guarantees substitutability. The implications for derivation relationships of replacing a type with a subtype, and the definition of composite objects, need further study.

Acknowledgements Michael Lai is thanked for his contribution to the early stages of this work. Steve Rudkin acted as a patient and helpful sounding board as the ideas developed.

References

[1] J-R Abrial, S Schumann and B Meyer, *Specification language*, in R McKeag and A Macnaghten (eds),*On the construction of programs: an advanced course*, Cambridge University Press, 1980

[2] Pierre America, *A behavioural approach to subtyping in object oriented programming languages*, ESPRIT Project 415 Doc No 443, January 1989

[3] Ed Brinksma, Giuseppe Scollo and Chris Steenbergen, *LOTOS specifications, their implementations and their tests*, Proc. Sixth International Symposium on Protocol Specification, Testing and Verification, Montreal, June 1986 (North Holland)

[4] Luca Cardelli and Peter Wegner, *On understanding types, data abstraction and polymorphism*, Computing Surveys 17, December 1985

[5] D Carrington, D Duke, R Duke, P King, G Rose and G Smith, *Object-Z : An object oriented extension to Z*, FORTE89 - International Conference On Formal Description Techniques, Vancouver, December 1989 (North Holland)

[6] William Cook, Jens Palsberg, *A denotational semantics of inheritance and its correctness*, Object Oriented Programming Systems, Languages and Applications 89, New Orleans, October 1989

[7] Elspeth Cusack, *Refinement, conformance and inheritance*, Formal Aspects of Computing Vol 3 No 2, April - June 1991

[8] Elspeth Cusack, Steve Rudkin and Chris Smith, *An object oriented interpretation of LOTOS*, FORTE89 - International Conference On Formal Description Techniques, Vancouver, December 1989 (North Holland)

[9] Elspeth Cusack and Mike Lai, *Object oriented specification in LOTOS and Z or, My cat really is object oriented!*, Workshop on the Foundations of Object Oriented Languages, Noordwijkerhout, The Netherlands, May 1990

[10] Elspeth Cusack, *Object oriented modelling in Z*, February 1991, submitted for publication

[11] David Duke and Roger Duke, *Towards a semantics for Object-Z*, VDM'90: VDM and Z, April 1990

[12] Roger Duke, Gordon Rose and Anthony Lee, *Object oriented protocol specification*, Proc Tenth International Symposium on Protocol Specification, Testing and Verification, Ottawa, June 1990 (North Holland)

[13] A Goldberg and D Robson, *Smalltalk-80:the language and its implementation*, Addison-Wesley (1983) reprinted 1985

[14] Joseph A Goguen and Jose Meseguer, *Unifying functional, object-oriented and relational programming with logical semantics* in *Research Directions In Object Oriented Programming*, Bruce Shriver and Peter Wegner (editors), MIT Press, 1987

[15] Ian Hayes (ed), *Specification Case Studies*, Prentice-Hall International Series in Computer Science, 1987

[16] C A R Hoare, *Communicating Sequential Processes*, Prentice-Hall International Series in Computer Science, 1985

[17] Carroll Morgan, *Programming from specifications*, Prentice Hall International Series in Computer Science, 1990

[18] T Mayr, *Specification of object-oriented systems in LOTOS*, International Conference on Formal Description Techniques - FORTE88, Stirling, September 1988 (North Holland)

[19] Peter Wegner and Stanley Zdonik, *Inheritance as an incremental modification technique, or what like is and isn't like*, European Conference on Object Oriented Programming, Norway, August 1988

[20] J M Spivey, *The Z Notation: A Reference Manual*, Prentice-Hall International Series in Computer Science, 1989

[21] ISO IS 8807, *LOTOS - a formal description technique based on the temporal ordering of observational behaviour*, 1989

[22] ISO JTC1 SC21 WG7 N315 *Basic Reference Model for Open Distributed Processing*, Draft Working Document, December 1990

[23] ISO JTC1 SC21 WG7 N314, *Architectural semantics, specification techniques and formalisms*, Draft Working Document, December 1990

OOZE: An Object Oriented Z Environment

Antonio J. Alencar

Programming Research Group
University of Oxford
11 Keble Road
Oxford OX1 3QD, UK
E-mail: alencar@prg.ox.ac.uk
Tel: +44 (865) 273 869
FAX: +44 (865) 273 839

Joseph A. Goguen

Programming Research Group
University of Oxford
11 Keble Road
Oxford OX1 3QD, UK
E-mail: goguen@prg.ox.ac.uk
Tel: +44 (865) 272 567
FAX: +44 (865) 273 839

OOZE, which stands for "Object Oriented Z Environment," is a generalized wide spectrum object oriented language that builds on the notation and style of Z. OOZE supports requirements, specifications, interpretable programs, and compilable programs. The OOZE system is based on OBJ3, and provides rapid prototyping and theorem proving facilities over a module database. OOZE modules can be generic, can be organized hierarchically, and can be used for structuring and reusing requirements, specifications, or code. Modules can be linked by views, which assert relationships of refinement. Module interfaces can be precisely specified using theories. Abstract data types, multiple inheritance, complex objects, overloading and dynamic binding are supported. Data types, objects, classes and modules are clearly distinguished from one another, and the entire language has a precise and relatively simple semantics based on order sorted, hidden sorted algebra.

Key Words: Object Orientated, Specification, Requirement, Rapid Prototyping, Algebraic Semantics, Z.

1 Introduction

OOZE, which stands for "Object Oriented Z Environment," is primarily intended for the requirement and specification phases of the system life cycle. It uses the graphical notation and comment convention of Z, formalizes its style, and adapts it to fit the object oriented paradigm, allowing declarations for *classes*, *attributes* and *methods* within modules. Attributes can be class-valued, i.e., *complex objects* are supported. Also, unlike other object oriented adaptations of Z, *objects* (which are instances) are carefully distinguished from *class declarations* (which serve as templates for objects). Objects are also organized into *meta-classes*, for ease of identification and iteration. Multiple inheritance is supported for both classes and modules. Abstract data types, overloading, and exception handling are also supported. OOZE has an interpretable sublanguage that can be used for rapid prototyping, and a compilable sublanguage that can be used for implementation. All of this has a precise semantics that is based upon order sorted algebra.

Formal methods emerged in the mid-seventies as an attempt to add mathematical rigour to the development of computer systems. It is claimed that their use can significantly increase quality by permitting accurate design at a high level of abstraction. Consequently, design errors can be reduced and confidence in the system behaviour increased. Formal specifications can also provide a reliable basis for documentation, implementation and maintenance.

Despite these attractive properties, formal methods have the reputation of being hard to use, because a reasonable understanding of computer science and discrete mathematics is required, and unfortunately, the average computer professional seems not to meet this requirement. Also, communication with clients can be difficult, because they may not easily understand the syntax and semantics of formal specification languages. Moreover, the time spent on design may increase, and it is not obvious that the extra cost is returned in all cases[1].

The present work describes a programming environment that can take advantage of the attractive properties of formal methods while reducing the burden associated with their use. This environment includes not just a syntax and type checker, but also an interpreter for an executable sublanguage, a theorem prover, and a module database; all of this is based on facilities provided by the OBJ3 [14] system. OOZE can be considered a syntactic variant of FOOPS [11], and indeed, it has the same semantics as FOOPS. However, OOZE is intended to be used in a different way by a different constituency, and it has a very different appearance. Thus, although OOZE looks and acts like a model-based language, it actually has a relatively simple equational semantics. However, unlike most other equational languages, OOZE supports the encapsulation of states, and more generally, is truly object oriented.

By providing animation facilities for rapid prototyping, OOZE helps to improve communication with the client, and makes it easier to master its mathematical basis. As a result, OOZE should reduce the time and cost of formal methods, and also increase confidence in correctness. OOZE can also help with subsequent phases of system development, including design, coding and maintenance.

2 Z

Z is a model-based specification language that has been primarily developed in the Programming Research Group at the Oxford University Computing Laboratory [18, 25], and has been widely used in industry. Z is based on set theory and the first-order predicate calculus, and has been successfully used for applications to distributed computing, transaction processing, operating systems, large information systems, etc. The heart of Z is its use of schemas to describe state spaces and state-changing operations. Schemas are the basis for the incremental presentation of Z specifications. They encourage structuring, and are syntactically integrated with informal prose, to help the reader understand what has been specified. Schemas also provide a graphically elegant way of delimiting the parts of a specification.

Although modularity is widely recognized as helpful in all phases of software development, Z provides only rather weak modularity. Z specifications do not have clearly delimited beginnings or ends, cannot be made generic or instantiated, and lack the ability to import and export. Schemas are not modules, because they do not hide information, and they have no natural meaning that is independent of context. Also, schema scope conventions are subtle, and can cause complex specifications to be misinterpreted. Therefore Z specifications can be hard to read and maintain, and their parts can be hard to reuse in new developments; see [22, 6] for related discussion.

A Z specification of a large and complex system may contain many state and operation schemas, which can be dispersed arbitrarily through the specification, because schemas do not enforce any association of operations with states. All state space schemas and operation schemas are global within the specification, i.e., they can be used in any other state space or operation schema. Therefore the

---

[1]See [4] for a discussion of the pros and cons of using formal methods.

dependency relations that exist between schemas can only be determined by examining all schemas in a specification. In addition, the schema calculus [25] allows schemas to be combined in a large variety of ways, some of which seem quite unnatural, especially from a logical point of view. Thus, understanding and updating specifications can be very hard in some cases.

The best ideas of Z are in its style. These ideas include its comment conventions, its graphical layout, its use of ordinary set theoretic and logical notation, its conventions for decorating input and output variables, and some uses of schemas.

3 OOZE

OOZE formalizes and enforces these attractive ideas, and combines them with other good ideas in software engineering, such as object orientation, modularization and algebraic semantics, yielding an environment that strongly supports reusability and the subordination of complexity. A summary of differences from Z appears in Section 7.

While numbers and other data elements do not change, objects have attributes that may change. For example, the natural number 7 is fixed and eternal; it does not change. But the amount of money in one's bank account may vary with time. Failure to make this distinction can cause confusions with undesirable practical consequences. For example, in Smalltalk72 [16], addition is not commutative; e.g., $2 + 2.0$ is 4 whereas $2.0 + 2$ is 4.0, because in each case the second number is sent as a message to the first, and so a different addition method is used.

3.1 Objects

By convention, a Z schema with non-decorated variables represents the state space of some system component, and is followed by another schema defining the initial values for those variables, and by other schemas that define operations on these variables. But these conventions are not enforced, and it is very easy to write specifications that violate them.

OOZE groups the state space schema, the initial state schema and operation schemas into a single unit[2]. Only the operations defined in the unit are allowed to act upon the objects of that class. Syntactically, such a unit is an open-sided named box in which the features of the class are defined, with the following general form,

```
┌─ class-name < ancestor-names ──────────────────────────────
│   constants
│   ┌─ State ───────────────────────────────────────────────
│   │   class attributes
│   │   ───────────────
│   │   class invariant
│   │
│   ┌─ Init ────────────────────────────────────────────────
│   │   initial values
│
│   methods
└────────────────────────────────────────────────────────────
```

where class-name is the name of the class. The symbol < indicates that the class being defined is a subclass of one or more previously defined classes, named in ancestor-names. The constants are fixed values which cannot be changed by any method, and are the same for all instances of the class. The

---

[2]This structure is similar to that used in Object-Z [6], but its semantics is quite different.

class attributes are variables that can take values either in another class or in a data type. The class invariant is a predicate that constrains the values that the attributes can take; it must hold for all objects of the class, before and after the execution of methods and in the initial state. *Init* gives the initial values that attributes take. methods are given in schemas that define operations involving one or more attributes of the same class, and possibly input or output variables; these define the relationship between the state of an object before and after the execution of a method. (Differences between the syntax and semantics of schemas in OOZE and Z are discussed in Section 3.8).

3.2 Encapsulation of Classes in Modules

To build a large system, we must overcome the difficulties of manipulating huge amounts of information. Explicit mechanisms for modularization are needed to support this in a natural way, allowing the system to be defined in small separate pieces that are easy to read and manage, and that can be easily combined [8]. Indeed, such mechanisms may significantly reduce the cost associated with system development, and are becoming common not only in languages for programming, but also in languages for prototyping and specification. There is no widely accepted agreement on an ideal mechanism, and several interesting alternatives have been proposed, including Clear [3], OBJ [14], Ada [1], SML [17], and the extension of VDM proposed by Bear [2].

In OOZE, classes of objects are encapsulated in modules, which can be generic and can contain any number of classes:

```
┌─ module-name[parameters] ─────────────────────────────────────────────
│   ┌─ Importing ──────────────────────────────────────────────────────
│   │ imported-modules
│   └──────────────────────────────────────────────────────────────────
│
│   ┌─ Class class-name₀ ──────────────────────────────────────────────
│   │ ⋮
│   └──────────────────────────────────────────────────────────────────
│
│   ⋮
│
│   ┌─ Class class-nameₙ ──────────────────────────────────────────────
│   │ ⋮
│   └──────────────────────────────────────────────────────────────────
└────────────────────────────────────────────────────────────────────────
```

Here module-name names the module; parameters is a list of formal names with their corresponding requirements on the actual parameters that instantiate the module; imported-modules lists the imported modules, and class-name$_0$, ..., class-name$_n$ are the classes defined in the module. Note the clear distinction between module importation and class inheritance. The former has to do with the scope of declarations; for example, a class cannot be used unless the module that declares it is imported. Note that module importation is *transitive*, so that if A imports B and B imports C, then everything in C is also available in A. See [8, 9] for more detailed discussions of the module concepts used in OOZE, including importation and genericity; they are evolved from those introduced in Clear [3] and implemented in OBJ [14], and are given a precise semantics using the theory of institutions.

In many object oriented languages, including Eiffel [20], Smalltalk [21] and Object-Z [6], modules and classes are identified, so that only one class can be encapsulated. Because of this, cases where several classes have interdependent representations are not easily captured. For example, consider a class Private-Teachers and a class Independent-Students, where each class has only one attribute, with a value involving the other class: teachers keep a list of their students, and students keep a list of their teachers. Because these two classes are interdependent, it is impossible to determine which should be defined first. If no order is established, then the object hierarchy is not properly enforced. A straightforward solution is to introduce both classes in one module. In OOZE, data, objects, classes and modules are distinct entities, carefully distinguished both syntactically and semantically. (This discussion follows [15]).

When encapsulating classes in modules, it is not rare to end up with modules with just one class. Moreover, the module and the class usually have the same name. As a result, for the sake of simplicity and conciseness, the class name and enclosing box for its space state and methods can be omitted in OOZE, as in Section 3.1.

3.2.1 Arrays

Consider the following code for arrays of real numbers[3]:

```
┌─ Array ──────────────────────────────────────────────────────
│  ┌─ State ──────────────────────────────────────────────────
│  │  array : Z ⇸ R [hidden]
│  │  lower_bound : Z
│  │  upper_bound : Z
│  └──────────────────────────────────────────────────────────
│  ┌─ Init ───────────────────────────────────────────────────
│  │  b₁?, b₂? : Z
│  │  ──────────────────────────────────────────────────────
│  │  ∀ j : min{b₁?, b₂?} .. max{b₁?, b₂?} • array' j = 0
│  │  lower_bound' = min{b₁?, b₂?}
│  │  upper_bound' = max{b₁?, b₂?}
│  └──────────────────────────────────────────────────────────
│  ┌─ Store ──────────────────────────────────────────────────
│  │  Δarray
│  │  j? : lower_bound .. upper_bound
│  │  z? : R
│  │  ──────────────────────────────────────────────────────
│  │  array' = array ⊕ {j? ↦ z?}
│  └──────────────────────────────────────────────────────────
│  ┌─ Get ────────────────────────────────────────────────────
│  │  j? : lower_bound ..upper_bound
│  │  z! : R
│  │  ──────────────────────────────────────────────────────
│  │  z! = array j?
│  └──────────────────────────────────────────────────────────
│  ┌─ Max_of ─────────────────────────────────────────────────
│  │  z! : R
│  │  ──────────────────────────────────────────────────────
│  │  z! = max(ran array)
│  └──────────────────────────────────────────────────────────
└──────────────────────────────────────────────────────────────
```

Following the notation of Z, we let Z, R and N denote the integers, reals and naturals respectively. Also, $f : A \nrightarrow B$ indicates that f is a finite partial function from A to B, while "ran f" denotes the range of f, and $x..y$ denotes the interval $\{n \mid x \leq n \leq y\}$. Finally, $f \oplus \{a \mapsto b\}$ denotes the partial function equal to f except that it takes value b on argument a. The notation "$\forall x : X \bullet ...$" for quantification over a variable x of sort X also comes from Z.

---

[3]The functions max and min are built in.

Arrays have attributes *array*, *lower_bound* and *upper_bound*. The *array* attribute is *hidden*, i.e., it is an internal state that is not visible outside the current module. This class does not inherit from any others, and it has no invariant. Only the methods *Init*, *Store*, *Get* and *Max_of* can be used on Arrays; these respectively create an array, store a value in an array, retrieve a stored value, and return the maximum value in an array.

Values of attributes before method application are indicated by undashed variables, and by dashed (') variables afterwards. Method inputs are indicated by variables with an interrogation mark (?), and outputs by variables with an exclamation mark (!). Δ heads a list of attributes whose values may be changed by the method; attributes absent from the list are unchanged, i.e., the dashed attribute value equals the undashed one. The absence of a Δ list means that no attribute value can be changed by the method[4]. Unlike Z, these are not mere conventions; they are part of the definition of OOZE, and are enforced by the implementation.

3.3 Parameters and Theories

It can be very useful to define precisely the properties that the actual parameters to a parameterized module must satisfy in order for it to work correctly; in OOZE these properties are given in a *theory*; theories are a second kind of module in OOZE, with the same syntactic form. In particular, theories can be parameterized and can use and inherit other modules. A theory is introduced in an open-sided box, and its name is preceded by the key word <u>*Theory*</u>.

Theories declare properties and provide a convenient way to document module interfaces. Understandability and correctness for reusability are improved by this feature. For example, the following theory requires that an actual parameter provide a totally ordered set with a given element:

```
┌─ Theory TotalOrder ─────────────────────────────────────────────────
│  [X]
│  v : X
│  ┌───────────────────────────
│  │  _ ⊏ _ : X ↔ X
│  ├──────────────────────────
│  │  ∀ x, y, z : X •
│  │      ¬ (x ⊏ x)
│  │      (x ⊏ y) ∧ (y ⊏ z) ⇒ (x ⊏ z)
│  │      (x ⊏ y) ∨ (x = y) ∨ (y ⊏ x)
│
└─────────────────────────────────────────────────────────────────────
```

Here the notation $[X]$ indicates that X is a set newly introduced for this specification.

The formal parameters of an OOZE module are given after its name in a list, along with the requirements that they must satisfy. The actual parameters of generic modules are not sets, constants and functions, but rather modules. The motivation for this is that the items that naturally occur in modules are usually closely related, so that it is natural to consider them together rather than separately. Moreover, by allowing parameters to be modules, OOZE incorporates the powerful mechanisms of parameterized programming [8]. In the syntax below, $P_0, P_1, \cdots, P_n$ are the formal module names, while $T_0, T_1, \cdots, T_n$ are theory names:

```
┌─ module-name[P_0 :: T_0, P_1 :: T_1, ⋯, P_n :: T_n] ─────────────────
│  ⋮
│  ⋮
└─────────────────────────────────────────────────────────────────────
```

---

[4] *Init* is an exception to this rule; its signature has no Δ list, and only dashed variables are available.

3.3.1 A Parameterized Array Module

The following parameterized version *NewArray* of *Array* is much more flexible, in that it can be instantiated to define arrays with different types and ranges:

```
┌─ NewArray[P :: TotalOrder] ──────────────────────────────────────────────
│  ┌─ State ──────────────────────────────────────────────────────────────
│  │  array : Z ⇸ X [hidden]
│  │  lower_bound : Z
│  │  upper_bound : Z
│  │  ──────────────────────────────────────────
│  │  Max : F₁ X → X
│  │  ∀ S : F₁ X; x, y : S •
│  │      Max(S) = x ⇔ y ⊑ x ∨ y = x
│  ┌─ Init ───────────────────────────────────────────────────────────────
│  │  b₁?, b₂? : Z
│  │  ──────────────────────────────────────────
│  │  ∀ j : min{b₁?, b₂?} .. max{b₁?, b₂?} • array' j = v
│  │  lower_bound = min{b₁?, b₂?}
│  │  upper_bound = max{b₁?, b₂?}
│  ┌─ Store ──────────────────────────────────────────────────────────────
│  │  Δarray
│  │  j? : lower_bound .. upper_bound
│  │  x? : X
│  │  ──────────────────────────────────────────
│  │  array' = array ⊕ {j? ↦ x?}
│  ┌─ Get ────────────────────────────────────────────────────────────────
│  │  j? : lower_bound .. upper_bound
│  │  x! : X
│  │  ──────────────────────────────────────────
│  │  x! = array j?
│  ┌─ Max_of ─────────────────────────────────────────────────────────────
│  │  x! : X
│  │  ──────────────────────────────────────────
│  │  x! = Max(ran array)
└──────────────────────────────────────────────────────────────────────────
```

Here $F_1 X$ denotes the set of all non-empty finite subsets of X, and $Max(\{a_o, a_1, \cdots, a_n\})$ denotes the maximum element of a non-empty totally ordered finite set.

3.4 Views for Parameterized Modules

A view can be used to say how a given module satisfies a given theory. A view is a mapping from the features (sets, methods, functions, constants, etc.) of the source module to the features of the target module, preserving subtype relations and the rank of methods and functions. Views are needed because an actual parameter may satisfy a given theory in more than one way. For example, the set of natural numbers is totally ordered with the relation $<$ or with $>$; these correspond to two distinct views. Views that are used for instantiating parameterized modules have the following general form,

$$M\{t_0 \mapsto m_0, t_1 \mapsto m_1, \cdots, t_n \mapsto m_n\},$$

in which M is the name of the parameterized module, while $t_0, t_1, \cdots, t_n$ are names of features in the source theory, and $m_0, m_1, \cdots, m_n$ are names of features in M.

Data types in OOZE are defined in modules similar to those used for classes, but they have initial order sorted algebra semantics[5]. For example, the module *Nat* gives the natural numbers, with the carrier N. Using the *NewArray* class and a view, we can get a class of arrays of natural numbers, with an operation that returns the maximum element, as follows:

$$NewArray\,[\;Nat\;\{X \mapsto N, v \mapsto 0, \sqsubset\, \mapsto\, <\,\}\,]$$

Because we already know that *TotalOrder* is the source theory for this view, its name is not needed. It is common to use an "obvious" view, and then it can be distracting to have to present it in detail. Some conventions for simplifying views ease this problem. For example, any pair of the form $S \mapsto S$ can be omitted[6].

3.5   Applying Methods

A basic principle of object oriented programming is that only the methods defined with a class may directly act upon its objects. Because attributes, method inputs and method outputs can be object valued, methods defined in other classes may be needed to define methods that manipulate the attributes of such complex objects. In OOZE, the following syntax indicates that a certain method acts on a certain object,

object.method($p_0, p_1, \cdots, p_n$)

where object is an object name, method is the name of a method on the class to which object belongs, and $p_0, p_1, \cdots, p_n$ are parameters whose types must agree with those of the corresponding formal parameters. Actual parameters are associated with formal parameters according to the order in which the latter are declared. For example, see the methods *Store* and *Get* in the *Matrix* class in Section 3.7 below. The method *Init* is an exception, because it acts on no objects, and its syntax is simplified to the form *Init*($p_0, p_1, \cdots, p_n$).

To actually create the object A of class *NewArray* from its "template" in the *NewArray* module, it is necessary to first instantiate the module with an actual value for P, say the natural numbers with 0 and $<$, yielding a *NewArrayNat* class, and then to apply the built in method *Init* with values for the parameters *lower_bound* and *upper_bound*,

A.*Init*(1, 10).

OOZE provides a selection function for each visible attribute of a class, indicated by a dot before the attribute name. So if A is the above object of the *NewArrayNat* class, then A.*upper_bound* yields the value 10 for the *upper_bound* of that specific array.

3.6   Overloading

OOZE has a strong but flexible type system. Strong typing is not only useful to catch meaningless expressions, but it also favours the separation of logically and intuitively distinct concepts (such as matrices and arrays) and enhances readability and reusability by documenting such distinctions. Moreover, strong typing supports *overloading*, i.e., attaching more than one meaning to a name. In particular, overloading allows simpler code, because the context can determine which possibility is intended.

---

[5]The semantics of data types is discussed in Section 6. Many data types including naturals, integers, reals, sequences, and tuples are built in, and can be used anywhere.

[6]Views in OOZE are derived from the OBJ3 [14] implementation of the ideas introduced in Clear [3]; see [8] for further discussion.

Overloaded attributes and methods of a class can be distinguished by the type required in a given context. For example, overloading resolution applies to the methods *Store*, *Get*, *Init* and *Max_of* in the Matrix class below.

3.7 Object-Valued Attributes

We illustrate complex objects using a class *Matrix* with an attribute that takes values in the *NewArray* class. Inheritance applies to all kinds of modules in OOZE and the effect is simply that the descendent module inherits all features of its parents. For example the module *Matrix* below inherits the module *NewArray*:

Matrix[P :: TotalOrder]

> **Importing**
> > NewArray[P]
>
> **State**
> > $matrix : \mathbb{Z} \nrightarrow NewArray$ [hidden]
> > $lower\_bound : \mathbb{Z}$
> > $upper\_bound : \mathbb{Z}$
>
> **Init**
> > $mb_1?, mb_2? : \mathbb{Z}$
> > $ab_1?, ab_2? : \mathbb{Z}$
> >
> > $\forall j : \min\{mb_1?, mb_2?\} .. \max\{mb_1?, mb_2?\} \bullet matrix' \, j = Init(ab_1?, ab_2?)$
> > $lower\_bound = \min\{mb_1?, mb_2?\}$
> > $upper\_bound = \max\{mb_1?, mb_2?\}$
>
> **Store**
> > $\Delta matrix$
> > $i? : lower\_bound..upper\_bound$
> > $j? : (matrix \, i?) \bullet lower\_bound .. (matrix \, i?) \bullet upper\_bound$
> > $x? : X$
> >
> > $matrix' = matrix \oplus \{i? \mapsto (matrix \, i?) \bullet Store(j?, x?)\}$
>
> **Get**
> > $i? : lower\_bound .. upper\_bound$
> > $j? : (matrix \, i?) \bullet lower\_bound .. (matrix \, i?) \bullet upper\_bound$
> > $x! : X$
> >
> > $x! = (matrix \, i?) \bullet Get(j?)$
>
> **Max_of**
> > $i? : lower\_bound .. upper\_bound$
> > $x! : X$
> >
> > $x! = (matrix \, i?) \bullet Max\_of$

3.8 Method Schemas

In both OOZE and Z, schemas are used to define some key aspects of systems, but OOZE schema syntax and semantics have been designed to enhance readability without loss of expressiveness.

In OOZE, the values of variables before and after method application are related by conditional equations. The *if* clause can be considered a pre-condition. The respective equations are required to hold if the condition, expressed by a predicate, is *true*. If the *if* clause is omitted, then the equations must hold in any circumstance. Method schemas have the following general form:

```
┌─schema_name─────────────────────────────────────────────
│   declarations
│ ─────────────────────────────────────────────────────────
│   equations
│   if predicate
│ ─────────────────────────────────────────────────────────
│   equations
│   if predicate
│ ─────────────────────────────────────────────────────────
│   ⋮
└───────────────────────────────────────────────────────────
```

In the *RegularAccount* class in Section 3.9.1 below, conditional equations say that after the *Debit* operation, the values of the attributes *bal* and *hist* are changed if the value of *bal* is greater than or equal to $m?$. On the other hand, the *Credit* method changes the value of *bal* and *hist* in any circumstance, because there is no *if* clause.

In OOZE, exceptional and non-exceptional behaviour for methods are defined in distinct schemas having the same name, with the exception schema name preceded by the key word *Error*. Moreover, the input variables appearing in the error schema must be among those appearing in the non-error schema. By this device, users need not understand both situations at once. Therefore code is simplified, readability is enhanced, and complexity is subordinated. The *Debit* method for the *RegularAccount* class illustrates this feature.

If the object that a method is supposed to act upon is omitted, then the method being used and the method being defined are regarded as sharing the same object, as in the *Interest* method in the *SavingsAccount* class below.

3.9 Class Inheritance

OOZE supports multiple inheritance for classes. When one class inherits from another, the attributes defined in the ancestor are added to those of the descendent. If the descendent class declares no attributes, it is assumed that ancestor and descendent have the same attributes. Class invariants defined in ancestors must hold in the descendant, and may also be strengthened. Initial values defined in the descendent take precedence over those of ancestors. All this is illustrated by the *SavingsAccount < RegularAccount* declaration below.

3.9.1 Bank Accounts

The *BankAccount* module to follow is parameterized, with parameter requirements defined by the *DateMoneyAndRate* theory below. Note that R_0^+ denotes the positive real numbers union $\{0\}$.

```
┌─Theory DateMoneyAndRate───────────────────────────────────
│   [DATE, MONEY, RATE]
│   MONEY ⊂ R_0^+
│   RATE ⊂ R_0^+
│   ∀ m : MONEY • ⌊100 * m⌋ = 100 * m
└───────────────────────────────────────────────────────────
```

Every object of the *RegularAccount* class has a balance and a history which records credit and debit transactions; these appear in the attributes *bal* and *hist*. *today* is a built in function that returns the current date. As in Z, $^\frown$ denotes sequence concatenation, and $\langle(a,b)\rangle$ is the singleton sequence consisting of the ordered pair (a, b).

```
_ BankAccount[P :: DateMoneyAndRate] _____

   _ Class RegularAccount _____

      _ State _____
      bal : MONEY
      hist : seq DATE × MONEY

      _ Init _____
      bal' = 0
      hist' = ⟨today, 0⟩

      _ Credit _____
      Δ bal, hist
      m? : MONEY
      _____
      bal' = bal + m?
      hist' = hist ⁀ ⟨(today, m?)⟩

      _ Debit _____
      Δ bal, hist
      m? : MONEY
      _____
      bal' = bal − m?
      hist' = hist ⁀ ⟨(today, −m?)⟩
      if bal ≥ m?

      _ Error Debit _____
      m? : MONEY
      error! : Report
      _____
      error! = Overdrawn
      if bal < m?

   _ Class SavingsAccount < RegularAccount _____

      _ State _____
      rate : RATE

      _ Interest _____
      Δ bal, hist
      _____
      bal' = Credit(rate * bal)·bal
      hist' = Credit(rate * bal)·hist
```

Note that because there is no *Init* method for *SavingsAccount*, the *Init* method for its superclass *RegularAccount* will be used; however, a value must be given for the attribute *rate* whenever a new

SavingsAccount is created, because there is no default value. The parameterized module *BankAccount* can be instantiated with *DateMoneyAndRate* modules to yield banks operating under various conventions for currency and date. Also, using a notational short cut, the specification of the method *Interest* could have been simplified to *Interest* $\equiv$ *Credit*(*bal* $*$ *rate*).

3.10 Animation

In order for an OOZE module to be executable, its axioms must have a special form,

$$
\boxed{
\begin{array}{l}
m \\
\hline
\Delta L \\
p_1 : T_1 \\
\vdots \\
p_n : T_n \\
\hline
a_1' = e_1 \\
a_2' = e_2 \\
\vdots \\
\underline{if}\ P
\end{array}
}
$$

where $a_1, a_2, \ldots$ are attributes changed by the method m and listed in L, where $p_1, \ldots, p_n$ are parameters of m with types $T_1, \ldots, T_n$, where $e_1, e_2, \ldots$ are expressions in $p_1, \ldots, p_n$ and the state of the object, including $a_1, a_2, \ldots$, and where P is a predicate in the same variables. The *if* clause is optional, and there could even be more than one such clause, each giving a set of conditional equations. These equations have a declarative interpretation, and in fact are referentially transparent. They define a method by its effects on attributes. Alternatively, methods can be defined as compositions of other already defined methods. The operations for composing methods include sequential and parallel composition.

Animation is useful for rapid prototyping during the requirement and early specification phases. If the attributes associative or commutative are used for any operation, then the resulting program cannot be compiled, but only interpreted (Section 5 contains an example using the attribute associative). Also, some forms of abstract data type definitions can only be interpreted.

4 Requirements

Usually the process of building a system starts from some very high level requirements. In this initial stage, it is quite common that attributes and methods are not completely determined, and so these initial definitions are satisfied by a large class of models, some of which may not fit the client's expectations; also, animation cannot in general be provided at this early stage. For example, the initial requirements for a bank might simply say that it should be possible to debit and credit accounts, and that these methods should respectively decrease and increase the balance. One can easily imagine models of this theory that are not among those really intended by the bankers, such as a deposit method that always increases the balance by one million currency units.

OOZE uses theories to express requirements, and also for the initial stages of specification. In many typical applications, an OOZE text will evolve until theories are only used to specify properties that parameters should satisfy (however, theories can also be retained to document the earlier stages of the development cycle). At this point, it is possible to use the specification itself as a rapid prototype. Let us consider the following theory of bank accounts[7]:

```
┌─ Theory LooseAccount ────────────────────────────────────────────
│
│   [DATE,MONEY]
│
│   MONEY ⊂ R₀⁺
│   ┌─ State ──────────────────────────────────────────────────────
│   │ bal : MONEY
│   │ hist : seq DATE × MONEY
│   │            #hist
│   │ bal =      ∑    second(hist(i))
│   │           i=1
│   ┌─ Init ───────────────────────────────────────────────────────
│   │ bal' = 0
│   │ hist' = ⟨today, 0⟩
│   ┌─ Credit ─────────────────────────────────────────────────────
│   │ Δ bal, hist
│   │ m? : MONEY
│   │ bal' ≥ bal
│   ┌─ Debit ──────────────────────────────────────────────────────
│   │ Δ bal, hist
│   │ m? : MONEY
│   │ bal' ≤ bal
│
└──────────────────────────────────────────────────────────────────
```

The theory box contains the following formal specification:

$MONEY \subset R_0^+$

State

$bal : MONEY$

$hist : seq\ DATE \times MONEY$

$$bal = \sum_{i=1}^{\#hist} second(hist(i))$$

Init

$bal' = 0$

$hist' = \langle today, 0 \rangle$

Credit

$\Delta\ bal, hist$

$m? : MONEY$

$bal' \geq bal$

Debit

$\Delta\ bal, hist$

$m? : MONEY$

$bal' \leq bal$

Although the attributes *bal* and *hist* are related by a state invariant, their value after the execution of the methods *Debit* and *Credit* is not completely determined. For example it is possible to credit or debit more money to an account than the argument indicates, and it is also possible to put arbitrary values in the history.

When creating large systems, it is important to relate the different stages of the development process. For example, the *BankAccount* module in Section 3.9.1 satisfies the requirements of the *LooseAccount* theory, and it might represent a more recent stage in the evolution of the same system. In OOZE, this satisfaction relationship is described by a view. Although views were previously used to describe how an actual parameter satisfies a theory, they can also express refinement relationships between any kind of module. However, in this context a more comprehensive notation is needed. The view *Account* that follows asserts how the class *RegularAccount* described in the module *BankAccounts* satisfies the theory *LooseAccount*[8]:

---

[7]The function *second* extracts the second component of a pair [25].

[8]Note that according with the conventions established in Section 3.2, the theory *LooseAccount* encapsulates the description of a class also named *LooseAccount*.

```
┌─ View Account ──────────────────────────────────────────────────────
│   LooseAccount → BankAccount
│  ──────────────────
│
│   [MONEY ↦ MONEY, DATE ↦ DATE]
│  ┌─ Class ──────────────────────────────────────────────────────────
│  │   LooseAccount ↦ RegularAccount
│  ├─ Attributes ─────────────────────────────────────────────────────
│  │   bal ↦ bal, hist ↦ hist
│  ├─ Methods ────────────────────────────────────────────────────────
│  │   Credit ↦ Credit, Debit ↦ Debit
└──────────────────────────────────────────────────────────────────────
```

OOZE texts are hierarchically organized into modules, and a complete OOZE system can be encapsulated in one final module. This allows the use of views to express satisfaction (i.e., refinement) relations between different levels of development of the same system. Views between such conglomerates can also be constructed from individual views between component modules. This makes it possible to build views between conglomerates by combining views between their components which are easier to understand and modify. In this way, each phase of the software life cycle can be precisely and quickly documented. Multiple implementations of a single specification or requirement can also be accommodated within a single OOZE text, encapsulated then in different modules.

5   Data Types

OOZE provides a large library of basic "built in" data types, intended to be rich enough for the vast majority of applications. For the most part, these are modelled after Z. However, it is important to provide a way for defining new data types in case those available in the library do not fit current needs. Data types in OOZE are defined in open-sided boxes in which the module name is preceded by the key word *Data*. Data modules can be parameterized and can import other data types. For example, consider the following definition of the parameterized data type *Seq* that defines sequences along with some of their basic operations; its parameter requirement is defined by the *Triv* theory below.

```
┌─ Theory Triv ───────────────────────────────────────────────────────
│   [X]
└──────────────────────────────────────────────────────────────────────
```

Thus, any module P that satisfies *Triv* must have a set X.

```
┌─ Data Seq[P :: Triv] ──────────────────────────────────────────────────
│  [Seq, Seq₁]
│
│  X ⊂ Seq₁ ⊂ Seq
│
│  ┌──────────────────────────────────────────────────────────────────
│  │ ⟨⟩ : Seq
│  │ _ ^ _ : Seq × Seq → Seq   [assoc, id : ⟨⟩]
│  │ _ ^ _ : Seq₁ × Seq → Seq₁   [assoc]
│  │ head : Seq₁ → X
│  │ tail : Seq₁ → Seq
│  │ ────────────────────────────────────────────────────────────────
│  │ ∀ S : Seq; z : X •
│  │    head(x ^ S) = x
│  │    tail(s ^ S) = S
│  └──────────────────────────────────────────────────────────────────
│
│  ┌──────────────────────────────────────────────────────────────────
│  │ #_ : Seq → N
│  │ rev : Seq → Seq
│  │ ────────────────────────────────────────────────────────────────
│  │ ∀ S : Seq; z : X •
│  │    #⟨⟩ = 0
│  │    #(x ^ S) = 1 + #S
│  │    rev(⟨⟩) = ⟨⟩
│  │    rev(S ^ x) = x ^ rev(S)
│  └──────────────────────────────────────────────────────────────────
└───────────────────────────────────────────────────────────────────────
```

Here *Seq* has just one constant, namely $\langle\rangle$, the empty sequence. Seq_1 is the set of all non-empty sequences. $X \subset Seq_1 \subset Seq$ indicates that an element of set X is a sequence and that a non-empty sequence is also a sequence. The operations $^\frown$, # and *rev* respectively denote concactenation, lenght and reverse, while *head* and *tail* have their expected meanings. The key words "assoc" and "id:" indicate that the operations are associative and have an identity. The constant introduced after "id:" is an identity element for that operation. This is a *specification* for an abstract data type whose enriched version is actually built into OOZE. Its conventions are those of initial algebra semantics, as discussed in Section 6 below, rather than those of set theory.

Other basic data types that define naturals, integers, rationals, tuples, etc., along with their respective operations can be defined in a similar way[9].

6   Semantics of OOZE

Although object and data elements are distinguished in OOZE, they share the important common feature of inheritance. At the data level inheritance is subtype inclusion, while at the object/class level, inheritance is subclass inclusion. For example, *Dog* is a subclass of *Canine*, and *Canine* is a subclass of *Mammal*. Similarly, we may say that the naturals are a subset of the integers, and that the integers are a subset of the rationals. It is also important to provide semantics for operations, that is, for functions at the data level (such as addition, division and multiplication for naturals, integers, rationals, etc.), and for methods at the class level (for updating, interrogating and manipulating objects).

---

[9]See [14] for an introduction to specifying data types in a similar context. It is perhaps worth remarking that the reals cannot be defined using ordinary initial algebra semantics; however, floating point numbers can be defined this way, and other techniques can be used for the "real" reals if they are really desired.

Order Sorted Algebra (OSA) [12] gives a powerful theory of inheritance for both data and objects, as well as for overloading functions and methods. OSA also has an operational semantics that can be used to animate specifications under certain conditions [10]. See Section 6.1.

It is also important to give a precise semantics for the large grain programming features of OOZE. Although the details of this are too complex for this paper, they have already been worked out in developing semantics for Clear, OBJ and FOOPS. The essential ideas are that modules are theories (i.e., sets of sentences) over the order sorted, hidden sorted, equational institution [15], and that the calculus of such modules is given by colimits. Views are theory morphisms, and a generic module is a theory inclusion. Furthermore, modules that define structures and operations are distinguished from those that define requirements by whether or not they involve data constraints. Data constraints are also used to define abstract data types, which are distinguished from classes in that their sorts are not hidden. Data constraints generalize initiality.

OOZE builds on FOOPS[10], an object oriented specification, programming and database language conceived by Goguen and Meseguer [11]. Both OOZE and FOOPS take OSA as a basis for their semantics, and specifically FOOPS is used to animate OOZE. FOOPS, in turn, is implemented by a translation into an enrichment of OBJ3 [24]. Both the OOZE and FOOPS implementations are still under construction, and are expected to see completion during 1991.

6.1 Data Types

The basic syntactic unit of the functional part of OOZE is the *Data* module, which defines abstract data types, including their constructor and selector functions. Such modules can be understood on the basis of two different semantics, one denotational and the other operational. The former is based on OSA and the latter on order sorted term rewriting [10] (see [19] for a survey of term rewriting). Following OBJ3, built in functional modules can also be implemented directly in the underlying Lisp system; for example, OBJ3 numbers are implemented in this way.

Consider the specification of sequence of natural numbers obtained by instantiating the data type *Seq* introduced in Section 5 with the module *Nat* which gives the natural numbers, i.e. *Seq* [*Nat* $\{X \mapsto \mathbb{N}\}$]. The basic idea of the term rewriting operational semantics of OOZE is to apply the given axioms to *ground terms*, i.e., terms without variables, as left-to-right rewrite rules, and progressively transform them until a form is reached where no further axioms can be applied; this form is called a *normal* form. Let us take a specific ground term as an example, and let the symbol $\Rightarrow$ indicate that a rewrite rule has been applied:

```
rev(head( 1 ^ 2 ^ 3 ) ^ tail (4 ^ 5 ^ 6)) ⇒
rev(1 ^ tail (4 ^ 5 ^ 6)) ⇒
rev(1 ^ 5 ^ 6) ⇒
6 ^ rev (1 ^ 5) ⇒
⋮
6 ^ 5 ^ 1
```

Two basic properties of term rewriting systems are termination and confluence. A term rewriting system is *terminating* if there are no infinite rewriting sequences on ground terms, and is *confluent* if any two rewrite sequences of a given ground term can be continued to a common term. A rewriting system that is both terminating and confluent is called *canonical*.

An OOZE functional module is an equational specification consisting of an order sorted signature Σ, which gives the sort and function symbols, and a partial ordering on the sorts, plus a set $\mathcal{E}$ of

---

[10]FOOPS stands for Functional and Object Oriented Programming System. It was first introduced in 1987 at SRI International, and is now under development in the Programming Research Group [24].

equations which involve only the symbols in Σ. The class of all algebras that satisfy $\mathcal{E}$ has initial algebras, i.e., algebras that have a unique homomorphism to any algebra that satisfies $\mathcal{E}$. OOZE takes initial algebras as the denotational semantics of its functional modules [13].

If a set $\mathcal{E}$ of equations is confluent and terminating as a term rewriting system, then the set of all its normal forms constitutes an algebra which is initial among the algebras satisfying $\mathcal{E}$ [7], and so the denotational (initial algebra) and operational (term rewriting) semantics agree. Since an abstract data type is an isomorphism class of initial algebras, it follows that an OOZE functional module defines an abstract data type. By contrast, Z and other model based languages, including Object-Z, have *concrete* data types, which have excessive implementation bias.

6.2   Classes and Objects

Many aspects of the data level of OOZE are mirrored at its object level. For example, OSA gives meaning to class inheritance and method overloading. Also, equations are used to define how methods modify attributes. Note that the types for data and the classes for objects form entirely separate hierarchies in OOZE, each with its own partial ordering.

Some axioms about objects appear not to be satisfied by all of their intended models. For example, the implementation of a stack by an array and a pointer does not satisfy pop(push(S,N)) = S for all states S: If the state before a pop is pop(push(push(push(empty,1),2),3)) then the state after the pop is pop(push(S,4)), which differs from the state before in that the number 4 occupies the position above the pointer, instead of the number 3. On the other hand, top(pop(push(S,N))) = top(S) is satisfied.

The solution is that rather than demanding axioms to be strictly satisfied, we only demand that their *visible consequences* are satisfied. This is justified by the fact that objects do not actually appear as such, because only their attributes are visible. While the functional level of OOZE has initial algebra semantics, the object level uses classes of algebras with the same observable behaviour as denotations; these need not be isomorphic to one another. More formally, given an order sorted signature Σ, a set of visible sorts and a set of hidden sorts, then two algebras are *behaviourally equivalent* if the result of evaluating any expression of a visible sort is the same for each of them [15, 9, 11].

Such algebras are *abstract machines* whose states are elements of hidden sorts; each object of a given class is a different copy of such a machine, with its own state, and creating an object produces a new copy of the machine in its initial state, while methods change the state, and attributes observe the state. When all sorts are visible, the concepts of abstract machine and abstract data type are identical. At the object level, OOZE takes behavioural equivalence classes of algebras as its denotational semantics. [11] gives an operational semantics based on the reflection of the object level into the data level; this provides on alternative way to support animation.

6.3   Theories and Views

Modern programming languages have many different kinds of entity, such as arrays, procedures, functions, operations, and records; hence, types are useful to separate and classify entities. The use of types helps to avoid meaningless expressions, and also makes it easier to understand code. In OOZE, theories are used to classify modules and to express requirements. This approach can be applied to both specification and programming languages, and is especially useful for building large systems.

Formally, a *theory* is a pair $\langle \Sigma, \mathcal{E} \rangle$; its denotation is the collection of Σ-algebras that satisfy $\mathcal{E}$. In OOZE, an algebra satisfies a data module if it is an initial algebra of the corresponding theory. At the object level, behavioural satisfaction is used instead. In both cases, *views* are morphisms from one pair $\langle \Sigma, \mathcal{E} \rangle$ to another pair $\langle \Sigma', \mathcal{E}' \rangle$ such that each equation in the first is (behaviourally) satisfied in the models of the second. See [15] for an introduction to behavioural satisfaction, and [9] for a more comprehensive discussion.

7 Related Work

OOZE is not the first proposal for an object oriented extension of Z. The oldest work in this area seems to be that of Schuman, Pitt and Byers [23]. The semantics of that language is based on set theory, first-order logic, events and histories. There are many differences between OOZE and this proposal, one of which is the absence of a specific syntactic construction for classes. As a result, classes and their associated operations may be dispersed freely throughout a specification, and it may be hard to discover what dependencies exist.

Object-Z, which is being developed at the University of Queensland, Australia [6], is based on *class histories* for each object, which record the operations executed on it[11]. In Object-Z, class histories are not only restricted by class invariants, and operations by pre- and post- conditions, but also by history invariants, which are temporal logic predicates. Although temporal operators make Object-Z unique among the object oriented extensions of Z, they may be hard to animate. For example, predicates of the form *eventually α will occur* are not easily checked. Also, maintaining a history for each object would require significant amounts of memory and processing time. Moreover, the semantics of Object-Z seems not to be very precise; however, recent work of Cusak [5] goes some way towards filling this gap.

In comparison with Z and other languages based upon it, OOZE is more abstract, more flexible, and more compact. This is largely because the model-based semantics is too concrete for many purposes, and in particular is not very well matched to some aspects of object orientation. For example, it can be difficult to tell whether a subset relationship is intentional or accidental, and what implications it may have for implementation. Given a *Flag* class whose state is a finite set of natural numbers in a certain range, it may be unclear whether *Flag* must be a subclass of a previously defined class of finite sets of integers. As a result, it will be unclear whether or not flags can be implemented by arrays of bits.

```
┌─ IntSet ──────────────────────────────
│  st : F Z
└───────────────────────────────────────
```

```
┌─ Flag ────────────────────────────────
│  st : F N
├───────────────────────────────────────
│  n ∈ st ⇒ 1 ≤ n ≤ N
└───────────────────────────────────────
```

where N is a positive integer constant assumed to be previously defined.

Z and Object-Z do not support classes of objects, but only single instances of each class; that is, they conflate the notions of class and object. In particular, they do not support the creation and deletion of objects. As a result, when there is more than one instance of a class, specifications in Z and Object-Z can be considerably longer.

Some other significant differences arise from OOZE's powerful module facility. These include: localizing variables and operations to modules, yielding simpler scoping conventions and eliminating the "global variable problem" (which is that all variables have global scope); parameterized (or "generic") modules; module importation; module expressions; a distinction among classes, objects

---

[11]There are differences between this approach and that of [23].

and modules; a distinction among modules used for interfaces and requirements, modules used for defining classes, and modules used for defining data types; relegating schemas to a minor rôle; eliminating schema combinators; clearly distinguishing between module inheritance and class inheritance; and using views to express refinement, satisfaction and inheritance at the module level. Finally, some significant differences arise from the semantic foundation in order sorted, hidden sorted equational logic. These include: precise and general ways of defining and handling exceptions; operation overloading; precise notions of abstraction and encapsulation; and simple criteria for when a refinement is correct.

8 Conclusion

OOZE is a generalized "wide spectrum" object oriented language with both *loose* specifications and *executable* (compilable or interpretable) programs. These two aspects of the language can be encapsulated in *modules* and may be linked by *views*, which assert refinement relationships. Modules are organized according to an *import hierarchy*, and can also be generic, i.e., *parameterized*. A system of modules, which may be loose and can even have empty bodies, can be used to express the large-grain *design* of a system. A single, very high level module can be used to express overall *requirements*, via a view to a module that encapsulates the whole system, or at earlier stages of development, just its design or specification. Rapid prototypes can be developed and precisely linked to their specifications and requirements by views. The use of loose specifications to define interfaces can be seen as a powerful semantic type system. Theorem proving is supported by the underlying OBJ system. OOZE is truly object oriented, allowing varying numbers of objects to a class, and complex objects (i.e., object valued attributes), as well as multiple inheritance and dynamic binding. The precise semantics based on order sorted algebra supports exception handling and overloaded operations. These characteristics are unique among the proposals for extending Z, and along with its animation and database facilities, make OOZE a very attractive language for developing large systems.

References

[1] American National Standards Institute, Inc. The programming language Ada reference manual. In *Lecture Notes in Computer Science 155*. Springer-Verlag, 1983. ANSI/MIL-STD-1815A-1983.

[2] S. Bear. Structuring for the VDM specification language. In *Lecture Notes in Computer Science 328*. Springer-Verlag, 1988.

[3] R.M. Burstall and Joseph A. Goguen. The semantics of Clear, a specification language. In *Lecture Notes in Computer Science 86*, pages 292–332. Springer-Verlag, 1980.

[4] Dan Craigen. Position paper for FM 89. In *Proceedings of Formal Methods '89, Workshop on Formal Methods*, Halifax, Nova Scotia, Canada, July 1989.

[5] Elspeth Cusack. Inheritance in object oriented Z, November 1990. British Telecom.

[6] David Duke, Roger Duke, Gordon Rose, and Graeme Smith. Object-Z: An object-oriented extension to Z. In *Proceedings of Formal Description Techniques (FORTE'89)*, 1989.

[7] Joseph A. Goguen. How to prove algebraic inductive without induction: With aplications to the correctness of data type representations. In Wolfgang Bibel and Robert Kowalski, editors, *Lecture Notes in Computer Science 87*, pages 356–373. Springer-Verlag, 1980.

[8] Joseph A. Goguen. Parameterized programming. *IEEE Transactions on Software Engineering*, SE-10(5), September 1984.

[9] Joseph A. Goguen. Types as theories. In *Proceedings of Symposium on General Topology and Applications*, Oxford University, June 1990. To appear, Oxford University Press, 1991.

[10] Joseph A. Goguen, Jean-Pierre Jouannaud, and José Meseguer. Operational semantics of order-sorted algebra. In *Lecture Notes in Computer Science 194*. Springer-Verlag, 1985.

[11] Joseph A. Goguen and José Meseguer. Unifying functional, object-oriented and relational programming with logical semantics. Technical Report SRI-CSL-87-7, SRI International - Computer Science Lab, July 1987.

[12] Joseph A. Goguen and José Meseguer. Order-Sorted Algebra I: Equational deduction for multiple inheritance, overloading, exceptions and partial operations. Technical Report SRI-CSL-89-10, SRI International, Computer Science Lab, July 1989.

[13] Joseph A. Goguen, James Thatcher, and Eric Wagner. An initial algebra approach to the specification, correctness and implementation of abstract data types. In Raymond Yeh, editor, *Trends in Programming Methodology IV*, pages 80–149. Prentice Hall, 1978.

[14] Joseph A. Goguen and Timothy Winkler. Introducing OBJ3. Technical Report SRI-CSL-88-9, SRI International -Computer Science Lab, August 1988.

[15] Joseph A. Goguen and David Wolfram. On types and FOOPS. In *Proceedings of Working Conference on Database Semantics*, Windermere, Lake District, United Kingdom, July 1990. (To appear).

[16] Adele Goldberg and Alan Kay. Smalltalk72 instruction manual. Technical report, Learning Research Group, Xerox Palo Alto Research Center, 1976.

[17] Robert Harper, David MacQueen, and Robin Milner. Standard ML. LFCS Report Series ECS-LFCS-86-2, University of Edinburgh, March 1986.

[18] Ian Hayes, editor. *Specification Case Studies*. International Series in Computer Science. Prentice Hall International, 1987.

[19] Gerard Huet and Derek Oppen. Equations and rewrite rules: A survey. In Ronald Book, editor, *Formal Language Theory: Perspective and Open Problems*, pages 349–405. Academic Press, 1980.

[20] Bertrand Meyer. *Object-Oriented Software Construction*. Prentice Hall International, 1988.

[21] Lewis J. Pinson and Richard S. Wiener. *Object Oriented Programming and Smalltalk*. Addison-Wesley, 1988.

[22] Augusto Sampaio and Silvio Meira. Modular extension to Z. In *Lecture Notes in Computer Science 428*. Springer-Verlag, 1990.

[23] S.A. Schuman, David Pitt, and P.J. Byers. Object-oriented process specification. Technical report, University of Surrey, 1989.

[24] Adolfo Socorro. An implementation of FOOPS. Programming Research Group, Oxford University Computing Laboratory, 1990.

[25] J. Michael Spivey. *The Z Notation, A Reference Manual*. International Series in Computer Science. Prentice Hall International, 1989.

Issues in the Design and Implementation of a
Schema Designer for an OODBMS

Jay Almarode

Instantiations, Inc.

Portland, Oregon

1. Introduction

In an earlier paper [Almarode Anderson 90], we described the GemStone Visual Schema Designer, a graphical schema editor for the GemStone† object-oriented database management system. The GemStone Visual Schema Designer (GS Designer) allows the user to interactively define classes and relationships between them by drawing a graphical object model of the class definitions. GS Designer allows the user to create, modify and delete GemStone class definitions using a mouse and keyboard interface and bit-mapped graphics in a windowing environment. The tool utilizes state of the art user interface primitives and direct graphical manipulation to provide an easy-to-use, intuitive interface to operations. GS Designer is a commercial product designed to meet the needs of real application development.

In the course of designing and implementing the tool, a number of issues were encountered that are unique to object-oriented databases. These issues include order of database update, references to classes external to a particular schema, and concurrency conflict. This paper discusses some of the key problems encountered, proposed solutions to the problems, and a rationale for the solutions that were chosen. This paper is organized as follows. Section 2 gives an overview of the GS Designer. Section 3 discusses the order of updating class definitions in the database and Section 4 discusses the problems of external references to classes outside the schema. Section 5 discusses concurrency conflicts that can arise under optimistic concurrency control. We conclude with a brief discussion of future directions for the GS Designer.

2.   Overview of the GemStone Designer

The main organizing principle of the GS Designer is the class graph. A class graph is a named collection of classes related to one another by various kinds of relationships. A particular class may be contained in more than one class graph, and a schema may consist of many class graphs. Collectively, all of the class graphs may be thought of as the schema for the application. The relationships currently implemented include generalization (realized by the superclass / subclass hierarchy), constrained instance variables, and constrained collections. Future relationships to be implemented include aggregation and association. All classes are part of a single superclass / subclass hierarchy (rooted at class **Object**), so any class class graph that the user creates or manipulates is a subgraph connected to the class hierarchy, although these connections may not be displayed. Class graphs are used to partition all the classes of an application schema into logical subdivisions. Within a class graph, relationships between classes may selectively be displayed or hidden. Thus, a class graph is a versatile mechanism for viewing the meta-data of an application, and for managing the complexity of large schemas. An important design principle of the GS Designer is that the user should not be allowed to create an invalid class graph. All class graphs should represent a consistent database state, and the user should not be allowed to draw an incorrect schema given the information currently available to the GS Designer.

Figure 1 illustrates the various windows of the GS Designer. The bottom window is the schema window. It contains an icon for each class graph in the schema. All schemas automatically include the four GemStone class graphs that

contain built-in classes, such as **Integer, String, Dictionary**, etc. The right-most
window is a class graph window. In this window, each rectangle represents a
class in the schema. An arrow represents a relationship between two classes.
The solid single-headed and double-headed arrows represent named instance
variables for a class. The arrow labeled **IsA** represents the superclass
relationship between classes, and the arrow labeled **holds** represents a
constrained collection. The top window is a class form window. This window
allows the user to define a class textually rather than by drawing relationship
arrows. An important feature of the GS Designer is that all windows are
consistent and are updated dynamically. This means that a change in one
window will be reflected in all windows that are appropriate.

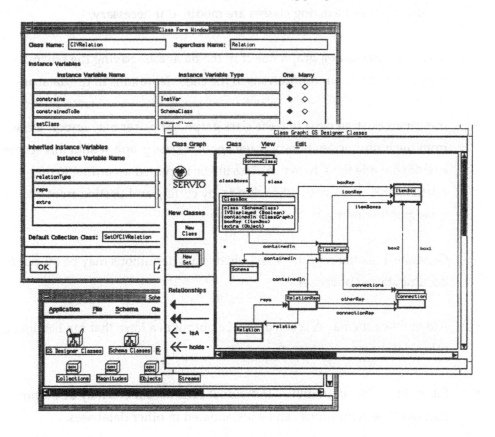

Figure 1.
The various windows of the GS Designer

The following list describes some of the main operations that can be performed by users of the GS Designer.

- Create a new class graph in the application schema. The new graph initially contains no classes.

- Delete the class graph. The class graph is deleted from the schema but classes in the graph remain, since they may be referenced by classes in other graphs.

- Create class definitions in the database. New classes are instantiated in the database and existing classes are modified if necessary.

- Save the schema as a graph object in the database. Saving the schema does not make any modifications to the class definitions in the database.

- Import an existing class into the class graph. The user may import a class from the built-in class library, from another class graph within this schema, or from outside the schema. A class my be imported according to the relationships it has with other classes, by cutting and pasting from another class graph window, or by name look-up.

- Generate a textual report. A text file of class definitions may be output for documentation purposes.

- File out the schema. A schema may be output in a form that can be input to other databases.

- File out the class definitions. Individual class definitions may be output so that the class definitions can be instantiated in other databases.

Another important feature of the GS Designer is that class and relationships may have multiple representations that can be manipulated. For example, a class may be represented in a class graph as a simple rectangle with its class name displayed and some of its instance variables displayed as arrows emanating from the rectangle. Another representation for a class in a class graph is a rectangle with all of the class's instance variables and their constraining classes listed inside. Still another representation for a class is a separate window which shows its superclass and lists all instance variables defined by the class and all its inherited instance variables. Since classes and relationships have multiple representations, it is possible to perform the same conceptual operation in many ways. For example, to reconstrain an instance variable, the user may type in a new constraint in the class form widow, or may graphically drag an arrow representing the instance variable from one class rectangle to another. A principle of good user interface design is to allow the user a number of ways to perform the same operation. Dynamic updating of all windows provides instant feedback of the results of the operation.

The remainder of this paper discusses some of the issues that were addressed during the design and implementation of the GS Designer.

3. Updating Class Definitions in the Database

One of the first issues that was addressed in the design of the GS Designer was when to update class definitions in the database. One alternative is to update a class definition in the database immediately after each operation on a class. Another alternative is to allow a number of operations to be performed and then allow the user to explicitly update the database with all class modifications. Most schema editors for non-traditional data models, including ISIS [Goldman et al. 85], Pasta3 [Kuntz Melchert 89], Siderius [Albano et al. 88], SNAP [Bryce Hull 86], and VILD [Leong et al. 89], have chosen the latter approach. We are aware of only one schema editor, the PSYCHO schema editor [KimH 88], that provides both alternatives.

For the first release of the GS Designer, we chose to provide an explicit operation to update the database. We felt it was desirable for the user to be able to save the schema design separately from actually updating the definitions in the database. This allows the user to modify and view private changes in the schema without changing classes that may be contained in other schemas. In addition, the user may file out the private changes and create the class definitions in a different database without updating the actual definitions in the original database. Another reason is performance. Some class modifications are expensive, potentially causing the recompilation of numerous methods in the class hierarchy. This delay can be noticeable with an interactive graphical tool, and discourages the user from exploring alternative designs. The next release of the GS Designer will cause us to re-evaluate whether to provide the first solution (continuously updating the database as changes are made) in addition to the second solution. The next release will provide integrated capability for defining and compiling methods for a class. Before a method can be compiled, any changes the user has made will need to be transmitted to the database, so that references to instance variables will be valid. In such a scenario, when the user opens a window for method definition for a class, an implicit operation will update the class's definition in the database.

Given that the user can make many modifications to more than one class before updating those changes to the database, the order that the changes are made in the database is important. The order of updates must ensure that the database is always in a consistent state, especially since methods may be invoked during the update operations. The ordering problem is particularly evident when a subclass reconstrains an instance variable inherited from a superclass. This reconstraining is allowable as long as the new constraint is a subclass of the superclass's constraint. Figure 2 illustrates an example of a subclass reconstraining an inherited instance variable. In this example, **Class2** may reconstrain inherited instance variable y as long as the new constraint is a subclass of **Dictionary**. When multiple deletions and additions of instance variables are performed, the order of class modifications must be performed correctly or this rule could be broken. This is best illustrated with an example. Figure 3 show two classes: **Class1** with no instance variables, and its subclass, **Class2**, with a single instance variable named x constrained to be a string. Now suppose that the user deletes instance variable x and redefines it for **Class1** to be constrained to an integer. The resulting class graph is pictured in Figure 4. When the class definitions are updated in the database, there are two operations to be performed: deleting x defined on **Class2** and adding x defined on **Class1**. If the addition of x is attempted first, it would not be allowed since x would be defined in a subclass and the constraint in the subclass would not be valid.

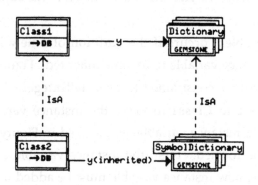

Figure 2.

An example of a correctly reconstrained inherited instance variable

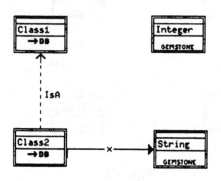

Figure 3.

A subclass with an instance variable

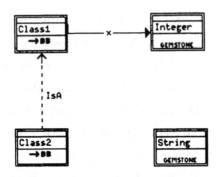

Figure 4.

After the instance variable has been moved to the superclass

A similar ordering problem occurs if the addition of a new instance variable causes a subclass's instance variable to become inherited. Figure 5 shows **Class2** with an instance variable z constrained to be **SmallInteger**. If the user adds a new instance variable z to **Class1** to make the instance variable in **Class2** a reconstrained inherited instance variable, as pictured in Figure 6, the following operations must be performed. First, the instance variable z must be deleted from **Class2**. Next, the new instance variable must be added to **Class1**. Finally, the inherited instance variable z for **Class2** must be constrained to SmallInteger.

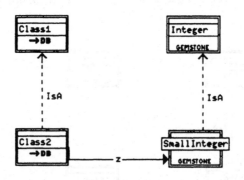

Figure 5.

A subclass with an instance variable

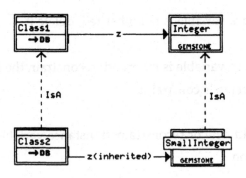

Figure 6.
After the instance variable has been made inherited

Although the user did not explicitly delete instance variable z for **Class2**, it must implicitly be deleted before z is added to **Class1**; otherwise, an error would occur for attempting to add a same-named instance variable that is defined by a subclass.

In light of the ordering problems described above, we have developed a general algorithm to perform multiple schema modifications. The purpose of the algorithm is to modify the actual class definitions in the database to conform to the definitions as pictured in the GS Designer. The pseudo code to perform multiple schema modifications is as follows:

1. Create any new class definitions in the database

2. For each class, remove any instance variables from the database definition that are not in the schema definition

   2a. Find an instance variable in the database definition that is not in the schema definition

   2b. Check all superclasses to see if this instance variable is inherited

2c.   If the instance variable is not inherited, delete it

2d.   If the instance variable is inherited, reconstrain the instance variable
       to the superclass's constraint

3.   For each class, add new or reconstrained instance variables to the
      database definition

3a.   Find an instance variable in the schema definition that is not in the
       database definition

3b.   Check all subclasses to see if this instance variable makes a subclass's
       instance variable become inherited

3c.   If so, delete the subclass's instance variable

3d.   Add the new instance variable

3e.   Reconstrain any subclass's instance variables that were removed in
       step 3c.

4.   External References

As mentioned previously, the GS Designer provides an operation to import
classes that are defined outside the schema. This provides a way to bring classes
defined in other schemas or by other tools under the control of the GS Designer.
However, importing external classes leads to some problems in handling
external references. When a class is imported into a schema, it is possible that
the class references other classes not in the schema. One solution is to import

the referenced class also, but this class may also reference a class outside the schema and so on. Unless some discipline is placed on how external classes are imported into the schema, a potentially large number of classes may be imported. This is unnecessary if all the user wishes to do is to reference a single class, for example, to constrain an instance variable.

The GS Designer solves this problem by giving the user control over how deeply nested the import operation is invoked. The user is allowed to import a class whose definition with respect to the GS Designer is 'incomplete', i.e. the class is imported although not all of its instance variables (and their constraining classes) may be included or displayable. When a class is imported incompletely, the class is read only; only complete classes may be modified. The GS Designer provides three levels of nesting for the import operation, as follows:

- Import the class only. The class definition in the GS Designer may be incomplete if it references classes not in the schema. This operation is useful if the user only plans on referencing the imported class.

- Import the class and its connections. The class definition is guaranteed to be complete. If it references external classes, those will be imported as 'class only' as described above. This operation is useful if the user plans on modifying the imported class.

- Import the class and its network. The class and all other classes imported will be complete. This operation imports the transitive closure of all classes and their references. This is useful if the user wants to bring a number of inter-related classes under the control of the GS Designer.

In all of the operations above, importing a class will implicitly import its superclass at the same nested level. The GS Designer also supports promoting incomplete definitions by providing a 're-import' operation. This allows an incomplete class definition to be changed to a complete definition by importing its external references. Two operations are provided to promote an incomplete class: re-import with connections, and re-import with network. These operations work on incomplete classes already in the schema and will import their referenced classes according to the semantics described above.

Though the import operation is both useful and flexible, problems can arise when the schema designer has only a partial definition of a class available to it (i.e., when a class within the schema references a class outside the schema or vice versa). An example of this occurs when a class within the schema has a subclass created in another schema by a different user of GS Designer, or through another interface to the database (such as the C language interface, Smalltalk interface, or the command line interpreter interface). In this situation, the GS Designer cannot recognize name conflicts and other errors between the superclass and its external subclasses until the superclass's modifications are updated in the database definition and the compiler determines the conflict. GS Designer then informs the user that an error resulted from an external class definition. The error message gives the name of the external class that caused the error, and also suggests that the user re-import the class into the schema to avoid future errors of the same type.

The import feature can also give rise to a deadlock situation. This problem is best illustrated with an example. Figure 7 shows two class graph windows for two different users of the GS Designer (i.e. two different sessions interacting with the database). The background window shows user 1's schema with class **Person** instantiated in the database. The foreground window shows user 2's schema which also contains class **Person**. Note, however, the class is locked by user 1 and is therefore not editable by user 2. (GS Designer locks class definitions when the schema is loaded, and doesn't allow modifications to classes with subclasses locked by another user). Figure 8 shows that user 2 has created the class **Employee** as a subclass of **Person** in the database. At this point, user 1's schema does not include class **Employee**, and name conflict errors could result, as described earlier. The deadlock situation is illustrated in Figure 9, when user 1 imports the subclass **Employee** into his/her schema. Once the subclass is imported, the GS Designer recognizes that class **Employee** is locked

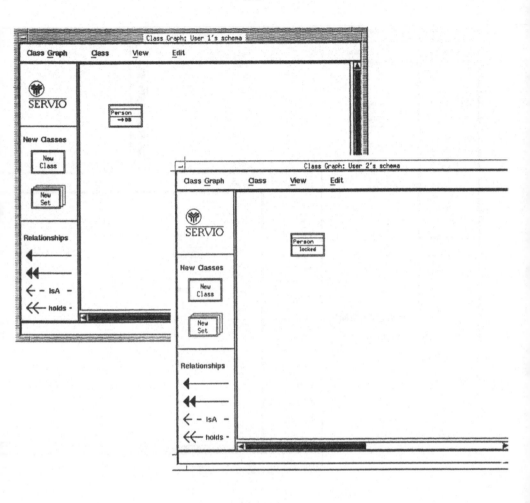

Figure 7.

Two class graphs with the same class for two different users

by another user and disallows any modification of class **Person**. This is
appropriate behavior because a change in the superclass may affect the subclass,
and the subclass is currently locked by user 2. Importing **Employee** eliminates the
possibility of name conflict errors as described earlier; however, no
modifications may be made to **Person** by either user until one of the users exits
his/her schema.

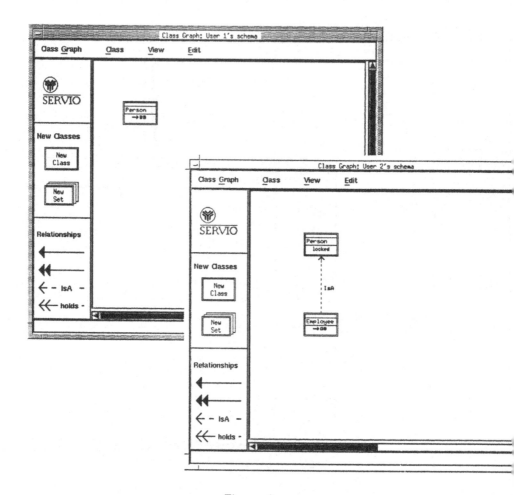

Figure 8.

User 2 creates a subclass

5. Concurrency Conflicts

As mentioned previously, the GS Designer acquires locks to prevent concurrency conflicts between multiple uses of the system. An important issue is how much of a class definition to lock without limiting other users. This is especially important in database management systems, such as GemStone, that use optimistic concurrency control (as described in [Maier et al. 86]) as well as locking. With this mechanism, concurrency conflicts are recognized at commit

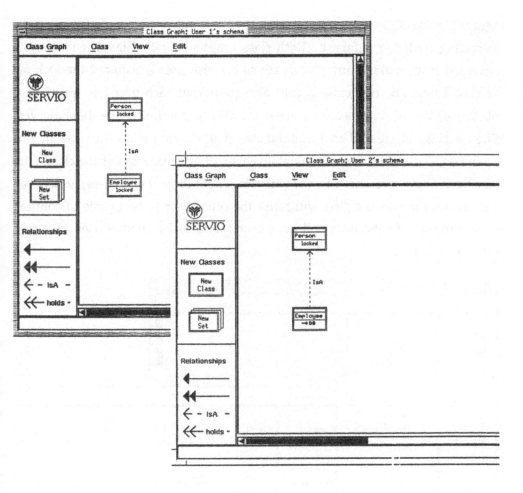

Figure 9.

User 1 imports the subclass

time if an object that was read or written has since been modified by another user. Although the GS Designer locks class definitions, schemas, and dictionaries that may be updated by the user, it is still possible for the operation that updates class definitions in the database to be unable to commit due to optimistic concurrency control. This is because the class creation and modification methods may alter nested objects that are not locked. The GS Designer could lock these nested objects, but doing so would limit other users. An example illustrates how this might happen.

Figure 10 shows two class graph windows belonging to two different users interacting with the database. Both class graphs contain **Class1**, with user 1 prevented from making any modifications because user 2 acquired the lock on the class first. The two class graphs also show that each user has specified a subclass of Class1, but has not created the class definition in the database yet. When a class is created in the database, it updates a class variable in the superclass. This class variable maintains a set of all subclasses of the class, and is a nested object referenced by the superclass definition. In this case, whichever user creates the subclass first will cause the other user to be unable to commit because the set of subclasses will have been modified by another user since this transaction began.

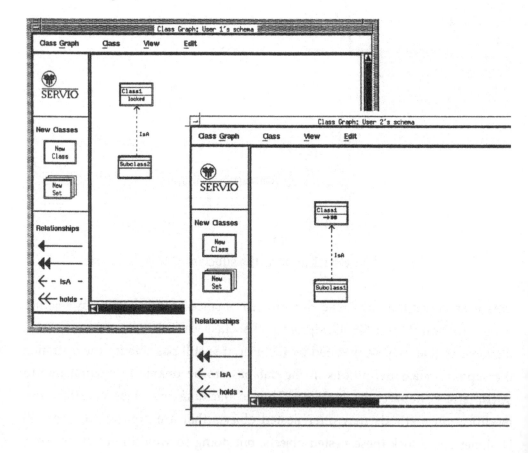

Figure 10.

Both user 1 and user 2 create subclasses of the same class

One solution to the problem would be to lock all nested objects that may be modified by other users. However, we felt this would be too limiting. As demonstrated in the previous example, if the set of subclasses were locked by user 2, then user 1 or any other users would not be able to create a subclass of **Class1**. The solution that is used by the GS Designer is to abort the current transaction when an optimistic concurrency control conflict occurs and then retry the operation again. Aborting the current transaction refreshes the database cache so that any modifications that occurred are now visible to the user. The GS Designer reduces this possibility by locking all class definitions, the schema, and the dictionary from which the schema was read. Locking the dictionary guarantees that the user will always be able to save the schema (i.e. no work is lost).

6.   Conclusion

This paper has discussed some of the issues that were addressed in the first release of the GS Designer. We have shown how the order of class modifications can lead to problems unless performed in the correct order, and given an algorithm of how the GS Designer performs multiple class modifications in the database. We have also shown how references to classes external to the schema can lead to problems when multiple designers are updating the database, and discussed the *import* operations to support incomplete definitions in the schema. Finally, we have illustrated problems with locking and optimistic concurrency control when subclasses are created by multiple users in different database sessions.

The emphasis throughout the design and implementation of the tool has been on providing intuitive, consistent operations for the user without limiting other users of the database. The tool is intended to aid in the sharing of class definitions as well as in their creation and modification. To this end, we expect to add a number of additional features in the next release. We expect to integrate the GS Designer with a database administration tool that will allow the user to set authorizations and to easily move objects to different name spaces. In the future, we also expect to couple the GS Designer with a forms package and a query tool, so that users will be able to specify indices and query the database graphically. With the increased complexity of inheritance, behavior, and complex objects in the database, building such tools for an object-oriented database management system will provide a challenge to all database researchers and implementors.

7. Bibliography

Almarode, J., Anderson, L. "GemStone Visual Schema Designer: A Tool for Object-Oriented Database Design", IFIP TC2 Working Conference on Database Semantics, Windermere, UK, 1990.

Albano, A., L. Alfo, S. Coluccini, R. Orsini. "An Overview of SIDERIUS: A Graphical Database Schema Editor for GALILEO", Proc. of the Int. Conf. on Extending Database Technology - EDBT '88, Venice, Italy, 1988.

Bryce, F., R. Hull. "SNAP: A Graphics-based Schema Manager", Proc. of the IEEE 2nd Int. Conf. on Data Engineering, Los Angeles, 1986.

Goldman, K. J., S. A. Goldman, P. C. Kanellakis, S. B. Zdonik. "ISIS: Interface for a Semantic Information System", Proc. of ACM-SIGMOD 1985 Int. Conf. on Management of Data, Austin, Texas, 1985.

Kim, H. J. "Issues in Object-Oriented Database Schemas", The University of Texas at Austin, PH.D. 1988.

Kuntz, M., R. Melchert, "Ergonomic Schema Design and Browsing with More Semantics in the Pasta-3 Interface for E-R DBMSs", 8th Int. Conf. on Entity-Relationship Approach, Toronto, Canada, 1989.

Leong, M.,S. Sam, D. Narasimhalu. "Towards a Visual Language for an Object-Oriented Multi-Media Database System", Proc. of the IFIP TC2/WG 2.6 Working Conf. on Visual Database Systems, Tokyo, 1989. Published as Visual Database Systems, Elsevier Science Publishers B .V, 1989.

Maier, D., J. Stein, A. Otis, A. Purdy. "Development of an Object-Oriented DBMS", OOPSLA '86.

Object Integrity Using Rules

Claudia Bauzer Medeiros[*]

DCC-IMECC-UNICAMP-CP 6065

13081 Campinas SP

Brazil

cmbmedeiros@dcc.unicamp.ansp.br

Patrick Pfeffer[†]

Department of Computer Science

University of Colorado

Boulder, CO 80309-0430

U.S.A.

patrick@cs.colorado.edu

Abstract

Integrity maintenance in object-oriented systems has so far received little attention. This paper is an attempt to fill this gap. It describes a mechanism for maintaining integrity in an object-oriented database, implemented for the O_2 system, and which uses the production rule approach to constraint maintenance. Object integrity is ensured by objects themselves – the *rules* which are activated when selected events take place. The approach presented is original, in the sense that it takes full advantage of the object-oriented paradigm, considering constraints as first-class citizens which can be inherited, and defined independently of any application. Furthermore, we support maintenance of not only static but also some types of dynamic constraints, as well as constraints on object behavior.

1 Introduction

As remarked by [JMSS89], a great part of the properties that define the consistency of a database can be represented by predicates on the database state (the so-called *static integrity constraints*). If all these predicates are evaluated as true for a given state, then the state is consistent. Most of the work published on database constraint maintenance is dedicated to ensuring this type of constraint.

Dynamic integrity constraints, on the other hand, are predicates specified over a *sequence of states*. Research in this area goes in the direction of transforming each dynamic constraint into a set of static constraints (e.g., [Via88]) sometimes using state transition graphs (e.g., [Kun85, Lip88]) where the terminal nodes are consistent states. Again as remarked by [JMSS89], a considerable amount of dynamic constraints can be expressed in terms of the initial and final states of a transaction. A *transaction* is a sequence of actions conducting from one initial (or input) database state to a terminal (output) state. Dynamic constraints that can be expressed in terms of only initial and final states of a single transaction are called *two-state predicate constraints*. The monitoring of other dynamic constraints is still a matter of research, and demands maintaining historical information on the database states ([HS90]).

Static constraints are usually expressed by means of first order logic expressions, and dynamic constraints by means of *temporal logic*. Temporal logic extends first order logic by incorporating modal operators *always*, *sometime* and *next*. These operators may vary, since authors who do research in the area define their own operators to better express dynamic constraints.

---

[*]This research was developed while the author was on sabbatical leave at GIP Altaïr, BP 105, 78153 Le Chesnay-Cedex, France. The support of this research was provided by GIP Altaïr and by grant CNPq - Brazil - 200.168-89.4

[†]This research was partially developed while the author was working for Gip Altaïr. The support for this research was provided by GIP Altaïr and by ONR under Contract N00014-88-K-0559

Most mechanisms for constraint enforcement support only a very limited set of constraints. This support consists usually in either forbidding or rolling back operations that violate constraints. A more flexible approach to enforcement is that of performing *compensating actions*, whereby the once forbidden operations are allowed to take place, followed by other operations which re-establish consistency.

Integrity maintenance in object-oriented systems is still an unexplored topic. This paper presents a solution to this problem, which has been implemented on the O_2 database system, and which can be generalized to other object-oriented database systems. The constraint maintenance mechanism takes advantage of the production rule subsystem which has been integrated into the O_2 prototype [Da90]. Though this rule mechanism is general, this paper is only concerned with the features relevant to the consistency problem. The reader is referred to [BMP91] for a more detailed description of rule treatment in O_2.

The key issues discussed here are based on the following:

- **Constraints supported.** The mechanism supports the maintenance of any constraint that can be expressed as a sequence of predicates on sequences of database states using the O_2 query language. This means that we allow static constraints and some classes of dynamic constraints. For dynamic constraints, we restrict ourselves to cases where state history can be checked in terms of one state transition (i.e., we support two-state predicate constraints). We do furthermore consider constraints on object behavior.

- **Integrity enforcement.** It is ensured by performing compensating actions, determined by database and application semantics. It uses the production rule solution to constraint maintenance.

- **Exploiting the object-oriented paradigm.** Our mechanism takes advantage of the object-oriented paradigm in three aspects. First, each constraint is transformed into a set of special objects, called *rules*, which will monitor integrity. Thus, object integrity is supported by objects themselves. Second, the system takes inheritance into account, and a constraint defined for a given class is automatically enforced in all its subclasses. Third, constraints can be inserted, deleted and modified at will, independent of any application. They are considered first-class citizens, and need not be encoded in the body of any application. The last point is an answer to the remark in [fADF90], where it is claimed that this independence cannot be supported in object-oriented systems.

The rest of this paper is organized as follows. Section 2 presents an overview of the O_2 system. Section 3 presents a brief description of the O_2 rule system. Section 4 points out some of the problems of constraint maintenance in an object-oriented environment, presents our framework and gives an overview of research in the area. Section 5 shows how the rule system is used to maintain constraints. Section 6 gives examples of constraint support. Finally, Section 7 contains conclusions and directions for future work.

2 A brief overview of the O_2 system

This section contains a short presentation of the O_2 object-oriented database system. The interested reader will find further detailed information in [Da90].

The O_2 data model [LR89] relies on two kinds of concepts: *complex values*, defined as in standard programming languages, and *objects*. Objects are instances of classes, and values are instances of types. Objects are encapsulated (i.e., their value is only accessible through methods), whereas values are not – their structure is known to the user, and they are manipulated by primitive operators. Manipulation of objects is done through *methods*, which are procedures attached to the objects. Objects sharing structure (*type*) and behavior (*methods*) are grouped into classes. Users can define *names* for given objects.

Types are constructed recursively using the O_2 atomic types (e.g., integer or bitmap), classes from the schema and the *set, list* and *tuple* constructors. An O_2 *schema* is a set of classes related by inheritance links and/or composition links, as well as the attached methods, and allows multiple inheritance.

Though O_2 is multi-language, the methods discussed here are coded in the CO_2 language. CO_2 is a C-like programming language which allows (i) class declaration, (ii) object manipulation (i.e., message passing) and (iii) value manipulation by means of primitive operators.

The O_2 system has a functional first order query language [BCD89] which can be used either in an interactive mode or included in the body of methods. This language supports access to O_2 structures, thus being able to manipulate O_2 constructors and make use of methods. The result of a query is a complex value whose type is defined by the query itself. The result of a query can be used in a program as any complex value.

3 The O_2 rule mechanism

3.1 General concepts

Active databases (e.g., [DBB+88]) are database systems that respond automatically to events generated internally or externally to the system itself, without user intervention. The nature of the response is arbitrary, and depends on application semantics. The desired behavior is commonly specified by *production rules*, which are pairs of the form < predicate $\rightarrow$ action > to be triggered at specific events.

Our solution to integrity enforcement uses the active database paradigm, where a constraint is enforced by means of O_2 *production rules*. This section gives a brief overview of the rule mechanism in O_2. A complete description of this mechanism is given in [BMP91].

Rules are considered to be schema components and can be kept independently from applications on the database. Furthermore, the inheritance property applies – i.e., rules defined for a given class are inherited by all of its subclasses. Like any other schema component, rules also suffer evolution: they can be added, deleted and modified. They differ from other schema components in the sense that they can be enabled or disabled at times, which does not apply to the other components. Some rules may be local to one transaction (which creates them at its beginning and deletes them at its end).

Rules are implemented as objects, with priorities and access rights, and are instances of O_2 builtin classes, whose root is the class *Rule*. Following the terminology of [DBB+88], their activation occurs upon some *Event*, in which case a *Condition* is checked and some *Action* is optionally undertaken.

3.2 Rules as objects

The O_2 rule system is not restricted to verifying integrity constraints. Whereas most active systems restrict events to be update requests, in O_2 they may be associated with *message sending* or with the *passing of time*.

Rule objects are tuples <**Name, E, Q, A, P, S, AP**>, where
Name is a string that identifies the rule;
E(vent): is an expression describing one event which triggers rule verification;
Q(uery): is an O_2 query. It contains the predicate to be tested in order to execute the action;
A(ction): is a sequence of CO_2 operations and corresponds to the action to be performed if the condition is met. It may itself involve operations which will trigger further rules, in nested execution;
P(riority): is an integer that ranks the rule, to be used when there is more than a rule applicable for a given event;
S(tatus): indicates whether the rule is enabled or disabled;
AP(plicability): indicates when to check the rule, e.g., pre- or post-method execution.

Message-related events are expressed as [*Receiver, Method*] – i.e., the event is signalled when there is a request for *Method* to be executed on *Receiver*. *Receiver* can be either an object name or a class name. Time-related events are specified as *TIME(value)*. Accepted time values are those of the O_2 builtin classes Date and Duration (which respectively allow expressing points in time or time intervals in years, months, days, hours, minutes and seconds). An event may trigger the verification of a set of rules, according to their priority. Verification of a rule's applicability corresponds to performing query **Q** followed by the arbitrary action **A** which is itself an O_2 method.

Rules can be examined or updated. Rule operations are methods attached to the *Rule* builtin class hierarchy. They can be invoked inside an application program or interactively using the graphical user interface. The update operations on rules are Add, Delete, Enable, Disable, Fire and Change_priority.

4 Constraints in an object-oriented DBMS

4.1 Related work

The analysis and support of constraints for object-oriented systems has so far merited little attention and has been restricted to static constraints. Most of the integrity maintenance problems already existing in the relational world can be translated into equivalent (or often the same) problems when one comes to the object-oriented model. However, the object-oriented model has brought an additional type of constraint into existence: constraints imposed on the *behavior* of objects (i.e., controlling method definition and execution). Some systems (e.g., [KGBW90]) support constraint maintenance for schema (structural) update operations; others (e.g., [DBB+88, KDM88]) describe constraint maintenance in the framework of active databases, but without details about types of constraint supported or their transformation into rules.

Recent research in constraint maintenance in relational and logic databases uses the active database approach, and is usually restricted to static constraint support. Examples are the constraint equations of [Mor84] (expressed as path expressions over relations), the POSTGRES rule system [SJGP90] (where rules are used to define views, compute aggregate fields and translate update requests), or the work of [SLR89] (concerned with different algorithms for improving the checking of conditions upon one-tuple relational updates). [CW90] describe a framework in which constraints specified in an SQL-like language can be translated into rules that detect integrity violation. Logic database rule based systems include PRISM [SK84] and TAXIS [MBW80].

In the object framework, [LR90] suggest how static constraints might be stated in a database programming language, to be checked as post-conditions to a transaction. Production rules are suggested for constraint maintenance in [DBB+88, KDM88]. In [DBB+88], ECA (Event Condition Action) rules are supported, where Event triggers the rule, Condition is a collection of queries evaluated when a rule is triggered by an Event, and Action is a sequence of database and application program operations. [KDM88] describes an extended trigger mechanism on top of the DAMASCUS system which has three components: Event, Action and Trigger. The Trigger is the means of connecting an Event with a given Action. Events have pointers to Trigger chains, organized according to Trigger priority.

Constraints and rule execution in object-oriented environments are also found in the CACTIS system [HK89] where derived attribute instances are defined in terms of triggers, and updated only on request. The work of [UD89] proposes specification and maintenance of integrity constraints as rules in an NF2 system, where constraints are defined on the schema or for specific application needs. Finally, in [NQZ90] a rule system for semantic modelling is implemented on top of Gemstone, allowing the handling of some types of static constraints.

4.2 Constraints supported in O_2 - assumptions and terminology

We support both static and two-state transition constraints. This section describes the framework of this support.

In the relational model, constraints are often classified into intra-relation (e.g., functional dependencies) or inter-relation (e.g., referential integrity). Inter and intra-relation constraints exist both at the static and the dynamic level. Analogously, we support constraints that are defined on the objects of one class (*intra-class*) or several classes (*inter-class*). We consider constraints between objects as a special case of intra-class constraint. We also support constraints defined on object behavior, as long as they can be stated as pre or post conditions to methods. Finally, constraints can be *global* – i.e., they hold for all applications that run on a database; or *local* – they are defined locally to an application, and their verification is only enabled when the application is active.

Another issue we consider is that of *flexibility*. In commercial database systems, constraint enforcement depends on the programmer adding the appropriate integrity checks throughout all applications that use the database. This type of enforcement requires a huge maintenance effort, not only to correct errors, but also to accompany evolution of the database or the applications. Furthermore, one would like flexible constraint management, allowing enabling and disabling of constraint verification.

In order to respond to this need for flexibility, we define constraints to be first-class citizens. They are conceptually considered to be *properties* of an O_2 database schema and can be kept independently from applications on the database. They may be defined over classes, methods or named objects, as well as as over *computed* or *aggregate* values, that is, values that are not effectively stored.

We handle both static constraints (expressed as first order logic predicates on a state) and some dynamic constraints (those that can be stated as two state predicates). Two-state constraints are formalized in [CCF82], where they are stated in terms of transactions that lead from an input $State_i$ to an output $State_o$, and where the predicate is transformed into a first order expression.

We thus deal with situations involving just first order logic predicates: static constraints, constraints on input and output states of methods, and two-state constraints. In the latter case, we use [CCF82]'s technique to transform the constraint into a transaction where predicates are to be verified as pre and/or post conditions.

We take the remedial approach to integrity maintenance. Thus, rather than defining constraints as assertions over database states, they are specified as *production rules*. These rules are implemented using the O_2 rule system and the predicates are expressed within O_2 queries: first order logic expressions, using methods, composition and iterators.

A constraint statement is transformed in a production rule expression as follows. Consider first static constraints, stated as first order logic predicates $\mathcal{P}$. They give origin to rule statements of the form $< \neg\, \mathcal{P} \rightarrow \mathcal{A} >$ for some designer-defined action $\mathcal{A}$. If one assumes the state of a database is consistent before any operation that may violate a static constraint, then this constraint need only be checked after a state change.

The dynamic constraints supported are expressed using modalities "sometime" and "always" (see [CCF82])

$$sometime\ \mathcal{P}i\ before\ \text{Transaction}$$
$$sometime\ \mathcal{P}o\ after\ \text{Transaction}$$
$$always\ \mathcal{P}i\ before\ \text{Transaction}$$
$$always\ \mathcal{P}o\ after\ \text{Transaction}$$

Each such dynamic constraint is transformed into a *set* of static constraint declarations, to be checked both as pre and post-conditions:

$$< \neg\, \mathcal{P}i\ (State_i) \rightarrow \mathcal{A}i >\ \text{and}\ < \neg\, \mathcal{P}o\ (State_o) \rightarrow \mathcal{A}o >$$

where i and o indicate input and output states, $\mathcal{P}i$ and $\mathcal{P}o$ are first order logic predicates and $State_i$ and $State_o$ are input and output states of Transaction.

5 Maintaining constraints through O_2 rules

As pointed out in [SLR89], one of the problems in maintaining constraints through rules is how to execute rules in the appropriate order for events where more than one rule applies. We adopt the solution described in, among others, [SLR89, DBB+88, CW90, WF90, NQZ90]: rules are assigned execution priorities to disambiguate execution order.

As stated in Section 4, we only consider constraints where the predicate to be checked is a first order logic statements. Constraint statements, expressed as $< \neg \mathcal{P} \to \mathcal{A} >$, are transformed into O_2 rules where $\neg \mathcal{P}$ is the selector clause within an O_2 query statement and $\mathcal{A}$ is the name of a CO_2 method. The answer to the query gives enough information on the state of the database to indicate if the constraint has been violated. Since O_2 queries return complex objects and values, the answer is also used, in some cases, to indicate which objects satisfy $(\neg \mathcal{P})$ and thus might need to be processed by $\mathcal{A}$. For details on the syntax of the query language, see [BCD89].

5.1 Checking constraints at message passing events

Like all other researchers who have examined the problem of integrity violation, we only analyze constraints whose violation is caused by schema or by state *updates* (insertions, deletions or modifications). We only consider therefore message-related events, where the methods perform some update action.

It must be stressed that this represents a subset of the constraints that can be enforced by the O_2 rule system (we ignore, for instance, time-related events). We have not yet, however, been able to completely characterize other kinds of constraints. One such example is the class of constraints that are violated by the *absence* of an update, another corresponds to constraints on history-bound relationships, which require keeping auxiliary structures to monitor state sequences.

5.2 Transforming a constraint into a set of objects

This section describes how a constraint stated as a production rule is transformed into an initial set of O_2 rules. This process is at the moment done manually, since automation would require restricting the types of constraint that can be enforced (e.g., [Mor84, CW90]). Once this initial set of rules is specified and inserted into the database, the rule support system takes over, and further transformations are executed, automatically.

The first step consists in *determining the pair* $< Q, A >$. Recall that the constraint is stated as (a set of) productions $< \neg \mathcal{P} \to \mathcal{A} >$. Predicate $\neg \mathcal{P}$ is transformed into an O_2 Query. The Action to be taken is determined by database and application semantics. It corresponds either to the name of a method supplied by the user, or to system-provided actions in the cases of cancelling or undoing of an operation.

The execution of the pair $< Q, A >$ may be triggered by different update events. Thus, the next step in transforming a constraint into rule objects corresponds to *the determination of all* Events that require constraint verification. This is done in two stages. The first stage is *path analysis*, in a fashion similar to the one described in [CW90]. The query predicate is treated as a path expression, where all objects or class names mentioned in the path are potential sources of constraint violation. The determination of these sources is automated, since this corresponds to syntactically analyzing a query statement. Unlike [CW90]'s relational constraints, however, our predicates are on classes and objects that interact, and static analysis is not enough. We must then go through the next stage and *examine the database schema* to identify all methods which, sent to the potential sources of violation, may indeed cause violation. The event description pairs *[Receiver, Method]* are the output of this second stage.

The steps described above correspond to transforming a constraint into a set of rule objects R1, ..., Rn, all having the same $< Q, A >$ and different Event components. Finally, some Queries can be simplified, given the restrictions imposed by the Events.

```
           Structural/Inheritance Information

class Person type
   tuple (Name:string, Birth:Date, Lives:Address)

class Employee Inherits Person type
   tuple (Salary:Money, Dept:Department)

class Client Inherits Person type
   tuple (Credit:Money, Status:string)

class Department type
   tuple(Name:string, Personnel:set (Employee), Manager:Employee)

             Behavior Information

method change_birth (Newbirth:Date) in class Person;
method hire () in class Employee;
method change_sal (newsal:Money) in class Employee;
method change_dept (Oldep:Department, Newdep:Department)
                       in class Employee;
method change_manager (Newman:Employee) in class Department;
method buy () in class Merchandise;
```

Figure 1: Example Schema

Once these steps are taken, the rule objects can be inserted into the database. The rule support mechanism then takes over and creates additional rules to ensure constraint inheritance. If rule R1 is created for an event [Rec, M], then other rules with the same components Q and A are automatically created for events [Rec', M] for all subclasses Rec' of Rec. This corresponds to a phenomenon of *constraint propagation by inheritance*. The user may later assign different priorities to each such rule, as well as enable, disable or delete them individually.

6   Example of constraint maintenance

There follows an example of constraint maintenance in the system. We use the classical "Employee" - "Department" example, with a few minor additions, which will allow the reader to easily grasp the details of constraint management, without having to understand a particular application. Consider the O_2 schema in Figure 1, with classes Person (subclasses Employee, Client) and Department. Address, Money, Date and Merchandise are classes defined elsewhere.

This schema is submitted to the following Static and Dynamic constraints, and respective corrective actions:

- S_IC1: an Employee who is a Manager must earn at least \$10,000 ⇒ Force Manager salary to be 10,000.

- S_IC2: (exception to S_IC1) constraint S_IC1 does not apply to Employee "Smith".

- D_IC3: a Person's age may never decrease ⇒ Forbid violation.

- S_IC4: the salary of a Manager is greater than the salary of all Employees of the Department ⇒ Non-Manager's salaries must always be kept to salary of Manager minus 1.

- D_IC5: a Client's status must be "good" before Client is allowed to buy Merchandise ⇒ Warn user and forbid operation.

The following sections show rule generation steps, pointing out relevant details. The use of O_2 queries and CO_2 methods is straightforward. We assume classes have extensions with the same name. For ease of understanding, a rule's components (E,Q,A) are numbered according the constraint they maintain - e.g., E1, Q1 and A1 refer to maintaining constraint number 1.

6.1 Processing S_IC1

- Determining Q and A components
  $\mathcal{P}$ is ($\forall$ d in Department, d.Manager.Salary $\geq$ 10,000)

  Q1: Q_result = select set(d.Manager)
                from d in Department
                where (d.Manager.Salary < 10,000)
  A1: for emp in Q_result { [emp change_sal(10,000)];}

  Notice the query returns an O_2 complex value, Q_result, whose type is defined in the select clause as being "set of Managers". This set contains all managers that violate the constraint. Also notice A1 is performed on the objects which are returned by the query.

- Determining Events
  Possible sources of violation are extracted from Q1's predicate
  "(d.Manager.Salary < 10,000)", i.e., Manager or a Manager's Salary. Manager is of type Employee and is a component of class Department, so this analysis just tells us that updating Employees or Departments may violate the constraint. This is obviously not a fine enough control to determine events. An examination of the schema (and method semantics) shows that the only events that must be checked for are
  E1.1: [Employee change_sal(Newsal)]
  E1.2: [Department change_manager(Newman)]
  This corresponds to the creation of two rules, R1.1 and R1.2, one for each event, which need only be checked after execution of the corresponding methods.

- Q and A simplification
  At event E1.1, the rule needs only be applied if method "change_sal" applies to an Employee who is also a Manager. Furthermore, Q1 is too general, since it always checks all Managers, whereas only one Manager is being affected at each event. Query and action are thus modified to:

  R1.1 (self is of type Employee), and for event E1.1:
  Q1.1: Q_result = (self $\rightarrow$ Dept.Manager == self
                AND
                self $\rightarrow$ Salary < 10,000)
  A1.1: if (Q_result) then [self change_sal(10,000)]
  R1.2 (self is of type Department), and for event E1.2:
  Q1.2: Q_result = (self $\rightarrow$ Manager.Salary < 10,000)
  A1.2: if (Q_result) then [self $\rightarrow$ Manager change_sal(10,000)]

- Detection of cycles
  The rule management system detects some types of cycles and warns the database designer. Here, one can immediately detect a cycle since R1.1 is both triggered by and executes the method "change_sal" and thus R1.1 activates itself. This is solved by using disable and enable rule operations in A1.1 as follows

  A1.1: if (Q_result) then { disable R1.1;
                          [self change_sal(10,000)];
                          enable R1.1;}

6.2 Processing S_IC2

This exception to S_IC1 can be handled in two ways. The first is to define pre (and post) method execution rules, where if Employee is "Smith" then both R1.1 and R1.2 are disabled (and enabled). The second (simpler) solution is to *compose* the two constraints, by modifying Q1.1 and Q1.2, adding to each the clause "AND self→Name != "Smith". The first choice maintains the independence between S_IC1 and S_IC2, but is less efficient in terms of processing time.

6.3 Processing D_IC3

This constraint predicate is stated as *"always* Birth > Newbirth", and is an example of a case where two-state constraints are expressed in terms of old (input) and new (output) values. Event, **Query** and Action after simplification are respectively:
   E3: [Person change_birth(Newbirth)]
   Q3: Q_result = (self → Birth ≤ Newbirth)
   A3: if (Q_result) then *Break*
   where *Break* is a special system method that results in not allowing the execution of "change_birth". This rule is to be checked before execution of "change_birth".

   Here a new phenomenon can be observed: *constraint inheritance.* The user defines rule R3 for class *Person.* Two other rules are automatically created by the system, to account for the fact that this class has two subclasses (*Employee, Client*) to which "change_birth" can also be applied. This finally results in three rules, one stated by the system designer and the other two generated by the system, with the components < Q3, A3 > and for events [Employee change_birth] and [Client change_birth].

6.4 Processing S_IC4

Query, Action and Events are

Q4: Q_result = select set(emp)
                from emp in Employee
                where (emp.Salary > emp.Dept.Manager.Salary)
A4: for e in Q_result
          { [e change_sal(e →Dept.Manager.Salary - 1)];}

Events are those that affect Salary, Managers and Employees
   E4.1 [Employee hire()]
   E4.2 [Employee change_sal(Newsal)]
   E4.3 [Employee change_dept(Oldep, Newdep)]
   E4.4 [Department change_manager(Newman)]
   Notice the query cannot be simplified to its predicate component in all four cases, because for certain events (e.g., change of Department's Manager) more than one Employee may be affected. If we had taken the approach of other authors, constraint violation would be signalled by having the constraint's predicate return the value of "false". Then, we would have to navigate through the database to perform corrective actions. Our approach is more efficient in that the query result itself already shows where to perform such actions. Query simplification to a boolean predicate can be made for events E4.1 and E4.3, only.

6.5 Processing D_IC5

This constraint can be stated as *"sometime* Client.status = "good" *before* Client buy Merchandise". This is another case of rule processing before method execution. Rule components after simplification are:

Q5: Q_result = (self → Status != "good")
A5: if (Q_result) { Warn user; Break; }
E5: [Merchandise buy]

6.6 General comments

In previous research about maintaining constraints through rules, each constraint gives origin to one rule (since updates and their effects are localized, and are not performed across classes). Here, one constraint may give origin to several rules, applied to distinct classes.

Each of the previous constraint transformations is an instance of the different issues covered. Processing of S_IC1 shows simplification of query and action, as well as the fact that part of an action may include the temporary disabling of the constraint itself. Enable and disable operations allow controlling constraint scope. Thus, constraints may be enabled only within an application or a transaction. One may want, for instance, to disable constraint S_IC1 for a transaction that will change all salaries of a company, and perform a global verification of Manager's salaries at the end.

Processing of S_IC2 shows exception handling options and that constraint composition is transformed into query and action composition. Processing of D_IC3 shows processing of an "always" dynamic constraint, the special system action *Break*, and the feature of automatic constraint inheritance. S_IC4 is an example of the need for a query that returns a complex value and not just a boolean. Again in this our system differs from the proposals of most authors that are limited to checking boolean expressions. Finally, D_IC5 shows handling of a "sometime/before" dynamic constraint.

7 Conclusions and future work

This paper presented a solution for maintaining integrity constraints in an object-oriented system, which was implemented using the O_2 production rule mechanism. The approach described here is original in that constraints are transformed into objects and therefore managed as database components by the database management system itself. Constraints are considered as part of a schema and are treated as first-class citizens. This permits supporting object-oriented characteristics such as constraint inheritance and independence, and which are ignored by most researchers.

Unlike previous work on constraint maintenance in object-oriented databases, this solution considers not only static but also some two-state dynamic constraints, as well as constraints on behavior. Also unlike previous work, we consider both global and local constraints, as well as inter-class constraints. Other aspects that distinguish our approach from others' are the ability to treat exception handling, considering one constraint as enforced by sets of rules (and not just one) and support to system evolution, where modification of the set of database constraints is transparent to the applications. Finally, constraint enforcement can be disabled and enabled for different transactions.

Future work will consider extending the set of allowable constraints, as well as partially automating the determination of the set of events which correspond to a constraint statement.

Acknowledgements

The authors thank Guy Bernard and Christophe Lécluse for their careful reading of previous versions of this paper, and their insightful comments.

References

[BCD89]   F. Bancilhon, S. Cluet, and C. Delobel. A query-language for an object-oriented database system. In *Proceedings of the Second Workshop on DataBase Programming Languages*, Salishan, Oregon, USA, June 1989. Morgan Kaufman.

[BMP91]   C. Bauzer-Medeiros and P. Pfeffer. A Mechanism for Managing Rules in an Object-Oriented Database. Technical Report 65-90, GIP Altaïr, Rocquencourt, France, 7 janvier 1991.

[CCF82]   J. Castilho, M. Casanova, and A. Furtado. A Temporal Framework for Database Specifications. In *Proceedings of VLDB*, pages 280–291, 1982.

[CW90]   S. Ceri and J. Widom. Deriving Production Rules for Constraint Maintenance. In *Proceedings of the 16th VLDB*, pages 566–577, 1990.

[Da90]   O. Deux and al. The Story of O_2. *Special Issue of IEEE Transactions on Knowledge and Data Engineering*, 2(1), March 1990.

[DBB+88] U. Dayal, B. Blaustein, A. Buchmann, U. Chakravarty, M. Hsu, R. Ledin, D. McCarthy, A. Rosenthal, S. Sarin, M.J. Carey, M. Livny, and R. Jaurhy. The HiPAC Project: Combining Active Databases And Timing Constraints. *SIGMOD RECORD*, 17(1), March 1988.

[fADF90] The Committee for Advanced DBMS Function. Third Generation Data Base System Manifesto. In *Proceedings of SIGMOD'90*, Atlantic City, May 1990.

[HK89]   S. Hudson and R. King. Cactis: a Self-Adaptive, Concurrent Implementation of an Object-Oriented Database Management System. *ACM TODS*, 14(3):291–321, 1989.

[HS90]   K. Hulsmann and G. Saake. Representation of the Historical Information Necessary for Temporal Integrity Monitoring. In *Proceedings of the 2nd EDBT*, pages 378–392, 1990.

[JMSS89] M. Jarke, S. Mazumdar, E. Simon, and D. Stemple. Assuring Database Integrity. Submitted for publication, 1989.

[KDM88]   A. Kotz, K. Dittrich, and J. Mulle. Supporting Semantic Rules by a Generalized Event/Trigger Mechanism. In *Proceedings of the 1st EDBT*, pages 76–91, 1988.

[KGBW90] W. Kim, J. F. Garza, N. Ballou, and D. Woelk. Architecture of the ORION Next-Generation Database System. *IEEE Transactions on Knowledge and Data Engineering*, 2(1):109 –124, March 1990.

[Kun85]   C. Kung. On verification of database temporal constraints. In *Proceedings of the ACM SIGMOD*, pages 169–179, 1985.

[Lip88]   U. Lipeck. Transformation of Dynamic Integrity Constraints into Transaction Specifications. In *Proceedings of ICDT*, pages 323–337, 1988.

[LR89]   C. Lécluse and P. Richard. Modeling Complex Structures in Object-Oriented Database. In *Proceedings of PODS*, 1989.

[LR90]   Christophe Lécluse and Philippe Richard. Data Base Schemas and Types Systems for DBPL. Rapport Technique 55-90, GIP Altaïr, Rocquencourt, France, 29 août 1990.

[MBW80]   J. Mylopoulos, P. Bernstein, and H. Wong. A Language Facility for Designing Database-Intensive Applications. *ACM TODS*, 5(3):185–207, 1980.

[Mor84]   M. Morgenstern. Constraint Equations: Declarative Expression of Constraints with Automatic Enforcement. In *Proceedings of the 10th VLDB*, pages 291–300, 1984.

[NQZ90]   R. Nassif, Y. Qiu, and J. Zhu. Extending the Object-Oriented Paradigm to Support Relationships and Constraints. In *Proceedings of the IFIP Conference Object Oriented Database Systems - Analysis, Design and Construction*, 1990.

[SJGP90]   M. Stonebraker, A. Jhingran, J. Goh, and S. Potamianos. On Rules, Procedures, Caching and Views in Database Systems. In *Procedings of the ACM SIGMOD*, pages 281–290, 1990.

[SK84]   A. Shepherd and L. Kerschberg. PRISM: a Knowledge Based System for Semantic Integrity Specification and Enforcement in Database Systems. In *Proceedings of ACM SIGMOD*, pages 307–315, 1984.

[SLR89]   T. Sellis, C. Lin, and L. Raschid. Implementing Large Productions Systems in a DBMS Environment: Concepts and Algorithms. In *Proceedings of ACM SIGMOD*, pages 404–412, 1989.

[UD89]   S. Urban and L. Delcambre. Constraint Analysis for Specifying Perspectives of Class Objects. In *Proceedings of the 5th IEEE Conference on Data Engineering*, pages 10–17, 1989.

[Via88]   V. Vianu. Database Survivability Under Dynamic Constraints. *Acta Informatica*, 25:55–84, 1988.

[WF90]   J. Widom and S. Finkelstein. Set Oriented Production Rules in Relational Database Systems. In *Proceedings of the ACM SIGMOD*, pages 259–270, 1990.

Hybrid Group Reflective Architecture for Object-Oriented Concurrent Reflective Programming

Satoshi Matsuoka   Takuo Watanabe
Akinori Yonezawa
Department of Information Science, The University of Tokyo*

Keywords and Phrases:
Actors, Object-Based Concurrency, Object Groups,
Reflection, Resource Management, Virtual Time

Abstract

The benefits of computational reflection are the abilities to reason and alter the dynamic behavior of computation from within the language framework. This is more beneficial in concurrent/distributed computing, where the complexity of the system is much greater compared to sequential computing; we have demonstrated various benefits in our past research of *Object-Oriented Concurrent Reflective (OOCR)* architectures. Unfortunately, attempts to formulate reflective features provided in practical reflective systems, such as resource management, have led to some difficulties in maintaining the linguistic lucidity necessary in computational reflection. The primary reason is that previous OOCR architectures lack the ingredients for group-wide object coordination. We present a new OOCR language with a *hybrid group reflective architecture*, ABCL/R2, whose key features are the notion of heterogeneous object groups and coordinated management of *group shared resources*. We describe and give examples of how such management can be effectively modeled and adaptively modified/controlled with the reflective features of ABCL/R2. We also identify that this architecture embodies *two* kinds of reflective towers, *individual* and *group*.

1   Introduction

Concurrent and distributed computing embodies multitudes of aspects not present in sequential computing. Various system resources such as computational power, communication, storage, I/O, etc. are naturally distributed and limited, and thus must be managed within the system in a coordinated manner; computational power, for example, is limited by the number of CPUs in the system, and thus scheduling and load-balancing become necessary. Such coordinated resource management (in a broad sense) of the system usually become little manifest at the language level; as a result, its control is only available in a fixed, ad-hoc fashion, with little possibility for user extensibility. This is not favorable, since concurrent/distributed architectures are much more complex compared to sequential ones, and the system must be *open* to structured dynamic extensions/modifications for adapting to new problems and environments.

Here, as were pointed out in [24] and [15], *computational reflection* can be beneficial in order to encompass such tasks within the programming language framework for the following reason: A (strict) reflective system embodies the structure and computational process of itself as appropriate abstractions, called the *Causally-Connected Self-Representation(s) (CCSR)*. By introspecting and altering

---

*Physical mail address: 7-3-1 Hongo, Bunkyo-ku, Tokyo 113, Japan. Phone 03-812-2111 (overseas +81-3-812-2111) ex. 4108. E-mail: {matsu,takuo,yonezawa}@is.s.u-tokyo.ac.jp

the CCSR, the abovementioned objectives can be realized at the language level, while maintaining the flexibility and portability.

Such uses of reflection are already proposed in distributed OS such as Muse[22], and window systems such as Silica[13]; they are important in that they demonstrate the effectiveness of *reflective techniques*. There, the meaning of 'reflection' is broader — their CCSRs are of the elements of the OS or of the window system, that is, their meta-systems are used to describe the implementation of the OS or the window system, and not the programming language. In the traditional linguistic sense, computational reflection is *linguistically lucid* — the view of the CCSR of language entities is intensional from within the language itself. That is to say, CCSR describes the computational process of the language itself. We would like our reflective architecture to be in the latter sense, thereby being able to achieve the necessary level of abstraction for various elements of CCSR at the language level. For an OOCP language, for example, it would be possible to define monitoring of objects within the language in a portable way, without resorting the underlying implementation details.

Our previous research of reflection[20, 21, 11] in *Object-Oriented Concurrent Programming (OOCP)* proposed several different kinds of *Object-Oriented Concurrent Reflective (OOCR)* architectures. For each OOCR architecture, we demonstrated the its applications to various features in concurrent and distributed computing, such as object monitoring and object migration. However, for wider classes of coordinated resource management, we have found some difficulties in maintaining the linguistic lucidity. The primary reason is that the architectures only had partial ingredients for realizing group-wide coordination of objects. By combining the architectures, we could attain more power — but doing so cannot be done without careful design, in order to maintain the lucidity as much as possible.

This paper demonstrates that linguistic lucidity can accompany reflective operations that practical systems require: First, we discuss the limitations of the previous OOCR architectures with respect to group-wide coordination of objects. Second, we present an OOCR language with a *hybrid group reflective architecture*, ABCL/R2, which incorporates heterogeneous object groups with group-wide object coordination and *group shared resources*. It also has other new features such as *non-reifying objects* for efficiency. We describe how these reflective features of ABCL/R2 allow coordinated resource management to be effectively modeled and efficiently controlled — as an example, we study the scheduling problem of the Time Warp algorithm[7] used in parallel discrete event simulations. Third, we contribute feedback to the conceptual side of OOCR architectures and object groups by (1) showing that (heterogeneous) object groups are not ad-hoc concepts but can be defined uniformly and lucidly, and (2) identifying that hybrid group architectures embody *two* kinds of reflective towers, instead of one: the *individual tower* which mainly determine the structure of each object, and the *group tower* which mainly determine computation.

2 Previous OOCR Architectures

Past research works analyzing and classifying metalevel and reflective architectures include those by Maes[10], Harmelen[18], Ferber[6], and Smith[15]. But so far to our knowledge no work has discussed issues in reflection *particular to concurrency*.

The two aspects of CCSR in OO languages are the *structural aspect*, indicating how objects or group of objects in the base-level and the meta-level are constructed and related, and the *computational aspect*, indicating how meta-level objects represent the computation of the base-level objects. The major key in the distinction of the structural aspect is the notion of *metaobjects*, introduced by Pattie Maes for a sequential OO language 3-KRS in [9]. For brevity, we will only briefly state that a *meta-level object* is an object which resides at the meta-level of the object-level computation as an element of the CCSR, and a *metaobject* is an object which reflects the structural, and possibly also the computational aspect of a *single* object. Note that a metaobject is a meta-level object, while the converse is not necessarily so; furthermore, there could be multiple metaobjects representing a single object.

2.1 Individual-based Architecture

In this architecture, each object in the system has its own metaobject(s) which solely govern(s) its computation. The threads of computation among metaobjects become naturally concurrent. By 'individual-based' we mean that an individual object is the unit of base-level computation that has a meaningful CCSR at the meta-level.

An example of this architecture is ABCL/R[20], a reflective version of ABCL/1[23]. Each object has its own unique metaobject, $\uparrow x$, which can be accessed with a special form [meta x]. Conversely, given a metaobject $\uparrow x$, [den $\uparrow x$] denotes the object it represents. Correspondence is 1-to-1, i.e., [meta [den $\uparrow x$]] $\stackrel{\text{def}}{=} \uparrow x$ and [den [meta x]] $\stackrel{\text{def}}{=} x$. The structural aspects of x — a set of state variables, a set of scripts, a local evaluator, and a message queue — are objects held in the state variables of $\uparrow x$ (Figure 1). The *arrival* of a message M at object x is represented as an *acceptance* of the message [:message $M\ R\ S$] at $\uparrow x$, where R and S are the *reply destination* and the *sender*, respectively. Customized metaobjects can be specified on object creation with the optional form (meta ...). A metaobject has its own metaobject $\Uparrow x$, naturally forming an infinite tower of metaobjects (Figure 1). Reflective computation in ABCL/R is via message transmissions to its metaobject and other objects in the tower.

Note that the individual-based architecture is independent from the issue of inter-level concurrency. In a sequential OO-reflective architecture, there is only a single computation thread in the tower of metaobjects. This thread performs the interpretation of a certain level, and a reflective operation causes a 'shift' of this level. By contrast, in ABCL/R, the interpretation of x by $\uparrow x$ is carefully designed so that the concurrency of the (individual) object activity defined by the the computational model of ABCL/1 — the message reception/queueing, and the execution of the user script — is preserved.

Other examples[1] include Tanaka's Actor language[16], Merling III[5], and X0/R[11].

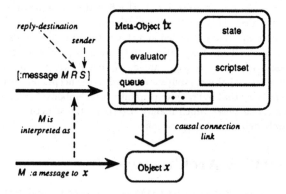

Figure 1: Reflective Architecture of ABCL/R

2.2 Group-wide Reflective Architecture

In this architecture, the behavior of an object is not governed by a single particular metaobject; rather, the collective behavior of a *group* of objects is represented as the coordinated actions of a group of meta-level objects, which comprise the *meta-group*. By 'group-wide' we mean that the entire object group is the unit of base-level computation that has a meaningful CCSR at the meta-level (as

---

[1] Both Merling III and Tanaka's Actor Language do not employ the term 'metaobject'. However, they do have the notion of some meta-level structure representing the structure and the computation of each object, which we regard as metaobjects in our terminology.

a meta-group); thus, there are *NO* intrinsic meta-relationships between an object and a particular object at the meta-level.

ACT/R[21] is an Actor-based language based on this architecture. The underlying formalism is Gul Agha's Actor model[1]. The meta-architecture of ACT/R is conceptually illustrated in Figure 2. Notice that there are no metaobjects, because the behavior of a single Actor is realized at the meta-level by coordinated action of multiple meta-level Actors. All reflective operations are performed solely via message sends, which are interpreted at the meta-level concurrently with interpretations of Actors at the base level; for various technical details including the faithfulness of the model to the Actor semantics, see [21].

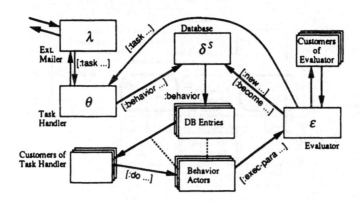

Figure 2: Reflective Architecture of ACT/R

2.3 Limitations of Both Architectures

The limitation of individual-based architectures is that it lacks the 'global view' of computation. Each metaobject is self-contained in a sense that it only controls the computation of its denotation; other objects can only be indirectly introspected or affected through their respective metaobjects. Thus, implicit coordination among the group of objects become difficult.

The limitation of group-wide architectures is that the identity of a base-level object is lost at the meta-level, i.e., identity is not intrinsic to the meta-level, but is implicit. To perform a reflective operation on a particular object, the identity of the object must be constructed explicitly from dispersed objects of the meta-system. As a consequence, what is natural with the individual-based architecture become difficult, for (1) explicit programming is required, and (2) causal connection is expensive to maintain, because it is difficult to obtain the true representation of the current state of the object in the meta-level due to the time delays in the message sends and the concurrent activities of the other parts of the meta-system.

Furthermore, both architectures lack the inherent notion of bounded resources, that is, computation basically proceeds in the presence of an unbounded number of objects representing resources, which would be bounded in real-life. For example, for the individual based, the infinite reflective tower can be constructed for all the objects in the system; for the group-wide, the amount of computation increases by the order of magnitude for the meta-level interpretation, but this is absorbed in the increased parallelism inherent in the basic Actor formalism.

2.4 Hybrid Group Reflective Architecture

In order to overcome the limitations, we propose an amalgamation of both architectures, called the *Hybrid Group (Reflective) Architecture*: In order to preserve the explicit identity and structure of

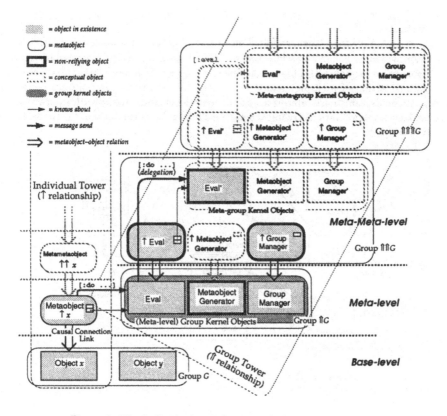

Figure 3: The Individual and Group Reflective Towers in ABCL/R2

objects at the meta-level, we maintain the tower of metaobjects in the same manner as the individual-based architecture. For coordinated management of system resources such as computational resource, we introduce object groups, whose meta-level representation is a group of meta-level objects that are responsible for managing the collective behavior of its member objects. The conceptual illustration of the resulting architecture is given in Figure 3. Note that there are two kinds of reflective towers, the *individual tower* for individual objects and the *group tower* for groups: the details will be described in the ensuing sections.

The hybrid group architecture does not merely combine the benefits of both architectures; the key benefit is that it is possible to model coordinated resource management which were otherwise difficult for previous OOCR architectures.

3 ABCL/R2: A Hybrid Group Architecture Language

ABCL/R2 is our prototype OOCR language with the hybrid group reflective architecture. It is a direct descendent of ABCL/R: each object x has its own meta-object $\uparrow x$, i.e., the unit of CCSR of an object is its metaobject. Also, as in ABCL/R, (1) the message reception and evaluation may proceed concurrently, preserving the ABCL/1 semantics, and (2) conceptually, there is an infinite structural (object-metaobject relationship) reflective tower per each object; the infinite meta-regression is resolved with lazy creation of the metaobject on demand.

3.1 Object Groups in ABCL/R2

The prime new feature of ABCL/R2 is the *heterogeneous object group*, or *group* for short. Members of a group participate in group-wide coordination for the management of system resources allocated to the group. Of special importance is the management of sharing of computational resources, which corresponds to scheduling in concurrent systems.

An object in ABCL/R2 always belongs to some group, with Default-Group being the default. A newly created object automatically becomes a member of the *same* group as its creator by default. The restriction is that an object cannot belong to multiple groups simultaneously. At the base-level, the structure of a group is flat in the sense that there are no base-level member objects which perform tasks specific to the group. Rather, analogous to the group-wide reflection, the structure and the computation of a group is explicitly defined at the meta- and higher levels of the group, by the objects called the *group kernel objects*. The group performs management of resources by coordinating among the metaobjects of the members and the group kernel objects.

Groups can be created dynamically with the group creation form as shown in Figure 4. The creation process of a group is not intrinsic, but is given given a concrete metacircular definition with ABCL/R2. As a result, not only that we have the tower of metaobjects, but we also have the tower of *meta-groups* as in ACT/R. We defer the details of group creation until Section 3.2.

```
[group  Group-Name    ;;; Group Definition.
   ;; a metaobject generator (required)
   (meta-gen Metaobject-generator)
   ;; a primary evaluator (required)
   (evaluator Evaluator)
   ;; additional resources (optional)
   (resources
       [name := expression]
       ;; example: a scheduler
       [scheduler := [scheduler-gen <= :new]]
       :
   )
   ;; extra (user definable) scripts definitions (optional)
   (script
       ;; Example: reflective operation to allocate more computational power on request
       (=> [:give-me-more-power Priority]
           ;;; Compute how much computational power can be given to the object.
           ;;;   Assume that the evaluator is extended to have a scheduler.
           [scheduler <= [:give-more-power-to sender computed-amount]])
       :
   )
   ;; initialization expressions
   (initialize
       Initialization-Expressions...
       ;; example: define an initial member of the group
       [object Root ...]
       :
   )
   ;; initialization for metalevel actors (set-up purpose)
   (initialize-meta
       Initialization-Expressions-for-Metalevel...
       ;; example: notify the initial scheduler
       [[meta evaluator] <= [:set-scheduler scheduler]]
       :
   )]
```

Figure 4: Group Definition in ABCL/R2

3.1.1 The Group Kernel Objects

The group kernel objects are the CCSR of the group and its management. They are identified with a dark shaded area in Figure 5:

- The *Group Manager* — represents and 'manages' the group. When a group is created, the identity of the group is actually that of the group manager object. It has two state variables holding the mail addresses of the primary evaluator and the primary metaobject generator of the group, but there are no inverse acquaintances. It also embodies the definition of itself for the creation of new groups. Its definition will be described in Section 3.2.

- The *(Primary) Metaobject Generator* — serves as the primary generator of the metaobjects for each member of the group. When a new object is created in the group, its metaobject is always created at the same time. The default metaobject generator of the system, **Metaobject-Generator**, is shown in Figure 6.

- The *(Primary) Evaluator* — represents the shared computational resource of the group. It purpose is to evaluate the methods of member objects. It is no longer a stand-alone, private object as in ABCL/R, but interacts with other group kernel objects and metaobjects for group management. The default definition is given in Figure 7. There could be multiple evaluators per group for parallelism.

Each metaobject of a group member object has state variables in its metaobject containing the mail addresses of group kernel objects for group membership; one is (the address of) the group manager, and the other is the primary evaluator (Figure 5). The group manager object can be accessed from the base-level with the special form [group-of ...]. Conversely, the metaobject generator is not directly known to the metaobjects of the group.

3.1.2 The Meta-Group

The group kernel objects are not members of the group they manage, because they reside at the meta-level of the member objects. But since the requirement that all objects belong to a group holds for group kernel objects as well (thus be able to compute in the first place), the *Meta-group* must exist to maintain the linguistic lucidity of reflective architectures. This is similar to ACT/R, where meta-actors comprised the meta-level group. In Figure 3, the metagroup of group G is identified as $\Uparrow G$. The group kernel objects are members of group $\Uparrow G$, while the metaobjects of the group kernel objects are members of $\Uparrow\Uparrow G$, etc. Here, the $\Uparrow$ tower forms a *group tower* distinct from the metaobject towers; we will discussed this in detail in Section 3.4.

In addition to the group kernel objects, there could be other meta-level objects that are members of the meta-group (or higher). In Figure 5, for example, the metaobjects of the evaluator and the group manager, in addition to the *scheduler* object, are members of the meta-meta-group of the base group.

3.1.3 Group Shared Resources

The member objects of a group share *group shared resources*, which are the CCSR of system resources, such as computational resource. The group-wide coordination of resource sharing by the member objects is controlled by the metaobject of each member object, with the aid of the group kernel objects. Coordination of sharing is thus done at the meta-level, and is basically invisible at the base-level. The homogeneity of metaobjects with respect to such coordinated behavior is guaranteed by the metaobjects being generated by the (primary) metaobject generator, which is unique to a group.

By default, the evaluator object is the CCSR of the shared computational resource of the group. By coordinating the evaluation with the metaobjects and the *scheduler* object, we can allocate more computational resources to certain objects in order to achieve higher execution efficiency. Other shared resources could be defined for the purpose of either adding new functionalities to the group, and/or making the implementation details manifest in order to alter some existing behavior. For this purpose, the user specifies a specialized metaobject generator. Examples currently under study include class database objects for distributed class management.

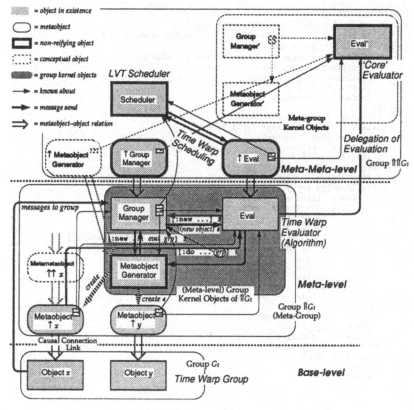

Figure 5: Reflective Architecture of ABCL/R2

3.2 Object and Group Creation in ABCL/R2

In ABCL/R2, the dynamics of object and group creation are manifest in the language; otherwise, the user would not be able to define more sophisticated groups tailored for his particular program and/or hardware architecture. Such extensibility via reflection distinguishes our work from previous works in object or process groups (see [8] for a survey), in which the functionalities of the group, especially its creation, were hard-wired and inalterable.

3.2.1 Object Creation Process

The default group membership of a newly created object is the same as its creator. This can be overridden, however, by explicit designation of a group in the object creation form. Similarly, a specialized metaobject for a particular object can be specified, overriding the primary metaobject generator of that group:

```
[object object-name
    (meta metaobject generator)      ;; optional, specify alternative metaobject
    (group group)                    ;; optional, specify alternative group
    ...
```

We show that the behavior results from our reflective architecture. Rather than to force the reader to follow through the details of the code, we give intuitive descriptions of the process of object x creating a new object y in group G_1, as illustrated in the lower part of Figure 5. The labeled message sends in the figure is numbered in correspondence to the explanations below:

```
[object Metaobject-Generator    ;; The 'Vanilla' Primary Metaobject Generator
 (script
  (=> [:new StateVars LexEnv Scripts Evaluator GMgr]
   ![object Metaobject    ;; The name 'Metaobject' is local to this method.
    (state [queue := [queue-gen <= :new]]
           [state := [env-gen <= [:new StateVars LexEnv]]]
           [scriptset := Scripts]
           [evaluator := Evaluator]
           [Group := GMgr]
           [mode := ':dormant])
     (script
      (=> [:message Message Reply Sender]
          [queue <= [:enq [Message Reply Sender]]]
          (when (eq mode ':dormant)
            [mode := ':active]
            [Me <= :begin]))
      (=> :begin
          (match [queue <= :deq]
           (is [Message Reply Sender]
               (match (find-script Message Reply scriptset)
                (is [Bindings ScriptBody]
                    [evaluator <=
                     [:do-progn
                       ScriptBody [env-gen <== [:new Bindings state]]
                       [den Me] GMgr] @
                     [cont
                       [Me <= :end]]])
                (otherwise
                 (warn "~S cannot handle the message ~S"
                   [den Me] Message))))))
      (=> :end
          (if (not [queue <== :empty?])
            [Me <= :begin]
            [mode := ':dormant]))
       ;; Methods implementing reflective operations.
       ;; see [20, 23] for details.
      (=> :queue
          !queue)
              :
      )])
  )]
```

Figure 6: Primary Metaobject Generator in ABCL/R2

1. Object x receives a message, and attempts to evaluate the corresponding script of x which contains an object creation form [object ...]. At the metaobject level, the script, the new environment, and the group (represented by the group manager) are sent to the evaluator object in the [:do ...] message (labeled 1 in Figure 5).

2. When the evaluator encounters the [object ...] form in the script, it sends a [:new ...] message to the target group manager object. If there is an explicit group specification with [group ...], then the target becomes the group manager object of the specified group; otherwise, the target is the group manager that was passed as a parameter in the [:do ...] message in Step 1, causing the group of the new object y to be the same as x (i.e., G_1). In both cases, the evaluator passes the specialized metaobject generator to the target metaobject generator in the message if and only if the object creation form has the (meta ...) option (labeled 2).

3. The group manager sends the [:new ...] message to the metaobject generator. If a specialized metaobject generator is passed in the message from the evaluator, that becomes the target; otherwise, the target is the primary metaobject generator of G_1. In both cases, the group manager passes the evaluator and itself in the message so that the new object would become the member of G_1 (labeled 3).

4. The metaobject generator creates the metaobject of the new object y, and returns it to the group manager of G_1. This metaobject creation would be interpreted as a creation of an object

```
[object Eval    ;; The Primary Evaluator — computational resource for the group.
 (script
  (=> [:do Exp Env Id Gid] @ C     ; Evaluation for a single expression.
     (match (parse-exp Exp)
      ;; Variables
      (is [:variable Var]
          (match Var
           (is 'Me ![den Id])    ; pseudo variable Me
           (is 'Group !Gid)      ; pseudo variable Group
           (otherwise [Env <= [:value-of Var] @ C))))
      ;; Past-Type Message Transmission
      (is [:send-past Target Message Reply]
          [Me <= [:do-evlis [Target Message Reply] Env Id Gid] @
           [cont [target* message* reply*]
            [C <= nil]
            (if (not (null target*))
             [[meta target*] <= [:message message* reply* [den Id]]])]])
      ;; Now-Type Message Transmission
      (is [:send-now Target Message]   (similar to above, omitted) )

      ;; Object Creation
      (is [:object-def Name Meta-gen-spec State Script]
          [Me <= [:do Meta-gen-spec Env Id Gid] @
           [cont meta-gen*
            (if (null meta-gen*)
             ;; if a metaobject generator is not explicitly specified, use default.
             [Gid <= [:new State Script] @
              [cont object
               (if Name
                [Env <= [:set Name object] @ C]
                !object)]]
             [meta-gen <= [:new State Env Script Me Gid] @ C)]])
          )
      ;; composite evaluation messages
      (=> [:do-progn (FirstExp . RestExps) Env Id Gid] @ C
       [Me <= [:do FirstExp Env Id Gid] @
        [cont first* [Me <= [:do-progn RestExps Env Id Gid] @ C]]])
      (=> [:do-progn (LastExp) Env Id Gid] @ C
       [Me <= [:do LastExp Env Id Gid] @ C])
      )]
```

Figure 7: Primary Evaluator in ABCL/R2

at the base-level due to the causal-connection property (labeled 4).

5. The group manager returns the new metaobject ↑y to the evaluator, which in turn returns it to ↑x; this is interpreted at the base-level as x receiving the new y. In the default case as illustrated in Figure 5, y belongs to G_1 — as a result, it shares the computational and other resources with x and other members of G_1 (labeled 5).

3.2.2   Dynamic Group Creation and Bootstrapping

A group is created dynamically at run-time with the evaluation of the group creation form in Figure 4. The name of the group is global; it actually refers to the group manager object. The two required objects are the primary metaobject generator and the primary evaluator of the group. Other shared resources are optional and are defined in the (resources ...) form. Next are the optional user-definable scripts of the group; they become the scripts of the group manager upon group creation. In Figure 4, the user defines a reflective method :give-me-more-power which allocates more computational resource to an object upon request. Finally, there are two initialization forms of the group: the former is the object-level initializer, whose prime purpose is the creation of the initial *fixed members* of the group; the latter is the meta-level initializer for initializing the meta-level objects of the group. Due to the dependency between the meta-level and the base-level objects, the latter is evaluated prior to the former.

The initial bootstrapping of a group is achieved in a manner similar to object creation: when the group creation form is detected, the evaluator object sends the group creation message to the group manager object. The group manager object then evaluates the object creation form (outlined in Figure 8) for the group manager of the new group. It roughly proceeds as follows: The mail addresses of the group shared resources are stored in the state variables, and the user-defined scripts of the group is merged with the default scripts of the new group manager. The generated initialization script includes the base-level and the meta-level initialization forms; the former is to be sent to the evaluator of the new group, while the latter is to be executed directly by the new group manager (and is thus evaluated by the meta-group evaluator). The newly created group manager object is then sent the :initialize message to start the above initialization sequence.

When an object of group G_1 creates a group G_2, the $\Uparrow G_1$ is identical to $\Uparrow G_2$; in other words, the group kernel objects of G_2 becomes a member of the same group as those of G_1.

```
[[object Group-Manager-Name
   (state [meta-gen := Metaobject-Generator]
          [evaluator := Evaluator]
          [name := expression]                    ;; additional resources
          [scheduler := [scheduler-gen <== :new]]  ;; the scheduler example
          )
   (script
    ;; initialization (bootstrap) method (automatically generated)
    (=> :initialize
        ;; initialization for metalevel can be directly executed by itself
        Initialization-Expressions-for-Metalevel...
        [[meta evaluator] <= [:set-scheduler scheduler]] ;; example

        ;; initialization codes must be sent to the new primary evaluator
        ;; Id is unspecified, (for there are no members)
        [evaluator <= [:do-progn '(Initialization-Expressions) global-env NIL Me]]
        )
    ;; default group manager methods (automatically generated)
    (=> :meta-gen
        !meta-gen)
    (=> :evaluator
        !evaluator)
    (=> [:new StateObj Env Script] @ C
        [meta-gen <= [:new StateObj Env Script evaluator Me] @ C])
    (=> [:new StateObj Env Script SpecialEvaluator] @ C
        [meta-gen <= [:new StateObj Env Script SpecialEvaluator Me] @ C])

    ;; user-defined methods: (the :give-me-more-power example)
    (=> [:give-me-more-power Priority]
        ;;; Compute how much computational power can be given to the object.
        [scheduler <= [:give-more-power-to sender computed-amount]])

    )]
<= :initialize]
```

Figure 8: Dynamic Group Creation and Bootstrapping

3.3   Non-reifying Objects

Another new feature of ABCL/R2 is the *non-reifying* object, whose purpose is to attain higher efficiency at the sacrifice for the loss of reflective capabilities. It is created with the following form:

```
[object object-name
   (meta non-reifying-meta)
   ...
```

The behavior of a non-reifying object is almost the same as that of a standard object. The difference is that reflective operations are disallowed — an attempt would result in an error.

The non-reifying object does not have a metaobject, i.e., the metaobject is only of 'hypothetical' existence, prohibiting actual reference to it within the script. (It is possible to have references to metaobjects of other standard objects.) Extensibility, as a consequence, is lost; however, non-reifying objects execute much more efficiently compared to the standard ones. In Figures 3 and 5, non-reifying objects are illustrated with thick borders; notice that they do not have metaobjects that actually exist. In our prototype implementation, a non-reifying object is actually an ABCL/1 object that mimics the interface of metaobjects in ABCL/R2. It runs faster compared to native ABCL/R2 objects due to optimized message handling.

As we see in the figures, some of the meta-level objects are not fully instantiated. This is because the members of the meta-group usually assume default behaviors identical to the ABCL/R objects, and the system thus can avoid the infinite meta-regression using standard techniques. However, the metaobject of the evaluator, for example, is instantiated; this requires that the evaluator of the meta-group be instantiated in order to process *its* evaluation. Other meta-level objects, such as the metaobject generator of $\Uparrow G$, is instantiated lazily at run-time when a new group is created.

3.4 The Two Kinds of Reflective Towers

Before proceeding, let us discuss the relationship between the individual tower and the group tower. The term 'tower' implies that there are some kind of structural relationships between the computations at each level. For example, the reflective tower in LISP is the tower of evaluation[14]. The state of the computation at level n can be given as a triplet data structure $<$ *expression, environment, continuation* $>$ at level $(n-1)$, which can be reified/reflected at each level.

The reflective tower of an ABCL/R object is an individual tower of object-metaobject relationship $\uparrow$, where each metaobject solely determines the structure of the object it denotes. This is also the case for ABCL/R2as we have seen.

In addition, in ABCL/R2, the meta-group relationship $\Uparrow$, which is structural, forms the group tower as illustrated in Figure 3. This tower parallels the meta-evaluation relationship, which is computational, in the following way: Let G_x be the group of a given object x, and E_x (labeled Eval) be the primary evaluator of G_x, which is a member of $\Uparrow G_x$. Since E_x is an object itself, it needs some computational resource, provided by the primary evaluator E_{E_x} (labeled Eval') of the group G_{E_x} to which it belongs. This group is the meta-group of $\Uparrow G_x$, i.e. $\Uparrow\Uparrow G_x$. Now, E_x has a metaobject, $\uparrow E_x$ (labeled $\uparrow Eval$). In our current architecture, we define this object to be also a member of $\Uparrow\Uparrow G_x$, so that the evaluations of both E_{E_x} and $\uparrow E_x$ are performed by the evaluator of the group $\Uparrow\Uparrow G_x$ (labeled Eval"). This forms a homogeneous tower-like structure of meta-groups as seen in the figure.

The above indicates that the reflective towers might not be solely in the direction of the $\uparrow$ relationship, but also in the direction of the $\Uparrow$ relationship. Since this was not manifest in the previous OOCR architectures, we attempt to place some distinctions between them:

- The individual tower mainly determines the structure of the object, including its script. Thus, reflective operations to alter the script is in the domain of the individual tower.

- The group tower mainly determines the group behavior, including the computation (evaluation) of the script of the group members. Thus, changes to have different *interpretations* of the same script are in the domain of the group tower.

The above distinctions correspond to the issue whether a reflective operations would affect the program itself, or affect the *interpretation* of the program. However, we cannot merely say that the individual tower only represents structure, and the group tower only represents computation; for example, we could modify the metaobject via the meta-metaobject so that it would suddenly deadlock after receiving k messages. We need more work to establish more sound conceptual distinctions, and develop the model into a formal one, as has been done for single reflective towers for LISP in the works by Friedman and Wand[19] and by Danvy and Malmkjær ([4], etc.).

Now, there is a choice in the construction of the individual tower of member object x: it can be made either distinct or parallel to the group tower. This corresponds to the issue of the *group membership of metaobjects*. We have deliberately avoided the discussion up to this point, because the membership is dependent on the scheme whereby the meta-circularity is broken. In the current implementation of ABCL/R2, the lazy creation of an metaobject is achieved with *self-reifying metaobject*. An regular ABCL/R2 object x (i.e., not non-reifying), upon evaluation of the form [meta x], does not cause the creation of a new meta-metaobject $\Uparrow x$. Rather, the self-reifying metaobject is essentially 'raised' to become the meta-metaobject, and it is properly initialized so that it would serve as the metaobject of $\Uparrow x$. This behavior is unfortunately not currently manifest as CCSR in the current implementation. As a result, the entire tower becomes a member of $\Uparrow G_x$, except for the base level x, as shown in Figure 5. Here, the individual tower is distinct from the group tower, in the sense that there are no correspondences between the meta-levels.

In order for the two towers to be parallel, the metaobject of level n needs to be created by the metaobject generator of the corresponding meta-group of level n. This requires a lazy creation scheme for the group kernel objects upon metaobject creation, which again is not manifest as CCSR in the current implementation. As a future work, we plan to extend the architecture so that the lazy creation of both objects and groups to be manifest, so that the user can have a choice on how to relate the two towers.

4   Reflective Programming in ABCL/R2

Reflective programming in ABCL/R2 is performed in two ways. One is to utilize its metaobject in the same way as ABCL/R, which were described in [20]. Another is to introspect and affect the group-wide coordinated behavior of the group the object is a member of. This is performed with a message to its group, [group-of x] (delivered to its group manager object). The two schemes are not contradictory; in practice, a combination of both schemes is effectively used.

For the remainder of the section, we present an example of computational resource management using reflective programming in ABCL/R2. Management of other resources can be performed analogously.

4.1   Time Warp Scheduling in ABCL/R2

In our previous work with ABCL/R, we have presented an example of how an OOCR architecture can be cleanly implement the *Time Warp* algorithm[7] (also known as the Virtual Time scheme) employed in parallel discrete event simulation. When objects model the entities and the message transmission/reception model the events in the simulation, the Time Warp algorithm serves to maintain the temporal consistency among the events. Consistency management is distributed and optimistic; each object has its own *Local Virtual Time (LVT)* (i.e., there is no global clock), and the messages are timestamped to be compared with the LVT of the recipient. When a conflict is detected, the object performs automatic *rollback* by sending *anti-messages* until it reaches the time just prior to the conflict occurrence.

In our previous implementation, the entire Time Warp algorithm was successfully encapsulated in the within the metaobject of each object, since Time Warp algorithm was meta-level to the execution of the simulation itself. One thing we did not address was the performance issues affected by different scheduling policies. A recent work by Burdorf and Marti[2], however, compared ten non-preemptive scheduling algorithms for the Time Warp algorithm, and discovered that there were orders of magnitude difference in their execution speed for some problems. Thus, we cannot ignore scheduling issues in practice when we implement the Time Warp algorithms with OOCP languages.

Burdorf and Marti made some simple assumptions in their performance measurement; for example, they did not allow interprocessor communication between the schedulers, which is necessary for inter-group load balancing. This is too restrictive for OOCP languages, where inter-scheduler communication would be simple. Also, they did not attempt any adaptive scheduling, that is, to alter the scheduling algorithm dynamically to adapt to better algorithms when excessive rollbacks occur during the simulation. For efficiency, we would like our language to be able to model these

```
┌─────────────────────────────────────────────┐
│   Time Warp Scheduling (Meta-Meta-level)     │
├─────────────────────────────────────────────┤
│    Time Warp Algorithm (Meta-level)          │
├─────────────────────────────────────────────┤
│   Application Code (Time Warp Group)         │
└─────────────────────────────────────────────┘
```

Figure 9: Meta-level Encapsulation of the Time Warp Algorithm

in a clean way; unfortunately, it was not easy with previous OOCP languages for the reasons we discussed in Section 2.3.

With ABCL/R2 we can obtain a clean solution: We define a *Time Warp group*, whose members are specialized with their individual metaobjects so that they coordinate in running the Time Warp algorithm. This is similar to the ABCL/R example, except that group membership automatically dictates Time Warp behavior, not requiring explicit metaobject specification. The actual definition of the Time Warp group are given in the Appendix. Messages sent within the group or to destinations within other Time Warp groups must be of the form:

$$[\textit{target} <\text{= } \textit{message} \text{ @ } \textit{reply-destination} \text{ :vrt } \textit{virtual-send-time}]$$

Since scheduling is meta-level to the execution of the Time Warp algorithm, we would want to encapsulate it in the *meta-level* of the Time Warp algorithm (i.e., meta-meta-level of the actual simulation algorithm), in the same manner that the algorithm itself was encapsulated in the meta-level of the simulation. The conceptual illustration of the encapsulation is given in Figure 9. For implementation, we utilize the group-reflective features of our architecture. We introduce the *Time Warp scheduler* object labeled Scheduler in Figure 5. It is responsible for controlling the allocation of the computational resource within a Time Warp group. For meta-meta-level encapsulation of scheduling, the scheduler does not interact with the evaluator of the Time Warp group; rather, it interacts with the *metaobject* of the evaluator. The metaobject of the evaluator is specialized so that the evaluation request to the evaluator sent from an object in the group is not directly executed, but instead sent to the scheduler. The metaobject then asks the scheduler for the next evaluation job as determined by the algorithm of the scheduler. This behavior is outlined in the abridged code of the evaluator below:

```
[object TW-Eval-meta   ;;; metaobject of the evaluator of the Time Warp group
  (meta non-reifying-meta)
  (state [scheduler := Scheduler])
  (script
  ;; meta-level reception of message to the evaluator
  (=> [:message [KeyWord Expr Env Id Time] R S]
        where (member KeyWord '(:do :do-evlis :do-progn))
      [scheduler <= [:schedule [KeyWord Expr Env Id Time] :with Id Time]]
      (if (eql mode 'dormant)
          [Me <= :begin]))
  (=> :begin
      (match [scheduler <== :next]
          :
      ))]
```

Aside from the behavior specific to Virtual Time, the behavior of the evaluator is almost identical to that of a standard evaluator. The TW-Eval-meta (labeled ↑Eval in Figure 5) delegates most of the scheduled evaluation requests directly to the evaluator of the meta-group (labeled Eval'). Since Eval' is a non-reifying object, the delegation would terminate there. In effect, Eval' is the sole computational resource for all the members of the group as well as the objects that comprise the group, including the group kernel objects[2]. So, in a sense, Eval′ is the native CPU hardware in an operating system; this is a generalization of the conceptual model of reflective operating systems such as Muse[22].

With this framework, dynamic change of the scheduler can be accommodated as given in the Appendix. Furthermore, it would be easy to extend the Time Warp group to add inter-scheduler communication, and/or to have scheduler controlling multiple meta-group evaluators to adapt to growth of computational resource in hardware.

Our plan is to measure the performance of more elaborate versions of Time Warp scheduling algorithms on ABCL/R2. We are not planning real-time benchmarks, however; instead, we plan to simulate the execution of the Time Warp algorithm using parallel discrete event simulation, employing the Time Warp algorithm itself. Treatment of such grossly intricate circularity would be significantly difficult for conventional non-reflective systems, but should be possible with our framework which permit meta-level encapsulation.

5. Discussions and Future Work

5.1 Relationship to Other Works

Here, we discuss the relationships with other works, those in object groups and reflective systems. The usefulness of the concept of an object group has been been widely recognized. But unfortunately, most work on object groups from the language aspect of OOCP has been for homogeneous groups[3, 12]; as for heterogeneous groups, its definition or construction has been mostly vague (for example, [8]). In this work, we have shown that heterogeneous object groups are not ad-hoc concepts, but can be defined constructively and lucidly in an OOCR language, and how cooperative actions of objects in a group with respect to resource management at the base-level can be described in the meta-level architecture. In a sense, our proposal would serve as one reference model for (heterogeneous) object groups.

As for reflective systems, the Muse distributed operating system[22] could be classified as a group-wide architecture, although it has some features of the hybrid architecture. The meta-level objects in the 'meta-space' 'support' the activity of the objects. There are specific meta-level objects responsible for message delivery, scheduling, memory management, etc. The reflective operation is performed by communicating with the meta-space via ports called *reflectors*. Although Muse uses the term 'reflection' in a more loose sense, it nevertheless incorporates many of the ideas from reflection, and thus enjoys their benefits not previously available in the traditional operating systems.

5.2 Current Status of ABCL/R2

The implementation of ABCL/R2 is underway. A subset is almost completely running on the parallel version of ABCL/1 on the IBM TOP-1, a shared-memory multiprocessor machine with ten 80386 CPUs. A program in ABCL/1 is compiled into a program in the parallel version of Common LISP running on TOP-1[17]. This version does not fully implement architecture in this paper, however. We are starting a complete version on Omron LUNA-88k, a multicomputer with four 88000 CPUs running Mach. We are also planning a distributed implementation on an Intel iPSC/2 Hypercube computer, based on the new distributed implementation of ABCL/1 in progress.

5.3 Future Work

Our work is by no means complete or our proposal ultimate. There are still some limitations with ABCL/R2 which we must strive to solve. For example, there is a difficulty in the management of two distinct resources exhibiting collaborative behaviors; this is necessary for realization of features proposed in advanced operating systems, where the virtual memory management coordinates with

---

[2]The situation would be analogous for multiple evaluators.

the thread scheduler. We could extend our architecture further, and/or make an approach from the group-wide reflection to the individual-based. In either cases, we feel that works in OOCR languages cannot avoid having strong emphasis on the architectural issues, for it is not the language but the language architecture that would contribute the most in solving the problems in practice. The search must go on for even more effective OOCR architectures.

6 Acknowledgements

We would like to thank Daniel Bobrow, Shigeru Chiba, Brian Foote, Mamdouh Ibrahim, Yutaka Ishikawa, Gregor Kiczales, Brian Smith, Jiro Tanaka, Tomoyuki Tanaka, Mario Tokoro, and numerous other people, the discussions with whom truly inspired us. We would also like to thank the comments from the anonymous referees which helped us to clarify and organize our work. Finally, we thank the members of the ABCL project group for their assistance with our everyday research.

References

[1] Gul Agha. *ACTORS: A Model of Concurrent Computation in Distributed Systems*. The MIT Press, 1986.

[2] Christopher Burdorf and Jed Marti. Non-preemptive time warp scheduling algorithm. *Operating Systems Review*, 24(2):7-18, April 1990.

[3] Andrew Chien and William J. Dally. Concurrent aggregates. In *Proceedings of ACM SIGPLAN Symposium on Principles and Practice of Parallel Programming (PPOPP)*, pages 187-196. SIGPLAN Notices, March 1990.

[4] Olivier Danvy and Karoline Malmkjær. Intensions and extensions in the reflective tower. In *Proceedings of the ACM Conference on LISP and Functional Programming*, pages 327-341. ACM Press, 1988.

[5] Jacques Ferber. Conceptual reflection and Actor languages. In Pattie Maes and Daniele Nardi, editors, *Meta-Level Architectures and Reflection*, pages 177-193. North-Holland, 1988.

[6] Jacques Ferber. Computational reflection in class-based object-oriented languages. In *Proceedings of OOPSLA'89*, volume 24, pages 317-326. SIGPLAN Notices, ACM Press, October 1989.

[7] David R. Jefferson. Virtual Time. *ACM Transactions on Programming Languages and Systems*, 7(3):404-425, July 1985.

[8] Luping Liang, Samuel T. Chanson, and Gerald W. Newfeld. Process groups and group communications: Classifications and requirements. *IEEE Computer*, pages 56-66, February 1990.

[9] Pattie Maes. Concepts and experiments in computational reflection. In *Proceedings of OOPSLA'87*, volume 22, pages 147-155. SIGPLAN Notices, ACM Press, October 1987.

[10] Pattie Maes. Issues in computational reflection. In Pattie Maes and Daniele Nardi, editors, *Meta-Level Architectures and Reflection*, pages 21-35. North-Holland, 1988.

[11] Satoshi Matsuoka and Akinori Yonezawa. Metalevel solution to inheritance anomaly in concurrent object-oriented languages. In *Proceedings of the ECOOP/OOPSLA'90 Workshop on Reflection and Metalevel Architectures in Object-Oriented Programming*, October 1990.

[12] Flavio De Paoli and Mehdi Jazayeri. FLAME: a language for distributed programming. In *Proceedings of the 1990 IEEE International Conference on Programming Languages*, pages 69-78, 1990.

[13] Ramana Rao. Implementational reflection in Silica. In *Proceedings of ECOOP'91*. Springer-Verlag, July 1991.

[14] Brian C. Smith. Reflection and semantics in Lisp. In *Conference Record of the ACM Symposium on Principles of Programming Languages*, pages 23–35. ACM Press, 1984.

[15] Brian C. Smith. What do you mean, meta? In *Proceedings of the ECOOP/OOPSLA'90 Workshop on Reflection and Metalevel Architectures in Object-Oriented Programming*, October 1990.

[16] Tomoyuki Tanaka. Actor-based reflection without meta-objects. Technical Report RT-0047, IBM Research, Tokyo Reserach Laboratory, August 1990.

[17] Tomoyuki Tanaka and Shigeru Uzuhara. Multiprocessor Common Lisp on TOP-1. In *Proceedings of the IEEE Symposium on Parallel and Distributed Processing*, 1990. (to appear).

[18] Frank van Harmlen. A classification of meta-level architectures. In Abramson and Rogers, editors, *Meta-Programming in Logic Programming*, chapter 5, pages 103–122. The MIT Press, 1989.

[19] Mitchell Wand and Danel P. Friedman. The mystery of the tower revealed: A non-reflective description of the reflective tower. In Pattie Maes and Daniele Nardi, editors, *Meta-Level Architectures and Reflection*, pages 111–134. North-Holland, 1988.

[20] Takuo Watanabe and Akinori Yonezawa. Reflection in an object-oriented concurrent language. In *Proceedings of OOPSLA'88*, volume 23, pages 306–315. SIGPLAN Notices, ACM Press, September 1988.

[21] Takuo Watanabe and Akinori Yonezawa. An actor-based metalevel architecture for group-wide reflection. In *Proceedings of the REX School/Workshop on Foundations of Object-Oriented Languages (REX/FOOL), Noordwijkerhout, the Netherlands*, Lecture Notes in Computer Science. Springer-Verlag, May 1990.

[22] Yasuhiko Yokote, Fumio Teraoka, and Mario Tokoro. A reflective architecture for an object-oriented distributed operating system. In Stephen Cook, editor, *Proceedings of ECOOP'89*, pages 89–106. Cambridge University Press, 1989.

[23] Akinori Yonezawa, editor. *ABCL: An Object-Oriented Concurrent System*. Computer Systems Series. The MIT Press, 1990.

[24] Akinori Yonezawa and Takuo Watanabe. An introduction to object-based reflective concurrent computations. In *Proceedings of the 1988 ACM SIGPLAN Workshop on Object-Based Concurrent Programming*, volume 24, pages 50–54. SIGPLAN Notices, ACM Press, April 1989.

A   Appendix: Definition of the Time Warp Group

Figures 10, 11, and 12 are the skeletal definition of the Time Warp group. The scheduling algorithm is the Lowest LVT (Local Virtual Time) First scheduler[2], but it can be interchanged dynamically with any valid Time Warp scheduler.

;;; The Time Warp group

```
[group TW-group
 (meta-gen TW-meta-gen)
 (evaluator [TW-eval-gen <== [:new Lowest-LVT-First-Scheduler]])
 ;; ... additional scripts & initialization expressions here ...
 ]
```

;;; The Lowest Local Virtual Time First Scheduler

```
[object Lowest-LVT-First-Scheduler
 (state [queue := [priority-queue-gen <== [:new :test-fun #'<]]])
 (script
  (=> [:schedule Message :with Id LVT]
      (match Message
       (is [:anti-message . ARGS]
            ;; Anihiration of the positive of this anti-message.
            (if [queue <== [:have? [:message . ARGS]]]
                [queue <= [:remove [:message . ARGS]]]
                [queue <= [:enq Message :with LVT]]))
       (otherwise
        [queue <= [:enq Message :with LVT]]))))
  (=> :next @ C
      [queue <= :deq @ C])
  (=> :contents @ C
      [queue <= :listify @ C])
  (=> [:copy List]
      [queue <= [:enq-list List]])
 )]
```

Figure 10: The Time Warp Group

```
[object TW-Meta-Gen    ;;; The Metaobject Generator of the Time Warp group
 (script
   (=> [:new StateVars LexEnv Script Evaluator GMgr]
       ![object TW-meta
         (state [queue := [queue-gen <== :new]]
                [pqueue := [priority-queue-gen <== :new]]
                [state := [undoable-env-gen <== [:new StateVars LexEnv]]]
                [output-history := [output-history-gen <== :new]]
                [scriptset := Script]
                [evaluator := Evaluator]
                [group := GMgr]
                [mode := ':dormant]
                [LVT := 0])
         (script
           ;; Ordinary messages (omitted)
               :
           ;; TimeWarp messages
           (=> [Type Message Reply Sender VST VRT]
                   where (member Type '(:message :anti-message))
               [pqueue <= [:enq [Message Reply Sender VST VRT] :with VRT]]
               (when (eq mode :dormant)
                 [mode := ':active]
                 [Me <= :begin-tw]))
           (=> :begin-tw
               (if [queue <== :empty?] ; check the ordinary message queue first
                   (match [pqueue <== :next]
                     (is [Message Reply Sender VST VRT] where (>= VRT LVT)
                         [state <= [:push LVT]]
                         [LVT := VRT]
                         (match (find-script Message scriptset)
                           (is [Vars Body]
                               [evaluator <= [:do-progn Body
                                                [env-gen <== [:new Bindings state]]
                                                [den Me] GMgr output-history LVT] @
                                           [cont ignore
                                                 [Me <= :end]]])
                           (is NIL
                               (warn "~A cannot handle the message: ~S"
                                     [den Me] Message)
                               [Me <= :end])))
                     (is [Message Reply Sender VST VRT] where (< VRT LVT)
                         ;; State rolls back itself to the most recent time
                         ;; before VRT and returns the value of the time.
                         [LVT := [state <== [:rollback-to VRT]]]
                         ;; Input queue for TimeWarp messages shold also be rewinded
                         [pqueue <= [:rollback-to VRT]]
                         ;; Send anti-messages.
                         (dolist (h [output-history <== [:history-since VRT]])
                           (match h
                             (is [Target Message Reply VST VRT]
                                 [Target <= [:anti-message Message
                                              Reply [den Me] VST VRT]])))))
                   [Me <= :begin]))
           (=> :begin
               ... same as 'vanilla' meta objects ...)
           (=> :end
               (if (not [queue <== :empty?])
                   [Me <= :begin]
                   (if (not [pqueue <== :empty?])
                       [Me <= :begin-tw]
                       [mode := ':dormant])))
         )])
 )]
```

Figure 11: Group Kernel Objects of the Time Warp Group (1)

```
[object TW-Eval-gen        ;;; The evaluator of the Time Warp group
 (script
   (=> [:new Scheduler]
       [object TW-eval
        (meta TW-eval-meta-gen)
        (script
         (=> [:do Exp Env Id Gid Outputs LVT] @ C
             (match (parse-exp Exp)
              (is [:variable Var]   ; variables and pseudo-variables
                  (match Var
                   (is 'Me ![den Id])
                   (is 'Group !Gid)
                   (is 'LVT !LVT)
                   (otherwise [Env <= [:value-of Var] @ C])))
              (is [:send-tw-mesg Target Message Reply VRT]
                  [Me <= [:do-evlis [Target Message Reply VRT] Env Id Gid Outputs LVT] @
                  [cont [target* message* reply* vrt*]
                   [C <= ()]
                   (if (not (null target*))
                       (progn
                        [[meta target*] <= [:message message* reply* LVT vrt*]]
                        [Outputs <= [:push [target* message* reply* LVT vrt*]]]
                        ))]])
              (is [:object-def Name Meta-gen-spec State Script]
                  [Me <= [:do Meta-gen-spec Env Id Gid Outputs LVT] @
                  [cont meta-gen*
                   (if (null meta-gen)
                       [Gid <= [:new State Script] @
                       [cont object
                        (if Name
                            [Env <= [:set-global Name object] @ C]
                            !C)]])]])
              )))]
       [[meta TW-eval] <= [:set-scheduler Scheduler]]
       !TW-eval
   ))]

[object TW-Eval-meta-gen   ;;; The special metaobject for TW-Eval
 (script
   (=> [:new StateVars LexEnv Scripts Evaluator GMgr]
       ![object Eval-Meta
        (meta non-reifying-meta)
        (state [scheduler := nil]
               [evaluator := Evaluator]
               [scriptset := Scripts]
               [mode := ':dormant])

        (script
         (=> [:message Message Reply Sender]
             (match Message   ; = [:do Exp Env Id Gid VRT]
              (is [_ _ _ Id _ _]
                  [scheduler <= [:schedule Message :with Id Time]]))
             (if (eql mode ':dormant)
                 (progn [mode := ':active]
                        [Me <= :begin])))
         (=> :begin
             ... almost same as 'vanilla' meta objects ...)
         (=> :end
             ... same as 'vanilla' meta objects ...)

         ;; Additional methods
         (=> [:set-scheduler NewScheduler]
             [scheduler := NewScheduler])
         (=> [:change-scheduler NewScheduler]
             [NewScheduler <= [:copy [scheduler <== :contents]]]
             [scheduler := NewScheduler])
       )]))]
```

Figure 12: Group Kernel Objects of the Time Warp Group (2)

Implementational Reflection in Silica

Ramana Rao

Xerox Palo Alto Research Center

3333 Coyote Hill Road; Palo Alto, CA 94304

Email: rao@parc.xerox.com

Abstract

The value of computational reflection has been explored in a number of programming language efforts. The major claim of this paper is that an ostensibly broader view of reflection, which we call implementational reflection, can be applied to the design of other kinds of systems, accruing the same benefits that arise in the programming language case. The domain of window systems in general, and the Silica window system in particular are used to illustrate how reflection can be applied more broadly. Silica is a CLOS-based window system that is a part of the Common Lisp Interface Manager, an emerging user interface programming standard for Common Lisp.

Introduction

One meaning of the word reflect is to consider some subject matter. Another is to turn back something (e.g. light or sound). Punning on these two meanings, we get the notion of turning back one's consideration or considering one's own activities as a subject matter. Our ability as humans to reflect in this sense has been credited, since Aristotle, with our success in adapting to new situations and mastering our environment. Naturally, it was widely conjectured in the artificial intelligence community that by providing reflective capabilities to computational systems, we would obtain systems with greater plasticity and consequently, enhanced functionality.

Hence, this notion was introduced in a number of languages including the procedural language 3-LISP[Smi84], the logic-based languages FOL[Wey80] and META-PROLOG[Bow86], and the rule-based language TEIRESIAS[Dav80]. These various efforts have shown that facilities for reflecting on the computational process can offer users the ability to control or monitor a language's behavior and to extend or modify its semantics in an elegant and principled way.

More recently, reflection has been gaining momentum as a major topic in the design of object-oriented languages. A number of object-oriented languages including CLOS[BKK+86, KdRB91], 3-KRS[Mae87], ObjVlisp[Coi87], ABCL/R[WY88], and KSL[IC88] have embraced reflection as a first class concern. Besides adding to the general understanding of reflection's benefits, these efforts have elaborated on the use of object-oriented programming technology for building reflective systems.

The primary purpose of this paper is to establish that reflection can be applied to the design of systems other than programming languages and that this endeavor can attain the same benefits for the users of such systems. We reformulate the framework of reflection in terms of a system's implementation. In particular, we introduce the concepts of implementational reflection (as opposed to computational reflection) and open implementation (as opposed to a reflective architecture) in the next section. This reformulation helps clarify what it means for a system other than a programming language to support reflection.

We substantiate our thesis by considering the domain of window systems, and within this domain, offer the Silica system, designed and implemented by the author, as an example. Silica is the portable window system layer of the Common Lisp Interface Manager (CLIM) [RYD91], an emerging standard user interface programming interface for Common Lisp (which includes CLOS). Silica can be viewed as a window system for a single address space environment (analogous to Interlisp-D[BKM+80], Symbolics[Sym], or Smalltalk-80[KP88, LP91]), or alternatively as an extended window system model for an application address space in a multiple address space environment that provides a window library (e.g. SunWindows[Sun86]) or a window server (e.g. X 11[SG86]). Most pertinent to this paper's purposes, Silica supports reflection on its implementation, thus providing a structured framework for allowing users to explore various window system semantics or implementations.

After presenting an account of implementational reflection, we describe the functionality provided by window systems and two scenarios where reflection would be useful. Following that, relevant features of Silica's open implementation are described. Then the two scenarios are revisited to explain how Silica's reflective facilities can be used. The paper concludes with a discussion of various questions and issues that arise when building systems with open implementations, particularly in object-oriented languages.

1 Implementational Reflection

The notion of reflection describes a wide range of activities loosely characterized as some form of self-analysis, often in service of initiating or informing subsequent actions. Hence, a reflective system, besides computing about some base domain, must compute about itself. But what does it mean for a system to compute about itself? Since a system is represented as a program and is embodied in a computational process that arises from the execution of that program, the following view on reflection is typical:

> *Computational Reflection.* Reflection involves inspecting and/or manipulating representations of the computational process specified by a system's program.

Thus, computational reflection allows a system to participate in how its program is executed. For example, many of the language systems cited above allow a program to alter control flow in response to analysis of various runtime interpretation structures. In particular, these language systems provide a separate level, often called a *metalevel*, for computing about the current state of the *base level* computation and allow this metacomputation to alter the control flow of the base level computation.

Though the computational reflection view adequately describes the application of reflection to programming languages and their builtin mechanisms, most significant systems depend not only on these constructs, but also on other systems that they utilize. This suggests another view on reflection:

> *Implementational Reflection.* Reflection involves inspecting and/or manipulating the implementational structures of other systems used by a program.

Implementational reflection allows a program to participate in the implementation of systems that it utilizes. For example, the CLOS Metaobject Protocol specified in [KdRB91] allows users of CLOS to control the implementation of instance representation. This capability can be used to select an instance representation that is appropriate for a given specific situation. For example, Figure 1 illustrates two different instance representations tuned to different requirements: the point class has a small number of slots that need to be accessed quickly, whereas the person class has hundreds of slots, many of which may not be used in any given instance.

Two observations suggest that computational and implementational reflection are, in fact, just different characterizations of the same essential capability. First, a language interpreter, which generates a computational process from a program, is the implementation of a language. And second, the interface of any system can be seen as a language, and the system's implementation as

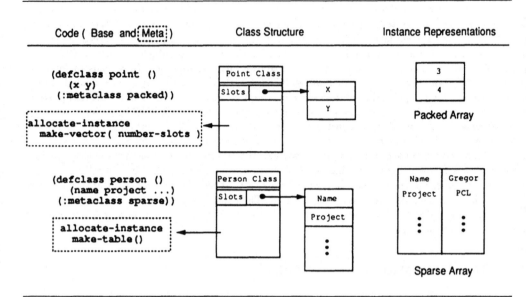

Figure 1: A metaobject protocol for CLOS allows the user to select instance representations tuned to their needs. The point class uses fixed storage, which is appropriate since slot access speed is important. The person class uses variable storage since for a given person object, many slots may not have a value and hence, space savings are the dominant factor.

an interpreter for that language. The first observation indicates that computational reflection is a special case of implementational reflection, and the second observation indicates the converse. In any case, the implementational reflection view allows us to recast much of the framework provided in the reflection literature in terms more familiar to system builders.

1.1 From Implementational Access to Open Implementations

To a certain extent, support for reflection is a matter of degree: many existing systems provide limited cases of reflective capability. In [Mae88], a valuable distinction is made between reflective facilities and a fully reflective architecture. A reflective facility is one that allows the user to query or manipulate some aspect of implementation using a set of predefined operations. As Smith and Maes have pointed out, many programming languages provide access to implementational constructs. For example, Common Lisp provides access to its interpreter (eval), its compiler (compile), its control stack (unwind-protect, catch and throw), and its special binding environment (boundp and makunbound).

Similarly, a number of existing non-language systems support operations which are about the implementation itself. The GKS graphics standard[ANS85] allows the user to query whether certain features are supported and thus adapt to different GKS implementations. The X window system[SG86] supports a more general version of this feature. The X11 protocol provides a request for determining whether a desired extension is supported. If the extension is supported, this request returns the information necessary to use the extension. This request is reflective because it supports a dialogue about functionality and implementation.

A *reflective architecture*, on the other hand, according to the discussion in [Mae87, Mae88], allows much more open-ended access to a language's implementation. In particular, a reflective architecture allows writing code that is invoked by the language interpreter. This reflective code participates in language interpretation by manipulating *causally connected* representations of the computational

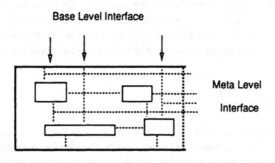

Base Level Interface

Meta Level

Interface

Figure 2: A system with an open implementation, besides providing a familiar interface to its functionality called a base level interface, reveals aspects of its implementation through a metalevel interface. The metalevel interface defines points in the implementation that can be tailored by the user.

process. Causal connection means, on one hand, that the representations accurately render the state of the computation and, on the other, that mutating the representations will influence subsequent computation.

The concept of a reflective architecture can be reformulated in terms of the implementation of a system. A system with an *open implementation* (depicted in Figure 2) provides (at least) two linked interfaces to its clients, a *base level interface* to the system's functionality similar to the interface of other such systems, and a metalevel interface that reveals some aspects of how the base level interface is implemented. In particular, the metalevel interface specifies points where the user can add code that implements base level behavior that differs in semantics and/or performance characteristics from the default base level behavior. Since this metalevel code directly implements aspects of the base level, the causal connection requirement of reflection is straightforwardly met.

Whereas features that provide limited access to a system's implementation provide some measure of system flexibility, an open implementation provides a more open-ended framework for exploring a space of implementations or semantics. Returning to earlier examples, whereas the primitives in Lisp do not support exploring alternative stack or environment implementations or semantics, a metaobject protocol for CLOS does allow implementing a range of instance representation strategies. And whereas the one request in the X window system does not facilitate exploring alternative window system implementations or semantics, a window system with an open implementation would.

1.2 Designing the Metalevel Interface

An obvious consequence of providing an open implementation is that a system is forced to make commitments to particular implementation details. This does not, however, mean that every aspect of its implementation is specified or that users can alter the implementation arbitrarily. In the parlance of the reflection community, an open implementation *reifies* some aspects of implementation, and *absorbs* others, meaning some aspects are made explicit and other are left implicit. In the sense of [Smi84, Smi82], an open implementation is based on a *theory* (i.e. model) which determines the reach of the system's metalevel, i.e. the extent to which base level behavior can be altered by the user. Smith calls this the *theory relativity* of reflection. This concept is illustrated in [Mae88] by contrasting several metacircular interpreters for Lisp, each of which reifies different aspects of Lisp interpretation.

In more traditional terms, just as a system provides an interface to its base functionality, an open implementation provides a well-defined interface (i.e. the metalevel interface) to the implementation of the system. The elaboration of a metalevel interface must address two, sometimes competing, sets of concerns. On one hand, the architecture or facilities prescribed by the metalevel interface must not prevent efficient and effective implementation of the base level. On the other, the metalevel interface must give the user access to aspects of the implementation which can be exploited to create either useful semantical variations or more efficient implementations for particular situations. Balancing these two sets of concerns is the major challenge in designing a system that supports implementational reflection.

2 Window Systems

In this section, we present an account of the functionality provided by window systems (i.e. what they are about) that provides the basis of a theory for Silica's open implementation. We also present two scenarios in which reflection on a window system's implementation would be useful. Later in the paper, we will explain how Silica can be used in these scenarios.

A window system allows multiple applications to share the bounded interactive resources of an computer system, in particular, its input devices and screen(s). The fundamental concept in window systems is a *windowing relationship*. A windowing relationship defines how a region in one coordinate system, either a real piece of screen real estate or a virtual region (arising from another windowing relationship), is divided or shared amongst a number of independent virtual regions called *windows*, each of which has its own coordinate system. Window systems often make assumptions in their support for windowing relationships. For example, most window systems provide windows that occupy a "two and a half" dimensional space that are stacked and thus may appear to overlap other windows, though some window systems just support tiled windows.

Many early window systems did not support the broad use of windowing relationships within an application, but rather focused on the desktop level as the primary client. However, others, especially more recent window systems (e.g. X and NeWS[Sun87]), allow the nesting of windows within other windows, thus creating many-level hierarchies of windowing relationships.

Besides managing one or more windowing relationships, window systems also provide output and input functionality. On the output side, window systems implement the graphics capabilities of windows, ensuring that output on one window does not affect the area allocated to other windows.[1] They generate repaint events on a window when window management causes it to be exposed. On the input side, window systems determine which windows to distribute input device events to, and how to deliver the events to the clients of those window. In short, a window system provides a basis for building graphical user interfaces by providing windows which support nesting or sharing of space, and output and input operations.

The first scenario illustrates that window system functionality is very similar to the functionality needed within applications for managing space, input, and output. Unfortunately, even though the needed functionality is of a kind provided by the window system, the user must often abandon the window system and build ad hoc support because it is impractical to use the monolithic window system implementation.

2.1 Building a SpreadSheet

In this scenario, we explore building a spreadsheet. In a spreadsheet, an array of cells is nested within a grid as illustrated in Figure 3. The relationship between the cells of the spreadsheet and the spreadsheet itself can be seen to be a kind of windowing relationship. The spreadsheet needs functionality for managing this nesting of regions, for generating repaints of subsets of the cells, and distributing input to cells.

Given these observations, the code shown in the figure accurately reflects the essence of the desired behavior. Unfortunately, this code is not likely to be practical in a window system with a

---

[1] If windowing is viewed as the virtualization of display space, this integrity constraint is analogous to not corrupting another application's memory in a virtual memory system.

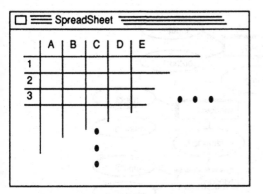

```
for row from 1 to 100
   for col from 1 to 100
      make-window( row * cell-width,
                   col * cell-height )
```

Figure 3: A spreadsheet application divides a grid region into a set of cell regions that display values and receive input. The code on the right succinctly captures the essence of this behavior.

closed implementation. The problem is that windows in the typical general-purpose window system implementation must support at least the desktop level of a window environment and maybe others. This requirement places demands on the algorithms and storage structures used within the window system that are not necessarily appropriate for spreadsheet cells. For example, X supports arbitrary overlapping of windows, which affects the implementation of various internal operations, whereas in this case, the cells never overlap. Furthermore, much of the storage associated with an X window is not necessary for every cell since they all, in general, can share a number of properties.

One possible solution to this problem is to provide other kinds of objects that address different. In fact, support for extremely light-weight window-like objects has been provided in a number of X toolkits including InterViews[CL90] and Motif[Ope89]. One problem with approach is that the new objects are now tuned to a different, but still quite specific set of needs.

A more fundamental problem is that the different implementations do not share structure, in code or necessarily in conception, and hence they do not lend support to one another. Besides the loss of conceptual clarity, this has the material consequence that code based on one system can't be easily mixed with that written for another. For example, suppose we now wanted to nest window system windows within the cell windows, so that window-based code, even entire applications, could be used within the cell. The problem is that this requires adding support to the cell window type for embedding window system windows.

An open implementation, on the other hand, provides an open-ended framework for introducing new types of windows and capturing commonalities across various types. It does this by allowing the user to participate in a well-chosen set of system design choices. Rather than providing a single implementation or a number of disconnected implementations, the user is allowed to specify a tailored solution within a design space.

2.2 Regenerating Output

As a second scenario, consider the problem of redisplaying a window when it becomes exposed by a user- or application-initiated window manipulation operation. Suppose the output on an application's window is particularly complex and that it takes substantial computation to regenerate. As a consequence, when the window is fully or partially exposed, this computation may lead to sluggish repaint of the window.

One solution is to write code for the application that caches the graphical results of this computation so that re-executing it during redisplay can be avoided. This solution places an additional requirement on the application and unless the programmer is disciplined, the redisplay issue can get

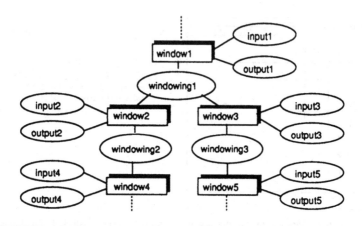

Figure 4: A representative Silica hierarchy. The rectangles represent windows. The ellipses represent contracts which implement part of the functionality of one or more windows. There are three kinds of contract: windowing, input, and output. A windowing contract implements the windowing relationship between a parent window and a set of children windows.

entangled with other application issues.

Moreover, the need for output recording or the choice of an appropriate output recording semantics or implementation may not be the same for all situations. For example, the same application may be used on machines with varying processor speeds or memory capacity, or even display architectures (e.g. one that supports display lists but not bitmaps). This could mean that the application programmer would need several mechanisms.

This type of output regeneration functionality is useful in a broad range of cases, and it seems a natural part of the window system. Specific functionality can clearly be built into the window system, but this approach will eventually lead to a bloated window system that is hard to implement, maintain, and use. On the other hand, we will show later that an open implementation allows adding this behavior in a modular and elegant way as a metalevel abstraction.

3   Silica's Open Implementation

In the last section, we presented an account of window systems and two scenarios that could potentially benefit from an open implementation. In this section, we describe the open implementation of the Silica window system. Silica is implemented in Common Lisp, which includes CLOS, though the aspects described here can be readily implemented in other object-oriented languages.

Silica provides a *base level interface* that is similar to the interface of other window systems. In addition to this base level interface, Silica specifies an architecture that prescribes the skeleton of the base level interface's implementation. In particular, this architecture is specified as a *metalevel interface* that consists of two parts: (i) the *components* that implement the base level behavior and (ii) the object-oriented *protocols* that govern how these components interact to achieve this end. We cover each of these aspects in turn.

Silica's base level interface is based on the same fundamental abstraction as many existing window systems: a tree of light-weight windows that support input and output operations. This interface, among other things, supports constructing and managing window trees;[2] querying their structure; and performing output operations on and receiving input from windows.

---

[2]Windows are actually called sheets in the existing version of Silica.

- output contract—determines the output capabilities of the window (i.e. how the client can draw images on the window) and how repaint of the window is invoked (e.g. how the client is notified of repaint requests).

- input contract—determines the input interface of the window (i.e. how the client is notified of input events which are distributed to this window).

- youth windowing contract—determines how the window's youth windowing relationship, the one in which it is a child, is managed (i.e. determines how a window behaves as a child). It must be the same or compatible with the adult windowing contract of the window's parent.

- adult windowing contract—determines how the window's adult windowing relationship, the one in which it is the parent, is managed (i.e. determines how a window behaves as a parent). It must be the same or compatible with the youth contracts of the window's children.

Table 1: The responsibilities of a window's four contracts.

In previous window systems, the input, output, and windowing functionality provided for all windows is the same. Silica departs from these window systems by implementing the three areas of window system functionality as distinct manipulable metalevel objects called *contracts*,[3] that can be selected for each window independently. This departure allows clients to select the functionality and implementation of their windows according to their needs, either statically or dynamically to accommodate changing runtime needs.

Figure 4 depicts a metalevel view of an exemplar Silica window hierarchy. Each rectangle represents a window; and each ellipse, a contract of one or more windows. As is shown for window2 or window3 in the figure, each window has four contracts, each responsible for a different portion of the window's implementation as described in Table 1. The specific mechanism that associates windows with their four contracts is described in Appendix A.

Contracts are Silica's primary metalevel objects. Input and output contracts implement the input and output functionality respectively of a single window. The case with windowing contracts is more complex (and more interesting) since they implement a windowing relationship involving more than one window. In particular, a windowing contract implements the functionality of one window vis-a-vis its role as a parent, and also the functionality of a number of other windows vis-a-vis their roles as children. A windowing contract, an input contract, and an output contract, thus, comprise the bulk of a local window system for a single window.[4]

The implementational responsibilities of each metalevel component as well as the interactions among components are specified as a set of object-oriented protocols. A *protocol* consists of one or more functions that together perform some subtask in the implementation of the base level interface. In CLOS, protocols include both ordinary Common Lisp functions for fixed portions of the protocol and CLOS generic functions that take one or more of the metalevel objects as specializable arguments for specializable portions of the protocol. Some protocol functions may actually be part of the base level interface, while others implement necessary supporting services. Table 2 presents most of Silica's major protocols, along with the metalevel objects involved in the protocol and a description of the protocol. The details of these protocols are not relevant here; what is important is that each of these protocols performs some task in the implementation of the base level interface and that they circumscribe the aspects of Silica's base level interface that can be changed at the metalevel by the

---

[3]This term may be unfortunate, since Silica contracts are actually real objects that provide methods rather than declarative specifications. The contracts of [HHG90] are actually more related to what we call a protocol here.

[4]The rest is provided by components that manage global resources. In particular, two other key components are ports and event distributors. Ports manage a connection to a host or remote window system. A port can also be seen as a software port of Silica to a particular host window system or display architecture. Event distributors oversee the distribution of raw input events coming in from ports.

Protocol	Responsibility
Window Construction *global*	Provides a simple interface for constructing windows and establishing windowing relationships. This interface hides the details of realizing a window's contracts. This protocol consults all contract classes to obtain implementation parts for the window.
Windowing Relationship *windowing contract*	Provides functions for adopting, disowning, and "enabling" children; and query methods for asking about parents and children. It also provides functionality for managing window region and coordinate system mapping.
Viewing Parameters *windowing contract*	Provides functions for calculating clipping regions and composing transformations from a window to any of its ancestors (and vice versa) and maintaining a cache for these values. These values are used by, among others, the output protection and the input distribution protocols.
Mirroring *port, windowing contract*	Provides the means for allocating and managing host (or remote) window system windows. Allows implementing top level windows and other kinds of windows that can benefit from the full functionality of a typical heavyweight window.
Output Protection *output*	Ensures that graphics operations applied to a window are transformed and clipped as appropriate for the window's region and position in the window hierarchy; and that they are appropriately synchronized with changes to the window hierarchy.
Graphics Functionality *output contract*	Provides graphics routines that can be applied to windows and ancillary functionality (e.g. drawing state or graphic context construction and manipulation).
Repaint *windowing contract, output contract*	Provides mechanism for repainting a window when portions are exposed that were previously covered or otherwise not visible.
Input Distribution *port, distributor, windowing contract, input contract*	Determines which window should be the recipient of user input events. Protocol supports extensive participation by local windowing and input contracts.
Input Delivery *input contract*	Translates from port specific event representations (the lowest level representation available) to a representation appropriate for the recipient window. Defines how input is delivered to the client of the recipient window.

implementing objects

Table 2: An Overview of Major Silica Protocols.

user.

Each of Silica's metalevel objects plays a well-defined role in the architecture that is specified by the protocols in which they participate. Some areas of functionality are largely implemented by a single metalevel component, but others are the shared responsibility of several metalevel objects. For example, access to graphics primitives and the delivery of input are primarily the responsibility of the output and input contracts respectively, whereas hit detection and window repainting involve interactions between these contracts and windowing contracts.

An important and familiar technique used to allow responsibility to be divided amongst a number of objects is the *layering* of protocols. A layered protocol invokes subprotocols which implement various subtasks within the protocol's overall task. For example, the repaint protocol invokes subprotocols to calculate what subwindows need repainting and in what order, and to repaint them. Another important benefit of layering is that it allows users to specialize protocols at a level of granularity appropriate to and a cost commensurate with their requirements (discussed further below).

In summary, Silica's metalevel components and protocols provide an architecture for implementing Silica's base level interface and for using this implementation to build window systems with specialized functionality or implementations. Since most Silica protocols are implemented by or consult one or more of a window's contracts and each window has its own contracts, a window's implementation can, to a large degree, be altered locally without affecting distant windows or windowing relationships.

4 Reflection in Silica

An important property of Silica is that its objects and protocols divide into two separate levels, one implementing the other. The collection of windows (the rectangles in Figure 4) form the base level and the collection of contracts (the ellipses) form the implementational or meta level. Similarly, Silica's protocols are layered with their base layer providing standard functionality to the user, and lower meta layers performing various subtasks in the implementation of that functionality.

This separation of Silica into two levels is the basis for allowing users to participate in design and implementation decisions, either statically or dynamically, either implicitly or explicitly. A program that uses Silica reflects when it provides contracts which variously define or implement some aspect of the base level interface or an extended or reduced interface. This form of reflective act, where a system (an interpreter) invokes user code at specific points during its implementation (the interpretation process), has been called implicit in [Mae88]. Silica also supports so-called explicit reflective acts by allowing users to manipulate window system functionality explicitly at runtime. This, for example, means that window system behavior like logging input can be added temporarily.

The two scenarios described above can each be handled in Silica by providing reflective code that defines a window system more suited to particular needs. Both cases involve defining a new contract (a windowing contract in the first and an output contract in the second) that specializes one or more Silica protocols. Though in both cases, the code written for the new contracts could clearly be written outside of a window system, Silica allows the framework provided by the window system to be reused by adding such code inside the window system.

4.1 SpreadSheet Revisited

In Silica, the spreadsheet scenario can be handled by implementing a windowing contract specifically tuned to its needs. In particular, this contract can make assumptions about its windowing relationship that can be exploited in its implementation. For example, a windowing contract for this scenario can make two assumptions: first, its children are laid out in a uniform 2-d grid and second, they do not overlap. An appropriate storage representation for storing the children of this contract is a 2-d array indexed by location in the grid.

As part of picking a tuned storage representation, the contract provides specialized methods for various protocol functions. For example, as illustrated in Figure 5, the general purpose method for

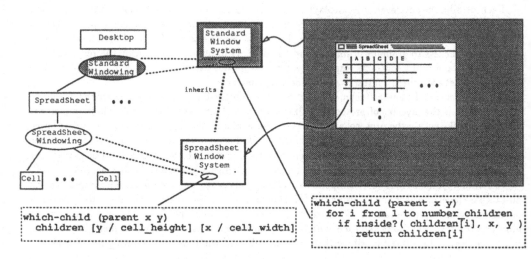

Figure 5: A tailored window system that exploits the regularity of the spreadsheet layout is created by combining a specialized windowing contract with the default input and output contracts. In this way, the spreadsheet window system inherits much of the behavior of the standard window system—only the windowing behavior is specialized. (The projection of the windowing contracts into the window system indicates that windowing contracts form only part of the total window system behavior.)

hit detection (invoked by the input distribution protocol) can be replaced by a special one that uses simple arithmetic and array reference. Similarly, a special method like the following can be provided for a function in the repaint protocol.

```
repaint-children (parent x y w h)
  . . .
  for col from (y / cell-height) to ((+ y h) / cell-height)
   for row from (x / cell-width) to ((+ x w) / cell-width)
    repaint( children[col][row] )
  . . .
```

An important point to note is that the methods provided by the specialized contract are metalevel code: they are about the implementation of a new kind of windowing relationship, not about the use of a windowing relationship. Metalevel code is like the code system implementors write to implement a window system rather than the code that users typically write to use one.

Using the specialized windowing contract, the spreadsheet application can efficiently create a window for each cell. However, this implementation does require each cell of the spreadsheet to be explicitly created as an object. Though the overhead associated with the window-ness of the cell was reduced significantly, there is still overhead associated with its object-ness. This issue can be addressed in two ways. One, the reflective capabilities of CLOS can be used to reduce unnecessary overhead associated with the cell window as an object.[5] An alternative approach would be to implement a windowing contract which avoids explicitly creating children objects unless or until they are necessary (e.g. for cells that actually have subwindows).

This spreadsheet example suggests an even more ambitious reuse of the window system design and implementation. Traditionally, window systems and toolkits have dealt with the part of the hierarchy

---

[5]This suggests that reflection on at least partially orthogonal system's used by a program can accumulate benefits.

that deals with objects that act as surfaces to be drawn on, and applications have built their own local mechanisms for dealing with their own hierarchies of objects. Alternatively, window systems have provided a number of predefined window types or user interface toolkits have provided extensive libraries of new window-like objects outside the window system. In contrast, Silica supports adding such facilities (e.g. display lists) as metalevel abstractions by defining new windowing contracts.

4.2 Output Regeneration Revisited

Output capture facilities are not provided primitively in Silica, but rather can be implemented as special output contracts. Such output contracts can extend the standard output semantics to manage the process of output recording. Different implementations of these semantics that optimize this behavior variously can be provided. If the code is running on a very fast processor and performance is not a problem, then a simple implementation that ignores output recording operations can be used. Other output contracts can make other implementation choices: maintaining a backing store (a pixmap) to regenerate the output; recording the output primitives as a display list; and recording output as host display lists in systems that directly support them. Moreover, since Silica supports switching contracts at runtime, different output recording mechanisms can be selected based on changing situations.

Though support for output recording or backing stores could be built directly into the window system, building them as metalevel extensions provides a better solution for several reasons. First, new implementations and semantics for this extension can be explored not just by the implementor of the window system, but also by users. Furthermore, the extensions can be used in cases where they are indeed useful without complicating the base level window system or increasing the builtin overhead for all users. Finally, there are a large number of other possible extensions which may be of equal value to other users. Supporting all such extensions would make any single interface and implementation extremely complex and even then, the single interface could not address the range of needs that an open implementation could.

The metalevel interface provides a separate level for introducing new abstractions. Just as 3-Lisp allows constructs like catch and throw to be implemented as metalevel abstractions rather than being built into the language, Silica allows constructs that would ordinarily be built into the window system to be introduced as implementation extensions. The primary advantage of having two separate levels for building such libraries is that each of the levels can be used to implement different portions of the required behavior. Window system metalevel code is for handling issues that window systems typically deal with, and base level code handles application computation.

5 Discussion

Many object-oriented languages that support reflection on their implementation—including CLOS, 3-KRS, and ObjVLisp—represent their metalevel as objects in the same object-oriented language as used at the base level. This metacircularity is advantageous for several reasons. The reason of primary concern here is that the benefits object-oriented programming provides to the user at the base level can be equally valuable at the metalevel. For example, the user can localize changes to the implementation to specific base level objects or to specific aspects of base level objects.

Silica's metalevel, also, is implemented using the same object-oriented language as is used at its base level interface. However, unlike the reflective object-oriented languages mentioned above, Silica is not metacircular. Silica's metalevel is not written in the base level language that it provides, nor does it even make sense to write a window system in the "window system language" it implements.

Silica's use of object-oriented programming raises the following question. What distinguishes Silica's design from that of other object-oriented systems? After all, any object-oriented implementation can be said to provide a representation of its implementation since it contains objects that provide implementation methods in addition to interface methods. However, object-oriented programming in itself does not guarantee an open implementation. For example, neither the Smalltalk window system nor the Symbolics window systems had the expressed goal of exposing aspects of the window system implementation, though to a certain degree both do.[6] Rather, object-oriented programming is a technology that is particularly well suited to our purpose; three aspects of object-oriented languages, in particular, are relevant.

1. Object-centered specification of behavior allows building an implementation that closely maps onto an understanding of the important design and implementation issues. Object-oriented languages are similar to knowledge representation languages in this regard.

2. Polymorphism helps partition the world in a manner that allows multiple implementations to peacefully coexist. This means users can implement their own version of the system without disturbing existing versions of the system used by other users.

3. Inheritance provides a powerful mechanism for incrementally specifying new or different behaviors, such that clients can reuse portions of the standard implementation or incorporate stock behaviors from available metalevel libraries.

The framework of implementational reflection provides a particular conception of how to build a malleable system and to some degree a prescription that guides the use of object-oriented programming. Many of the benefits generally attributed to object-oriented programming are, in fact, benefits arising from opening up implementation or more precisely structuring the implementation well enough to allow users to benefit from access to it. Many object-oriented techniques can be cast more specifically in terms of how they give access to a system's implementation.

A salient example of this is the layering of object-oriented protocols, which greatly increases their utility. Layering involves elaborating the substructure of a protocol by specifying auxiliary functions that are invoked by the protocol to perform subtasks within the protocol's overall task. The various layers of a protocol can provide, on one hand, differing degrees of predefined behaviors (and hence structure or functionality), and, on the other, greater latitude in specializing or recombining behaviors at varying degrees of granularity. However, layering has costs and consequences. The process of layering a protocol is exactly the process of refining, and hence further constraining, a system's implementation. Hence, the definition of a layered protocol has to take into account concerns of effective implementation as well as potential utility. Many of these issues are discussed by [KdRB91] in the context of the CLOS Metaobject Protocol and CLOS implementation.

A related point is that providing explicit representations of any aspect of a system's implementation may have consequences for the system's efficiency. Lazy reification or reification on demand is a typical strategy used for making implementation state explicit. This approach can help ensure a "Don't use, don't lose" policy.[7] However, there is still potentially a disadvantage in this area if a promise to reify some aspect of the implementation has a constant or continual cost.

Layering a protocol is, in fact, a form of reification. It involves making explicit various internal places for attaching or installing tailored behaviors or decision-making machinery. An interesting observation is that lazy reification techniques for layered protocols can be implemented using the reflective capabilities of an underlying object-oriented language. In CLOS, this involves developing optimization techniques that bypass entire subprotocols in cases where it is known the standard behavior applies. Such techniques are in fact used in later versions of the PCL implementation of CLOS[KR90].

---

[6]Similarly, Smalltalk or Flavors do not give the same level of access to the object system implementation as CLOS does.

[7]Of course, a "Use, don't lose" policy is also important.

Conclusion

In this paper, we have argued that reflection can provide a conceptual framework for building not just programming languages but malleable systems of all kinds. A typical consequence of broadening a framework is that it can start to lose some of its resolution and hence may not seem much different from some other set of concepts. Many of the ideas discussed, especially in the terms used here, are probably familiar. Many systems do, in fact, open up aspects of their implementation. For example, the Mach operating system allows users to write code that participates in an open-ended way in decisions regarding secondary storage management and page replacement[YTR+87].

What, then, is the benefit derived from the framework of implementational reflection? Though, we ourselves are not yet convinced that it is the only or even the best way of thinking about systems that open up their implementation, we do believe that, for the time being, it provides intellectual scaffolding in a number of significant ways. First, explicitly focusing on the metalevel as a separate and first class interface to export to the user forces a greater attention to exposing important design and implementation choices. For example, Silica carefully separates the various aspects of windows— its roles as an output surface, as an input stream, and as participant in two different windowing relationships. Second, this benefit is also exported to the client. The disciplined division of the window system into its base level and a partial implementation as specified by a metalevel interfaces provides the programmer with two separate levels for introducing abstractions.

Perhaps most important in the long run is that the separation of the implementation methods into a metalevel allows a more radical shift from procedural reflection to declarative reflection. Currently, a Silica client programs at the metalevel by specializing various methods on their own contract types (i.e. in the same way that they program at the base level). A natural next step is to move from this procedural specification of metalevel statements to one that is more declarative. For example, users could state their requirements for a window system in a higher level language, and the system could then automatically pick or even construct appropriate contract types. Though the causal connection requirements are hard to meet in such a system, and some may argue should be loosened, such an approach promises great value.

Acknowledgements

I am greatly indebted to Richard Burton, Gregor Kiczales, and John Seely Brown who have actively (and patiently) supported my work on Silica in many ways. Other colleagues at PARC, especially Jim des Rivières, Mike Dixon, John Lamping, Luis Rodriguez, and Brian Smith, have helped develop these ideas on reflection and their presentation in this paper.

References

[ANS85]   ANSI, New York, NY. *Graphical Kernal System (GKS) Functional Description*, 1985. ANSI X3.124-1985 and ISO 7942.

[BKK+86] D.G. Bobrow, K. Kahn, G. Kiczales, L. Masinter, M. Stefik, and F. Zdybel. Common-Loops: Merging Lisp and Object-Oriented Programming. In *OOPSLA '86 Conference Proceedings, Sigplan Notices 21(11)*. ACM, Nov 1986.

[BKM+80] R. Burton, R. Kaplan, L. Masinter, B. Sheil, A. Bell, D. Bobrow, L.P. Deutsch, and W.S. Haugeland. Papers on Interlisp-D. Technical report, Xerox PARC, 1980.

[Bow86]   K. Bowen. Meta-level Techniques in Logic Programming. In *Proceedings of the International Conference on Artificial Intelligence and its Applications*, 1986.

[CL90]   Paul Calder and Mark Linton. Glyphs: Flyweight Objects for User Interfaces. In *Proceedings of the ACM SIGGRAPH Symposium on User Interface Software and Technology*, pages 92–101. ACM Press, Oct 1990.

[Coi87]   P. Cointe. Metaclasses are First Class: the ObjVlisp Model. In *OOPSLA '87 Conference Proceedings, Sigplan Notices 22(12)*. ACM, Dec 1987.

[Dav80]   R. Davis. Meta-rules: Reasoning about Control. *Artificial Intelligence*, 15, 1980.

[HHG90]   Richard Helm, Ian M. Holland, and Dipayan Gangopadhyay. Contracts: Specifying Behavior Compositions in Object-oriented Systems. In *OOPSLA/ECOOP '90 Conference Proceedings, Sigplan Notices 25(10)*. ACM, Nov 1990.

[IC88]   M.H. Ibrahim and F.A Cummins. KSL: A Reflective Object-Oriented Programming Language. In *Proceedings of the IEEE Computer Society International Conference on Computer Languages*, 1988.

[KdRB91]   Gregor Kiczales, Jim des Rivières, and Daniel Bobrow. *The Art of the Metaobject Protocol*. MIT Press, 1991.

[KP88]   Glenn Krasner and Stephen Pope. A Cookbook for Using the Model-View-Controller User Interface Paradigm in Smalltalk-80. *Journal on Object-Oriented Programming*, August/September 1988.

[KR90]   Gregor Kiczales and Luis Rodriguez. Efficient Method Dispatch in PCL. In *Proceedings 1990 ACM Conference on Lisp and Functional Programming*, pages 99–105. ACM, June 1990.

[Lie86]   H. Lieberman. Using Prototypical Objects to Implement Shared Behavior in Object-Oriented Systems. In *OOPSLA '86 Conference Proceedings, Sigplan Notices 21(11)*. ACM, Nov 1986.

[LP91]   Wilf LaLonde and John Pugh. *Inside Smalltalk: Volume II*. Prentice-Hall, Inc, Englewood Cliffs, NJ, 1991.

[Mae87]   P. Maes. Concepts and Experiments in Computational Reflection. In *OOPSLA '87 Conference Proceedings, Sigplan Notices 22(12)*. ACM, Dec 1987.

[Mae88]   Pattie Maes. Issues in Reflection. In P. Maes and D. Nardi, editors, *Meta-Level Architectures and Reflections*. North Holland, 1988.

[Ope89]   Open Software Foundation, Cambridge, MA. *OSF/MOTIF Manual*, 1989.

[RYD91]   Ramana Rao, William York, and Dennis Doughty. A Guided Tour of the Common Lisp Interface Manager. *Lisp Pointers*, 4(1), 1991.

[SG86]   R.W. Scheifler and J. Gettys. The X Window System. *ACM Transactions on Graphics*, 5(2), 1986.

[Smi82]   Brian Smith. Reflection and Semantics in a Procedural Language. Technical Report 272, Massachusetts Institute of Technology, Laboratory for Computer Science, Cambridge, MA, 1982.

[Smi84]   Brian Smith. Reflection and Semantics in Lisp. In *Proceedings of the 1984 ACM Principles of Programming Language Conference*, pages 23–35. ACM, Dec 1984.

[Sun86]   Sun Microsystems, Mountain View, CA. *Programmer's Reference Manual for the Sun Window System*, 1986.

[Sun87]   Sun Microsystems. *NeWS Technical Overview*, 1987.

[Sym]   Symbolics, Inc, Burlington, MA. *Programmer's Reference Manual Vol 7: Programming the User Interface.*

[Wey80]   Richard Weyhrauch. Prolegomena to a Theory of Mechanised Formal Reasoning. *Artificial Intelligence*, 13, 1980.

[WY88]   T. Watanabe and A. Yonezawa. Reflection in an Object-Oriented Concurrent Language. In *OOPSLA '88 Conference Proceedings, Sigplan Notices 23(11)*. ACM, Nov 1988.

[YTR+87]   M. Young, A. Tevanian, R. Rashid, D. Golub, J. Chew J. Eppinger, W. Bolosky, D. Black, and R. Baron. The Duality of Memory and Communication in the Implementation of a Multiprocessor Operating System. In *Proceedings of the 11th Symposium on Operating System Principles*. ACM, Nov 1987.

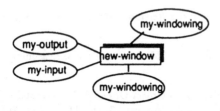

output	parent
input	child

```
(define-window-class new-window-class        (defclass new-window-class
      (extra-behavior :parts)                      (extra-behavior
   (... <slots> ...)                                window
   (:youth-contract 'my-windowing-contract)        my-child-part
   (:adult-contract 'my-windowing-contract)        my-parent-part
   (:output-contract 'my-output-contract)          my-output-part
   (:input-contract 'my-input-contract))           my-input-part)
                                              (... <slots> ...))
```

Figure 6: The conceptual model as shown in the code and picture on the left is actually implemented in CLOS in the manner shown on the right. Implementational part classes (provided by the contracts) are inherited by a window class. However, because of various features of CLOS, no power is actually lost by this choice.

A   Implementation of Contracts in CLOS

An inheritance-based strategy is used to allow contracts to provide implementation methods to their windows in the current CLOS-based implementation. Contracts, though conceptually separate objects, are not allocated separately from the windows that use them. Rather contract implementation parts (i.e. classes defined by a contract implementor) are inherited by or "mixed-in" to the window objects. In the case of a windowing contract, different implementation part classes are mixed in depending on whether the window is to be a parent or a child controlled by that contract.

The essence of this strategy for the case of a statically defined combination of contracts is depicted in Figure 6. In addition, a window class can be constructed dynamically by make-window which takes the same keyword options as the define-window-class form. Automatically constructed classes are cached so that subsequent attempts to use the same combination of contracts will reuse them.

This implementation strategy was appropriate for CLOS, since CLOS does not directly support delegation[Lie86], but it does support changing an object's class dynamically and constructing classes at runtime. This strategy avoids the inefficiency of allocating several objects as opposed to a single larger one and of trampolining functions from windows to their contracts. CLOS's runtime class construction and change-class allow selecting and changing contracts at runtime. Furthermore, since CLOS implements classes as objects, contract classes can be manipulated by Silica's metalevel interface.

Exceptions in Guide, an Object-Oriented Language for Distributed Applications

Serge Lacourte

Unité Mixte Bull-Imag, Z.I. de Mayencin, 38610 GIERES, FRANCE

email: Serge.Lacourte@gu.bull.fr

Abstract:

This paper describes the design of an exception handling mechanism for Guide, an object-oriented language based on a distributed system. We confront the usual exception techniques to the object formalism, and we propose conformance rules and an original association scheme. A specific tool to maintain the consistency of objects in the face of exceptions is provided. System and hardware exceptions are integrated to the mechanism, and parallelism is handled in an original manner. Some details of the implementation are given.

Key words: exceptions, consistency, object-oriented languages, concurrency

1 Introduction

The concept of exception handling has been refined in the last decade and is now an integral part of most high-level languages. Exceptions provide a means to separate a "normal" flow of control from an "exceptional" one, where the semantics of "normal" and "exceptional" may be predefined in the language or specified by the programmer. The advantages are twofold: the textual separation of the exception handling code from the normal one greatly improves the structure and readability of the program, while the semantical separation ensures that the normal flow is stopped when an exception occurs, and may resume only after the proper exceptional handling code has been executed.

1.1 Issues

Most of the work on exception mechanisms has been done for traditional languages. Experience with exceptions in object-oriented languages is still limited. The integration of an exception mechanism in an object-oriented model should be coherent with the structuring principles of that model, especially as regards the delegation of responsibility and the internal consistency of the objects. This axiom has constantly directed our design, built around the method invocation on an object, the basic executing unit in object-oriented languages. An exception becomes an exceptional variation of the invocation, allowing the dialogue between caller and callee to be enriched.

When an operation cannot fulfil its requirements, it raises an exception. Control is then transferred to a calling entity which provides an exception handler. The handler executes some code and may choose between three main policies; *resumption* resumes the execution at the level of the signalling entity, *termination* (or *alternate* policy) resumes at the level of the handling entity, *propagation* signals a possibly different exception to a higher calling entity. The handler may also retry the failed call, as a variation of *termination*. Handlers are associated to invocation statements in the caller. These are parts of a standard mechanism that needs to be refined in an object-oriented language. Is resumption to be provided? How does exception raising relate to interface checking? What is the scope of handlers? What is the precise effect of termination? What is the impact of inheritance on all these points? How do we declare default handlers?

An object-oriented language must also address the issue of the consistency of the objects, particularly if they are persistent. Are the standard mechanisms sufficient, or do we need a specific one? There is also the specific issue raised by concurrency. How is the normal termination of two parallel invocations related to the normal termination of the same invocations in sequence? The underlying system can also fail. How does it report exceptions? How are system and hardware exceptions handled?

This paper is an attempt to contribute to these issues. It is based on our experience of integrating an exception mechanism in Guide [1], a strongly typed object-oriented language for distributed applications, jointly developed with a supporting operating system environment [2].

1.2 Previous work

Most current object-oriented languages offer an exception handling mechanism similar to those of modular languages. Ada, CLU and Modula2+ have all three chosen a termination model. Their main characteristic is that they associate a handler with a block of instructions, syntactically as well as semantically. A handler with a termination policy resumes the execution at the instruction following the block. In Guide, execution resumes just after the call. Another point is the propagation "as is" of an exception through operation frontiers, except in CLU, where the *FAILURE* exception is propagated. In a similar way, the frontier of method invocation is not bypassed in Guide.

1.2.1 A termination model

The mechanisms offered in Modula-3 [9], Trellis-Owl [12], ANSA [3], Argus [4], NIL [10], are more or less related to the model shortly described above. Their main improvement consists of a strict control of the exceptions a method may raise, or propagate. Usually, when an exception is not handled by the caller, a special exception is propagated, like the *FAILURE* exception of CLU. Only Modula-3 does not conform to this rule. Guide propagates the *UNCAUGHT_EXCEPTION* system exception.

But all the above languages have kept the association of a handler with a block of instructions, with the related termination behaviour explained above. The drawback of this model is that the control flow depends on the place where the handler is declared. In particular if the handler offers an alternate computation to a precise method call, then it has to be associated to a block which contains only this call. In fact the advantage of this model is to avoid the handler having to execute a local control transfer instruction to exit the block. However it prevents a clear separation of the exception handling code from the main algorithm. In Guide the handler just applies to the raising invocation, without relation to its declaration.

Few of these languages answer the issue of the consistency of objects. Argus integrates a mechanism whose purpose is to restore the state of a guardian and to restart it after a failure, but nothing is done for internal objects. Modula-3 keeps the **try ... finally** tool provided in Modula2+, that ensures the **finally** part being executed whatever happens during the execution of the **try** body. This is more a finalization tool than a restoration one, because the code is executed even if the body ends normally.

1.2.2 Eiffel

Exceptions in Eiffel [7] are handled in a very specific way. The **rescue** clause can be simulated by a handler associated to the method with the above semantics. The only authorized policies are either to retry the execution of the whole body, or to propagate the exception. This tool is rather primitive, but it turns out to be appropriate to ensure the consistency of objects. In fact it has been designed for that purpose: it ensures the correctness of the postconditions of the method, which include the invariant of the object. However nothing special is offered to deal with an exception raised during the execution of this rescue code, as we have tried to do in Guide with the *RESTORATION_FAILED* exception.

1.2.3 Exceptions as data objets

The model proposed in C++ [5] is close to those described in section 1.2.1. The semantics of association is still related to the syntax, the control of propagated exceptions may be bypassed, and nothing is done to ensure consistency. However there is a major change with exceptions being considered as objects. To raise an exception is to pass an exception object as a parameter to a handler. The handler declares its parameter as being of a given class, but may catch exception objects of any subclass. It allows the signaller to pass any type of parameters by declaring them in the state of the object. It allows the catching of specialized exceptions by general handlers. However it gives an exception a universal meaning, and allows two unrelated classes to raise a similar exception. In Guide an exception depends on the type that may raise it.

We call these objects data objects despite the possible definition of methods on them because behaviours specific to exception raising and handling are not offered through methods defined on a root exception class (see the following section).

1.2.4 Exceptions as full objects

The object orientation of exceptions has been developped to its completeness in some Lisp-based languages and also recently in Smalltalk-80 [11]. To raise an exception is to create an instance of the related class, then to call it with a *raise* method. The behaviour of any of the *termination*, *retry*, *resumption* policies can be defined as a method of a root *Exception* class from which all exception classes inherit. The conclusions from the Lore proposition are summarized in [8].

This approach is interesting because it tries to integrate exceptions into the standard invocation mechanism; however by doing so it complicates its semantics. A *raise* method call eventually resolve into a **return** (*termination*), a normal call (*resumption*), or something more complicated (*retry*). How then can such a method be formally defined? Keeping the exception as a possible response to the method invocation, as we have done in Guide, leads to a semantically simpler model.

The remainder of this paper is organized as follows. Section 2 describes the main features of the mechanism. We first present in section 2.1 the Guide project, and the relevant concepts of the language. We then describe the core of the mechanism in three sections, touching in turn on exception raising, handler association, and handling policies. Section 2.5 tries to bring new arguments to the debate about resumption, and it is followed by a concise summary of our proposal in section 2.6. Section 3 touches on more specific issues. Section 3.1 shows how we integrate system and hardware exceptions to the main scheme. Section 3.2 describes a specific tool to maintain the consistency of objects. Relationship with inheritance and conformance is developed in section 3.3. Section 3.4 reports on the integration of exceptions in the parallel construct of Guide. In the final part of the paper, section 4, we discuss three future developments of the mechanism.

2 The Guide proposal: general features

2.1 The Guide language and system

The Guide programming language has been designed and implemented for the programming of distributed applications. Its run-time support is provided by the Guide object-oriented distributed operating system, designed and implemented at the University of Grenoble as a joint project of IMAG and Bull Research Center [2].

The object model implemented in Guide is characterized by the following main features:

- Objects are typed. A type describes a behavior shared by all objects of that type, in terms of the signatures of the operations applicable to the objects. Objects are accessed through views. A view is essentially a typed pointer; the effective type of the object must conform to that of its view. The conformance rule is statically checked. Types are declared apart from classes, which describe specific implementations of types.

- Subtyping defines a hierarchy of types. The subtyping hierarchy is paralleled by a subclassing hierarchy, with single inheritance. Subtyping and inheritance ensure conformance.

- Objects are persistent. They are named by system references (system-wide uniquely generated internal names). Complex structures may be constructed by embedding references to objects within other objects.

- Concurrency is provided by a **co_begin** ... **co_end** construct allowing for the creation of parallelly-executed sub-activities.

The execution model involves distributed jobs and activities. Execution structures extend to a remote site when needed.

The characteristics of our proposal are described in the following sections. We first present an example which will be extensively used throughout our presentation. A basic *Editor* allows the user to browse through a *Document, Page* by *Page*. It caches the *Page*s it has read into *ShadowPage*s until *Commit*. It gets the needed *ShadowPage*s from an *ObjectManager* of *ShadowPage*s, to lighten the load of the garbage collector. A *Garbage* method allows it to free its clean *ShadowPage*s. Two other methods are described to print the current *ShadowPage* and to create a new one. A *Page* is read *Char* by *Char*, and a *ShadowPage* is a *Page* with a "dirty" flag. An *ObjectManager* provides and gets objects back with the methods *Get* and *Free*. The keyword **type** introduces the definition of an interface. The keyword **class** introduces an implementation. Only state variables are shown below in the implementation of *Editor*, the methods are described later in the document.

```
type Editor is                    type Page is
   method Commit;                    method GetChar: Char;
   method PrintPage;                 signals end_of_line,
   method CreateNewPage;                end_of_page,
   method Garbage;                      error;
end Editor.                        end Page.

type Document is                   type ShadowPage
   pages: ref List of              subtype of Page is
      ref Page;                       isDirty: Boolean;
end Document.                      end ShadowPage.

class Editor implements Editor is
   // state variables
   shadowPages: ref List of ref ShadowPage;
   shadowPageManager: ref ObjectManager of ref ShadowPage;
   currentPage: ref ShadowPage;
end Editor.
```

2.2 Exceptions in the object-oriented design

Object-oriented languages encapsulate data and code in an object (an instance of a class). The basic computation unit is the method invocation on an object, in which a message is sent to and interpreted by the called object; this allows polymorphism. Exceptions naturally fit in this scheme, as a possible response to this message. Thus the exception handling mechanism should also be defined at object level.

Due to the choice of a termination model (see section 2.5), the calling object does not answer to the raising of an exception. Raising an exception exits the method in the same way as a **return** statement does.

This dialog between caller and callee is controlled by the interface of the called object. As this interface is explicitly defined in Guide, it must include exception declarations. This affects the conformance rules checked by the compiler, which are detailed in section 3.3.

The nature of Guide exceptions are mere symbols. In this way an exception remains attached to the method, and more generally to the type, where it is declared. However this does not help to solve the parameter passing issue. We chose not to allow extra parameter passing, but to give sense in the handler to the standard "out" parameters of the signalling method. When a method whishes to pass parameters while raising an exception, it can use its standard "out" ones. This solution has the advantages of allowing parameter passing, while keeping the simplicity of exception raising and the attachment of an exception to a type.

The implementation uses a string variable for each activity. Raising an exception sets this variable and returns the control to the calling entity, which is in charge of testing the variable. Since an activity may be distributed (see section 2.1), the system ensures that this variable remains consistent across multiple nodes. The compiler generates code to test it after each system/object call.

2.3 Handlers in the object-oriented design

We have just seen that exception raising is associated to a method call. This holds as well for exception handling. What it means is that the alternate or retry policies mentioned in section 1.1 apply only to the method call itself and not to a possible block in which the call would be located. A characteristic of our proposal is that a handler may be semantically associated only to a method call, and not to a block of instructions. When the call *currentPage.GetChar* raises an *end_of_line* exception, the handler supplies a replacement value (**replace** is discussed later) and *PrintPage* continues with a call to *output.WriteChar* to print it.

```
method PrintPage;     // of class Editor
begin
    while TRUE do
        output.WriteChar(currentPage.GetChar);
    end;
except
    end_of_line from Page: replace '\n';
        // gives the printable character for a newline
    end_of_page from Page: return;
        // exits the method PrintPage
end PrintPage;
```

A handler can be associated to one instruction. Its declaration can be syntactically factorized to a block of instructions, to the whole method as in *PrintPage*, or even to a class of objects, but the handler is semantically associated to each operation (method call) of the block, or of the method, or of each method of the class. The programmer can then declare semantically precise handlers at the method level, and that allows him to clearly separate exception handling from the main flow of control.

In order to help the user to precisely define the scope of his handlers, we allow a handler to be associated not only to an exception name, but also to a type and a method name. The handler may only handle exceptions of the given name, raised by a method call of the given name on a reference to a type which conforms to the given one. The type and method name can be omitted when unnecessary. Besides, the keyword **ALL** may be used in each field, in order to factorize the declaration. Note that the handler in *PrintPage* is associated to the type *Page*, but it can handle the *end_of_line* exception raised by *currentPage* which is a *ShadowPage*, because *ShadowPage* is a subtype of *Page* and conforms to *Page* (see section 2.1 about the Guide model).

The implementation uses a stack variable, local to each method call, which refers the in scope handlers with a mask of the exceptions (and optionally the related method and type) that they may handle. This stack is updated once for each handler declaration, and the order is significant, high priority first. When an exception is raised, the first handler with a matching mask is executed.

2.4 Exception handling policies

Separating the exceptional code from the normal one seems a clean technique, but it raises the following problem. In Guide a method may return a value, which may be used as parameter in another method call. This is the case with *GetChar*. If it raises an exception, the handler may want to do the work by other means, so it must be able to provide an alternate character to be printed. This is the aim of the **replace** keyword used in the handler. The conformity relationship between the replacement value and the one expected by the operation is checked at compile time.

The retry policy is provided through the **retry** keyword that only a handler may use. This is a generic way to ask for a new execution of the call that raised the exception; so it allows general fault recovery policies to be programmed. The new execution should be done in the same environment as the first one, with optionally new handlers set by the programmer. However this induces a risk of recursively calling the same handler. To prevent this, the system ensures that a handler cannot be called again while it has not terminated. The following handler associated to the class *Editor* tries to recover from a failure of the *ObjectManager* (called in method *CreateNewPage*).

```
class Editor implements Editor is
    ...
    method Garbage;
        page: ref shadowPage;
    begin
        page := shadowPages.First;
        while page do
            if page.isDirty then
                shadowPageManager.Free(page);
                page := shadowPages.Delete;
            else
                page := shadowPages.Next;
        end; end;
    end;
except
    noObjectLeft from ShadowPageManager.Get: begin
        self.Garbage;
        retry;
        end;
end Editor.
```

We also provide a default handler to handle otherwise unhandled exceptions. The encapsulation of code guarantees that the calling object knows only the signature of the called method. So, when the method *CreateNewPage* of *Editor* calls the method *Get* of the *ObjectManager*, it does not know how it is implemented. The *ObjectManager* can use a memory allocator which may raise a *NO_MORE_MEMORY* exception, but the *Editor* cannot understand this exception. It must be handled by the *ObjectManager*, or a default policy has to be applied, but it cannot be propagated unchanged. The Guide system provides a default handler which propagates the *UNCAUGHT_EXCEPTION* system exception (cf section 3.1). This insures that an exception will either be handled or will eventually terminate the task.

```
method CreateNewPage;    // of class Editor
begin
    currentPage := shadowPageManager.Get;
end;
```

The implementation of **retry** and **replace** is allowed by the generic access respectively to the last method invocation, and to the optional return parameter of this invocation.

2.5 Resumption versus termination

Let us now explain why we have chosen a termination model in Guide. Whether resumption should be provided or not is an old debate. It has been supported in [13] and rejected in [6]. We now try to bring new arguments to this discussion, in relation to the object-oriented formalism.

We identify two main uses of resumption, depending on the provider of the handler. The handler may be provided by the user, through a debugger or a specialized shell, or it can be included by the programmer in the original code. The question is: what is the meaning of resumption after handler execution, and does it preserve the object encapsulation principle?

When an exception is raised inside the debugger, the stack of the nested calls is somehow saved, and control is given to the user. He can browse the stack, change a value at some level, and then resume at a possibly different level, perhaps the deepest. This means that the part of the saved stack between the level of the changed value and the resumption level is considered to be valid. This supposes a complete analysis of the concerned code, so it violates the frontier between the calls. However it could be left to the user's responsibility, in such specialized tools as the debugger. But to supply basic tools allowing other applications to do the same is another issue.

The call of a resumption handler must then be viewed from the other side, as the invocation in a nested context of code provided by the calling entity. The question becomes: do this code passing and invocation respect the encapsulation principle of objects? The aim of encapsulation is to allow to prove (formally or informally) the correctness of the implementation of an object interface, using only the interfaces called by this object. The correctness of an object may not depend on the implementation of the objects that use it. In that particular case, the signalling method would have to be proved using the interface of the handler, defined as a procedure argument passed to the signaller.

In a standard object-oriented environment a procedure is always associated to an object. A resumption handler must then be a closure, which embodies both a procedure and an environment. This notion of closure must appear in the language, because the callee has to provide the interface of the awaited closure in order to allow the control of the validity of the proposed handlers. A language which does not offer this notion will be reluctant to define it just for handling resumption handlers. Closures are defined in Lisp-based languages, where methods are or tend to be first class objects [8], and in a less rich way in Smalltalk with the *Block* class. However it is generally not the case in strongly typed object-oriented languages like Trellis-Owl, Eiffel or Guide.

We can conclude from this discussion that resumption is related to the existence in the language of closures, blocks of code including an environment. If the latter is provided by the language, then the former may be provided. In Guide this is not the case, so we adhere to a termination model, with the retry variation.

2.6 Summary

Exceptions are associated to object methods. Exceptions potentially raised by a method appear in its interface. Conformance rules are modified to take exceptions into account.

Handlers are associated to method invocations. The normal continuation after the execution of a handler is from the point just after the raising method invocation. It has nothing to do with the syntactic declaration of the handler, which may be factorized at the method or class level. A type and a method modifier help to refine the scope of the handler.

We have chosen a termination model. A handler may provide a replacement value when the raising method invocation is functional. The **retry** keyword allows a handler to reexecute the raising call in a generic manner. A default handler guarantees that an exception, once detected, cannot be unintentionnally discarded.

3 The Guide proposal: specific issues

3.1 System and hardware exceptions

Up to now we have only considered exceptions raised by method calls. However programs also ask services from the system, which may not be able to provide them. The problem is how to report these exceptions to the programmer.

In Guide we have decided to consider the system as a special class, and each instruction as a method call to the system class. In this way we handle system exceptions in the same way as other exceptions. They are predefined and may be handled with the keyword **SYSTEM** as a type, which may be omitted.

Examples of hardware exceptions are segmentation fault or arithmetic overflow. Such exceptions also appear as exceptions raised by the system. However this raises an implementation issue because such exceptions can effectively occur at nearly each instruction, so it is no longer possible to detect them by a test after each call, as it is done for system exceptions.

Interrupts are asynchronous events. They are not provided in Guide, except when an activity aborts. The system converts this event into a *QUIT* exception, which is detected later on, at the following system/method call.

3.2 The need for consistency

Our exception handling mechanism allows the programmer to implement alternate or retry policies when a call fails. However it does not insure that the called object is in a consistent state after it has raised an exception. Consistency depends on the validity of data relationships called invariants that are assumed to be true, except for the periods when an object operation is executed. The invariant must be restored at operation exit. This is especially needed in a parallel environment where the object can be used by another task, or in a persistent object system in which objects may be reused.

A (seemingly) obvious way to achieve this is for the programmer to declare some restoration code before each normal or exceptional exit point of the object. The problem is that an exception handling mechanism spills exit points throughout the whole code. They are **raises** and **return**s from the main code, and also from handlers which in turn may be called from various points of the main code if they are general (for example if they are defined at the method level), and also from handlers which could be inherited or from the default system handlers. The last cases show that restoration code specific to the object cannot be provided before each exit point of the object. This is why we need a specific restoration mechanism.

In Guide, the **restore** keyword allows to define a restoration block which is executed whenever the method exits abnormally (raises an exception). The block is not executed if the method returns normally, as would do a finalization mechanism, because we want to address the problem of consistency, and the object is assumed to be consistent in this case. The block is executed just after the raising of the exception and prior to the search for and execution of the handler. In turn if the handler propagates an exception then a restoration block of the calling object is executed before the search for a new handler. As an example, a restoration block associated to the class *Editor* allows us to save the dirty *Pages* of the *Editor* whenever it exits abnormally.

```
class Editor implements Editor is
    ...
restore
    page: ref ShadowPage;
    shadowDocument: ref Document;
begin
    page := shadowPages.First;
    while page do
        if page.isDirty then
            shadowPageManager.Free(page);
        else
            shadowDocument.pages.Append(page);
        end;
        page := shadowPages.Delete;
    end;
    if shadowDocument.pages.nbItem > 0 then
        output.WriteString("abnormal exit\n");
        output.WriteString("modifications saved in " + <name>);
        ... (shadowDocument, <name>);
end; end;
end Editor.
```

The programmer can optionally associate a restoration block with a class and with a method. If the method raises an exception, then the block associated to it is executed, after which the block associated to the effective class of the object is executed. Note that this class may be different from the definition class of the executed method, if this method is inherited.

A last characteristic of the Guide proposal is related to exception handling in the restoration code. Class handlers and method handlers are active during the execution of the restoration block associated to the method. Only the former are active for the restoration code of the class.

The block can also declare its own additional handlers. The main point is that if the restoration code does not handle an exception, or if it raises an exception itself, then the system propagates the *RECOVERY_FAILED* system exception. This ensures that the caller will not try some recovery operations on a called object which has not restored a consistent state. This is a first step to address an issue which is further discussed in section 4.2.

The implementation is different depending on the association. The compiler ensures that a method has only one exit point, tags it with a flag, and puts the method restoration code just after the flag. The class restoration code is directly called by the system.

3.3 Inheritance and conformance

The conformance rule between types has to be modified to take exceptions into account. It has been stated that an exception cannot be raised by an operation if it was not declared in its signature. Thus, in the method *PrintPage*, the call *currentPage.GetChar* cannot raise any other exception than *end_of_line*, *end_of_page* or *error* which are declared in and inherited from the type *Page*. It implies that the method *GetChar* of any type that conforms to *ShadowPage* may raise only a subset of the three exceptions. This is the same rule as for output parameters. In Guide a subtype conforms to its super-type, so the definition of type *ShadowSpecialPage* below is not correct.

```
type ShadowLongLine              type ShadowSpecialPage
subtype of ShadowPage is         subtype of ShadowPage is
   method GetChar: Char;            method GetChar: Char;
      signals end_of_line,             signals end_of_line,
         error;                           end_of_page,
end ShadowLongLine.                       unprintable, error;
// this type is correct          end ShadowSpecialPage.
                                 // this type is incorrect
```

Inheritance is also a tool to factorize code, and it impacts the handling code and the restoration code. Handlers that are associated with a method or with some instructions of a method are not inherited apart from the method. This means that either the subclass inherits the method and then it gets the related handlers, or it redefines the method and then it has to redefine handlers. This is natural because these handlers are supposed to heavily depend on the method code. On the other hand, handlers that are associated with a class are automatically inherited in the subclasses. This would be the case with the "garbage handler" for a subclass of *Editor*. This also allows to define default handlers for an application by the means of a common super-class.

We conclude this section with the inheritance of restoration code. As for handlers, only the block associated to the class is inherited. However a restoration block defined in a subclass overrides the one defined in the class.

3.4 Managing concurrency

A sequential algorithm assumes that an operation has succeeded before executing the next one. This is no longer the case with a parallel algorithm where one may want to perform simultaneously two operations and be satisfied with the first that returns a useful result.

In Guide, the **co_begin** statement enables the programmer to make concurrent calls. One variable per sub-activity is available, yielding *TRUE* if and only if the associated branch has terminated normally, i.e. without raising an exception. The programmer can express the termination condition with a **and** and **or** combination of these variables. If this condition yields *TRUE* after the normal termination of a branch, then the remaining branches are stopped and the parallel statement exits normally. On the other hand, if the failure of a branch prevents the normal termination condition from ever being verified, then the remaining branches are stopped and the system raises the *JOIN_FAILED* system exception.

This mechanism must be used with care: a *TRUE* branch variable means "I have successfully terminated", and not only "I have terminated". In the following example of a parallel producer and consumer, the condition **co_end**(*producer* **and** *consumer*) means that the two tasks must correctly terminate. If one of them terminates abnormally, then *JOIN_FAILED* is raised and *<handler>* is executed. The condition that the consumer has to terminate when the producer has terminated must be expressed in another way, because a **co_end**(*producer*) termination condition would induce an abnormal and rather rough termination of the consumer, and this would not detect a previous abnormal termination of the consumer.

```
method Main;
begin
   co_begin
        producer: ...    // producer code
        consumer: ...    // consumer code
   co_end(producer and consumer);
except
   JOIN_FAILED: <handler>;
end Main;
```

Note that the parallel block may either satisfy its termination condition, or be sure that it will never satisfy it, while some of its branches still run. In this case the system stops them softly by raising a *QUIT* exception (see section 3.1). It allows them to perform some restoration before exiting.

The parent activity cannot access the possible exception raised by a branch in the termination condition. However it can interpret this exception by providing a new handler specific to the branch.

To implement the failure detection, the system maintains another array of boolean variables, one per branch, that yields *TRUE* if and only if the corresponding branch has failed. When a branch fails, the system applies the termination function to the negation of these variables, and a *FALSE* result indicates that the parallel block has failed. The proof is simple. The negation of the variables identifies the activities that have terminated or may still terminate normally. This is clearly a superset of the positive variables in the final state. As we use only AND and OR modifiers, if the termination function yields true in the final state, it yields true with this superset.

4 Future work

We have discussed so far the current design of the exception handling mechanism in Guide, and the reasons behind the choices. Everything that is described in the two previous sections is implemented and works, except for the aspects related to hardware exceptions. We now present the extensions we plan to implement.

4.1 Exception hierarchy

Exceptions currently are simple strings associated to a type. This solution has the major drawback that an overloaded method in a subclass cannot raise another exception than those declared by the method in the superclass (cf section 3.3). In fact what we want in a subclass is to specialize each exception of the superclass. Exceptions must then be organized in a hierarchy respecting the subtype hierarchy of the corresponding types. It now becomes possible to declare *ShadowSpecialPage* as a subtype of *ShadowPage* (cf example in section 3.3), given the needed syntax which could be:

```
method GetChar: Char;
    signals end_of_line, end_of_page,
        unprintable isa error, error;
```

This gives a new task to the system because when *PrintPage* is compiled, the compiler does not know that *currentPage* may be a *ShadowSpecialPage* . So the system must be able to turn a possible *unprintable* exception raised by the call *currentPage.GetChar* into an *error* exception known to *Editor*.

Another advantage of this solution is that it would be easier for the compiler to check the validity of an exception raised in a handler defined at the class level, because this exception could be defined directly at the type level. Each exception would be a specialization of a primary *error* exception defined in type *Top*, which is the supertype of every Guide type. In the current design, one would have to check that the exception is declared in each method which can potentially cause the handler to be activated; this check is not done because it is complicated.

In addition this solution preserves the attachment of exceptions to a type. A subtype may only specialize an exception which has been declared in one of its supertypes. Conceptually, two unrelated types cannot raise the same exception, even if their exception names are identical.

4.2 Restoration

The current design is also too rigid, because the restoration code is executed when the method raises any exception, even when the programmer is sure that the object is in a consistent state. We describe below how we plan to refine our mechanism.

The restoration code defined at the method level can be made dependant on the raised exception. When an exception is raised the corresponding part of the restoration code is executed, and if this part executes normally the functionality we offer is close to that of a finalization tool. However when an exception occurs during execution of the restoration code then the object is declared being in an inconsistent state.

At the time the object is declared inconsistent, each activity executing on the object is stopped. The faulty activity then executes the restoration code associated with the class of the object. If this code executes normally then the activity and all other stopped activities raise the

FINALIZATION_FAILED system exception. If the class restoration code executes abnormally then the activities raise the *BAD_OBJECT_STATUS* system exception. To complete this scheme, an activity which calls an object which is in an inconsistent state is notified of the failure by a *BAD_OBJECT_STATUS* system exception.

This solution seems to solve the issue introduced in section 3.2, about failure occurrence during the execution of the restoration code. However it remains to be implemented and evaluated.

4.3 Hardware exceptions

The aim is to handle hardware exceptions as the other system exceptions (cf section 3.1). In fact we want to be able either to continue the execution after the raising point if the handler exits normally, or to propagate the exception (i.e. to return with the exception parameter set). We can then attempt to provide the retry, but it is not imperative.

Using C on Unix makes the propagation difficult. A hardware exception is turned into a signal and the programmer can execute a standard procedure call, the signal handler. When the call ends, the execution automatically continues. In the next phase of the project, we will use a low-level distributed kernel, Mach or Chorus, which can make the problem easier. In Mach and Chorus, a hardware exception stops the thread and is turned into a message sent to the exception port of the thread. Another thread can then read this message, take some action such as touching the stack of the stopped thread, and then restart it. To implement Unix signals is to push a procedure call onto the stack. We propose instead to change the program counter of the stopped thread, so that it executes the handler when it resumes. The return and the propagation become easier to implement, and the continuation needs to get the former program counter to be able to resume correctly.

5 Conclusion

This paper has described the exception handling mechanism we have designed and implemented for Guide, a strongly typed object-oriented language supported by a distributed system. The choices have always been directed by the encapsulation principle of the object formalism, and by a concern for orthogonality to the other concepts of the language. This resulted in the following characteristics:

conformance : exceptions are associated to object methods. Exceptions potentially raised by a method appear in its interface. Conformance rules are modified to take exceptions into account.

association: handlers are associated to method invocations. The normal continuation after the execution of a handler is the invocation that immediately follows the invocation of the method in which the exception was raised. It has nothing to do with the syntactic declaration of the handler, which may be factorized at the method or class level. This contributes to satisfying the main goal of an exception handling mechanism: to separate exceptional cases from the main algorithm.

inheritance : a handler defined in a class is automatically inherited in the subclasses. This is a convenient means of declaring default handlers.

restoration: restoration code may be provided at the method and class level. It is executed whenever the method exits abnormally. This is a useful tool to ensure the consistency of objects.

parallelism : exceptions are integrated in a natural and powerful way in concurrent computations, allowing complex termination policies to be implemented.

Everything that is described in section 2 and 3 is implemented. The rather primitive current implementation induces an additional cost of one assignment and one test per method call, inducing a small executing overhead when no exception is raised, and even no overhead considering the tests needed after the invocations when no exception handling mechanism is available, but increasing the code size by 25 per cent. It also adds a few assignments per handler declaration, but uses more execution time when an exception is raised, in order to find the right handler to execute.

Acknowledgments

I have been constantly supported by the whole Guide team while specifying and implementing this mechanism. I wish to thank Sacha Krakowiak, Véronique Normand and Xavier Rousset for their detailed criticisms of previous drafts of this paper. Project Guide is partly supported by the Commission of European Communities under the Comandos ESPRIT Project (no 2071).

Bibliography

[1] S. Krakowiak, M. Meysembourg, H. Nguyen Van, M. Riveill, C. Roisin and X. Rousset. Design and implementation of an object-oriented, strongly typed language for distributed applications. *Journal of Object-Oriented Programming*, 3(3), pp. 11-22, September-October 1990.

[2] R. Balter and al. Architecture and Implementation of Guide, an Object-Oriented Distributed System. *to appear in Computing Systems*, 1991.

[3] *ANSA Reference Manual*. Architecture Projects Management Limited, 24 Hills Road, Cambridge CB2 1JP, United Kingdom, March 1989.

[4] B. Liskov, M. Herlihy, P. Johnson, G. Leavens, R. Scheifler and W. Weihl. *Preliminary Argus Reference Manual*. October 1983.

[5] M.A. Ellis and B. Stroustrup. *The Annotated C++ Reference Manual*. Addison-Wesley, 1990.

[6] B. Liskov and A. Snyder. Exception Handling in CLU. *IEEE Transactions on Software Engineering*, SE-5(6), pp. 546-558, November 1979.

[7] B. Meyer. *Object-Oriented Software Construction*. Series in Computer Science Prentice Hall International, 1988.

[8] C. Dony. Exception Handling and Object-Oriented Programming: towards a synthesis. *Proc. ECOOP/OOPSLA '90*, pp. 322-330, October 1990.

[9] L. Cardelli, J. Donahue, L. Glassman, M. Jordan, B. Kalsow and G. Nelson. *Modula-3 Report (revised)*. DEC SRC, October 1989.

[10] W.F. Burger, N. Halim, J.A. Pershing, R. Strom and S. Yemini. *Draft NIL Reference Manual*. (42993), IBM, TJ Watson RC, P.O. Box 218, Yorktown Heights, NY 10598, December 1982.

[11] Objectworks Smalltalk-80 V2.5. *Advanced User's Guide*. Parc Place Systems, 1550 Plymouth Street, Mountain View, California 94043, 1989.

[12] C. Schaffert, T. Cooper and C. Wilpolt. *Trellis Object-Based Environment, Language Reference Manual*. (DEC-TR-372), DEC, Eastern Research Lab, Hudson, Masachusetts, November 1985.

[13] S. Yemini and D.M. Berry. A Modular Verifiable Exception-Handling Mechanism. *ACM Transactions on Programming Languages and Systems*, 7(2), pp. 214-243, April 1985.

Representation of Complex Objects :
Multiple Facets with Part-Whole Hierarchies

Francis Wolinski & Jean-François Perrot
LAFORIA, Institut Blaise Pascal,
Université Paris VI & CNRS, Paris
Boîte 169, 4 Place Jussieu, 75252 Paris Cedex 05, France

1- INTRODUCTION

1.1- General

We study a problem in object-oriented knowledge representation. The traditional class/instance and inheritance paradigms form a sound basis for a computer simulation of real-world objects "as they are described", thereby giving a tool for expressing knowledge about the world in a specific way which is neither procedural nor declarative, and which we propose to call "object-oriented". In our opinion, knowledge representation differs from programming in that it has to be practised by experts of the domain and not by professional programmers. Hence, the programming tools it uses must be designed to fit the intellectual processes of the domain expert rather than to suit the needs of the implementer. In this respect, we consider that the class/instance mechanism is a very satisfactory machine realization of the "general concept"/"specific instance" way of thinking, whereas inheritance (simple or multiple) is far less acceptable as a classification scheme. As a consequence, we shall concentrate on improving the instanciation process and use inheritance in a standard way purely as a programming tool.

Anyhow, this well-known, well-implemented and well-understood paradigm must be extended in at least two ways in order to become a really usable tool for representing substantial amounts of knowledge about complex objects. Namely, it has to deal with two dimensions of structural complexity. First, objects usually must be considered from various points of view. Second, many objects are thought of as being composed of various parts that are themselves considered as sub-objects (and not as attributes). These two dimensions have been repeatedly explored in the past (Points of view : Goldstein & Bobrow in PIE [9], Bobrow & Stefik in LOOPS [2] and lately Carré in ROME [5] [6]. Part-whole : the LOOPS and Thinglab [3] systems, lately Blake & Cook [1]). But nowhere have they been treated together: for instance the LOOPS primitives dealing with points of view (classes Node and Perspective) are not easily combined with metaclass Template catering for part-whole hierarchies.

1.2- Aim of paper

In this paper, we propose to bring these two dimensions together in an analysis and an implementation based on a restricted application domain, that of robot representation. We claim that by restricting the field we are able to formulate some proposals about the intellectual processes used by domain expersts and thus to motivate our solutions.

More precisely, the aim of this paper is to study both dimensions together and to propose a set of tools which insures their harmonious cooperation. Our proposal extends the approach of Goldstein & Bobrow in PIE [9] on the multi-facet aspect by integrating the part-whole hierarchy aspect.

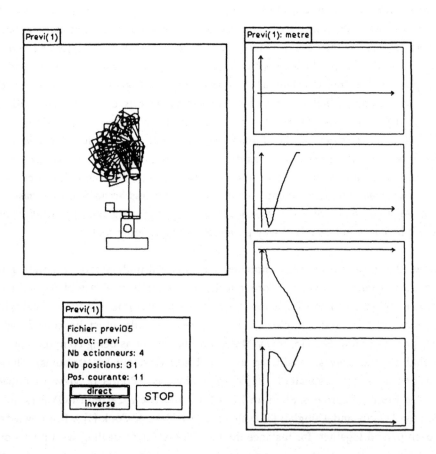

Fig. 1 : A view of manipulator Previ as represented in *Systalk*

2- CONTEXT OF WORK

2.1- Robotics at EDF

The work partially reported here was done in the Robotics Group of Electricité de France (EDF). Its aim was to provide the various specialised teams dealing with robots at EDF (mechanics, control, sensing, CAD, trajectory generation) with a computer system where their various approaches would be housed in a uniform way. The requirements included an interface with CAD tools for reading in robot specifications as well as input of trajectories computed off line and their execution. We chose Smalltalk-80 as a base and developed the *Systalk* system [15].

About 12 different operational domains totalling 40 classes or so were covered, with 50 predefined robotic components. The system was used in two main robotic fields :
   - manipulators, with execution of off-line computed trajectories and force and torque calculation (see [14]). All manipulators used or studied by EDF were modelled in *Systalk*.
   - mobile robots, with simulation of sensors and qualitative control (see [7]).

2.2- User specification

Our application caters for 4 levels of user competence :
   - (a) the *system developer* : he has full knowledge of the architecture of *Systalk* at its various levels of implementation, he is able e.g. to improve on implementation efficiency.
   - (b) the *programming specialist* : he is a Smalltalk programmer, but only knows the outward description of *Systalk*, he is therefore unable to modify structural implementation choices. His task is to manage and extend the set of specialised classes that represent the various facets of robots (see under § 3 for more details). Typically, he would have to improve the speed of computation of forces and torques, and to program a new facet "robot compliance under external contraints". He also may have to extend the library of predefined robotic components (such as various sorts of primitive geometric bodies and more sophisticated joints).
   - (c) the *robot conceptor* : he knows nothing of Smalltalk, but has a complete knowledge of *Systalk'* s functionalities. His task is to build classes modelling actual robots, using the representation tools we propose via the user interface.
   - (d) the *basic user* : he knows neither Smalltalk nor the full structure of *Systalk*, but is well acquainted with *Systalk'* s user interface. His job is to instantiate one or several robot classes and to use the instances for simulation purposes and thereby derive informations of interest for his project.

Systalk was designed mainly to accomodate user (c). We assume that our robot conceptor thinks of the robot he has to represent as a hierarchy of sub-systems ultimately made up of standard robot components to be picked off the shelf. The various facets of the complete robot (visible form to be drawn on screen, articulated motion, constraints that are applied at various points of the structure etc.) are correspondingly built up from those of the sub-systems **in an automatic way**, provided the communication schemes that link the various sub-system facets are specified. Note this simulation of the mounting of a robot results in a kind of multiple reuse of software components, since robotic components are re-used whereas each of them does reuse more elementary software components corresponding to its facets.

2.3- Example : A construction of a "simple" robot : the *Previ* manipulator (figs. 1 and 2)

2.3.1- *Facets*

Robots in our application context have a number of facets, or activities, which will be implemented as independent objects (see infra § 3.1). Here are the most important :

- *Cartesian frame* : The position of the robot in space is given by a three dimensional coordinate system bound to the robot, expressed in the coordinates of the supersystem of the robot. Accordingly, a move of the robot relative to its supersystem will be appear as a transformation of its cartesian frame. Class `cartesianFrame` defines 4 instance variables O, X, Y, Z with values in R^3, as well as methods for algebraic computation of translations, rotations and transpositions.
- *Shape* : The visible shape of the robot, to be drawn on the screen. The actual drawing is obtained by top-down activation of the `Shape` facet objects attached to the subsystems that make up the robot (see § 4). Eventually, each elementary component has its own shape, described by some subclass e.g. `Cylinder`, `Cone`, `Parallelepiped`, which defines the necessary instance variables (e.g. for `Cylinder`, variables `height` and `radius`) as well as the display methods (which of course will make use of the `cartesianFrame` facet).
- *Solid* : Mass and centre of gravity, the last being recomputed at every instant in function of the state of the (articulated) robot.
- *Kinematics* : Expresses the role of each part of the robot as a motion transformer : when a move is applied to it, it executes the move (transforming its `cartesianFrame`) and transmits it to the objects with which it is bound.
- *Force (and Torque)* : Computes the forces from which elastic deformation may be deduced.
- *Control* : Logical organization of motion operators.
- *Measurements* : *idem* for motion, speed and stress sensors.

2.3.2- *Subsystems*

Robots are usually analysed in 3 levels : the robot is composed of a number of articulated bodies, each of which is made up of a few geometric solids and joints, which are all predefined and available in store. Constructing a robot is thus accomplished in two steps, first the building of the individual parts, second the assembly of the parts.

In our example the following standard elements will be used :
- Geometric solids : bars, boxes and fingers
- Joints : static and revolute

Our *Previ* robot is made up of five articulated bodies :
- a *base*, comprising 3 bars, one static joint and one revolute joint.
- one link of kind *link1*, of 4 bars, 2 boxes with one static joint and one revolute joint.
- two links of kind *link2*, of 2 bars, one static joint and one revolute joint.
- a *gripper*, made up of 2 boxes, 2 fingers and one static joint.

According to this analysis, the *Systalk* user of type (c) wishing to represent a *Previ* manipulator involves:
- making sure that classes `Bar`, `Box` and `Finger`, as well as `SJoint` and `RJoint` are predefined in the system ;
- defining 4 new classes `PreviBase`, `PreviLink1`, `PreviLink2` and `PreviGripper` ;
- defining a new class `Previ`.

Then any number of instances of Previ may be created by instantiating class `Previ` (the work of a *Systalk* user of type (d), and used *ad libitum* via the various facets (executing trajectories, displaying motion etc).

The essence of *Systalk* is to give means to express that class `Previ` is obtained by composing classes `PreviBase`, `PreviLink1` etc. in an intelligible way, and that in turn `PreviBase` is composed of classes `Bar`, `SJoint` and `RJoint` in an analogous way etc. To formulate the structural and functional relationships that constitute the definition of these entities, we introduce three categories of discourse :

- a system (robot) has several *facets*, or activities ;
- a system is composed of several *subsystems* ;
- facets of the same kind in different subsystems are linked by *communication schemes*.

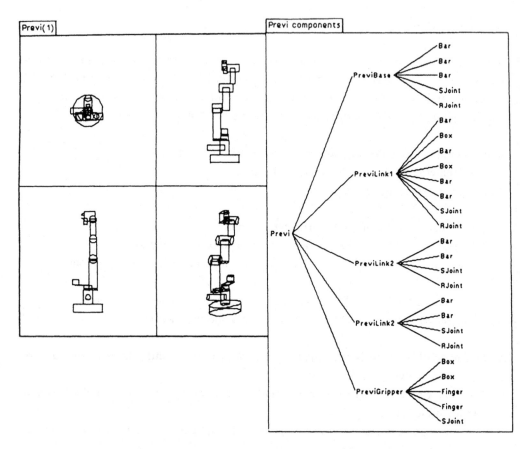

Fig. 2 : Manipulator Previ : its Shape facet (top left), its decomposition tree (top right), and (the Shape facets of) its five components (below)

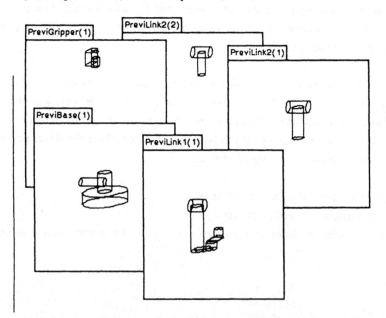

As we said before, the first two have been considered many times, whereas the third is (to our knowledge) new. It is needed to link facets and hierarchy together. The originality of our work is to present an integrated architecture with all three aspects working smoothly together.

One might choose to translate this analysis directly at the level of the implementation language (supposing it powerful enough). That is, part-whole hierarchy and multi-facets could be rendered using the standard object-oriented techniques of aggregation of attributes and (multiple) inheritance. See B. Carré [5] for a thorough discussion.

Clearly, the programming tools at the disposal of users (c) and (d) must be distinct from the general-purpose Smalltalk primitives accessible only to (a) and (b).

3- MULTI-FACETS

3.1- Explicit delegation

3.1.1- *Our choice*

The traditional choice for implementing multi-faceted objects is between multiple inheritance and explicit delegation. Rather than endowing Smalltalk with a refined multiple inheritance scheme such as the point-of-view approach of Carré [6] , we chose to materialize each facet by an independent object, to which the messages corresponding to its activities are delegated, and which in turn is able to delegate parts of its work to other facet-objects. Apart from its comparative easy implementation in Smalltalk, it has the advantage of allowing dynamic modification of the facets. In this we follow the approach of PIE, whose conclusion we adopt

"In most cases, we have found that the sender knows the point of view that the recipient should employ to understand the message" [9, p. 77]

Our syntax for delegation uses a method function:, to send message msg to a given facet of a certain system, write :

```
(system function: facetName) msg
```

3.1.2- *"Contractual backing" between facets*

Facets possess a backward pointer to the system to which they belong (an instance variable called system), thus they have indirect access to the other facets of the same system. For instance, facets of the Shape kind have recourse to the facet cartesianFrame of the system for display. We call this kind of cooperation between facets *contractual backing*.

Although it was virtually present in PIE, its authors don't seem to have made use of it, since they defined functionally independent facets such as resistor and plane location. Here is a simple example for facet Solid which defines the instance variable mass :

```
!Solid methodsFor: 'access' !
density
      ^ mass/(system function: #Shape) volume !!
```

Communication between facets using contractual backing accurately reflects the laws of physics and in the same time allows a high degree of code sharing.

3.2- Prototypes

3.2.1- *Problem statement*

The problem is then to write only one class hierarchy per facet (e.g. for the "visible shape" facet Shape, classes Cylinder, Parallelepiped, Cone, Sphere etc.), which will be "used" by all the robot classes that possess the facet. This raises a well-known problem which we summarize as follows.

Creating a multi-faceted object is a rather heavy process, since it demands the creation of all facet-objects, hence the creation method must provide all their relevant instance variable values for due initialization. This is admissible when the object is created for the first time, much less so when it is to be reused. Hence, one would wish to adopt another approach and be able to duplicate complex object instead of buiding them *ex nihilo*. However, physical copying (deepCopy) carries with it more information than is actually needed (irrelevant details about the actual state of the object). So we are led to defining equivalence relations between complex objects that are intermediate between complete identity (equal values of attributes) and belonging to the same class. For instance, the general notion of a cylinder (class Cylinder, with attributes height and radius), may be refined as cylinder-with-radius-10, cylinder-with-height-50, cylinder-with-radius-10-and-height-50, this last notion being clearly distinct from any given instance of a cylinder having those values in its instance variables. Whereas the general notion is adequately represented by class Cylinder, the other three don't seem to require independent classes to represent them, since they do share most of the information they carry with the said class. Therefore a new implementation concept is needed, different from class as well as from instance. In PIE, this concept was called *contextualization* and implemented as a pair (class, dictionary).

3.2.2- *Multi-parameter classes*

We follow here the same line with a different terminology : PIE contextualizations are called here **prototypes**, and seen as named contexts, i.e. pairs (name, dictionary). To use them we introduce **multi-parameter classes**, the metaclasses of which define an instance variable (for this technique, see Cointe [4, 8]) called prototypes, pointing toward a dictionary of contexts (dictionaries). In these classes the instantiation method new: takes as an argument a contextName and yields as a result an instance of the class initialized according to the context which is the value of contextName in the dictionary prototypes. They are defined as subclasses of the abstract class MultiParaObject, and all facet classes of *Systalk* belong to this hierarchy.

```
Object subclass: MultiParaObject
    instanceVariableNames: ''
    classVariableNames: '' !

!MultiParaObject methodsFor: 'initialization'!

init:  aPrototype
    aPrototype associationsDo:
        [:a | self perform: (a key, ':') asSymbol
            with: a value]!!

MultiParaObject class
    instanceVariableNames: 'prototypes'!

!MultiParaObject class methodsFor: 'creation'!

new:  contextName
    ^super new init: (prototypes at: contextName) !!
```

For instance, class Cylinder will inherit from MultiParaObject, and the value of its variable prototypes is the dictionary containing all the cylinder prototypes corresponding to all the various robot parts of cylindrical shape that are currently available in the system. The names to be used as keys for this dictionary are generated automatically as the path (see section 4.2.2) referencing the part in the part-whole hierarchy of the robot being built. Actually the dictionary itself will have a hierarchical structure (see section 4.2.3).

For the Previ manipulator only there will be no less than 11 such prototypes, corresponding to PreviBase (3 parts), PreviLink1 (4 parts) and PreviLink2 (2 parts, used twice). When an instance of Previ is created, class Cylinder is accordingly instanciated 11 times:

```
Cylindre new: 'Previ.1.1' asSymbol      (first part of the base)
Cylindre new: 'Previ.1.2' asSymbol      (second part of the base)
Cylindre new: 'Previ.2.2' asSymbol      (second part of first link)
etc ...
```

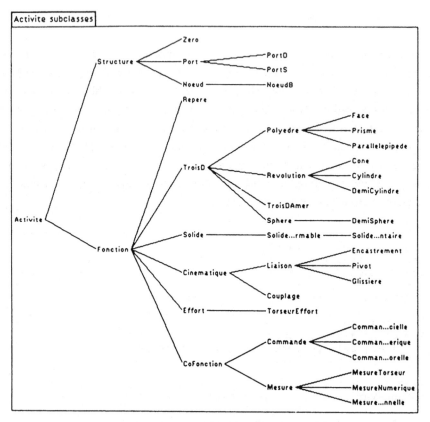

Fig. 3: The class hierarchy of *Systalk* facets
(note that *3D* is French for *Shape*, *Effort* idem for *Force&Torque*, and *Repere* for *CartesianFrame*)

4- PART-WHOLE HIERARCHIES

4.1- Problem statement

In some sense, giving the set of facets of a system (robot) amounts to defining its type. Once this type is fixed, the structure of the system is defined by its decomposition in subsystems. It is therefore natural to try and describe a system in terms of its subsystems and relations between them, without explicitly mentioning the facets. Such a description will be formalized as the writing of a class (e.g. class Previ).

At the class level, only the classes of the subsystems will appear. This implies a certain loss of information that must be compensated by an equivalent injection of knowledge in those classes on the one hand and into the composition methods on the other hand. Our purpose is to give some techniques for doing so (preliminary report in [12]). Typically, we must be able to specify that a certain subsystem not only belongs to a certain class, but also has some fixed parameters, or that it must satisfy some constraints. Since most of the properties of our systems are attached to their facets, our first task will be to get together part-whole hierarchies and our multi-facet technique.

The hierarchical decomposition of a system induces a corresponding hierarchical structure for each of its facets. The corresponding trees are identical to the decomposition tree of the system where a label nil at a node denotes the absence of the facet for the corresponding part (compare fig. 4 with fig. 2 top right).

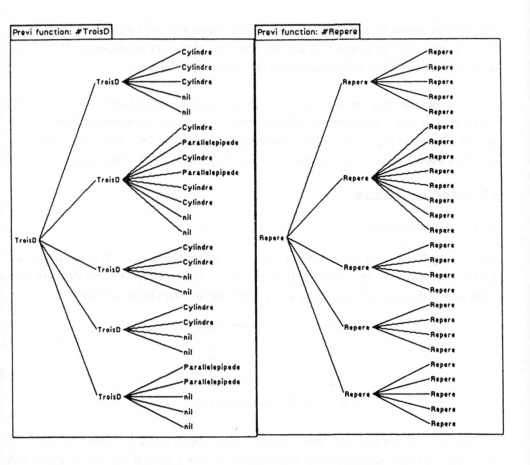

Fig. 4 : The decomposition trees of *Previ*'s facets Shape(= TroisD)
and CartesianFrame(= Repere)

As an example of the hierarchical structure of facets consider the Previ manipulator, defined as the composition of 5 articulated bodies (one base, one gripper, three links):

- its Shape facet (visible shape) is clearly composed of the Shape facets of the 5 bodies.

- its Solid facet is composed in a way that is less visible, but not less real, via an algebraic summation of the masses and the centres of gravity of the subsystems (i.e. from their Solid facets).

- the strucure of its facet cartesianFrame, on the contrary, is not to be seen as a decomposition, but in the expression of the cartesian frames of the 5 subsystems with respect to that of the system.

This example shows that the induced hierarchical structure is not the same for every facet. Actually, the way this structure is derived from that of the system depends on the facet class, but only on it. It is an integral part of the definition of the facet.

At the implementation level, the hierarchical structure of a facet is not explicitly represented. It is computed on first demand from the structure of the system, then (to save computation time) it is stored in its associated communication link (see § 5.1.). We must now find means to automate the definition of subfacets from the definition of subsystems.

4.2- Hierarchical prototypes

4.2.1- *Lazy instanciation*

We start again from the instanciation problem. Creating a system involves creating all its subsystems, hence all the facets of its subsystems. The facets of a subsystem are also subobjects of the facets of the system, so that there are two ways to create them :

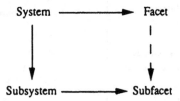

In order to save memory and speed up the instanciation process, we use a kind of lazy instanciation, where all subsystems are instantiated, whereas facets are created only when required. Therefore, subfacets will be reached through the subsystem they belong to and not from their "superfacet".

4.2.2- *Paths*

Now subsystems are referred to as paths (following Thinglab) in the decomposition tree. If
S is the name of the system, its subsystem n° *i* will be denoted by *S.i*, and subsystem n° *j*
of *S.i* will be denoted by *S.i.j* etc. Such a path (e.g. 'Previ.3.1') is the only name of the
subsystem known to *Systalk*. Hence we must deduce from it all the prototypes that we
need for the different facets of the subsystem it refers to. Recall that, for each facet, these
prototypes are to be found inside the class of the facet. Thus we must set up an
interpretation scheme for subsystem paths that works with every such (multi-parameter)
class.

Now, we have to take into account the fact that a component may be considered at various
levels of integration. In the same way as we refined (in § 3.2.1) the general notion of a
cylinder as cylinder-with-radius-10 etc, we want to consider Bar (1) in itself, (2) as the first
element of PreviLink2 in itself, (3) as the first element of PreviLink2 taken as the third
component of Previ in itself and (4) should Previ be used as n^{th} component of a
supersystem X, as the first element of the third component of the nth component of X in
itself, etc. These different notions of a bar are naturally denoted by paths 'Bar',
'PreviLink2.1', 'Previ.3.1' and 'X.n.3.1', etc.

We want to provide an explicit representation of those various notions in order to allow
the full reuse of them. Clearly, they have to be represented as prototypes attached to class
Bar. Moreover, each of these prototypes is included (as a dictionary) in the next one in the
above integration order. This order corresponds to an incremental specification of the
prototypes:

- path 'Bar' says nothing more than "it is a bar", leaving all parameters undefined
(generic bar).
- path 'PreviLink2.1' says that this bar is the first element of a super-system that is of
kind PreviLink2. This specifies the relative orientation of the bar, which is reflected in its
facet cartesianFrame, but not its geometric dimensions.
- path 'Previ.3.1' says that the abovesaid supersystem is indeed the third subsystem of
Previ and which completes the specification of the bar.
- other paths (like 'X.n.3.1') won't add any specifications to the bar.

4.2.3- *Utilization trees*

So, when referring to a bar, path 'Previ.3.1' can be interpreted as a sequence of
increasingly constrained contexts, starting with the empty context and ending with a fully
specified one. We call each of these contexts a **utilization** of the bar. We further observe
that all such paths concerning a given system can be assembled as a tree, which we call the

utilization tree of the bar in the system. In some sense, the family of those trees for the various subsystems is dual to the decomposition tree of the system. At the level of class Bar, the utilization trees corresponding to the various robots available in *Systalk* are collected as a single tree, with the empty context as root, which we call the **utilization tree** of subsystem Bar.

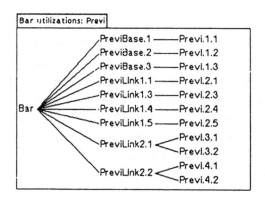

Fig. 5 : The utilization tree of Bar in Previ

This solves our problem : suppose our subsystem Bar owns facet F, the utilization tree is readily converted into a tree of prototypes to be given as a value to the variable prototypes of class F. We only have to make a slight change to the mechanism of multi-parameter classes in order to accomodate a tree of prototypes instead of a dictionary of contexts.

This requires the introduction of a class Prototype, subclass of Dictionary, which will define the hierarchical tree structure by means of an instance variable superPrototype, and to modify method init: of class MultiParaObject as follows :

```
!MultiParaObject methodsFor: 'initialization'!

init:  aPrototype
     aPrototype associationsDo:
          [:a | self perform: (a key, ':') asSymbol
                with: a value].
     self init: aPrototype superPrototype  !!
```

5- COMMUNICATION SCHEMES

5.1- The idea and the three classes

So far, our implementation captures the structural relationships between subsystems. There remain to express the functional ones. For instance, facet Kinematics works with a number of contacts between homologous facets of static joints, revolute joints, links etc. These communications between facets of the same kind are organized in *communication schemes* which we represent by specific objects (which we call *communication links*) having as attributes several *communication channels* (symbolized by mere numbers) and an *interconnection matrix* [13]. They fall into three main classes which we call Zero (vertical communication of a father with all of its sons collectively), Port (vertical communication of a father with each of its sons individually) and Node (horizontal communication between brothers).

Communication links of classes Zero and Port answer to messages :

```
propagate: aSelector
propagate: aSelector arguments: anArray
```

those of class Node to messages (one for emission and one for reception) :

```
propagate: aSelector arguments: anArray target: aChannel
propagate: aSelector arguments: anArray source: aChannel
```

To each type of facet corresponds one type of communication scheme. For instance, facet Shape communicates in mode Zero, Kinematics in mode Node. This correspondence is expressed by an instance variable called structure in all the facet classes (defined in the metaclass), with value the associated class of communication schemes. Every facet instance accesses its own communication link through a method called comLink : here is a simple example :

```
!Measurement methodsFor: 'work' !

getValue
      ^self comLink propagate: #getValue !!
```

where it is understood that Measurement facets of elementary components have specific getValue methods.

Conversely, every communication link accesses the facet object with which it is associated through a method called function (with no argument). It owns an instance variable subComLinks with value the set of the communication links of the subfacets, thus representing in an indirect way the hierarchical structure of the facet as indicated in § 4.1.

5.2- An example of communication

Propagation of the display message to facet Shape. : displaying a shape needs a cartesian frame which has to be transformed down the communication line according to the relative positions of the subparts. This transform belongs to facet Shape but is operated by the communication scheme thanks to a compound selector (**trans**. <propagated selector>). As usual, Shape subclasses will have their own specialized display methods.

```
!Shape methodsFor: 'display' !

displayAt: aPoint frame: aCartFrame scale: aNumber
    self comLink propagate: displayAt:frame:scale:
            arguments: (Array with: aPoint
                              with: aCartFrame
                              with: aNumber)!!

!Shape methodsFor: 'transform'!

trans.displayAt: aPoint frame: aCartFrame scale: aNumber
    ^Array with: aPoint
        with: ((system function: #CartesianFrame)
                            transform: aCartFrame)
        with: aNumber!!
```

Method trans.display of Shape is operated by method transform:arguments: of Zero as shown in the code for propagate:

```
!Zero methodsFor: 'propagation'!

propagate: aSelector arguments: anArray
    self subComLinks isEmpty
        ifTrue: "rock-bottom facet : execute"
                [self function perform: aSelector
                              withArguments: anArray ]
        ifFalse: "intermediary facet : transform then propagate"
                [self subComLinks do:
                    [:cl| cl propagate: aSelector
                      arguments: (cl transform: aSelector
                                        arguments: anArray ) ]] !!
```

5.3- Prototypes with translation

In the hierarchical contruction of a system S, if no coupling occurs, the channels of the communication links of the various facets of the subsystems of S become automatically channels of the links of the facets of S. For instance, assembling two robots with p resp. q degrees of freedom (i.e. p resp. q input-output channels for facet kinematicControl) yields a robot with $p+q$ degrees of freedom, i.e. $p+q$ channels in the same facet. Coupling between subsystems represents physical bindings and reduces the total amount of channels in the supersystem. For instance, a rigid binding between subsystems A and B results in identifying a channel of A with a channel of B, submitted to compatibility relationships (e.g. male/female parts, see [14] for details).

Hence we have to set up some sort of algebra for interconnection matrices, which is part of the definition of our communication scheme classes :

- Schemes of class Zero have no channel at all, hence no matrix. They address directly the subfacets of the same kind and establish a collective communication with them (as demonstrated by the code for propagation above).

- In schemes of class Port, each channel of the subsystem corresponds to a channel of the supersystem, through an automatic renumbering process. The interconnection matrix is trivial.

- In schemes of class Node, the interconnection matrix may be arbitrary, and must be explicitly given by the user.

Here is the matrix for the Kinematics facet of our Previ example. Each line corresponds to one of the 5 subsystems (see § 2.3.2 and fig. 2), all of which happen to have the same number of channels, namely 2. Each channel c appears as a pair of integers $(x\ y)$, indicating that channel c is connected to channel number y of subsystem number x (0 meaning the supersystem).

PreviBase :   [(0 1) (2 1)]   the 1st channel of the base is the input channel of Previ,
                                  the 2nd one is connected to the 1st channel of PreviLink1

PreviLink1:   [(1 2) (3 1)]

PreviLink2:   [(2 2) (4 1)]

PreviLink2:   [(3 2) (5 1)]

PreviGripper: [(4 2) (0 2)]   the 2nd channel of the gripper is the output channel of
                                  Previ.

As a consequence, Previ has two kinematics channels left instead of the 10 channels provided by its 5 subsystems.

Communication scheme classes are submitted to the same process of incomplete instanciation via prototypes as facet classes. However, what is practically needed are prototypes that specify the total number of channels as well as the interconnection matrix, but leave open the exact identity of the subsystems that they are going to interrelate. These subsystems are represented by *ad hoc* placeholders (their numbers). The symbolic matrices (such as the one above) are stored in instances of a special class, a variant (but not a subclass) of Prototype. This class also supports the translation process of the placeholders into the actual subsystems during instanciation.

In our example, in the course of instantiating class Previ, numbers 0 to 5 appearing in the symbolic connection matrix will be replaced by the actual subsystems of the instance of Previ that is created.

6- CONCLUSION

We have presented a working system that integrates in a homogeneous way multi-facets and part-whole hierarchies. Of course many improvements are in order, notably some form of compilation to gain speed.

The main direction to be explored, in our opinion, is the meta-knowledge needed to implement reasoning about the system. Our first attempt was to couple *Systalk* with our version of OPUS [10], a Smalltalk-80 interpretation of OPS-5 (see Pachet [11]) and to have OPUS production rules control a *Systalk* robot. The next will be to integrate a powerful semantic network. Work is going on in this way.

ACKNOWLEDGEMENTS

We wish to thank Mr Michel Delbos, formerly head of the Robotics Group of the Sureillance, Diagnostics and Maintenance Dept, Electricité de France, for his help and support while developing *Systalk*.

REFERENCES

[1] Blake, E. and Cook, S : On including part hierarchies in object-oriented languages, with an implementation in Smaltalk, ECOOP '87, p. 45-54.

[2] Bobrow, D. and Stefik, M. : The LOOPS Manual, Xerox Corp. (1983).

[3] Borning, A. : THINGLAB - A Constraint-Oriented Simulation Laboratory, Ph.D. thesis, Stanford 1979.

[4] Briot, J.-P. and Cointe, P. : A Uniform Model for Object-Oriented Languages Using the Class Abstraction, IJCAI '87, vol.1, p. 40-43.

[5] Carré, B. : Une méthodologie orientée objet pour la représentation des connaissances - concepts de point de vue, de représentation multiple et évolutive d'objets, Thèse, Université de Lille, 1989.

[6] Carré, B. and Geib, J.-M. : The Point of View notion for Multiple Inheritance, OOPSLA-ECOOP '90, p. 312-321.

[7] Coiffet, Ph., Zhao, J., Zhou, J., Wolinski, F., Novikoff, P., Schmit, D. : About qualitative robot control, Nato Workshop on Expert Systems and Robotics, Corfu 1990.

[8] Cointe, P. : Metaclasses are First Class : the ObjVlisp Model, OOPSLA '87, p. 156-167.

[9] Goldstein, I. and Bobrow, D. : Extending Object Oriented Programming in Smalltalk, First Lisp Conference, Stanford 1980, p. 75-81.

[10] Laursen, J. and Atkinson, R. : OPUS : a Smalltalk Production System, OOPSLA '87, p. 377-387.

[11] Pachet, F. : Mixing Rules and Objects : an Experiment in the World of Euclidean Geometry, 5th International Symposium on Computer and Information Sciences, Nevsehir (Turkey) 1990, p. 797-805.

[12] Wolinski, F. : Gestion des contraintes induites dans la structuration des objets en sous-objets, Reconnaissance des Formes et Intelligence Artificielle (RFIA), Paris 1989, p. 163-171.

[13] Wolinski, F. : Modeling and simulation of robotic systems using the Smalltalk-80 environment, TOOLS '89, p. 141-149.

[14] Wolinski, F. : Représentation de systèmes robotiques en Smalltalk-80, Convention IA 1990, Paris (Hermes publ.) p. 685-699.

[15] Wolinski, F. : Etude des capacités de modélisation systémique des langages à objets appliquées à la représentation de robots, Thèse, Université Paris VI, 1990.

Multi-Methods in a Statically-Typed Programming Language

Warwick B. Mugridge, John Hamer, John G. Hosking

Department of Computer Science, University of Auckland,

Private Bag, Auckland, New Zealand

rick@cs.aukuni.ac.nz   jham1@cs.aukuni.ac.nz   john@cs.aukuni.ac.nz

ABSTRACT:

Multivariant functions in Kea are a statically-typed form of the multi-methods of CLOS (Keene, 1989) but encapsulation is retained. Multivariants permit fine typing distinctions to be made, allow despatching to be avoided in some cases, and may be used to avoid some restrictions of the contravariance rule.

Once multivariant functions are introduced by example, the semantics of the despatch of multivariants are provided, based on the generation of despatching variants. Three issues arise with despatching: redundancy, ambiguity, and exhaustiveness of a (partially-ordered) set of variants with respect to a function call. It is shown that the approach taken here is consistent with separate compilation.

KEYWORDS: object-oriented, multi-methods, static-typing, polymorphism, contravariance

1. Introduction

A form of multi-methods is introduced in the context of Kea[1], a statically-typed object-oriented and functional programming language which is currently being extended to include higher-order and (implicitly) polymorphic functions. Multivariant functions in Kea are a statically-typed form of the multi-methods of CLOS, in which despatching depends on the class of all arguments to a function (Keene, 1989). Unlike CLOS, however, Kea retains a notion of encapsulation. Multivariants permit fine typing distinctions to be made, allow despatching to be avoided in some cases, and may be used to avoid some restrictions of the contravariance rule (Cook, 1989).

In the Simula despatching model, an object is the implicit first argument to a procedure (or function) call; the class of this object determines the procedure that is executed (Dahl and Nygaard, 1966). This model is

---

[1] *Kea* was previously known as *Class Language*; a kea is an inquisitive New Zealand alpine bird.

inherited by Smalltalk and most other object-oriented languages (Goldberg and Robson, 1983). In class-based approaches, methods are associated with classes in a class hierarchy or partially-ordered set, and encapsulation is provided in some form, giving the benefits of abstract data types.

The Common Lisp Object System (CLOS) introduced the multiple-despatch model, in which the selection of the method to be executed depends on the class of all arguments to the message, not just the object (Keene, 1989). CLOS provides for multiple despatch with generic functions in a dynamically-typed setting but where encapsulation has been ignored.

The advantages of a statically-typed programming language are well known. The most important is that many errors can be detected at compile-time; such errors have to be found at run-time in a dynamically-typed language like Smalltalk or CLOS, sometimes long after a program is "complete". However, the disadvantages of an inflexible typing system, and/or the need to supply type information, lead many to prefer dynamically-typed languages. An important aim is to find typing systems which do not place unnecessary demands or restrictions on a programmer; automatic type inference and bounded parametric polymorphism are steps towards this goal (Cardelli and Wegner, 1985).

Section 2 of this paper briefly introduces Kea to provide a context for multivariant functions. Section 3 introduces multivariant functions by example and shows that there is not a clear distinction between overloading and inclusion polymorphism. Multivariants may be used to avoid some of the restrictions of the contravariance rule. Section 4 defines the semantics of despatching multivariant functions with a scheme for the automatic generation of *despatching* variants. Three issues that arise with despatching are defined: redundancy, ambiguity, and exhaustiveness of a (partially-ordered) set of variants with respect to a function call. Section 5 raises compilation issues, including provision for separate compilation. The final section concludes the paper and suggests future work.

2.   Introduction to Kea

Kea inherits from the object-oriented paradigm the notions of information-hiding, abstract data types, inclusion polymorphism, method overriding, and multiple inheritance. In addition, it introduces dynamic classification (Hamer et al, 1989; Hamer, 1990a; Hosking et al, 1990). From the functional language paradigm, Kea inherits higher-order and polymorphic functions, type inference, and lazy evaluation.

A class consists of a signature and an implementation. The signature consists of public features of the class. A public feature of a component object is referenced using the "^" operator. The implementation consists of expressions for public and private (non-public) features. A feature of a class is typed; its expression is evaluated when a value is required, such as in the evaluation of another expression. An object is created on demand with the pseudo-function *new*. The arguments to *new* are lazily evaluated; they pass information to the new object (as object parameters) from the context in which it was created.

A class inherits the signatures and implementations of all its generalisation classes (superclasses); it may extend either. A class inherits a feature only once from a superclass even when there are several inheritance paths. Generalisation relationships between classes define a (partial) type ordering, similar to Trellis/Owl (Halbert and O'Brien, 1987). There is no notion of inheritance without a type relationship, in contrast to Smalltalk (Goldberg and Robson, 1983).

Classification expresses sufficient conditions for object class membership; for example, a rectangle with equal sides can be treated as a square. A classification attribute specifies a *cluster*: a set of mutually-exclusive subclasses (Smith and Smith, 1977). If class A has a cluster {B, C}, classification ensures that any object of class A will also belong to either class B or C (but not both). In this way, clusters constrain types; for example, the presence of cluster {B, C} means that no class can inherit from both B and C. Multiple classification is achieved with independent classification attributes, so that an object can be classified to several independent subclasses.

Dynamic classification of an object permits its type to be elaborated at run-time. An object may be explicitly classified as also belonging to other classes, based on the evaluation of its classification attributes. This process of classification is carried out on demand, whenever a possible classification may lead to code which can affect the current evaluation of an expression. Classification is lazy in that it is only carried out to the extent that is necessary. Classification need not mirror inheritance, allowing for "classification leaps" down the class inheritance structure. Hosking et al (1990) provides further details.

2.1   Higher-Order and Polymorphic Functions in the List Classes

Kea is currently being extended to include higher-order, (implicitly) polymorphic functions with multiple despatch. The use of higher-order and polymorphic functions in class *List* and its subclasses is shown in Fig. 2.1. The three classes here together define a data structure for a list of integers. The class *List* specifies the signatures of the public functions available (corresponding to "virtuals" in Simula (Dahl and Nygaard, 1966)), as well as defining the constructor function *cons*.

Class *EmptyList* provides code for the empty list case. Class *ListNode* defines the non-empty list case with object parameters *head* and *tail*. The classification feature *defaultEmpty* in class *List* specifies that the two subclasses of *List* are mutually exclusive. An object of class *List* will be classified to class *EmptyList*, as defined by the expression for *defaultEmpty*, on the first access to a public function of the object (other than *cons*). Thus, class *List* is not an abstract class; the default classification makes "new List" operationally equivalent to "new EmptyList".

```
class List.
 public    cons, filter, map, fold, append.
 classification defaultEmpty: [EmptyList, ListNode]
     := EmptyList.
 cons(front: integer) := new ListNode(front, self).
 filter(keep: integer -> boolean): List.
 map(trans: integer -> integer): List.
 fold(accum: (integer, Any) -> Any, identity: Any): Any.
 append(other: List): List.
 end List.
```

```
class EmptyList.
 generalisation List.
  filter(keep) := self.
  map(trans) := self.
  fold(accum, identity) := identity.
  append(other) := other.
 end EmptyList.
```

```
class ListNode.
 generalisation List.
 parameter head: integer.
          tail: List.
 public head, tail.
  filter(keep)
     := tail^filter(keep)^cons(head) if keep(head)
     |  tail^filter(keep).
  map(trans) := tail^map(trans)^cons(trans(head)).
  fold(accum, identity)
     := accum(head, tail^fold(accum, identity)).
  append(other) := tail^append(other)^cons(head).
 end ListNode.
```

Figure 2.1   The *List* Classes[2]

Functions in Kea may be higher-order and/or polymorphic, as is usual in functional languages (Field and Harrison, 1988). For example, the higher-order function *map* in class *ListNode* in Fig. 2.1 is inferred to be of type "ListNode → (integer → integer) → ListNode". This function returns the list resulting from applying the function *trans* to each of the elements of the provided list. The *map* function call in Fig. 2.2 returns the increment of each of the integers in a list, using an anonymous function. Similarly, the function *filter* is used in Fig. 2.2 to select the positive integers from a list.

```
ints := new List^cons(-1)^cons(2).
positives := ints^filter(lambda(i: integer) => i > 0).
increment := ints^map(lambda(i: integer) => i + 1).
sum := ints^fold(add, 0).
add(i: integer, total: integer) := i + total.
```

Figure 2.2   Using functions *filter*, *map*, and *fold*

---

[2] The symbol "|" is read as "or" in function expressions.

Parametric polymorphism for functions is implicit, both in bounded and unbounded forms (Cardelli and Wegner, 1985). For example, the function *fold* in Fig. 2.1 has the type *Any* specified for some of the parameters. The type of this function is inferred to be "List → (integer → x → x) → x → x", in which *x* is a type variable. The function *fold* is used in Fig. 2.2 to sum the elements of an *List*; the actual type of the function application here is "List → (integer → integer → integer) → integer → integer".

3.   Multivariant Functions by Example

Kea's multivariant functions are related to the multi-methods of CLOS (Keene, 1989). As with multi-methods, the code chosen for execution (during *despatching*) depends on the type of all function call arguments, rather than just the type of the primary object (self). Kea, however, is statically typed; multivariant functions and their calls are statically checked for type-correctness. The selection of the appropriate function *variant* can be made at compile-time if the types of function call arguments are suitable, as discussed below.

3.1   Overloading

Multivariant functions provide for overloading, where different variants have unrelated parameter types. For example, in Fig. 3.1 the function *div* accepts either integers or reals. The applicable variant (and hence the result type) can be determined at compile-time for a call of the function *div*. Thus the expression for *aList* in Fig. 3.1 is incorrectly typed because the *List* function *cons* requires an integer parameter; it is rejected at compile-time. Compile-time selection of the appropriate variant for a function call means that there need be no despatch at run-time.

```
div(r1: real, r2: real) := r1 / r2.             % real
div(r: real, i: integer) := r / toReal(i).      % real
div(i: integer, r: real) := toReal(i) / r.      % real
div(i1: integer, i2: integer) := i1 div i2.     % integer

anInt := div(4,2).                   % integer
aReal := div(4, 2.0).                % real
aList := new List^cons(div(2.0, 4)). % Type error
```

Figure 3.1 Overloaded Function

Overloading also arises naturally from the coincidental matching of function names from unrelated classes.

3.2   Despatching

Type information about the parameters of a function call may not be sufficient to select the appropriate function variant at compile-time. For example, consider the function *equal* in the classes *Point* and

ColorPoint in Fig. 3.2 (adapted from Canning et al, 1989). The types of the two variants are "Point →
Point → boolean" and "ColorPoint → ColorPoint → boolean". With a function call in which the types of
the arguments are only known (statically) to be of type *Point*, a selection must be made at run-time between
the two relevant variants, based on the type of the actual parameters. For example, if the actual parameters
to the function call are both of class *ColorPoint*, the variant in class *ColorPoint* is dynamically selected.

Encapsulation is enforced: a function within a class may access any parameters and functions of an object
of that class. However, access is only permitted to public functions of the arguments of a function.

```
class Point.
 public x, y, move, equal.
 parameter x, y.
  x: float.
  y: float.
  equal(p: Point) := x = p^x and y = p^y.
 end Point.
```

```
class ColorPoint.
 generalisation Point.
 public color.
 parameter color: Color.
  equal(p: ColorPoint) := x = p^x and y = p^y and color = p^color.
 end ColorPoint.
```

Figure 3.2   Despatching

Cook (1989) points out that the contravariance rule[3] is violated in Eiffel, a statically-typed language which
uses the Simula despatching model (Meyer, 1988). Multivariant functions in Kea allow the benefits of
subclassing to be retained without violating this rule. The contravariance rule is satisfied because the
function *equal* in class *ColorPoint* does not completely override the inherited function; instead, it provides
code to handle the case when the object and the function parameter are both of type *ColorPoint*.

The two uses of *equal* in the expression for *consistent* in Fig. 3.3 provide the same result; if either the
object or the parameter (or both) are of type *Point*, the function variant in class *Point* is called.

```
a := new Point(x := 0.0, y := 0.0).
b := new ColorPoint (x := 0.0, y := 0.0, colour := red).

consistent := a^equal(b) = b^equal(a).
```

Figure 3.3   Consistency of Result from *equal*

---

[3] The contravariance rule specifies that a function f of type "AA → B" is a subtype of function g of type
"A → BB" (i.e. $f \leq g$) if and only if $A \leq AA$ and $B \leq BB$. That is, the subtype may "narrow" the result
type but can only "widen" the parameter type.

Functions that access objects need not be defined within a class; in this case access is only permitted to publics of those objects supplied as parameters. This is illustrated with the function *firmEqual* in Fig. 3.4 which provides a different notion of equality: an object of class *Point* can not be equal to an object of class *ColorPoint*. The order of variants defines the sequence in which they are considered during despatching.

```
firmEqual(p: ColorPoint, q: ColorPoint)
   := p^x = q^x and p^y = q^y and p^colour = q^colour.
firmEqual(p: ColorPoint, q: Point) := false.
firmEqual(p: Point, q: ColorPoint) := false.
firmEqual(p: Point, q: Point) := p^x = q^x and p^y = q^y.
```

Figure 3.4   A Different Notion of Equality

3.3   Overloading and Despatching

The need for despatching may depend on the particular function call. For example, consider the function *addList* in Fig. 3.5, which extends the *List* classes of Fig. 2.1. This function takes two lists and adds them element by element; the resulting list is the length of the shortest of the two lists. The types of the three variants in Fig. 3.5 are "EmptyList $\rightarrow$ List $\rightarrow$ EmptyList", "ListNode $\rightarrow$ EmptyList $\rightarrow$ EmptyList", and "ListNode $\rightarrow$ ListNode $\rightarrow$ ListNode" respectively.

```
class List.
...
    cons(front: integer) := new ListNode(front, self).
...
    addList(other: List): List.
end List.

class EmptyList.
...
   addList(other) := self.
end EmptyList.

class ListNode.
...
parameter head: integer.
          tail: List.
...
   addList(other: EmptyList) := other.
   addList(other: ListNode)
      := tail^addList(other^tail)^cons(head + other^head).
end ListNode.
```

Figure 3.5   Function *addList*

Consider the example function calls in Fig. 3.6 (with result types shown as comments). Despatching is not needed for the expressions of *v1*, *v2*, and *v3*, as adequate type information is available to select the appropriate variant statically. In addition, the specific type of these expressions is determined. For example, the function call in the expression for *v3* is "ListNode → ListNode → x"; given that the third variant is selected statically, the type variable *x* is determined to be *ListNode*.

```
empty := new EmptyList.                              % EmptyList
one := empty^cons(1).                                % ListNode
positives := one^filter(lambda(x) => x > 0).         % List
v1 := empty^addList(one).                            % EmptyList
v2 := one^addList(empty).                            % EmptyList
v3 := one^addList(one).                              % ListNode
v4 := one^addList(positives).                        % List
v5 := positives^addList(positives).                  % List
```

Figure 3.6 Overloaded and Despatching Function Calls

Despatching is required for the calls to *addList* in the expressions of *v4* and *v5*. The expressions are both of type *List*; this type is based on the types of the variants involved in the selection.

4. Semantics of Despatching Multivariant Functions

We define the semantics of multivariant functions through their translation to a lazy functional language. *Despatching* variants are generated during this translation; these define the selection between variants that is carried out at run-time. For functions within a class, the object is made explicit as *self*, the first parameter. For example, the function *addList* from Fig. 3.5 is translated to the code shown in Fig. 4.1 (in which redundant conformance tests have been removed).

```
addList1(self, p1) := self.    % EmptyList → List → EmptyList
addList2(self, p1) := p1.       % ListNode → EmptyList → EmptyList
addList3(self, p1)              % ListNode → ListNode → ListNode
    := cons(addList5(tail(self), tail(p1)), head(self) + head(p1)).
addList4(self, p1)              % ListNode → List → List
    := addList2(self, p1) if conforms(p1)(EmptyList)
    |  addList3(self, p1).
addList5(self, p1)              % List → List → List
    := addList1(self, p1) if conforms(self)(EmptyList)
    |  addList4(self, p1).
```

Figure 4.1 Generated Code for *addList*

Two *despatching* variants *addList4* and *addList5* have been generated to select between other variants. For example, the variant *addList4* (called by *v4* in Fig. 3.6) selects at run-time between the variants *addList2* and *addList3* depending on the type of the second actual parameter; this variant is of type "ListNode → List → List". The function *conforms* takes an object and returns a function which in turn takes a class identifier as parameter; the latter function returns true if the object is of that class.

To assist in defining the semantics of multivariant despatching, we informally introduce a "first pass" translation. The results of this translation are used to define the generation of despatching variants. Three important properties of sets of variants are defined: redundancy, ambiguity, and exhaustiveness. We stress that the aim here is to define the semantics of despatching; an implementation will use rather different techniques. For example, *conforms* information and the results of unary functions are cached in the current system (Hamer, 1990b).

4.1   The "First Pass" Translation

The first pass takes a Kea program and produces:

- Function variants in a functional form in which the object is included as an explicit first parameter (self) to encapsulated functions. This means that the implicit parameter can be treated the same as other parameters in Section 4.2.

- The partial order of the variants of each function;

- Functions for object creation and access to object parameters; and

- Subtyping and classification information.

We ignore here a number of issues in this translation: signatures, checking that encapsulation is respected, and checking the constraints imposed by classification attributes.

For example, the definition of the function *addList*, which appears in the classes *EmptyList* and *ListNode* in Fig. 3.5, is translated to the functional form shown in Fig. 4.2. Function calls are later resolved to specific function variants, as defined in Section 4.2.

```
addList₁(self: EmptyList, other: List) := self.
addList₂(self: ListNode, other: EmptyList) := other.
addList₃(self: ListNode, other: ListNode)
     := cons(addList(tail(self), tail(other)), head(self) + head(other)).
```

Figure 4.2 Function *addList* in Functional Form

Information is gathered about the class relationships and clusters. Each class has zero or more clusters, where a *cluster* is a set of classes corresponding to a single classification attribute. For example, clusters(List) = {{EmptyList, ListNode}}. The subtype relation < is the transitive closure of immediate subclass; the relation ≤ is the reflexive transitive closure.

A multivariant function f is defined as a triple (P, V, Θ), where P is the number of arguments of the function, V is the set of variants with name f and P arguments, and Θ specifies the partial order of the variants in V. For the purposes of the following discussion, we are only concerned with the type of the variants.

The partial order is defined as follows. Let v_1, $v_2 \in$ V where v_1 appears in class C_1 and v_2 appears in class C_2. The set Θ contains the element $v_1 \ll v_2$ iff: $C_1 = C_2$ and v1 appears before v2; or $C_1 < C_2$. For example, the function *addList* in Fig. 4.2 is defined as the triple (2, {addList$_1$, addList$_2$, addList$_3$}, {addList$_2 \ll$ addList$_3$}). For the purpose of defining Θ, function variants which are declared outside of classes are treated as being defined within a class T, where for all C $\in$ the user-defined classes, C $\leq$ T.

For each class, there is a function to create new objects of that class. There is also a function to access each object parameter. For example, consider the class *ColorPoint* from Fig. 3.2. The function *new_ColorPoint*, shown in Fig. 4.3, creates an object of class *ColorPoint*. An object consists of a pair (M, P), where M is a class membership function and P is a sequence of actual object parameters.[4] The general function *conforms* selects M from the pair; it is used in depatching code. The argument to *conforms* is used when a class has one or more classification attributes.

```
new_ColorPoint(p1, p2, p3) := o where o :=
        (conformsCP(o), (p1, p2, p3)).
conformsCP(o) := lambda(c) => c = ColorPoint or c = Point.
x((c, (p1, ...))) := p1.
y((c, (p1, p2, ...))) := p2.
color((c, (p1, p2, p3))) := p3.

conforms((c,p)) := c.
```

Figure 4.3 Object Creation and Object Parameters

4.2 Despatching Function Calls

The second phase of translation involves the generation of despatching variants. Three issues arise in depatching function calls: redundancy, ambiguity, and exhaustiveness. A variant is redundant if it can never be selected; redundancy points to a programmer error. A set of variants is ambiguous with respect to a function call if different total orderings of the partial order of the relevant variants lead to different results. A set of variants is exhaustive with respect to a function call if the variants cover all possible subtypes of the arguments of the function call.

---

4 The treatment of object parameters is simplified here; under multiple inheritance they are partially ordered.

These properties of variant sets are defined in this section, along with the generation of despatching variants. These definitions do not take account of polymorphic or recursive function variants; see Mugridge et al (1991a) for further details.

<u>An Example</u>.

Consider the classes in subtype relations $B \leq D$, $B \leq A$, and $C \leq A$ and where clusters(A) ={{B, C}}. The function f is defined as the triple $(2, V_f, \Theta_f)$, where $V_f = \{f_1: D \rightarrow D \rightarrow T, f_2: A \rightarrow B \rightarrow T, f_3: B \rightarrow D \rightarrow T, f_4: C \rightarrow B \rightarrow T, f_5: C \rightarrow C \rightarrow T\}$, and $\Theta_f = \{f_3 << f_1, f_4 << f_2, f_4 << f_5, f_5 << f_2\}$. The function g is defined as the triple $(1, V_g, \Theta_g)$, where $V_g = \{g_1: D \rightarrow T, g_2: A \rightarrow T\}$, and $\Theta_g = \{\}$. This situation is illustrated in Fig. 4.4. In the remainder of this section, we consider a function call, such as f': $A \rightarrow B \rightarrow x$, as being a variant type in which the result type x is unknown.

The following problems arise:

- The variant f_2 is **redundant**; due to the variants f_3 and f_4 and the cluster, it can never be selected. A function call f': $A \rightarrow B \rightarrow x$ will match either f_3 and f_4 because an object of class A must also be either of class B or class C due to the cluster.

- The variants g_1 and g_2 are **ambiguous** with respect to a function call g': $B \rightarrow x$. Both variants apply but there is no order defined between them in Θ_g.

- The variant set V_f is not **exhaustive** with respect to the function call f': $A \rightarrow C \rightarrow x$. It would be with the addition of the variant $f_6: B \rightarrow C \rightarrow T$.

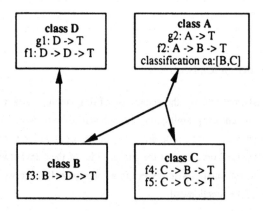

Figure 4.4 Redundancy, Ambiguity, and Exhaustiveness

Definitions.

Cover: The *cover* of a variant v: $t_1 \to ... \to t_n \to w$ is the set $\{s_1 \to ... \to s_n \mid s_1 \leq t_1, ..., s_n \leq t_n\}$. The *cover* of a set of variants V is $\{c \mid c \in cover(v')$ and $v' \in V\}$.

ExtendedCover: We can extend the variants in a cover by considering clusters. If $\{s_{i1}, ..., s_{in}\} \in clusters(s_i)$ and a cover of a variant contains all the classes $s_{i1}, ..., s_{in}$ in argument position i, then the variant must also cover the class s_i in that argument position.

The *extendedCover* of a set of variants V is the set C where C contains:

- all variants in $cover(V)$;

- $S \to t \to U$ if C contains $S \to t_i \to U, ..., S \to t_m \to U$ where $\{t_1, ..., t_m\} \in clusters(t)$, S is a type $s_1 \to ... \to s_i$ and U is a type $u_1 \to ... \to u_j$.

Relevant. Let a function f be (n, V, Θ). A variant $v \in V$ is *relevant* to a function call f' iff $cover(v) \cap cover(f') \neq \emptyset$.

Exhaustive: A set of variants E is *exhaustive* with respect to a variant v iff $cover(v) \subseteq extendedCover(E)$.

Redundant. There are two sources of redundancy. The simplest case is where a set of function variants from the same class (i.e. with the same first argument) cover all the argument types of a later variant from that class. The second case, illustrated in the example above, arises where a set of function variants from the classes in a cluster cover all the argument types of a variant from the cluster's class. These forms of redundancy are defined as follows:

(1) Direct Redundance: Let a function f be (n, V, Θ), $v \in V$, $V' = \{v' \in V \mid v' << v \in \Theta$ and v and v' have the same first argument type$\}$. The variant v is *redundant* if V' is exhaustive with respect to v.

(2) Extended Redundance: Let a function f be (n, V, Θ) and $v \in V$. The variant v is *redundant* if there exists a cluster C such that $V' = \{v' \in V \mid v' << v \in \Theta$ and the type of the first argument of v' is $C_i \in C\}$ and V' is exhaustive with respect to v.

Ambiguous: Let a function f be (n, V, Θ). The variant set V is *ambiguous* with respect to a function call f' iff there exists distinct variants $v_i, v_j \in cover(V)$ such that there is no ordering defined between v_i and v_j in Θ and $cover(v_i) \cap cover(v_j) \cap cover(f') \neq \emptyset$.

Despatch Variant: The generation scheme *despatch* generates code to select between an exhaustive set of variants as follows:

$$despatch(\{v_i: t_{1,1} \rightarrow ... \rightarrow t_{1,m} \rightarrow w_1, \ ... \ , v_n: t_{n,1} \rightarrow ... \rightarrow t_{n,m} \rightarrow w_n\}) =$$

```
v0(p1, ...,pm) := v1(p1, ... , pm) if conforms(p1)(t1,1) and ...
                                     and conforms(pm)(t1,m)
            | ...
            | vn(p1, ... , pm) if conforms(p1)(tn,1) and ...
                                     and conforms(pm)(tn,m).
```

Function Call Despatching: Let a function f be (n, V, Θ) and f': $t_1 \rightarrow ... \rightarrow t_n \rightarrow x$ be an application of function f. Code can be generated for f' iff R, the set of variants relevant to f', is exhaustive and not ambiguous with respect to f'. In this case, a call is made to the despatching variant generated by despatch(R).

Examples.

• The cover(f_2) = {A → B, B → B, C → B} and extendedCover({f_3, f_4}) = {B → D, B → B, C → B, A → B}. As cover(f_2) ⊆ extendedCover({f_3, f_4}), {f_3, f_4} is exhaustive with respect to f_2, and hence the variant f_2 is redundant.

• The cover of the function call g': B → x is {B}. The cover(g_1) = {D, B} and cover(g_2) = {A, B, C}. There is no ordering defined between g_1 and g_2 in Θ_g and yet cover(g_1) ∩ cover(g_2) ∩ cover(g') = {B}. Hence g_1 and g_2 are ambiguous with respect to g'.

• The cover of the function call f': A → C → x is {A → C, B → C, C → C}. However, B → C ∉ extendedCover(V_f) and so V_f is not exhaustive with respect to f'.

• Consider the function call f': A → B → x. The relevant variant set R = {f_2, f_3, f_4}, which is exhaustive and not ambiguous with respect to f'. A call is made to the the despatching variant v' defined as follows:

```
v'(p1, p2) := f3(p1, p2) if conforms(p1)(B)
           | f4(p1, p2) if conforms(p1)(C)
           | f2(p1, p2).      % This case is redundant
```

5. Compilation Issues

Problems with variant redundancy, ambiguity, and non-exhautiveness must be signalled during compilation. We now consider two issues: handling exhaustiveness and ambiguity at runtime, and separate compilation of a Kea program.

5.1 Runtime Checks

When a set of variants is not exhaustive with respect to a function call, a compilation error should result. As it is convenient to develop a partially-completed program, a better approach is to give a warning and extend the variant set so that it is exhaustive with respect to the function call. The extra variant produces an error message at run-time. For example, a program that calls the function *tail* with an argument that is only known to be of type *List* results in a warning and leads to the new variant shown in Fig. 5.1.

```
tail(self: List): List
    := exception("function tail can only be applied to a ListNode").
```

Figure 5.1 Automatically-Generated Error-Checking Variant

A warning could also be given when two or more variants are ambiguous with respect to a subset of the cover of a function call; an extra variant can be generated which gives an error if the ambiguity arises at runtime.

5.2 Separate Compilation

Provision is made for separate compilation. Consider the set of classes shown in Fig. 5.2, in which the classes *A* and *B* have been compiled within a library and the classes *C* and *D* appear in new code that uses the library.

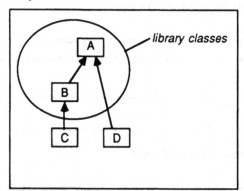

Figure 5.2 Library and Added Classes

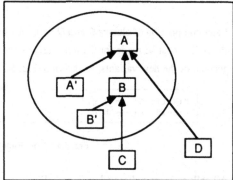

Figure 5.3 After Class Migration

The set of classes in a library is translated so that a class is not used to create objects if it is (or may become) a superclass of other classes. The translation, shown in Fig. 5.3, introduces an empty class *A'* as a subclass of *A*. Any object which previously would have been created as an object of class *A* is instead created as an object of class A'. This process of "class migration" automatically introduces an abstract class.[5]

Class migration opens the way for separate compilation by permitting subclasses to be introduced later. When a function call to a variant is compiled, the position of the call is added to a list of all calls to that variant. If a new subclass is introduced later, such as class C in Fig. 5.3, new despatch code is generated and all function calls are redirected to the new (despatching) variant which has been generated to take account of variants in new subclasses.

```
f(self: A) := h^g.
f(self: B) := g^h.
```

Fig 5.4 The Functions in the Library

For example, consider the two variants of the function f defined in the library, as shown in Fig 5.4. The generated code, along with a despatching variant, is shown in Fig. 5.5; this despatching variant is based on the assumption that A' and B are the only subclasses of A.

```
f₁(self) := g(h(self)).              % A'
f₂(self) := h(g(self)).              % B
f₀(self) := f₂(self) if conforms(self)(B)      % A
          | f₁(self).
```

Fig 5.5 Generated Code for the Library Variants

Later compilation of classes C and D with the library makes the original despatching variant f_0 incorrect. Provision must be made for the new variants shown in Fig. 5.6. New despatch code is generated, taking account of the new variants, as shown in Fig. 5.7.

```
f(self: C) := g^g.
f(self: D) := h^h.
```

Fig 5.6 The Functions in Classes C and D

All calls to f_0 are redirected to $f_{0'}$ and all calls to f_2 are redirected to $f_{2'}$. This is handled by re-linking the list of function calls from f_2 so that they are linked to the variant $f_{2'}$. A "code linking" phase runs through the lists and resolves the addresses. The links makes it possible to eliminate the code of unused variants in a "garbage collection" phase; this is important when using a small portion of a large library.

---

[5] The original motivation for class migration was "type loss" (Mugridge, et al, 1990b).

```
f₃(self) := g(g(self)).              % C
f₄(self) := h(h(self)).              % D
f₀.(self) := f₃(self) if conforms(self)(C)        % A
         | f₄(self) if conforms(self)(D)
         | f₀(self).
f₂.(self) := f₃(self) if conforms(self)(C)        % B
         | f₂(self).
```

Fig 5.7 The New Generated Code

Adding classes later can invalidate previously acceptable function calls. For example, if the subclass C were introduced without a variant for function f, the set of variants would be no longer exhaustive with respect to function calls to f_0. This is handled as in Section 5.1.

6. Conclusions and Future Work

Multivariant functions in Kea generalise the notion of despatching in statically-typed object-oriented languages; the ideas are also relevant to procedural object-oriented languages, such as Eiffel (Meyer, 1988). Multivariants are a statically-typed form of the multi-methods of CLOS (Keene, 1989) but where encapsulation is retained. As despatching can be avoided when there is adequate type information about arguments to a function call, there need be no unnecessary overhead on function calls. In addition, multivariant functions avoid the restrictions on subtyping imposed by the contravariance rule.

Cardelli and Wegner (1985) distinguish overloading (ad hoc polymorphism) and universal polymorphism (parameteric and inclusion polymorphism). However, multivariant functions show that the distinction is not so clear; whether overloading or inclusion polymorphism is involved can depend on the function calls concerned.

Encapsulation of multivariant functions is provided. Functions in Kea may be organised within classes (i.e. based on the object: the implicit first argument), where access is available to all functions of the class, both public and private. Functions that are written outside of classes may only access public functions. Hence the first argument to a function is still given special status, as in many object-oriented programming languages: Smalltalk (Goldberg and Robson, 1983), Eiffel (Meyer, 1988), and Trellis/Owl (Halbert and O'Brien, 1987). This is in comparison with CLOS, which discards the notion of encapsulation altogether in introducing multi-methods (Keene, 1989). Further work is needed in considering other ways to integrate encapsulation and multi-methods.

As Kea is currently defined, all function argument types must be specified. We are considering the introduction of further type inference so as to eliminate the need for explicit typing where it is unnecessary. For example, the signatures defined in class *List* in Fig. 2.1 could be inferred automatically. A related area of investigation is into "type loss", which prevents the full potential of static typing from being realised (Mugridge et al, 1991b). Unfortunately, bounded parametric polymorphism (Cardelli and Wegner, 1985) only avoids some forms of "type loss".

Multivariant functions provide a weak form of selection when compared to the pattern-matching of functional languages like Hope (Field and Harrison, 1988; Mugridge et al, 1990). It would be convenient to introduce a form of pattern-matching into Kea. We are considering the definition of patterns (consisting only of public functions) in a class and using those patterns in variants. For example, the function *addList* in class *ListNode*, from Fig. 3.5, is recoded in Fig. 6.1 to use a possible form of pattern-matching.

```
class ListNode.
 pattern (head, tail).
 ...
  addList(other: EmptyList) := other.
  addList((h,t): ListNode) := tail^addList(t)^cons(head + h).
 end ListNode.
```

Figure 6.1 Pattern-Matching in Function *addList*

Acknowledgements

The authors acknowledge the financial assistance provided by the Building Research Association of New Zealand, the University of Auckland Research Committee, and the New Zealand University Grants Committee.

References

Canning P S, Cook W R, Hill W L, Olthoff W G, 1989. Interfaces for strongly-typed object-oriented programming, OOPSLA'89, ACM SIGPLAN Notices, **24** (10) October, 1989, pp457-467.

Cardelli L, Wegner P, 1985. On understanding types, data abstraction, and polymorphism, *Computing Surveys*, **17**(4), pp471-522.

Cook W, 1989. A proposal for making Eiffel type safe, in Cook S (Ed), *ECOOP 89*, Cambridge University Press, pp57-70.

Dahl O J, Nygaard K, 1966. Simula - an Algol-based simulation language, *CACM* **9** (9), pp671-678.

Field A J, Harrison P G, 1988. *Functional Programming*, Addison-Wesley.

Goldberg A, Robson D, 1983. *Smalltalk 80: The Language and its Implementation*, Addison-Wesley.

Halbert D C, O'Brien P D, 1987. Using types and inheritance in object-oriented programming, *IEEE Software*, September 1987, pp71-79.

Hamer J, Hosking J G, Mugridge W B, 1989. Knowledge-based systems for representing codes of practice, Report 48, Department of Computer Science, University of Auckland, New Zealand.

Hamer J, 1990a. Expert Systems for codes of practice, PhD Thesis, Department of Computer Science, University of Auckland, New Zealand.

Hamer J, 1990b. Class Language runtime system: detailed specification, BRANZ Contract 85-024, Technical Report No. 9, Department of Computer Science, University of Auckland, New Zealand.

Hosking J G, Hamer J, Mugridge W B, 1990. Integrating functional and object-oriented programming, Procs. Pacific Tools 80 Conference, Sydney, Australia, November 1990.

Keene S E, 1989. *Object-Oriented Programming in Common Lisp: A Programmer's Guide to CLOS*, Addison-Wesley, 1989.

Meyer B, 1988. *Object-Oriented Software Construction*, Prentice Hall.

Mugridge W B, Hosking J G, Hamer J, 1990. Functional extensions to an object-oriented programming language, Report No. 49, Department of Computer Science, University of Auckland, New Zealand.

Mugridge W B, Hamer J, Hosking J G, 1991a. The semantics of multivariant functions, in preparation.

Mugridge W B, Hamer J, Hosking J G, 1991b. Type loss in statically-typed object-oriented proghramming languages, in preparation.

Smith J M, Smith D C P, 1977. Database abstractions: aggregation and generalization, *ACM Trans. on Database Systems*, 2 (2), 1977, pp105-133.

What is Type-Safe Code Reuse?

Jens Palsberg
palsberg@daimi.aau.dk

Michael I. Schwartzbach
mis@daimi.aau.dk

Computer Science Department
Aarhus University
Ny Munkegade
DK-8000 Århus C, Denmark

Abstract

Subclassing is reuse of class definitions. It is usually tied to the use of class names, thus relying on the order in which the particular classes in a program are created. This is a burden, however, both when programming and in theoretical studies.

This paper presents a structural notion of subclassing for typed languages. It is a direct abstraction of the SMALLTALK interpreter and the separate compilation technique of MODULA. We argue that it is the most general mechanism which can be supported by the implementation while relying on the type-correctness of superclasses. In short, it captures *type-safe code reuse*.

1 Introduction

An important goal of object-oriented programming is to obtain reusable classes without introducing significant compiling or linking overhead. A statically typed language should thus offer general mechanisms for reusing classes without ever requiring a compiler to re-type-check an already compiled class. Such mechanisms allow *type-safe code reuse*. Instead of suggesting new mechanisms and then later worry about implementation, we will analyze a particular implementation technique and from it derive the most general mechanism it can support. The result is a structural subclassing mechanism which generalizes inheritance.

In the following section we further motivate the notion of type-safe code reuse and discuss our approach to obtain mechanisms for it. In section 3 we discuss a well-known way of implementing classes and inheritance, and suggest a straightforward, inexpensive extension. In section 4 we show that the way code is reused in the implementation can be abstracted into a general subclass relation which captures type-safe code reuse. Finally, in section 5 we give an example.

2   Motivation

It is a useful property of an object-oriented language to be statically typed and to allow separate compilation of classes. The languages C++ [16] and EIFFEL [11] come close to achieving this, though the type systems of both have well-known loopholes. Similar to MODULA [17] implementations, a compiler for these languages needs only some symbol table information about previously compiled classes. In particular, this is true of the superclass of the class being compiled. Hence, the implementation of a subclass both reuses the *code* of its superclass and relies on the *type correctness* of the corresponding source code. We call this *type-safe code reuse*.

In the following we discuss our approach to type-safe code reuse, the concept of structural subclassing, and a novel idea of class lookup.

2.1   Our approach

From a purist's point of view, the loopholes in the C++ and EIFFEL type systems are unacceptable. In search for improvements, one can attempt to alter one or more of the subclassing mechanism, the type system, and the compilation technique. Previous research tends to suggest new type systems for languages with inheritance, but to ignore compilation.

This paper takes a radically different approach: We analyze the SMALLTALK [6] interpreter together with a well-known technique for separate compilation of MODULA modules, extend them, and derive a general subclassing mechanism for type-safe code reuse. This subclassing mechanism turns out to be exactly the one which we earlier have shown to be spanned by inheritance and type substitution (a new genericity mechanism) [13, 12]. Our analysis of the compilation technique is based on the assumptions that types are finite sets of classes and that variables can only contain instances of the declared classes [7, 8, 14].

2.2   Structural subclassing

Subclassing is usually tied to the use of class names. This means that a class is a subclass of only its ancestors in the explicitly created class hierarchy. In other words, a superclass must be created *before* the subclass. For an example, see figure 1A where Device must be created before Terminal-1 and Terminal-2.

Suppose that a new type of terminal, Terminal-3, is going to be implemented. An obvious possibility is to implement it as a subclass of Device, see figure 1B. Pedersen [15] discusses the case where the programmer realizes that all three terminals actually are ANSI terminals, i.e., they support the ANSI-defined control

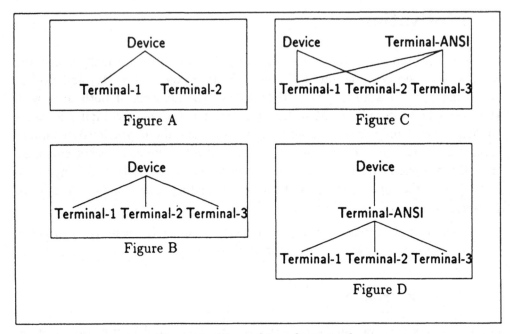

Figure 1: Hierarchies of terminals.

sequences. He argues the need for a new mechanism, *generalization*, which would allow the creation of a common superclass, Terminal-ANSI, which should contain all commonalities of the two existing classes. The programmer can then write Terminal-3 as a subclass of Terminal-ANSI, see figure 1C. This is of course not possible when only inheritance (tied to class names) is available, because it forces the class hierarchy to be constructed in a strictly top-down fashion.

Although the mechanism of generalization provides extra flexibility, it does not allow us to create Terminal-ANSI as *both* a common superclass of the three terminals *and* a subclass of Device, see figure 1D. We could of course restructure the class hierarchy by hand, but this may be undesirable or even practically impossible. Our conclusion is that tying subclassing (and generalization) to class names is too restrictive in practice. If subclassing was *structural*, then Terminal-ANSI could be created using inheritance or generalization, or it could even be written from scratch; the compiler will in any case infer the relationship in figure 1D.

We have summarized an informal definition of structural subclassing in figure 2. This notion of structural subclassing is envisioned to be useful in situations like the above, where classes are both specialized and generalized. It would, of course, be a miracle if two completely independently developed classes just happened to be in a subclass relationship.

Also in theoretical studies a structural notion of subclassing would be preferable. The point is that if all classes and subclass relations are given *a priori*—

Structural subclassing:

A relation ◁ on class definitions satisfying:

- reflexive and transitive

- independent of class names

- decidable at compile-time

- if $C_1 ◁ C_2$ then an implementation of C_1 can be extended into an implementation of C_2

Figure 2: Requirements of structural subclassing.

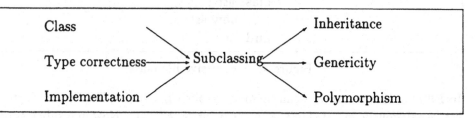

Figure 3: A development of ideas.

independently of the programmer's definitions—then they are easier to deal with mathematically. This idea lies behind almost all theories which study types independently of particular programs, see for example [1, 2, 5].

In this paper we derive a structural subclassing mechanism from existing implementation techniques; this a sound basis for theoretical investigations of subclassing and subtyping in object-oriented programming.

We have already reported some of these investigations in other papers [13, 12], see the overview in figure 3. Originally, we simply *defined* the subclassing mechanism that we have now derived. It turned out to have many nice mathematical properties and it lead us to discover a new genericity mechanism (type substitution) which is a significant improvement compared to parameterized classes. It also provided an appropriate setting for analyzing polymorphism and subtyping. All these results are now based on the well-understood concepts of class, type correctness, and implementation—rather than some random looking definition of subclassing.

We consider a core language for object-oriented programming with objects, classes, instance variables, and methods. Possible source code in methods include assignments, message sending, and the **new** expression for creating instances of a class.

We do not consider the issues of encapsulation and opacity; both seem independent of structural subclassing. Our approach does not permit multiple inheritance; two classes will in general not have a common structural subclass.

2.3 Class lookup

Our extension of the standard implementation technique is based on the observation that just as overriding of methods can be implemented by dynamic method lookup, then redefinition of the arguments of new expressions can be implemented by an analogous *class lookup*. This requires, in a naive implementation, an entry at run-time for each class occurring in a new expression. Our reason for introducing this extra flexibility is the following. When an instance of for example a list class is created by a method of the list class itself, see figure 4, then the occurrence of list in new list is a recursive one [3].

```
class list
    ... new list ...
end list
```

Figure 4: A recursive list class.

In EIFFEL, this recurrence can be made explicit by writing like Current instead of list. Analogously, in SMALLTALK, one can write self class. Now in a subclass of list, say recordlist, what kind of instance should be created? Meyer [11] argues that the programmer in some cases wants an instance of list and in others an instance of recordlist. In EIFFEL, a statement corresponding to new list would cause the creation of the former, and new (like Current) the latter. With our technique, an instance of recordlist will always be created—the choice that will most often be appropriate. The generality of EIFFEL can be recovered, however, using *opaque* definitions [13], but this will not concern us here. Our approach means that in recordlist the recursive occurrence of list is implicitly substituted by recordlist. But why, we ask, should only the class in *some* but not all new expressions be substitutable? By introducing class lookup, we remove this unpleasing asymmetry. The notion of *virtual class* in BETA [9, 10] is actually implemented by a variation of class lookup.

Let us now move on to a description of how to implement classes, inheritance, and instance creation.

3 Code Reuse

We will describe interpreters for three languages of increasing complexity. The first involves only classes and objects, and its implementation is essentially that of separately compiled modules in MODULA. The second language introduces inheritance which is implemented as in the Smalltalk interpreter, except that we retain separate compilation. The third language extends this with the possibility of redefining the arguments of new expressions. This is implemented using class lookup which is analogous to method lookup. Throughout, we focus solely on those concepts that have impact on the structural subclassing mechanism which we derive in a later section.

3.1 Classes

Classes group together declarations of variables and methods. An *instance* of a class is created by allocating space for the variables; the code for the methods is only generated once. The compiler uses a standard symbol table containing names and types of variables and procedure headers. At run-time three structures are present: The *code space* which implements all the methods, the *object memory* which contains the objects, and the *stack* which contains activation records for active methods. An *object* is a record of instance variables, each of which contains either nil or a pointer to an object in the object memory. The situation is illustrated in figure 5

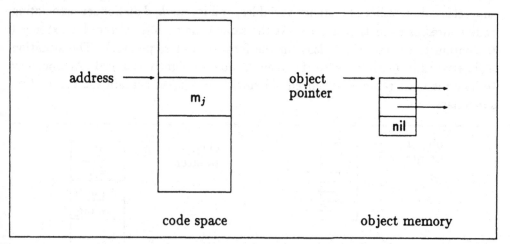

Figure 5: Implementation of classes and objects.

To present the workings of the interpreter, we shall sketch the code to be executed for two language constructs: message sends and object creations. A message send of the form $x.m(a_1,\ldots,a_k)$ generates the following code:

```
PUSH x
PUSH a₁
⋮
PUSH aₖ
CALL ADDRESS(m)
```

The activation record for a message send will contain the receiver; it can be thought of as an implicit actual parameter and will be accessible through the metavariable SELF.

Notice that the compiler can statically determine the address of the method, since the class of the receiver x is known. The code for the object creation new C is:

ALLOCATE(nil,...,nil)

with one argument for each instance variable in C. This operation returns an object pointer to a record with fields initialized by the arguments. Again, the number of instance variables is statically known by the compiler.

3.2 Inheritance

The concept of inheritance allows the construction of subclasses by adding variables and methods, and by replacing method bodies [4]. At run-time an important new structure is introduced: the *class table*, which for each class C describes its superclass, its number of instance variables, and its *method dictionary* associating code addresses to method names. At the same time an object record is extended to contain the name of its class (in the form of a class pointer). The situation is illustrated in figure 6. Also the symbol table is slightly changed. Analogously to how the class table is organized, all entries for classes contain the name of its superclass.

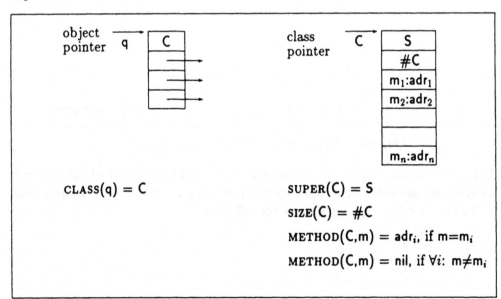

Figure 6: Implementation with inheritance.

The code for a message send is now:

```
PUSH x
PUSH a₁
⋮
PUSH aₖ
CALL M-LOOKUP(CLASS(x),m)
```

where the *method lookup* is defined as follows

$$\text{M-LOOKUP}(q,m) = \begin{cases} \text{message-not-understood} & \text{if } q=\text{nil} \\ \text{adr} & \text{if METHOD}(q,m)=\text{adr}\neq\text{nil} \\ \text{M-LOOKUP}(\text{SUPER}(q),m) & \text{otherwise} \end{cases}$$

The code for object creation comes in two varieties. For non-recursive occurrences, such as new C, we generate the code:

$$\text{ALLOCATE}(C,\text{nil},\dots,\text{nil})$$

which just includes the class in the object record. For recursive occurrences, we must generate the code:

$$\text{ALLOCATE}(\text{CLASS}(\text{SELF}),\text{nil},\dots,\text{nil})$$

with $\text{SIZE}(\text{CLASS}(\text{SELF}))$ nil-arguments.

3.3 Object Creation

We now depart from the standard interpreters by allowing a subclass to modify the classes that are used for object creation. For each occurrence of a new expression we introduce an *instantiator*. The class description now contains an *instantiator dictionary* associating classes to the instantiators. Finally, we introduce *instantiator lookup* analogously to method lookup. Instantiator lookup is the concrete implementation of class lookup. The situation is illustrated in figure 7.

The code for a non-recursive object creation, such as new z where z is now an instantiator, is:

$$C \leftarrow \text{I-LOOKUP}(\text{CLASS}(\text{SELF})),z)$$
$$\text{ALLOCATE}(C,\text{nil},\dots,\text{nil})$$

with $\text{SIZE}(C)$ nil-arguments. The instantiator lookup is defined as follows:

$$\text{I-LOOKUP}(q,z) = \begin{cases} \text{instantiator-not-found} & \text{if } q=\text{nil} \\ C & \text{if INSTANTIATOR}(q,z)=C\neq\text{nil} \\ \text{I-LOOKUP}(\text{SUPER}(q),z) & \text{otherwise} \end{cases}$$

The code for recursive occurrences is the same as before.

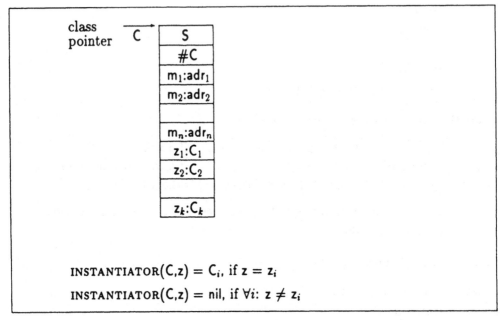

$$\text{INSTANTIATOR}(C,z) = C_i, \text{ if } z = z_i$$
$$\text{INSTANTIATOR}(C,z) = \text{nil, if } \forall i: z \neq z_i$$

Figure 7: Implementation with inheritance and instantiators.

4 Type-Safe Code Reuse

The separate compilation of a class C yields an extension of the symbol table, the class table, and the code space. A triple such as

$$(\text{symbol table}, \text{class table}, \text{code space})$$

we will call a *context* and usually denote by the symbol Θ. Thus, we can view the compilation process as a mapping from contexts to contexts. Notice that since we want the usual notion of separate compilation, only the symbol table and the class table can be inspected during the compilation of a new class.

We assume that the compilation ensures that the class is type-correct, which includes the usual syntactic checks as well as *early* checks and *subtype* checks. For every message send of the form $x.m(\ldots)$ an early check requires that a method m with the appropriate number of parameters is implemented in all classes in the declared type of x. For every assignment of the form $x:=y$, and similarly for parameter passings, a subtype check requires that the declared type of y is contained in that of x.

A context completely describes an implementation of a collection of classes. Obviously, there are many ways of achieving the same result, depending on how the class hierarchy is organized. Thus, we can introduce a notion of *equivalence* of contexts, $\Theta_1 \approx \Theta_2$, whenever the two respond alike to every request of the form SIZE, M-LOOKUP, and I-LOOKUP described in the previous section. The difference between two equivalent contexts is the degree to which the possibilities for code reuse have been exploited.

These possibilities can be expressed in terms of *extensions* of contexts. If C is a class defined in a context Θ, then a C-extension of Θ is just the information required to construct a new subclass in the class table. Hence, it is again a triple consisting of a symbol table, a class table, and a code space. The only difference between an extension and a context is that not all SUPER-pointers need to be defined in the former, whereas the latter is completely self-contained. This is illustrated further in figure 9 in section 5.

4.1   General Subclassing

A class C_2 is said to be a Θ-*subclass* of the class C_1 when they are both defined in Θ and C_1 occurs in the SUPER-chain of C_2. This is a concrete notion of subclassing. We can give another notion which captures the *potential* subclass relations.

Consider the source code of two classes C_1 and C_2. Whether they are in a subclass relation or not depends on Θ, as follows.

$$C_1 \lhd_\Theta C_2$$

$\Updownarrow$

$\exists$ a C_1-extension E such that the result of
- compiling C_1 in Θ and then extending with E; and
- compiling C_2 in Θ

are equivalent

This definition clearly expresses that C_2 *could* be implemented as a subclass of C_1. It is not the full story, however.

Because of our adherence to separate compilation, the extension above should be insensitive to changes in the implementation of methods in C_1.

Let us call C and E *compatible* in Θ if compiling C in Θ and extending with E is equivalent to the compilation of some other class in Θ. In the definition of $\lhd_\Theta$ above we will only allow extensions that are compatible with *all* classes that have the same symbol table as C_1.

Note that the definition of $\lhd_\Theta$ relies heavily on details of the implementation and programmer-defined names. We want a more abstract, *structural* notion of subclassing. To be able to define a such, let us introduce a slight abstraction of the source code of a class.

4.2 Classes as Trees

We shall represent a class as an ordered, node-labeled tree. Given a class name
C and a context Θ, we can reconstruct the untyped code of its implementation,
by short-circuiting the SUPER-chains and collecting all relevant information. By
untyped code we mean that all occurrences of class names have been replaced by
the special *gap* symbol •. This code will be the label associated with the root of the
tree. For each gap we supply the tree that represents the class corresponding to the
absent class name. This will in general yield an infinite tree, due to recursion; the
tree is obtained by repeated *unfolding* of the class definitions. However, since Θ is
always finite, the tree will be *regular*, i.e., it will only have finitely many *different*
subtrees. We shall denote this tree by $\text{TREE}_\Theta(C)$. Figure 11 shows examples of
such trees.

We can now lift the subclass relation to trees, as follows.

$$T_1 \vartriangleleft_{\text{IMPL}} T_2$$
$$\Updownarrow$$
$$\exists \Theta, C_1, C_2: \quad C_1 \vartriangleleft_\Theta C_2 \wedge$$
$$\text{TREE}_\Theta(C_1) = T_1 \wedge \text{TREE}_\Theta(C_2) = T_2$$

This definition expresses that two trees are related if there exists a context Θ in
which two classes corresponding to the trees are $\vartriangleleft_\Theta$-related. It follows directly
that

$$C_1 \vartriangleleft_\Theta C_2$$
$$\Updownarrow$$
$$\text{TREE}_\Theta(C_1) \vartriangleleft_{\text{IMPL}} \text{TREE}_\Theta(C_2)$$

Note also that we now have a structural equivalence on classes defined as equality
of the corresponding trees with respect to some Θ.

4.3 Structural Subclassing

Although the notion of a class has been made more abstract, by the representation
as a tree, the subclass relation is still explicit about contexts. Furthermore, it is
far from obvious that $\vartriangleleft_{\text{IMPL}}$ is decidable at compile-time, which is one of our
requirements of structural subclassing concepts. In the following we define a
relation $\vartriangleleft_{\text{TREE}}$ in a pure tree terminology. This relation will be a subset of $\vartriangleleft_{\text{IMPL}}$,
it will satisfy all the requirements for being a structural subclassing concept, and
it is—as far as the authors can see—the largest such one which is mathematically
attractive. It should be noted that $\vartriangleleft_{\text{TREE}}$ generalizes inheritance [12], and that it
seems possible to define a restriction of the legal contexts so that in fact $\vartriangleleft_{\text{IMPL}} =$

◁TREE. The required restriction on contexts is quite subtle: recursive classes may not be "unfolded" in the implementation.

We first need to define the notion of the *generator* of a tree. It is obtained by replacing all maximal recursive occurrences of the tree in itself by the special label ◇. If T is a tree, then GEN(T) is its generator—another tree.

We also need a bit of notation. A *tree address* is simply an indication of a path from the root to a subtree. We shall write $\alpha \in T$ when α is a valid tree address in T. In that case $T \downarrow \alpha$ denotes the corresponding subtree, and $T[\alpha]$ denotes the label in the root of that subtree.

We can now define

$$T_1 \triangleleft_{TREE} T_2$$
$$\Updownarrow$$
$$\forall \alpha \in T_1 : GEN(T_1 \downarrow \alpha) \triangleleft_G GEN(T_2 \downarrow \alpha)$$

where $\triangleleft_G$ is defined by

$$G_1 \triangleleft_G G_2$$
$$\Updownarrow$$

Monotonicity: $\forall \alpha \in G_1 : G_1[\alpha] \leq G_2[\alpha]$
Stability: $\forall \alpha, \beta \in G_1 : G_1 \downarrow \alpha = G_1 \downarrow \beta \Rightarrow G_2 \downarrow \alpha = G_2 \downarrow \beta$

Here $\leq$ is a straightforward prefix order on text; it is assumed that ◇-labels are incomparable with all others. The essence of $\triangleleft_G$ is that code can only be extended, and equal classes must remain equal.

This definition contains no mention of implementations; nevertheless, we can show that $\triangleleft_{TREE} \subseteq \triangleleft_{IMPL}$, see the following subsection. It is easy to see that $\triangleleft_{TREE}$ is reflexive, transitive, and independent of class names. Finally, $\triangleleft_{TREE}$ is decidable at compile-time using finite-state automata algorithmics [12]. Thus, it does satisfy our requirements of being an independent, structural subclass relation that is at the same time rooted in implementation practices. The above definition of $\triangleleft_{TREE}$ is the basis of the papers [13, 12].

4.4 Formalities

We now sketch a demonstration of the inclusion $\triangleleft_{TREE} \subseteq \triangleleft_{IMPL}$:

Assume that $T_1 \triangleleft_{TREE} T_2$. We must construct Θ, C_1, C_2 with the appropriate properties. We shall in fact provide an inductive method for doing this. The induction will proceed in the number of different subtrees of the T_i's; this is a finite number since the trees are regular. If they have no subtrees, then their implementation is trivial. Otherwise, we first compute the generators of the two trees, i.e., we discount their recursive occurrences. The remaining proper subtrees form a strictly smaller set, since at least two trees fewer need to be considered. To every remaining immediate subtree of T_1 there is a corresponding $\lhd$TREE-related immediate subtree of T_2. By induction hypothesis, we can implement all of these subtrees in some context. The extraneous subtrees of T_2 can be trivially implemented leading to the final, larger context Θ. We must now show how to extend this to T_1 and T_2. The code C_i for T_i is essentially a named version of the root label, with class names from Θ in place of subtrees, and the name of the code itself in place of the recursive $\diamond$-occurrences. It should be clear that $\text{TREE}_\Theta(C_i) = T_i$. The extension of C_1 that will be equivalent to C_2 is clearly a class table with C_1 as SUPER, with SIZE equal to the number of instance variables in C_2, with a method dictionary reflecting the extra code, and with an instantiator dictionary reflecting the substitution of classes from C_1 to C_2. From the previous construction we see that the instantiator dictionary only substitutes Θ-subclasses. From monotonicity and stability it follows that this extension is compatible with all modifications of C_1 that do not change the symbol table. The result follows.

5   Example

We have introduced three different views of classes: as program texts, as implementation contexts, and as trees. In this section we illustrate all three by means of an example, see figure 8.

Class D differs from C in having other arguments to the two occurrences of new and in declaring an extra variable and an extra method. This can be made explicit in the implementation by using C as the super part in the entries for D and then only specifying the differences from C, see figure 9.

This includes specifying that one of the instantiators is new boolean. It does *not*, however, include any specification of the replacement of new C by new D. This is because the occurrence of C is a recursive one; hence, the code for it is new class(self). Likewise, the occurrence of D is recursive; thus, we use the same code as before.

The incremental implementation shows that C and D should be subclass related. Indeed, we can specify D as explicitly being a subclass of C by using the standard syntax for inheritance together with the syntax for type substitution that we introduced in [13], see figure 10.

```
class C
  var x: integer
  method p(arg: boolean)
    ... new object
    ... new C ...
end C
class D
  var x: integer
  method p(arg: boolean)
    ... new boolean
    ... new D ...
  var y: integer
  method q
    ...
end D
```

Figure 8: An example program.

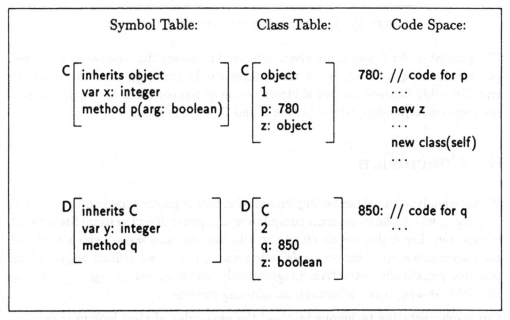

Figure 9: An implementation of the example program.

---

class D inherits C[object ← boolean]
    var y: integer
    method q
      . . .
end D

Figure 10: Class D as an explicit subclass of C.

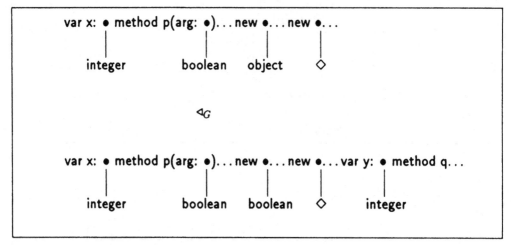

Figure 11: The generators for the example classes.

The generators for C and D are given in figure 11. To see that the two constructed generators are $\vartriangleleft_G$-related, notice that subtrees only get larger, and that stability trivially holds because no two subtrees in the generator for C are equal. Hence, the trees corresponding to the classes C and D are $\vartriangleleft$-related.

6 Conclusion

We have analyzed a particular implementation technique for typed object-oriented languages, which allows separate compilation and generalizes the usual SMALLTALK interpreter. From this we obtained the relations $\vartriangleleft_\Theta$ and $\vartriangleleft_{IMPL}$ which captured the maximal *potential* for type-safe code reuse. Finally, we defined $\vartriangleleft_{TREE}$ which is a mathematically attractive, pragmatically useful subset of $\vartriangleleft_{IMPL}$. We also showed that $\vartriangleleft_{TREE}$ is a structural subclassing concept.

Our implementation technique involved the novel idea of class lookup in connection with new expressions. In analogy with method lookup, class lookup helps avoiding recompilation of superclasses. Together, these two forms of lookup avoid all recompilation in connection with subclassing.

Structural subclassing provides more flexibility than subclassing tied to class names; it is also an appropriate basis for theoretical studies.

The implementation we have described cannot immediately cope with *mutually* recursive classes, but it can fairly easily be extended to deal with this complication—at a small cost on run-time. The theory of trees and ◁ can, however, handle such an extension without any changes at all. This is because ◇ can occur in any leaf and not just immediately below the root.

Acknowledgement: The authors thank Urs Hölzle and the referees for helpful comments on a draft of the paper.

References

[1] L. Cardelli. A semantics of multiple inheritance. In G. Kahn, D. MacQueen, and Gordon Plotkin, editors, *Semantics of Data Types*, pages 51–68. Springer-Verlag (*LNCS* 173), 1984.

[2] L. Cardelli and P. Wegner. On understanding types, data abstraction, and polymorphism. *ACM Computing Surveys*, 17(4), December 1985.

[3] William Cook, Walter Hill, and Peter Canning. Inheritance is not subtyping. In *Seventeenth Symposium on Principles of Programming Languages*. ACM Press, January 1990.

[4] William Cook and Jens Palsberg. A denotational semantics of inheritance and its correctness. In *Proc. OOPSLA'89, ACM SIGPLAN Fourth Annual Conference on Object-Oriented Programming Systems, Languages and Applications*, 1989. To appear in Information and Computation.

[5] Scott Danforth and Chris Tomlinson. Type theories and object-oriented programming. *ACM Computing Surveys*, 20(1), March 1988.

[6] A. Goldberg and D. Robson. *Smalltalk-80—The Language and its Implementation*. Addison-Wesley, 1983.

[7] Justin O. Graver and Ralph E. Johnson. A type system for smalltalk. In *Seventeenth Symposium on Principles of Programming Languages*, pages 136–150. ACM Press, January 1990.

[8] Justin Owen Graver. *Type-Checking and Type-Inference for Object-Oriented Programming Languages*. PhD thesis, Department of Computer Science, University of Illinois at Urbana-Champaign, August 1989. UIUCD-R-89-1539.

[9] B. B. Kristensen, O. L. Madsen, B. Møller-Pedersen, and K. Nygaard. The BETA programming language. In B. Shriver and P. Wegner, editors, *Research Directions in Object-Oriented Programming*, pages 7–48. MIT Press, 1987.

[10] Ole L. Madsen and Birger Møller-Pedersen. Virtual classes: A powerful mechanism in object-oriented programming. In *Proc. OOPSLA'89, Fourth Annual Conference on Object-Oriented Programming Systems, Languages and Applications*. ACM, 1989.

[11] Bertrand Meyer. *Object-Oriented Software Construction*. Prentice-Hall, Englewood Cliffs, NJ, 1988.

[12] Jens Palsberg and Michael I. Schwartzbach. Genericity And Inheritance. Computer Science Department, Aarhus University. PB-318, 1990.

[13] Jens Palsberg and Michael I. Schwartzbach. Type substitution for object-oriented programming. In *Proc. OOPSLA/ECOOP'90, ACM SIGPLAN Fifth Annual Conference on Object-Oriented Programming Systems, Languages and Applications; European Conference on Object-Oriented Programming*, 1990.

[14] Jens Palsberg and Michael I. Schwartzbach. Object-oriented type inference. In *Proc. OOPSLA'91, ACM SIGPLAN Sixth Annual Conference on Object-Oriented Programming Systems, Languages and Applications*, 1991.

[15] Claus H. Pedersen. Extending ordinary inheritance schemes to include generalization. In *Proc. OOPSLA'89, ACM SIGPLAN Fourth Annual Conference on Object-Oriented Programming Systems, Languages and Applications*, 1989.

[16] B. Stroustrup. *The C++ Programming Language*. Addison-Wesley, 1986.

[17] Niklaus Wirth. *Programming in Modula-2*. Springer-Verlag, New York, 1985.

Implementation Techniques for Integral Version Management

Ernst Lippe

Software Engineering Research Centre, University of Utrecht

Gert Florijn

Software Engineering Research Centre

P.O. Box 424

3500 AK Utrecht

The Netherlands

e-mail: lippe@serc.nl, florijn@serc.nl

Abstract

Version management services have traditionally focussed on versioning individual objects, and especially text files. This approach ignores the fact that (versions of) different objects are not independent from each other, and introduces the problem of finding consistent version combinations. One way to alleviate these problems is by expanding the unit of versioning, i.e. by applying integral version management to collections of objects.

This paper describes implementation techniques for integral version control. The techniques are applied to an object model which is characteristic for modern (engineering) object management systems, i.e. a model in which data is represented through objects and relationships. The techniques we propose support for both linear development and general, branching history. Furthermore, the techniques are incremental: they only store the difference with respect to the previous version.

1 Introduction

Object management systems (OMSes) have an increasing popularity, especially in engineering environments [PCT, BCG*87, BMO*89, F*88, KL89]. These object management systems provide mechanisms for storage of typed objects, plus mechanisms to handle references between objects. It is expected that they will replace traditional file systems for many applications, especially as a basis for engineering support environments.

Object management systems give new possibilities and new problems for version control. Traditional version control systems apply version control to individual files. The equivalent in object management systems would be that version control is applied to individual objects. We argue that version control should not be limited to individual objects but instead be applied to larger units (see section 2). We refer to this approach as *integral version management*. Integral version management forms the basis of the CAMERA system [LFB89, LF91], a version control system aimed at supporting (software) developers that use loosely coupled distributed networks. In CAMERA integral version management is applied to the entire contents of an OMS.

Efficient implementation of versioning is hard. Therefore, the main part of this paper is concerned with possible implementations of integral version management when applied to a data model consisting of objects and relationships. We will discuss data structures for storing and retrieving versions that can be used for linear (section 5) and non-linear (section 6) version history.

2   Version management

Version management is concerned with handling versions of objects in a systematic way. The main applications of version management are the recording of the history of developments, and support and coordination of parallel activities[1].

Versions (or revisions) are used to record the evolution of data. In software development for instance it is important to trace the modifications that were made to a set of programs. Modifications often introduce new bugs; and in such a case it is very important to know exactly what was changed. Another application for historical versions is release management. All entities that are needed to recreate a specific release of a software product are stored on a safe medium, so that this release can be recreated (and possibly corrected) at a later point in time. Historical version management can also be used to "undo" unwanted modifications, if versions are created sufficiently often. When a user has made a mistake, (e.g. deleted an important object) an old version can be used to continue work.

Version management can be used to support parallel activity, where a group of users is working on (a version of) a set of objects at the same time. In such situations users often want to have their private workspace, which they can modify without interference from others. If we look at a multi-user hypertext system, for instance, users may want to add new links without seeing the links that are added by others. However if each user has a private version of all data, it is very hard to discover when new versions of objects are created, and what the contribution of a single line of development is to the overall result. Version management systems can help in managing and tracing these parallel developments.

Units of version management

Traditionally, version control is applied to individual objects. In this section we provide some arguments for the claim that this is not sufficient (see also [LFB89]). Instead version control should be applied to collections of objects and their mutual references.

Versions of one object depend on specific versions of other objects, since a new version is developed using specific versions for the other objects. In general it is not possible to combine arbitrary versions of some objects, since these versions need not be mutually compatible. For example, in an object oriented environment, a version of a method in one class may depend on the existence of a method in second class. Inconsistency problems arise if a version of the second class has been selected that does not contain this method.

Ideally, a version management system should only allow "consistent" version combinations. This is a difficult problem since the number of possible combinations grows exponentially. Furthermore, it is in general impossible to determine automatically which combinations are consistent, because the definition of consistency depends on the semantics of the objects that are involved.

However, there seems to be a reasonable choice for obtaining consistent combinations. It is likely that the set of versions that were used to develop a new version of some object will form a consistent selection. This can be supported by recording which versions of related objects were used in the creation of a particular version of an object. One particular way to do so is by shifting the unit of versioning up to collections of objects, and the references between them.

This approach has an intuitive appeal. Often changes that are seen as a conceptual unit by a user will involve modifications to a group of related objects. For example, adding a new feature to a program may involve changes to several program modules. The changes to all these modules are of course closely related and can be seen as one compound modification to the group as a unit. Again, it seems more appropriate to apply version management to the group as a whole (see [NSE88, BGW89]).

---

[1]Traditionally variant management is also seen as a form of version management. Variants are different objects that share functionality. This notion is mainly used in program development were different variants of a program (e.g. for different machine architectures) may share a large portion of their source code. In our opinion variant management is orthogonal to history management, and should be solved by the modeling capabilities of the OMS.

Versioning larger units also provides a direct solution to the problems of versioning references between objects. Object systems provide mechanisms to store and manipulate references between objects. References can occur in two forms: as instance variables that act as pointers to other objects (most object-oriented languages), and in the form of relationships (some object-oriented databases and engineering object management systems). Since references constitute important information, they must be subject to version control, too. A problem here is, how version control on references is related to version control on the individual objects. For example, what must happen if a new version is created of an object that is referenced by another object. Must a new version of the referring object be created as well? This problem can be solved by putting both objects (and the reference) in one group and creating a new version of this group. Thus we version graphs of objects.

Certain object oriented systems use the notion of *composite* or *complex* object to define the sub-graphs that are subject to version management (e.g. [KBC*87, PAC89]). A disadvantage of this approach is that it makes it impossible to apply version control to references *between* objects that are not part of the same composite object. This places a rather severe restriction on the use of references. This is especially important since it is not always easy to define a particular composition structure, in advance. In hypertext systems, for instance, one often finds overlapping views, each of which could be a complex object. In some cases composition structures are even determined by the operations that are performed [Rum88]. Furthermore, the same combination problems that we saw for individual objects reoccur, but now on a different level. I.e. combining versions of several complex objects may give rise to consistency problems.

Consequently, a reasonable solution appears to be *integral version control*: version control is simultaneously applied to a self-contained collection of objects and the references among them.

Systems for integral version management

There are several systems that provide some form of integral version management. Systems like NSE [NSE88], and Plan 9 [PPTT90] store versions of (a part of) a file system, see also [Hum89]. Other examples of systems that provide integral version management on a graph of objects are Gandalf [BGW89], and [LCM*89]. Postgres [SR87] also offers a form of integral version management in a relational database. By tagging each tuple with the time at which it was created, the system supports linear history recording for a complete database.

In a certain sense it can be said that Smalltalk gives a form of integral version management in the Smalltalk images. But because images are large, it is highly impractical to store many of them. PIE [GB86] attempts to solve some of these problems by adding a notion of layers, a (sub)-graph of related objects that is treated as a unit, and that can be exchanged between users. A similar notion of layers can be found in [GMS89] for a software development system that is built on top of a traditional file system, Sun's Translucent File System [Hen88] where the notion of layer is incorporated into the file system itself, and [Pre90] for hypertext systems.

The CAMERA system, currently under development at SERC [LF91], also incorporates integral version management. CAMERA is aimed at supporting teams of (software) developers who cooperate across loosely-coupled networks. CAMERA has a two-level architecture. Integral version control is applied to object worlds containing the data (e.g. the design, the software) that is under development. Versions of these object worlds (called snapshots) are stored in a higher level object management system (called the Album), which supports and records the development process.

In the remainder of this paper we focus on implementation techniques for integral version management that were developed for the CAMERA system. This emphasis means that we will not discuss usage aspects of versioning service, such as whether version creation is implicit or explicit (via checkout/checkin), or policies that determine when new versions should be created. The reader is referred to [LF91] for further background on this.

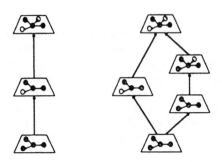

Figure 1: Examples of linear and branching history

3 A model for integral version management

In this section we will give a model for integral version management which is used in the description of the implementation techniques.

The example object model

This section describes the sample object model that will be used in the rest of this paper. We assume that data is stored in an object management system that is based on a hybrid data model, i.e. a model providing both objects and relations.

Objects are identified by an *object identifier* OID. The object identifier of an object remains the same when the object is changed. Every object has a *value*. The internal structure of the objects is not relevant for the rest of this paper, but we should point out that the internal structure cannot contain references to other objects.

References are handled via *relations*. Relations are sets of *relationships*, n-tuples of object identifiers or primitive values. Each relation is identified by a *relation identifier* RELID. We can use relations to describe how version control on inter-object references can be implemented. Relations are also treated separately because references between objects could change faster or slower than the contents of the object. This makes it more efficient to separate the version control of references from the version control of the contents.

Snapshots

Under integral version management versions of the entire contents of an object management system are recorded. Versions of the OMS are called *snapshots*. Since snapshots are used to record history we will assume that old snapshots (i.e. snapshots for which a successor has been created) are immutable. If errors are discovered in an old snapshot, a new snapshot with the modifications must be created. Possibly, the erroneous snapshot could be deleted.

Every snapshot is uniquely identified by a *time stamp*, also known as version identifier. The time stamps are unique labels, that need not have any relation to actual clock times. Time stamps have an ordering imposed on them, that describes the successor relation between the versions.

Two different types of history can be distinguished: *linear* and *non-linear* version history. In linear version history every version (except for the most recent one) has a single successor. This happens if there is one central version that is developed. The ordering that corresponds with linear history is a total ordering of the time stamps.

In a non-linear version history versions can have more than one successor, and more than one predecessor. This version history is characterized by branches and merges. This occurs during parallel development,

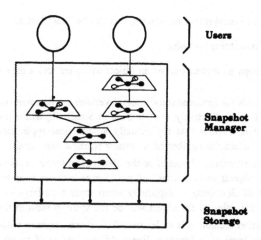

Figure 2: Architecture for integral version management

when several persons use the same version as basis for their work. The ordering in a non-linear version history is a partial ordering of the time stamps, i.e. the successor relation forms a directed acyclic graph.

As we have seen above inside the OMS every object has a unique object identifier (OID) and likewise every relation is identified by a relation identifier (RELID). Thus a version of an object (relation) can be identified by the combination of its object (relation) identifier and the time stamp of the snapshot to which this version belongs.

The two most important operations on snapshots, are creation and retrieval. Users can retrieve any existing snapshot, and use that as the contents of their workspace. At certain points in time a new snapshot is created of the entire contents of this workspace. Users can also examine parts of existing snapshots, e.g. to determine the values of objects and relations inside the snapshot.

4 The implementation model

An overview of the model for integral version management is given in figure 2. Versions of the entire contents of an OMS are stored by the system, and one such version is called a *snapshot*. Users operate on specific snapshots, each of which contains a particular state of the OMS. The snapshot manager handles operations on these snapshots, and maintains the successor relation between snapshots.

All snapshots are stored in one global snapshot storage, and this paper describes data structures for the efficient implementation of this global store. Different techniques can be used for objects and relations, and the following sections will introduce the functionality of these data structures. This section will introduce a global framework that will be used to describe the specific data-structures for linear and non-linear history, in sections 5 and 6, respectively.

Storing versions of objects

At an abstract level the functionality of an OMS can be described as a data structure that associates an object identifier of an object with the value (the contents) of this object, i.e.:

$$OMS : OID \rightarrow value$$

If we add integral version management on objects, this can be described as:

$$Index : OID \times TimeStamp \rightarrow value$$

i.e. this data structure maps a combination of an object identifier and a time stamp to the value of this object in the snapshot.

A straightforward approach for implementing integral version management is to store a complete copy of the entire snapshot. This is effectively what is done in Smalltalk, where the equivalent of a snapshot is a Smalltalk image. It is obvious that for virtually all practical applications this will soon become prohibitively expensive, unless the number of snapshots remains very small.

A somewhat more advanced solution is based on the observation that successive snapshots will tend to be very similar, since most objects and relations will not change between snapshots. It is therefore wasteful to make separate copies of all objects — especially when objects are large — for all snapshots in which the object occurs, since the value of the object will be the same in most of these snapshots.

An obvious implementation technique is to let snapshots share common values of objects. This can be done by adding an extra level of indirection. Every *different* value of an object is stored in a separate data structure, and can be identified by a value identifier (VALID). The data structure now consist of two parts:

$$VersionIndex : OID \times TimeStamp \rightarrow VALID$$

and

$$ValueIndex : VALID \rightarrow value$$

The ValueIndex contains for each object all values of this object. In order to retrieve a specific version, first the VersionIndex is searched to find the corresponding VALID, which is then used as key in ValueIndex to retrieve the value of this version. In a functional notation this can be described as

$$Index(oid, timestamp) = ValueIndex(VersionIndex(oid, timestamp))$$

The implementation of the ValueIndex will be dependent on the type of the values. With text files, for example, compression techniques such as delta compression ([Tic85]) can be used. For objects that contain fixed length records the techniques from [KL84] might be used. A data structure that can be used to store different versions of a set in a compressed way is described in sections 5.2 (linear history) and 6.2 (non-linear history).

For objects that are small or that have very dissimilar values, these compression techniques cannot be used: in this case the different values will be stored completely. Very small values (e.g. integers) can even be stored in the VersionIndex itself, instead of their VALID, thereby avoiding the extra overhead of using the ValueIndex.

In the rest of this paper we will ignore the ValueIndex, and concentrate on implementations for VersionIndex. These will be described in sections 5.1 and 6.1.

Storing versions of relations

It is of course possible to treat a relation as an object that has a set (of relationships) as its value, and then to use the techniques from the previous section. Special algorithms would be needed to compress the values of relations. Since relations are sets, we could use the techniques like the ones described in sections 5.2 and 6.2. However, the speed of access for relations can be greatly improved by defining special index structures, which reflect the common use of the relation.

A standard method for the implementation of relations is as one or more indexes on search keys of the relation. Such an index has the following functionality:

$$RELID \times Key \rightarrow \mathbf{P} \ Relationship$$

The index takes a relation identifier plus a search key, and returns the set of relationships with this key. These indexes are commonly found in databases but can also be used for the navigational behaviour found in most OMS applications, by using object identifiers as search keys.

A modified form of these indexes can be used to store old versions of relations. We define a two level index:

$$Relindex : RELID \times Key \rightarrow RVALID$$

$$RelVersionIndex : RVALID \times TimeStamp \rightarrow \mathbb{P} \, Relationship$$

RelVersionIndex implements versions of sets (of relationships). Specialized data structures for storing versions of sets will be described sections 5.2 (linear history) and 6.2 (non-linear history).

Relindex can be implemented using traditional indexing techniques, e.g. B-trees [Knu73].

Because these indexes have a key, fast access to the tuples is possible.

5 Linear version history

An important special type of history is the linear version history in which each time stamp (except for the last one) has precisely one successor. The restricted nature of the linear version history makes it possible to use more efficient data structures than those for the general non-linear version history, which will be described in section 6.

This section, that describes data structures for linear version history, is divided in two parts. The first part (section 5.1) concentrates on implementations for VersionIndex, the data structure that is used for integral version management on objects, while section 5.2 describes a data structure for storing versions of sets that can be used for integral version management on relations.

5.1 Sparse index

An obvious implementation for VersionIndex is to use a B-tree [Knu73], with the combination of OID and TimeStamp as key. If the index is sorted lexicographically on $\langle OID, TimeStamp \rangle$, all entries with the same OID will be adjacent in the index, and ordered by increasing TimeStamp.

It can be expected that successive entries in the index will tend to have the same value, since typically an object will not change between two snapshots. In a certain sense these repeated entries are redundant, and can be omitted.

A more precise definition of when an entry can be omitted is the following. We define that an entry $\langle oid, t \rangle$ *immediately precedes* an entry $\langle oid, t' \rangle$ in the index if there is no entry $\langle oid, t'' \rangle$ in the index with $t < t'' < t'$. An entry $\langle oid, t \rangle$ can be omitted from the index if there is an entry $\langle oid, t' \rangle$ that would immediately precede $\langle oid, t \rangle$ if it were present in the index, such that $indexval(\langle oid, t \rangle) = indexval(\langle oid, t' \rangle)$.

A *sparse index* is an index where the value of each entry is different from the immediately preceding entry. In order to handle deletions of objects correctly, the domain of object values is extended with the special object value null, i.e. an entry $(\langle oid, t \rangle \mapsto null)$ would indicate that at time t, object identifier oid was not referring to an existing object.

The insertion algorithm for a new entry $(\langle oid, t \rangle \mapsto val)$ is:

> **if** the index contains an entry $\langle oid, t' \rangle$ that immediately precedes $\langle oid, t \rangle$
> such that $indexval(\langle oid, t' \rangle) = val$
> **then** do nothing
> **else** insert $(\langle oid, t \rangle \mapsto val)$ in the index

Obviously, the deletion of an object *oid* at time *t* is indicated by inserting an entry $(\langle oid, t \rangle \mapsto \text{null})$ in the index.

The algorithm to retrieve the value of an object *oid* at time *t* is:

> if there is an entry for $\langle oid, t \rangle$
> then return *indexval*$(\langle oid, t \rangle)$
> else if there is an immediately preceding entry $\langle oid, t' \rangle$
> then return *indexval*$(\langle oid, t' \rangle)$
> else return null

This sparse index can be implemented using traditional data structures, e.g. the ubiquitous B-trees.

Performance

The index will only contain an entry for an object, if that object has been changed with respect to the previous snapshot. In general, it is to be expected that most objects will not change between snapshots. Therefore, a sparse index will be much smaller than the corresponding full index that stores all object values for all time stamps.

Searching the sparse index can be somewhat faster than with the full index due to the smaller size of the index. In a similar way the creation of a new snapshot can be faster because only objects that have been changed since the previous snapshot must be entered into the index.

5.2 Versions of sets

This section describes a data structure that can be used to handle versions of sets for a linear version history, that can be used to store versions of relations. This data structure is called *version list*. A version list consists of a list of 3-tuples $\langle el, birth, death \rangle$, where *el* is an element of the set, *birth* and *death* are both time stamps. The meaning of a 3-tuple is that *el* is a member of the set at all times *t* such that $birth \leq t < death$. All elements that are in the set at the most recent time stamp have a death time stamp of $+\infty$.

The 3-tuples in the version list are sorted on decreasing death time stamp. This means that all the entries that are currently alive are located near the head of the list. When a new element *r* is added to the set at time *t*, a new entry $\langle r, t, +\infty \rangle$ is added to the version list. For a deletion of a element *el* at time *t* the death time of the corresponding 3-tuple is changed to *t*. In order to keep the list sorted this 3-tuple may have to be moved to the rear of the list, this can be arranged by swapping this entry with the last 3-tuple that is currently alive.

The algorithm for reconstructing the set of elements for a given time t from a version list v is:

```
i := 1;
result := ∅
while i ≤ size(v) and v[i].death > t do
      if v[i].birth ≤ t
            then result := result ∪ v[i].el
      i:= i+1
```

Observe that we can terminate the search loop when an entry is found for which v[i].death < t because the list is sorted on decreasing death time. So we know that for all j > i, v[i].death < t.

Performance

Because old snapshots are immutable it is only possible to insert and delete elements for the most recent snapshot. Therefore, insertion and deletion operations will be $O(s)$ where s is the size of the current version of the set.

From the algorithm that retrieves old versions of the set, it can be seen that newer versions can be retrieved faster than older versions. This is desirable, because it can be expected that recent versions will be used much more frequently than older versions. The time needed to retrieve the most recent version is $O(s)$, where s is the size of the current version of the set, and this is of course the best achievable.

6   Non-linear version history

In the general case, version histories are not linear — i.e. timestamps can have more than one successor/predecessor — due to branching and merging. The techniques that were used in the previous section cannot be applied in this case. This section will describe some extensions that can be used in the non-linear case as well.

Like the previous section, this section is split into two parts. The first part describes techniques for storing objects. The second part describes data structures for storing versions of sets that can be used to implement versioned relations, as was explained in section 4.

6.1   Storing versions of objects

The sparse index technique, that was described in section 5.1, cannot be used immediately in the case of non-linear history. The most important problem is that in this case time stamps are not completely ordered. Therefore, they cannot be used as key in the sparse index. This problem can be solved by adding yet another indirection.

The procedure works as follows. There is one global mapping table: map : $TimeStamp \rightarrow N$, that is used to convert a TimeStamp to a (totally ordered) natural number. The resulting number is used to index the modified sparse index

$$VersionIndex' : OID \times N \rightarrow VALID$$

This mapping table will contain one entry per snapshot. It will thus be relatively small, and could be kept in core. It can be implemented e.g. as a hash table.

Example

An example sparse index for the data in figure 3 is shown in figure 4. In this example, we have two objects OID_1 and OID_2, and a set of snapshots with timestamps $T_a \ldots T_f$. The initial snapshot is T_a, that only contains the object OID_1 with value A. In one line of development (T_b, T_d, T_e), the object OID_2 is created and modified. In the other development line (T_c) object OID_1 is modified. The final snapshot T_f merges the results of both lines of development.

Insertion algorithms

The size of the index VersionIndex' depends on the mapping table in the following way : for all TimeStamps A and B let $d(A, B)$ be the number of objects that are different between snapshot A and snapshot B. The TimeStamps in the index are sorted by the increasing value of the mapping function. If we arrange all TimeStamps in a sequence $t_1 \ldots t_n$ such that $map(t_i) < map(t_{i+1})$, the total size of the index is

$$l = \sum_{i=1}^{n-1} d(t_i, t_{i+1})$$

Snapshot contents

T	OID_1	OID_2
T_a	A	–
T_b	A	B
T_c	D	–
T_d	A	B
T_e	A	C
T_f	D	C

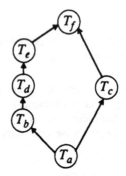

Figure 3: Example data for sparse index. This figure shows a partially ordered set of time stamps, and the contents of the corresponding snapshots.

map function

T	map(T)
T_a	1
T_b	2
T_c	6
T_d	3
T_e	4
T_f	5

VersionIndex'

OID	map(T)	Object-Version
OID_1	1	A
OID_1	5	D
OID_2	2	B
OID_2	4	C
OID_2	6	null

Figure 4: A sparse index

This table shows an example sparse index and the corresponding mapping function. null indicates a deleted entry.

A bad choice for the mapping table will give a very large index. Unfortunately it is not very easy to discover the optimal mapping table for a given set of snapshots, that gives a minimal value for l. Appendix A contains a proof that this problem is NP-complete. Because the problem of finding an optimal mapping table is NP-complete, for a practical insertion algorithm heuristic methods must be used. Which particular method is most suited depends very much on local branching patterns. The index will be relatively small if every snapshot is similar to its neighbors in the index. It can be expected that every snapshot is similar to its predecessor, thus a simple heuristic would be to insert every snapshot as a neighbor in the index of its predecessor.

It is not always possible to insert a successor of a snapshot with time stamp t as a neighbor, this happens if $\text{map}(t) + 1$ and $\text{map}(t) - 1$ are already used in the mapping table. In this case the new snapshot must be inserted elsewhere. A useful (greedy) heuristic, is to insert this snapshot at a place in the index where it causes the smallest increase in the total index size, i.e. between two snapshots to which it is very similar. Simulation experiments with this heuristic indicate that the size of the produced index is normally very close to the size with the optimal mapping table.

Performance

The performance of retrieval operations on this data-structure can be very similar to that of the standard sparse matrix for linear history. The only extra overhead is one lookup in the mapping table. When the relevant part of the mapping table is kept in core (as it probably will be) the additional overhead is negligible.

6.2 Implementations for versioned sets

This section describes implementation techniques that can be used to store versions of sets, in the case of non-linear version history. As was explained in section 4 this data structure can be used to store versions of relations.

Several standard data structures like lists and hash tables can be used to represent sets. But these data structures cannot be used to store multiple versions of the set in an efficient way. Two data structures, delta lists and modified AVL-trees, that are more space efficient will be described in the next sections.

Delta lists

A first data structure for the implementation of versioned sets makes use of *delta lists*. This data structure consists of two parts. Certain versions of the set are stored in full as *base versions*, using a traditional data structure (hash tables are suitable). Other versions are stored as sets of changes to a base version in the delta lists. A delta list is a list of *deltas*, every delta contains the differences (additions/deletions of elements) with respect to the previous version of the set. Every delta in a delta list is marked with a time stamp. The first delta in every delta list contains the modification with respect to a fully stored base version.

To retrieve a specific version of the set with a specific time stamp T, first the corresponding base version must be retrieved, and then all delta's that have time stamps between that of the base version and T must be applied. Thus the average access time will depend on the size of the delta lists. If base versions are made more often access time will get shorter, but storage demands will increase.

The average amount of storage per set with this data structure is:

$$c_1 \cdot f \cdot n + c_2 \cdot (1 - f) \cdot k$$

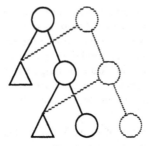

Figure 5: Shared subtree implementation for sets

The black tree and the shaded tree represent two different versions of the same set that share common subtrees.

where f = proportion of the versions that are stored as base versions
c_1 = storage size per element in a base version
n = average number of elements in a set
c_2 = storage size per element in a delta
k = average number of elements in a delta

The average access time is:

$$\tfrac{1}{2}d_1 \cdot (1 - f) \cdot k + d_2$$

where d_1 = time to access one element in a delta
d_2 = time to access one element in a base version

The proportion of versions that are stored as base versions (f) is an important parameter when implementing this data structure. It represents a classical space/time tradeoff, a low value for f gives a compact data structure while a high value gives good access performance.

Trees

Another standard way to implement sets is by using trees, e.g. AVL trees (see e.g. [Knu73]). This data structure can be used in a slightly modified form to store different versions of sets in an efficient way, by *sharing* common subtrees. In large trees successive different versions of a set, that differ in only a few elements, will have large subtrees in common, and these can be shared between the different versions, see figure 5.

The procedure for inserting/deleting elements is almost the same as that for a standard AVL tree, but instead of modifying existing nodes in the tree, a new copy of the node is made that contains the new value. When a node is copied, all of its ancestors must be copied as well. Each copied ancestor will point to the copies of its children, and if a child is not modified, the copied parent will use the original child node, which will then be shared between the old and the new version of the tree. If, for example, two successive sets differ only in one element, they will only differ in the nodes that form the path from the root to that element. All other nodes can be shared between the two versions.

Every individual tree is a normal balanced AVL-tree, so average access-times are logarithmic in the size of the tree. Also the worst case access-times are logarithmic, since the maximum depth of an AVL-tree of size N is $1.4404 \log_2(N + 2) - 0.328$ [Knu73].

For single deletions/insertions the storage requirement to store the new version is logarithmic in the total size of the set, since all elements of the path to the root must be copied. However when multiple additions/deletions are made the overhead per individual modification is less than log n.

Analysis of AVL-trees for versioned sets

An important question about the implementation of versioned sets with AVL-trees is the amount of storage that will be consumed by this data structure. This section attempts to give some approximate answers.

The storage requirements are determined by the overlap between successive versions. If they can share many common subtrees, they will require less storage. So the question is: how many nodes will on the average be shared between a tree and its successors?

The key observation for this analysis is that a node will only be shared with the next tree if the subtree that is rooted at this node, is left completely unchanged. Thus, the expected number of nodes that can be shared with the successor of tree T is:

$$\sigma(T) = \sum_{s \in T} p(s)$$

where $p(s)$ is the probability that subtree s will not be modified.

We now split the newly created nodes into two different groups: primary and secondary nodes; primary nodes are those that would also be changed in a normal AVL tree, while secondary nodes are those nodes which are not primary, but are created because one of their subtrees was modified. We assume that the possibility that a node does not undergo a primary change is the same for all nodes and equal to c, and that the probabilities for the different nodes are independent from one another. Under these assumptions the expected number of shared nodes becomes

$$\sigma(T) = \sum_{s \in T} c^{|s|}$$

where $|s|$ denotes the number of nodes in the tree s.

The value of $\sigma(T)$ depends on the shape of T. Therefore, we will analyze the two extreme shapes that an AVL tree can have: a fully balanced tree (best case) and the Fibonacci tree (worst case). These are the most balanced and most unbalanced shapes that an AVL-tree can have [Knu73].

Balanced trees

A fully balanced tree can be defined as a tree in which every node has either no children or two children that have the same height. In a fully balanced tree of height h there are 2^{h-n} subtrees of height n, each of which contains $2^{n+1} - 1$ nodes. Thus in this case:

$$\sigma(T) = \sum_{n=0}^{h} 2^{h-n} c^{2^{n+1}-1}$$

Fibonacci trees

Fibonacci trees are the most unbalanced AVL trees. The Fibonacci trees $\mathcal{F}_0, \mathcal{F}_1, \ldots$ can be defined in the following way:

$\mathcal{F}_0$ is the empty tree, $\mathcal{F}_1$ is the tree consisting of one node, and $\mathcal{F}_n$ is the tree that has $\mathcal{F}_{n-1}$ and $\mathcal{F}_{n-2}$ as children.

It can easily be proved by induction that $|\mathcal{F}_n| = Fib(n+1) - 1$ where Fib is the Fibonacci function. Thus we have

$$s(n) \stackrel{\text{def}}{=} \sigma(\mathcal{F}_n) = s(n-1) + s(n-2) + c^{Fib(n+1)-1}$$

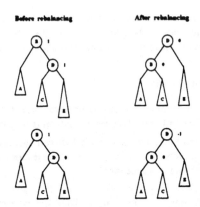

Figure 6: Rebalancing an AVL tree

In these 2 cases (and their mirror images) additional rebalancing can be performed without destroying the AVL property. The balance factors are indicated at the individual nodes.

This recurrence relation can be transformed to:

$$s(n) = \sum_{i=0}^{n} Fib(n - i) \cdot c^{Fib(n+1)-1}$$

This could be further transformed using the identity

$$Fib(n) = \frac{1}{\sqrt{5}}(\Phi^n - \overline{\Phi}^n)$$

where $\Phi = \frac{1}{2}(1 + \sqrt{5})$ and $\overline{\Phi} = \frac{1}{2}(1 - \sqrt{5})$:

$$s(n) = \sum_{i=0}^{n} \frac{1}{c\sqrt{5}}(\Phi^{n-i} - \overline{\Phi}^{n-i}) \cdot c^{\frac{1}{\sqrt{5}}\left(\Phi^{n+1} - \overline{\Phi}^{n+1}\right)}$$

Rebalancing

The algorithm can be further enhanced by performing some extra rebalancing to get a better weight balance. This will make the creation of new sets somewhat slower, but can speed up access to the new set, without incurring additional storage overheads. The enhancement is based on the fact that at certain places in an AVL tree it is possible to rebalance subtrees without loosing the AVL property. These cases are shown in figure 6 (the mirror images are not shown). In these cases rebalancing obviously does not disturb the AVL-property: the balance factor[2] for the individual nodes still remains within [-1,1]. However, the weight-balance for these nodes could be improved by this rebalancing operation. If we denote by #X the total number of nodes in subtree X, and by N the total number of nodes in the tree, then rebalancing will change the average path length by $\frac{\#A - \#E}{N}$. Thus, additional rebalancing is advantageous if #E > #A. Rebalancing can be done without causing any storage overhead if the operation is only performed on copied nodes. Thus in our example rebalancing would only be performed if nodes B and D were copied anyway.

---

[2]The balance factor of a node is equal to the difference in height between its left and right subtree.

A comparison of delta lists and AVL trees

There are two candidates for the implementation of versioned sets: delta lists and balanced trees. These data structures have different properties. The behavior of the delta list depends heavily on the value for the parameter f, the proportion of all versions that are stored in full as base version.

If storage space is at a premium, the delta list with a low value of f is better than a tree, due to the compact storage that is possible for delta-lists. But the access time will increase linearly with $(1 - f)$ so low values of f will give a bad access performance.

If, on the other hand, access time is more important than storage space, AVL trees will tend to be better, since their access time is always logarithmic in the size of the set. It seems likely that the delta list implementation with the same access speed as an AVL tree will consume more storage due to the large proportion of base versions.

Whether or not AVL trees are really superior in this case depends on implementation parameters and usage patterns.

7 Conclusions

Version management is an important ingredient of any software development process. It provides the basis for keeping track of changes to a system, and for managing and coordinating parallel development. Proper support for versioning is therefore a primary asset of any development environment.

In this paper we discuss an approach where version management is incorporated as a basic mechanism into an object system. Versioning is applied to complete, self-contained object worlds. This approach provides an intuitive and attractive way to improve consistency of version combinations, and avoids some of the problems that exist in other approaches, most notably that of version control of arbitrary references among objects.

Versioning does not come for free, and one of the main reasons that many systems do not provide version management is because it is too expensive. Of course, decreasing hardware costs, increased cpu power, cheaper storage media, such as WORM disks, make version control more attractive. Nevertheless, to make large scale application of versioning — and especially integral version management — viable, it is necessary to have suitable implementation techniques.

This paper presents several data structures and algorithms to implement integral version management which will be applied in the development of CAMERA. Although the techniques are applied to versioning of a self-contained object management system, we feel that it is possible to use them also in other situations, e.g. for the versioning of complex objects.

We expect that the data structures in this paper will give acceptable performance for frequent versioning during development. The results of our initial prototype implementations in this area are encouraging (some of this work is described in [Lip90]). More experience will be gained from the current prototype development of the complete CAMERA system.

This further research will also allow us to tune the algorithms to usage patterns. For example, the size of the index for a non linear history, that was described in section 6 depends on the chosen mapping function. Which mapping table performs best is determined by the actual usage patterns, e.g. the similarity between successive snapshots, the rate at which development lines branch and merge etc.

Acknowledgments

We would like to thank Jan Wielemaker and Doaitse Swierstra and the referees for their comments on versions of this paper.

References

[BCG*87] Jay Banerjee, Hong-Tai Chou, Jorge F. Garza, Won Kim, Darrell Woelk, Nat Ballou, and Hyoung-Joo Kim. Data model issues for object-oriented applications. *ACM Transactions on Office Automation Systems*, 5(1):3–26, January 1987.

[BGW89] David B. Miller, Robert G. Stockton, and Charles W. Krueger. An inverted approach to configuration management. In *Proceedings of the 2nd International Workshop in Software Configuration Management*, pages 1–4, November 1989. ACM SEN 17:7.

[BMO*89] Robert Bretl, David Maier, Allan Otis, Jason Penney, Bruce Schuchardt, Jacob Stein, E. Harold Williams, and Monty Williams. The GemStone data management system. In Won Kim and Frederick H. Lochovsky, editors, *Object-Oriented Concepts, Databases and Applications*, chapter 12, Addison-Wesley, 1989.

[F*88] Daniel H. Fishman et al. *Overview of the Iris DBMS*. Technical Report, Hewlett-Packard Laboratories, Palo Alto, 1988.

[GB86] Ira P. Goldstein and Daniel G. Bobrow. A layered approach to software design. In *Interactive Programming Environments*, chapter 19, Mc Graw-Hill, 1986.

[GMS89] W. Morwen Gentleman, Stephen A. MacKay, and Darlene A. Stewart. Commercial realtime software needs different configuration management. In *Proceedings of the 2nd International Workshop on Software Configuration Management*, pages 152–161, November 1989. ACM SEN 17:7.

[Hen88] David Hendricks. The translucent file service. In *EEUG Autumn*, 1988.

[Hum89] Andrew G. Hume. The use of a time machine to control software. In *Software Management Workshop*, Usenix, April 1989.

[KBC*87] Won Kim, Jay Banerjee, Hong-Tai Chou, Jorge F. Garza, and Darrell Woelk. Composite object support in an object-oriented database system. In *Proceedings OOPSLA '87*, 1987.

[KL84] Randy H. Katz and Tobin J. Lehman. Database support for versions and alternatives of large design files. *IEEE Transactions on Software Engineering*, 10(2):191–200, March 1984.

[KL89] Won Kim and Frederick H. Lochovsky. *Object-Oriented Concepts, Databases and Applications*. Addison-Wesley, 1989.

[Knu73] Donald Ervin Knuth. *The Art of Computer Programming 3: Sorting and Searching*. Addison-Wesley, 1973.

[LCM*89] Anund Lie, Reidar Conradi, Tor M. Didriksen, Even-Andre Karlsson, Svein O. Hallsteinsen, and Per Holager. Change oriented versioning in a software engineering database. In *Proceedings of the 2nd International Workshop in Software Configuration Management*, pages 56–65, November 1989. ACM SEN 17:7.

[LF91] Ernst Lippe and Gert Florijn. *CAMERA: a Distributed Version Control System*. Technical Report 91/1, Software Engineering Research Centrum, 1991.

[LFB89] Ernst Lippe, Gert Florijn, and Eugène Bogaart. *CAMERA: Architecture of a Distributed Version Control System*. Technical Report RP/DVM-89/4, Software Engineering Research Centrum, April 1989.

[Lip90] Ernst Lippe. *Index Structures for Integral Version Management*. Technical Report 90/2, Software Engineering Research Centre, 1990.

[NSE88]   *Network Software Environment: Reference Manual.* Sun Microsystems, March 1988.

[PAC89]   *Configuration Management Guide.* PACT, December 1989.

[PCT]   *PCTE: A Basis for a Portable Common Tool Environment.* European Economic Community, fourth edition.

[PPTT90]   Rob Pike, Dave Presotto, Ken Thompson, and Howard Trickey. Plan 9 from Bell labs. *EUUG Newsletter*, 10(3):2–11, 1990.

[Pre90]   Vasilis Prevelakis. Versioning issues for hypertext systems. In Dennis Tsichritzis, editor, *Object Management*, chapter 6, pages 89–106, Centre Universitaire d'Informatique, Université de Genève, 1990.

[Rum88]   James Rumbaugh. Controlling Propagation of Operations using Attributes on Relations. In *Proc. of the 1988 Object-Oriented Programming Systems and Languages Conference*, pages 285–296, September 1988.

[SR87]   Michael Stonebraker and Lawrence A. Rowe (editors). *The POSTGRES Papers.* Memorandum UCB/ERL M86/85, Electronics Research Laboratory, U.C. Berkeley, June 1987.

[Tic85]   Walter F. Tichy. RCS — a system for version control. *Software Practice and Experience*, 15(7):637–654, July 1985.

A   Proof of NP-completeness

Lemma: Finding an optimal mapping function for a sparse index, as described in section 6.1 is NP-complete.

Proof:

First observe that the corresponding decision problem is in NP, since if we are given an ordering and its path length, it can be checked in polynomial time whether this ordering has indeed this path length. Since the decision problem is in NP, the problem of finding an optimal ordering is in NP, too.

Now we will reduce a standard NP-complete problem, a version of the Hamiltonian path problem, to our ordering problem. The Hamiltonian path problem can be stated as follows: Given a graph consisting of a set of nodes: $N = \{\nu_1 \cdots \nu_n\}$ and a set of edges: $E = \{\epsilon_1 \cdots \epsilon_e\}$ without double edges between nodes, find a path that passes exactly once through all nodes.

Now we are going to construct an instance of the optimal ordering problem for an instance of the Hamiltonian path problem. We construct a set of snapshots $\overline{X} = \{\overline{x}_1 \cdots \overline{x}_n\}$, where

$$\overline{x}_i = \begin{pmatrix} x_{i,1} \\ \vdots \\ x_{i,e} \end{pmatrix}$$

Every snapshot corresponds with a node in the Hamiltonian path problem. We represent a snapshot by a column vector that contains the values of the objects, thus $x_{i,j}$ contains the value of object j at time stamp i. For this proof we only need objects that can have integer values.

The contents of each $\overline{x}_i$ is as follows:

$$\begin{aligned} x_{i,j} &= 0 \quad \text{if } \epsilon_j \text{ is connected to } \nu_i \\ &= i \quad \text{otherwise} \end{aligned}$$

This transformation can be performed in polynomial time.

Remember that the distance between two snapshots is equal to the number of objects that have different values in both snapshots. Observe that the distance between two points that represent two connected nodes is $e - 1$ while the distance for unconnected nodes is e. Now there exists a Hamiltonian path iff there exists an ordering of the $\overline{X}$ such that the total path-length is equal to $(n - 1)(e - 1)$.   □

Object-Oriented Analysis and Top-Down Software Development

Dennis de Champeaux

HP-Labs

1501 Page Mill Rd, 1U

Palo Alto, CA 94304-1181

USA

Abstract

In this paper, we address the issue of how to provide an analyst that uses the object-oriented paradigm with a top-down approach. An analyst gets this approach for free when working within the structured paradigm. Ensembles are introduced that differ from objects in that they connote entities with internal parallelism. Preliminary experimentation suggests that ensembles allow for information hiding.

electronic address: champeaux@hplabs.hp.com

telephone #: (415) 857 6674

key words: OO-Analysis, top-down, ensemble

1 Introduction

In this paper, we outline a top-down object-oriented analysis (OOA) method. Top-down OOA allows an analyst to employ well-established strategies like divide-and-conquer.

We start by clarifying some of our terminology:

Analysis is the activity that yields a description of *what* a target system is supposed to do; detailing functional, performance and resource requirements. This description could be the basis for a contract between the client and the developer and aims to be the unambiguous input to the designer.

Design is the activity which yields an artifact description of *how* a target system will work. The design satisfies the requirements, while it is still implementation language independent. The artifact description aims to be the unambiguous input to the implementor.

Object-oriented analysis describes a target system with a characterization of the entities in the domain, their inherent interrelationships, and their intended behavior in isolation as well as their interactions. The order in which these aspects are addressed varies, but usually the entity characterization precedes the behavior description. This contrasts with the order in which structured analysis deals with these aspects; behavior first and entity characterization (data dictionaries) second.

Our work is grounded on the assumption that neither structured analysis nor structured design provide a natural characterization for subsequent implementation in an object-oriented language, as supported by experience in Hewlett-Packard. At the same-time, we do not suggest that object-oriented analysis and design make sense only when a subsequent implementation employs an object-oriented programming language.

The necessity of analyzing a system in a top-down fashion arises specially in the characterization of large systems. While the analysis of a toy example like the popular car cruise control system yields only a "flat" set of objects, the analysis of a corporation like Hewlett-Packard, an airline reservation system or a bank will yield "objects" at different abstraction levels.

The problem that we encounter is caused - we conjecture - by an uncritical adoption of the notion of object from the realm of the object-oriented programming languages. We suspect that this is the core reason why identifying objects is a hard task. We can wonder for instance whether the following notions are proper objects:

In the realm of Hewlett-Packard:
a division, a department, an employee, a project, a production unit, a product, an order, a floor in a building, a location code, etc.

In the realm of an airline system:
a flight, an airplane, a flight attendant, a client, a flight schedule, a special meal order, a service schedule, a luggage door, a payment scale, etc.

In the realm of a bank:
an interest rate, a branch office, a teller machine, a corporate account, a loan officer, the overseas department, a monthly statement, etc.

One cannot immediately deny objecthood to any of those notions. However, their juxtaposition gives an uneasy feeling. We need different abstraction levels. The unhappy consequence is that we need to introduce objects that are "less equal", to paraphrase Orwell, than other objects. We propose *ensembles*, a different kind of abstract object, to facilitate a top-down analysis mode.

This paper is organized as follows: section 2 summarizes our current version of an object-oriented analysis method by outlining the notions for the models that the analyst can construct. In section 3, we introduce and discuss the notion of an ensemble. We illustrate ensembles in greater detail in section 4 by applying them to the example of a car, which we view as a hierarchy of multiple systems. The last section is devoted to a discussion of the pros and cons of the ensemble concept.

2 The Object-Oriented Analysis Method

Our analysis technique emerged from a variety of influences, among which are work in knowledge representation languages like KL-ONE ([2]), formal software development ([11, 5]), experiences gathered inside Hewlett-Packard at utilizing the object paradigm, and previous object-oriented analysis approaches ([9, 3, 8]). In particular, the work of Shlaer and Mellor ([9]) was the focus of our early efforts.

As mentioned above, we view the analysis process as "the activity that yields a description of *what* a target system is supposed to do by detailing functional, performance and resource requirements". The output of object-oriented analysis should satisfy two requirements:

- it should be a contract between client and developer

- it should be a contract between analyst and designer

Many approaches to OOA fail to satisfy the contract character, mostly because they fall short of providing two essential features: (1) the ability to be precise, i.e. to have a rich analysis language that allows, if desired, a rigorous and semantically unique description of the domain of discourse; (2) the provision of a development process, i.e. a framework in which a problem is composed and/ or decomposed.

Our method tries to overcome these deficiencies. It consists of the following steps:

- Developing an Information Model

- Developing a State-Transition Model

- Developing a Process Model

These will be discussed in greater detail in subsequent sections (see also [4]). The reason for using these models is to provide a variety of views of an object so as to capture as much data as possible during analysis. Many of the topics related to these views go beyond the scope of this paper, for example how to find objects, how to attach identified services to particular objects, or how to migrate from OOA to OOD. The interested reader can find further information in the cited literature.

The typical sequence of model development starts with information modeling and proceeds as diagramed below:

```
IM -------> ST -------> PM
```

Explanation of the symbols:
IM = Information Model
ST = State-Transition Model
PM = Process Model

In order to facilitate the transition to design an interface model, IFM, may be derived from the State-Transition Model and the Process Model:

```
IM -------> ST -------> PM
              \           \
               ---------------> IFM
```

We foresee that an interface model would generalize away the specific details of the object interactions in the process model and would produce the set of services that are associated with a prototypical instance of a class. (A service is not necessarily a synchronized interaction pair between an initiator and a recipient. Services subsume here as well trigger and send-and-forget interactions.)

2.1 Information Model

The IM consists of object class definitions, ensemble class definitions, and definitions of inter-object relations; the notion of ensemble is introduced in section 3.

Existing approaches to OOA typically define objects by listing a collection of attributes which are descriptive names (like BankAccount). There are shortcomings with this style of definition. For example, the analyst should be able to express what constitutes the legal value set of the deposit of a BankAccount. An attribute value may be dependent on the values of other attributes. Dependencies should be expressible as well. The occurrence of an attribute may be fixed or may vary over all instances of a class. It is worthwhile to register such a regularity also.

While attributes help to describe an object, we can elaborate the significance of an attribute by describing it beyond its name through its features. We have borrowed the following features from the KL-ONE knowledge representation language ([2]):

- cardinality: whether the attribute value is a singleton, enumeration, fixed or unbounded (sub)set.

- modality: whether this attribute always has a value (i.e. is mandatory), optional or whether this attribute is derived.

- value restriction: the named set of values out of which actual values have to be taken.

The analyst can also state an integrity constraint, here called *invariant* that applies to every instance of a class. Typically, an invariant is an implicitly quantified statement that refers to features of attributes. (In KL-ONE ([2]), invariants were captured by structure links; see an example in section 4, figure 1.)

Here is an example that provides attribute name, cardinality, modality, and value restriction for each attribute:

Object class BankAccount

- account owner, fixed-set, necessarily-present, Name

- account type, singleton, necessarily-present, (saving, checking)

- balance, singleton, necessarily-present, Amount

- connected_accounts, set, optional, BankAccount

An invariant for such an account would be:

$$balance + SUM(connected\_accounts.balance) > 0$$

saying that an overdraft in an account may be tolerated as long as sufficient funds are available in connected accounts.

An analyst may observe that two defined object classes have common attributes. In that case, the common attributes can be abstracted into a new object class, the common attributes can be removed from the initial classes and an inheritance relationship can be introduced between the new abstract object class and the modified classes. Inheritance can also be introduced initially as a consequence of inherent commonalities in the domain of discourse. In the banking world, we encounter checking accounts, saving accounts, commercial accounts, etc. This suggests that one introduces a generic account class and let the specific accounts inherit from it.

The graph constructed by taking the objects as vertices and the inheritance links as the arcs is directed and acyclic. This graph turns into a tree if no object inherits from multiple parents.

2.2 State Model

While the Information Model addresses the static aspects of an object, the dynamic (or behavioral) aspects are described in a State Model (SM).

The states of an object are derived from the set of all possible values of its attributes. A state is defined by a predicate on the state space spanned by the cartesian product of the value restrictions of the attributes. The predicates should be defined such that the states are mutually disjoint.

A transition corresponds with a directed pair of states. The set of states and transitions form a directed graph which is not necessarily connected. In case we have more than one component, we consider the components as independent. While an object occupies a state within each component, inside a component only one state at the time is visited.

OOA does not associate actions with states, as is done in [9], but with transitions. The state-transition model in [9] can be phrased as "states cause each other", while our method captures "transitions cause each other".

A transition carries a *condition* that is to be fulfilled before a transition can take place; that is, being in a state does not automatically enable a transition; such a condition can refer to attributes of "other" objects.

We augment the concept of state transitions by attaching:

- an *external* flag that indicates whether a triggering event is required;

- a *cause* list that describes the events that are generated as a consequence of the transition and act as triggers for subsequent transitions, usually in other objects.

In order to create objects that are reusable, we describe the dynamic dimension of an object *independently* of how it will interact with other objects in the context of the target system. This entails that a reference to an external object - to describe a causal consequence of a transition - should abstract away from the actual connections that the object has when integrated in the target system. To obtain proper generality, one may have to introduce attributes in an object whose role is to capture interaction "acquaintanceships" with peer objects.

As an example consider the domain of pipes, valves, junctions, pressure regulators, reservoirs, etc. In order to model the propagation of a pressure change in a pipe, we need to refer to a transition of an attached device. Since a generic pipe can't know what device it is attached to, we need a pipe attribute that stores this information.

The process model is responsible for "welding" the state models together through event descriptions.

2.3 Process Model

An analyst can express a causal connection between transitions in different objects by adding to a transition in an originator a causelist and in a recipient transition an indication that a preceding triggering event is required. In this section, we give an example to elaborate.

We describe the connection between a button object and a car cruise control object which is in a sense the "brain" of a car cruise control system. The button's responsibility is to switch the system from the off to the on state.

We model the button as a single state, single transition machine. The condition for the transition is always true. However, the transition needs a triggering event to fire. The source of this trigger is outside the system boundary and corresponds with the side effect of pushing the physical button on the dashboard. The transition has on its cause list a single event, On-Event(ccs, turn-on). The ccs argument describes the recipient of the trigger; we assume here that the button has an acquaintance attribute ccs. The second argument, turn-on, indicates which transition in the recipient is "invited" to fire. In general, the originator has no control on whether the recipient can honor the invitation. For example, pushing the (physical) button twice should have no effect the second time.

The recipient car cruise control object will have, among others an Off state and a Cruising state, and a turn-on transition between the two. This transition requires an external event to fire: On-Event. If necessary a transition may specify an additional condition to be fulfilled. In our turn-on transition, we may require, for example, that the car has a certain minimum speed.

This description is only the tip of the iceberg. The process model can employ as well more powerful modes of interaction than just send-and-forget triggering. We may want to trigger more than one object/ transition combination and insist, for example, that these transitions are synchronized. We may want to send data along with a trigger from the originator to the recipient(s). An originator may want to obtain an acknowledgement of reception, with or without time-outs. An originator may issue a blocking send which results in a suspension until return data is received, etc.

A recipient may be in the wrong state to honor a trigger/ send. There are different interpretations of such a situation:

An analyst has made an error; i.e. a condition has been omitted somewhere in the originator.

The trigger/ send is queued in the recipient and will be honored when the recipient arrives in the start state of the triggered transition.

The trigger/ send is lost.

Any of these interpretations can be appropriate, thus it is the analyst's responsibility to annotate a trigger/ send with the intended interpretation.

3   Ensembles

The different models that we described in the previous section allow the analyst to focus attention on different aspects of the task. The definition of the entities in the target domain is separated from the characterizations of the dynamics of the system. The description of the lifecycle of an entity is separated from the description of how an entity interacts with other entities. Still, we feel that the support for divide and conquer techniques provided by the method is insufficient. We should have the ability to acknowledge formally that certain groups of entities are tightly coupled and that these groups are entities by themselves with more or less similar features as the basic entities/ objects in the target domain. To phrase it in a more compelling manner: object-oriented analysis without an entity clustering technique is not a viable method for the characterization of large systems.

To stress the difference between clusters and basic entities, we propose *ensembles* as an alternative for objects. Ensembles share with objects the modeling apparatus that we outlined in section 2; i.e. an ensemble has attributes, has an associated state-transition machine, has the ability to interact with objects as well as with ensembles and can have an interface model. An ensemble differs from an object in that it stands for a cluster or bundle of less abstract entities which are either objects or lower level ensembles. These constituents interact only among each other or with the encompassing ensemble. I.e. the ensemble acts as a gateway/ manager between the constituents and the context. The relationship between an ensemble and its constituents can be thought of as subsuming abstract-part-of. While the dynamic dimension of an object can be conceptualized as a sequential machine, an ensemble connotes an entity with internal parallelism.

For example, in the bank domain, we can see an account as an object when only one transaction at a time is permitted on it. On the other hand, the loan department with several loan officers would be an ensemble because its constituents, the loan officers, are operating in parallel (presumably).

An ensemble hides details of its constituent objects/ sub-ensembles that are irrelevant outside the ensemble, somewhat in analogy with an object in the programming realm that hides its internal implementation details.

To make the notion of an ensemble more real, we will look in this section at its features in more detail. Section 4 discusses an example.

3.1 Ensemble Class

In the same way that we like to deal with classes of objects instead of individual objects, we will deal with classes of ensembles instead of individual ensembles. And as is the custom in the case of objects in which a class of objects is characterized with a prototypical member, called "an object", we will deal with classes of ensembles through a prototypical ensemble.

We have the following correspondences:

	descriptive notion	
target domain	atomic	cluster
entity	object	ensemble
concept	object class	ensemble class

3.2 Ensemble Constituents

Describing the constituent objects/ sub-ensembles of an ensemble is the primary task of its information model. Regular attributes can do this. An invariant relating a constituent in the value-restriction of such an attribute and the $self of the ensemble may elaborate the *abstract-part-of* relationship between the two.

Additional attributes in an ensemble may describe features that apply to the cluster of constituents as a whole. For instance, summary information of the constituents. Their number is an example. Or, as an another example, we can capture in an ensemble information that applies to each of its constituents. Consider a fleet to be represented by an ensemble. The individual ships share the direction in which they are going. Thus, we can introduce direction as an attribute of a fleet.

When an ensemble has non-constituent attributes, it may have a "life of its own"; i.e. we may develop a state-transition model for it. As an example we can maintain in a fleet an attribute that records the distance of the fleet to its home port. This allows us, for example, to introduce three states induced by a linear ordering suggested by: near-the-home-port, remote-from-the-home-port and far-away-from-the-home-port. These distinctions could have consequences in the process model for, say, refueling operations.

If an ensemble has been equipped with a state-transition model, we can describe inter-ensemble and/or ensemble - object interactions similar to the plain inter-object interactions. An example of an inter-ensemble interaction in our fleet domain, where a home-fleet is seen as the ensemble consisting of the home ports of the ships in the fleet, would be a fleet-home-docking trigger initiated by a fleet to begin the docking of the ships in the home ports. An example of an ensemble - object interaction would be the fleet giving a directive specifically to one of its ships.

4 Example

We will model fragments of a car to illustrate in greater detail the use of ensembles. A car can be seen as a single object only if one does not need to deal with its components. This would be the case, for instance, from the perspective of a car rental agency. Otherwise, when the internal aspects do matter, we better see a car as consisting of several systems, including: steering, suspension, electrical, transmission, brake, engine, heating, doors, controls, etc.

We can recognize that the entries on this list do not correspond with ordinary car attributes. They have behaviors of their own, while they operate semi independently and in parallel. In contrast, examples of regular attributes of a car are: chassis, coach-work, owner, license-number, speed, location, etc. Some of the entities on this list also have life cycles and operate semi independently, thus one may wonder why they are not constituents of a car. The justification for the different elements vary. For the chassis and coach-work one might argue that they have a state "being a part of a car assembly", which from the perspective of the car is too constant to be considered a system. For the owner, one might argue instead that the owner attribute is an artifact, the remnant of a binary Owner relationship between cars and persons that is realized ("implemented") via attributes. The other attributes refer to value restrictions which aren't objects, at least not from the perspective of a car.

In this paper, we adhere to the following graphic conventions:

```
 -----
/ XYZ \      : a trapezoid indicates an object class or ensemble class
 -------

U--->        : this arrow denotes class/ ensemble inheritance

|----{...} : a regular attribute of a class/ ensemble

|===={...} : a constituent attribute of an ensemble

{ / / / }  : see section 2.1 for the 4-tuple inside the brackets
```

With these conventions, we obtain the following fragment of the information model of a car:

```
  -----                  ---------
/ Car \   U----> / Vehicle \ ; Vehicle is a super class of Car
-------                  -----------
   |-------{chassis/ 1/ np/ Chassis}
   |-------{coach-work/ 1/ np/ Coach-work}
   |-------{owner/ [1, 00)/ np/ Person U ...}
   |            ; An owner can also be a here unspecified
   |            ; non-person, more than one owner is possible
   |-------{license-number/ 1/ np/ String}
   |-------{speed/ 1/ np/ [0, max-speed]}
   |-------{location/ 1/ np/ Place}
   |======={steering-sys/ 1/ np/ Steering-sys}
   |======={suspension-sys/ 1/ np/ Suspension-sys}
   |======={electrical-sys/ 1/ np/ Electrical-sys}
   |======={transmission-sys/ 1/ np/ Transmission-sys}
   |======={brake-sys/ 1/ np/ Brake-sys}
   |======={engine-sys/ 1/ np/ Engine-sys}
   |======={heating-sys/ 1/ np/ Heating-sys}
   |======={door-sys/ 1/ np/ Door-sys}
   |======={control-sys/ 1/ np/ Control-sys}
   |======={wheel-sys/ 1/ np/ Wheel-sys}
  ...
   + structure-links:
       wheel-sys.front-wheels.angle =
             angle-function(
                steering-sys.steering-wheel.angle)
       wheel-sys.wheel-rotation =
             wheel-rotation-function(speed)
  ...
```

Fig. 1 A fragment of the information model of a Car,
        when seen as an ensemble.

The structure-link in Car reaches inside the ensemble Front-wheels which is a constituent of the ensemble Wheel-sys. Front-wheels itself has a constituent Wheel-pair, which in turn has two Wheels as constituents. We obtain the following fragments:

```
 -----------
/ Wheel-sys \
 --------------
    |-------{wheel-rotation/ 1/ np/ [0, max-rotation]}
    |======={front-wheels/ 1/ np/ Front-wheels}
    |======={rear-wheels/ 1/ np/ Rear-wheels}


 --------------
/ Front-wheels \
 ----------------
    |-------{angle/ 1/ np/ [0, max-angle]}
    |======={wheel-pair/ 1/ np/ Wheel-pair}

 --------------
/ Rear-wheels  \
 ----------------
    |======={differential-gear-sys/ 1/ np/ Differential-gear}
    |======={wheel-pair/ 1/ np/ Wheel-pair}


 --------------
/ Wheel-pair   \
 ----------------
    |======={left-wheel/ 1/ np/ Wheel}
    |======={right-wheel/ 1/ np/ Wheel}
```

Fig. 2   A fragment of some constituents of the
         ensemble Car; these constituents are
         themselves ensembles.

Regular attributes and constituent attributes have much in common, see section 2. A constituent attribute also has a cardinality descriptor, a modality descriptor as well as a characterization of the value restriction, i.e. the kind of constituent(s) that is referred to in the attribute. For example, if we see the wheels of a Car as non-distinguished sub-constituents of the Wheel-sys constituent - unlike the modeling done above -, we can indicate that the cardinality feature is four (excluding here pathological vehicles), that the modality is necessary and that the kind is obviously Wheel. A structure link capturing an invariant can refer to a constituent attribute as well. For example, there is a constraint between the angle of the front wheels with respect to the chassis and the degree of rotation of the steering wheel as expressed above in the information model of Car.

Observe that we introduced a regular attribute wheel-rotation in Wheel-sys. A structure-link in Wheel-sys should express that the value of this attribute is the average of the rotations of the Wheels in the two constituting Wheel-pairs.

An ensemble can have a regular state-transition model (and possibly more than one, as is allowed for regular objects). For example, we can observe for our car whether it is insured or not, whether it is for sale or not, whether the manual transition indicates neutral, rear, first, second, third, fourth gear, whether the lights are off, on park lights, dimmed or full, etc. Some of these state-models are imported from lower level constituents through the control-sys constituent.

As a major difference between an object and an ensemble, we have associated with an ensemble a forwarding mechanism for triggers and messages that mediates between external entities and the constituents of an ensemble. Thus, we can hide aspects of the constituents of an ensemble which have significance only inside the ensemble. For example, the interface of the engine is an internal affair of a car and the outside world need not to know anything about it. On the other hand, the forwarding mechanism of the car ensemble should export the interface of the control constituent.

We will illustrate information hiding occurring within the car ensemble by sketching the description of starting a car. We will export through the Control-sys constituent the state transition diagrams of an Ignition-lock and of an Oil-pressure-indication-lamp, which are both (sub) constituents of Car.

The state-transition diagram of the ignition lock:

Ignition-lock:

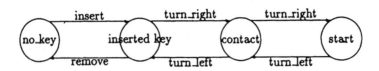

Fig. 3 The exported state-transition diagram of the
        ignition-lock.

The turn-right transition that leads into the contact state triggers the contacted transition in Oil-pressure-indication-lamp, see below.

Other relevant constituents that we consider are:

Start-engine, Engine-sys, and Oil-pressure-sensor.

Their state transitions will *not* be exported through the Control-sys. For the start-engine we have the following behavior description:

Start-engine:

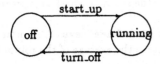

Fig. 4 The state-transition diagram of the start-engine.

We assume that the turn-right transition that connects the contact state with the start state in Ignition-lock has a trigger directed at the start-up transition in Start-engine. (The identity of the recipient object - in this example there is only one legal recipient - can be traced through the car ensemble.) We omit here conditions associated with the start-up transition, like the transmission being in neutral, etc. The start-up transition in its turn will generate a trigger aimed at the start-up transition in Engine-sys:

Engine-sys:

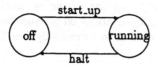

Fig. 5 The state-transition diagram of the engine.

To simplify matters, we assume that the start-up transition in Engine-sys directly triggers the go-high transition in Oil-pressure-sensor:

Oil-pressure-sensor:

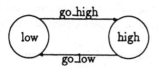

Fig. 6 The state-transition diagram of the
oil-pressure-sensor

The go-high transition finally triggers the start-up transition in:
Oil-pressure-indicator-lamp, which causes the lamp to go off again:

Oil-pressure-indicator-lamp:

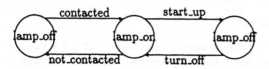

Fig. 7 The exported state-transition diagram of the
oil-pressure-indicator-lamp

Since the state-transition of the Oil-pressure-indicator-lamp is exported the driver will see the lamp go off.

When we look from the outside, we see *pseudo* causal consequences. For instance, the turn-right transition out of the inserted-key state "causes" the oil-pressure-indica-tor-lamp to go on. A similar pseudo causality turns this lamp off again when the ignition-lock moves into the start state (which signals the driver to turn the key out of the start position, which causes the ignition-lock, etc.)

However, when we look inside the Car ensemble, we will see a different triggering/ messaging pattern that ultimately achieves these pseudo causal consequences.

In summary (and without claim to automotive correctness): starting engine → running engine → actual pressure goes up → oil pressure sensor goes in high state → oil pressure lamp goes off. Consequently, the introduction of ensembles has allowed us to successfully hide low level mechanisms from higher order functionality.

5 Related work

Object-oriented analysis is a relatively new field. The first book in this area is from Shlaer & Mellor, [9]. Most of the book is devoted to the Information Model. One chapter discusses an example in which they illustrate the State Model and their Process Model. Their Process Model differs from ours in that they rely on data flow diagrams, borrowed from Structured Analysis, to describe the actions in their State Models. As a result, the interaction between objects is described in their method in an indirect way - the occurrence of an external data store in a data flow diagram. We feel that our triggers and messages allow us to express directly causal interactions between objects. A summary of their version of Object-Oriented Analysis can be found in [10].

In Ward,[12], an attempt is made to salvage Structured Analysis and Design when an implementation will be done in an Object-Oriented programming language. Ward acknowledges that the original version of SA/SD doesn't lend itself easily to the identification of objects, and certainly not to object hierarchies which deepen the insight in the understanding of the domain. However, he points to a refinement of SA/SD for real-time systems, [13], in which entity-relationship modeling is imported from the database realm. We remain doubtful whether unbiased object identification can be done *after* processes have been modeled.

Our comment on Ward's paper, [12], applies also to that of Bailin, [1].

In Wirfs-Brock et al, [14], the authors discuss the notion of a subsystem.

> A *subsystem* is a set of ... classes (and possibly other subsystems) collaborating to fulfill a common set of responsibilities.

They motivate their subsystems similarly:

> Subsystems are a concept used to simplify a design. The complexity of a large application can be dealt with by first identifying subsystems within it, and treating those subsystems as classes.

They take an explicit position regarding whether subsystems will show up ultimately in an implementation:

Subsystems are only conceptual entities; they do not exist during execution.

On the basis of our understanding of their subsystems, we have found here the most significant difference with respect to our ensembles. Certain ensembles introduced in the analysis phase may indeed be "compiled away" in the subsequent design phase, but we foresee that at least those ensembles which have their own regular attributes in addition to constituent attributes will show up in the implementation. This explains why we felt the necessity of introducing a forwarding mechanism for triggers/ messages in ensembles. In addition, we surmise that the encapsulation provided by ensembles - constituents cannot be reached directly from outside an ensemble - is not available in their subsystems.

In the European terrain, we see two approaches as relevant for the work described here. Jacobson [6] describes a development method for large object-oriented systems, called ObjectOry, that covers the analysis phase as well as the design phase. We discuss here only the analysis component. The core notions are: entities, interface objects and use cases. Entities correspond with the objects in the target domain. Interface objects are introduced to shield the "real" objects from the system interface with the users/ external world. Use cases - as far as we understand them - correspond with generic scenarios that define the target system's behavior from the perspective of a user. (A user is to be understood in a wide sense; i.e. it can be another system.) The material that we had available did not mention (sub)systems as a way to structure a target system. Use cases, however, do provide a global view. We suspect that a use case is a special case of the information captured by a state-transition model associated with the target system represented as an ensemble.

Beta [7] is a programming language and also a development technique. The Beta language simplifies the collection of object-oriented notions by simply providing *patterns* as the only concept for classes, methods, procedures and types. As a consequence, the analysis technique reflects this simplicity, and a lot of emphasis is put on modeling the communication between objects. Beta is one of the few object-oriented systems that emphatically supports concurrency in all steps of the development process. The Beta concurrency primitives for e.g. synchronization are similar to what we have suggested for triggers and services in our method. The difference is that they have already gained experience with implementing a particular communication scheme, and that they have restricted the analysis to that scheme (ADA-like rendez-vous). In our technique, the analyst has a degree of freedom to define and use his/her own communication scheme.

6 Summary and Conclusion

Object-oriented techniques, as practiced in OOP have a bottom-up flavor since OOP does not formalize and elaborate object decomposition. This is acceptable or even desirable in the programming phase. However, an analyst needs to operate - especially in the early phase - in a top-down fashion. In this paper, we have proposed ensembles as a mechanism for clustering tightly coupled objects. This mechanism supports top-down decomposition. We have illustrated ensembles with several examples.

A major distinction between ensembles and objects is that an ensemble connotes an entity with internal parallelism, while an object connotes - from the perspective of the task domain - a finite state machine. We associate with an ensemble a trigger/ message forwarding mechanism that mediates the interaction between external entities and the internal constituents of the ensemble. The examples discussed indicate that information hiding can be achieved indeed through ensembles.

Our ensembles resemble the sub-systems that are introduced for a similar purpose by Wirfs-Brock et al [14]. Their sub-systems appear to be a mental construct only while we foresee our ensembles to materialize ultimately in an implementation.

Experiments to validate the effectiveness of ensembles by applying the OOA method to larger real-life examples are ongoing.

Acknowledgement

George Woodmansee, Donna Ho, Penelope Faure and Teresa Parry provided illuminating feedback.

References

[1] Bailin, S.C., An Object-Oriented Requirements Specification Method, in *CACM*, vol 32, no 5, pp 608-623, 1989 May.

[2] Brachman, R.J., A Structural Paradigm for Representing Knowledge, Report 3605, BBN, 1978 May.

[3] Coad, P. & E. Yourdon, *Object-Oriented Analysis*, Yourdon Press, Prentice-Hall, 1990.

[4] de Champeaux, D., & W. Olthoff, Towards an Object-Oriented Analysis Method, *7th Annual Pacific Northwest Software Quality Conference*, pp 323-338, Portland OR, 1989.

[5] Goguen, J., Thatcher, J.W., Wagner, E.G., Wright, J.B., Initial Algebra Semantics and Continuous Algebras, *JACM*, vol 24, no 1, pp 68-75, 1977.

[6] Jacobson, I., Object-Oriented Development in an Industrial Environment, in *Proc. OOPSLA'87*, Orlando, Florida, pp 183-191, 1987 October.

[7] Kristensen, B., Madsen, O., Moller-Pedersen, B., Nygaard, K., Coroutine Sequencing in BETA, in Proceedings of the Twenty-First Annual Hawaii International Conference on System Sciences, vol II Software Track, pp 396-405, 1988 January

[8] Kurtz, B., Object-Oriented Systems Analysis and Specification: A Model-Driven Approach, M.Sc. Thesis, Brigham Young University, CS Dept., 1989.

[9] Shlaer, S. & S.J. Mellor, *Object-Oriented Systems Analysis*, Yourdon Press, 1988.

[10] Shlaer, S., S.J. Mellor, D. Ohlsen, W. Hywari, The Object-Oriented Method for Analysis, in *Proceedings of the 10th Structured Development Forum (SDF-X)*, San Francisco, 1988 August.

[11] VDM Specification Language Proto-Standard, SI VDM Working Paper IST 5/50/40, 1988.

[12] Ward, P.T., How to integrate Object Orientation with Structured Analysis and Design, in *IEEE Software*, pp 74-82, 1989 March.

[13] Ward, P.T. & S.J. Mellor, *Structured Development for Real-Time Systems*, Prentice-Hall, Englewood Cliffs NJ, 1985.

[14] Wirfs-Brock, R., B. Wilkerson & L. Wiener, *Designing Object-Oriented Software*, Prentice Hall, 1990.

Incremental Class Dictionary Learning and Optimization

Paul L. Bergstein and Karl J. Lieberherr
Northeastern University, College of Computer Science
Cullinane Hall, 360 Huntington Ave., Boston MA 02115
(pberg or lieber)@corwin.CCS.northeastern.EDU

Abstract

We have previously shown how the discovery of classes from objects can be automated, and how the resulting class organization can be efficiently optimized in the case where the optimum is a single inheritance class hierarchy. This paper extends our previous work by showing how an optimal class dictionary can be learned incrementally. The ability to expand a class organization incrementally as new object examples are presented is an important consideration in software engineering.

Keywords: Object-oriented programming and design, reverse engineering, class library organization, class abstraction algorithms.

1 Introduction

In class-based object-oriented languages, the user has to define classes before objects can be created. For the novice as well as for the experienced user, the class definitions are a non-trivial abstraction of the objects. We claim it is easier to initially describe certain example objects and to get a proposal for an optimal set of class definitions generated automatically than to write the class definitions by hand.

We have previously shown ([LBS90], [LBS91]) how the discovery of classes from objects can be automated, and how the resulting class organization can be efficiently optimized in the case where the optimum is a single inheritance class hierarchy. This paper extends our previous work in an important way: We show how an optimal class organization can be learned incrementally.

The algorithms discussed in this paper are a part of our research results in reverse engineering of programs from examples. In one line of research, we start with object examples and apply an abstraction algorithm described in this paper to get a set of class definitions. Then we apply a legalization algorithm to the class definitions to ensure that each recursive class definition is well behaved. Next, an optimization algorithm summarized in this paper makes the class definitions as small as possible while preserving the same set of objects. Then we apply an LL(1)-correction algorithm which adds some concrete syntax to the class definitions to make the object description language LL(1) for easy readability and learnability. The object description language allows very succinct object descriptions and the LL(1)-property guarantees that there is a one-to-one correspondence between sentences and objects. Finally we apply a C++ code generation algorithm to the class definitions which produces a tailored class library for manipulating the application objects (e.g., reading, printing, traversing, comparing, copying etc.).

This sequence of algorithms allows us to produce a tailored C++ library just from object examples. After the specific object implementations are injected into this library, we have the complete application code. The creative steps in this method of software development are 1) to find the right objects, 2) to find good replacements for the names which are generated by the abstraction programs, 3) to fine tune the object syntax and 4) to write the specific object implementations. However, it is much easier to start with a custom generated C++ class library than to proceed manually from the object examples. For further information on our research program in object-oriented software engineering, we refer the reader to the survey in [WJ90].

In section 2 the basic learning algorithm is formally presented. An informal presentation has been given in [LBS90]. This algorithm learns a correct (but not optimal) class dictionary graph from a list of object example graphs. An algorithm for learning class dictionary graphs incrementally is given in section 3. The ability to expand a class dictionary incrementally as new object examples are presented is an important consideration in software engineering. In section 4 the algorithm is extended to incrementally learn an optimal class dictionary graph when the optimum is a single inheritance class dictionary.

Our algorithms are programming language independent and are therefore useful to programmers who use object-oriented languages such as C++ [Str86], Smalltalk [GR83], CLOS [BDG*88] or Eiffel [Mey88]. We have implemented the abstraction algorithms as part of our C++ CASE tool, called the C++ Demeter System^{TM} [Lie88], [LR88]. The input to the abstraction algorithms is a list of object examples, and the output is a programming language independent set of class definitions. They can be improved by the user and then translated into C++ by the CASE tool.

We first describe our class definition and object example notations (the key concepts behind the algorithms we present in this paper), since they are not common in the object-oriented literature.

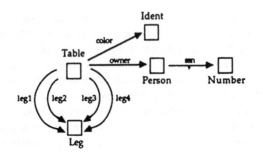

Figure 1: Construction class

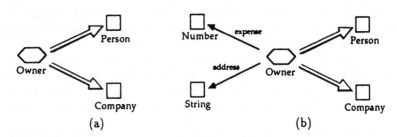

Figure 2: Alternation classes

1.1 Class notation

We use a class notation which uses two kinds of classes: construction and alternation classes.[1] A construction class definition is an abstraction of a class definition in a typical statically typed programming language (e.g., C++). A construction class does not reveal implementation information. Examples of construction classes are in Figure 1 for: Table, Leg, etc.

Each construction class defines a set of objects which can be thought of being elements of the direct product of the part classes. When modeling an application domain, it is natural to take the union of object sets defined by construction classes. For example, the owner of a table can be either a person or a company. So the objects we want to store in the owner part of the table are either person or company objects. We use alternation classes to define such union classes. An example of an alternation class is in Fig. 2a.

Person and Company are called alternatives of the alternation class. Often the alternatives have some common parts. For example, each owner had an expense to acquire the object. We use the notation in Fig. 2b to express such common parts.

Alternation classes have their origin in the variant records of Pascal. Because of the delayed

---

[1]In practice we use a third kind, called repetition classes, which can be expressed in terms of construction and alternation [Lie88].

binding of function calls to code in object-oriented programming, alternation classes are easier to use than variant records.

Alternation classes which have commc: parts are implemented by inheritance. In Fig. 2b, Person and Company inherit from Owner. Class Owner has methods and/or instance variables to implement the parts expense and address.

Construction and alternation classes correspond to the two basic data type constructions in denotational semantics: cartesian products and disjoint sums. They also correspond to the two basic mechanisms used in formal languages: concatenation and alternation.

Definition 1 *A class dictionary graph* ϕ *is a directed graph* $\phi = (V, \Lambda; \; EC, EA)$ *with finitely many labeled vertices* V. *There are two defining relations:* EC, EA. EC *is a ternary relation on* $V \times V \times \Lambda$, *called the (labeled) construction edges:* $(v, w, l) \in EC$ *iff there is a construction edge with label* l *from* v *to* w. Λ *is a finite set of construction edge labels.* EA *is a binary relation on* $V \times V$, *called the alternation edges:* $(v, w) \in EA$ *iff there is an alternation edge from* v *to* w.

Next we partition the set of vertices into two subclasses, called the construction and alternation vertices.

Definition 2 *We define*

- *the* construction vertices $VC = \{v \mid v \in V, \forall w \in V : (v, w) \notin EA\}$. *In other words, the construction vertices have no outgoing alternation edges.*

- *the* alternation vertices $VA = \{v \mid v \in V, \exists w \in V : (v, w) \in EA\}$. *In other words, the alternation vertices have at least one outgoing alternation edge.*

Sometimes, when we want to talk about the construction and alternation vertices, we describe a class dictionary graph as a tuple which contains explicit references to VC and VA: $\phi = (VC, VA, \Lambda; \; EC, EA)$.

Definition 3 *Vertex* $v_k \in V$ *in a class dictionary graph,* $\phi = (V, \Lambda; \; EC, EA)$, *is said to be* alternation reachable *from vertex* $v_0 \in V$ *via a path of length* $k \geq 1$, *if there exist* $k - 1$ *vertices* $v_1, v_2, ..., v_{k-1}$ *such that for all* j, $0 \leq j < k$, $(v_j, v_{j+1}) \in EA$. *The path consists of the sequence of alternation edges. We say that every vertex is alternation-reachable from itself.*

A legal class dictionary graph is a structure which satisfies two independent axioms.

Definition 4 *A class dictionary graph* $\phi = (VC, VA, \Lambda; \; EC, EA)$ *is* legal *if it satisfies the following two axioms:*

1. *Cycle-free alternation axiom:*

   There are no cyclic alternation paths, i.e., $\forall v \in VA$ there is no alternation path from v to v.

   The cycle-free alternation axiom is natural and has been proposed by other researchers, e.g., [PBF*89, page 396], [Sno89, page 109: Class names may not depend on themselves in a circular fashion involving only (alternation) class productions]. The axiom says that a class may not inherit from itself.

2. *Unique labels axiom:*

   $\forall w \in V$ there are no $p_1, p_2 \in V$ s.t. $\exists x, y \in V, l \in \Lambda$ s.t. $e_1 = (p_1, x, l) \in EC$ and $e_2 = (p_2, y, l) \in EC$, $e_1 \neq e_2$ and w is alternation reachable from p_1 and p_2.

   The unique labels axiom guarantees that "inherited" construction edges are uniquely labeled. Other mechanism for uniquely naming the construction edges could be used, e.g., the renaming mechanism of Eiffel [Mey88].

In the rest of this paper, when we refer to a class dictionary graph we mean a legal class dictionary graph.

We use the following graphical notation, based on [TYF86], for drawing class dictionary graphs: squares for construction vertices, hexagons for alternation vertices, thin arrows for construction edges and double arrows for alternation edges (see Figures 1 and 2).

1.2 Object example notation

The importance of objects extends beyond the programmer concerns of data and control abstraction and data hiding. Rather, objects are important because they allow the program to model some application domain in a natural way. In [MM88], the execution of an object-oriented program is viewed as a physical model consisting of objects, each object characterized by parts and a sequence of actions. It is the modeling that is significant, rather than the expression of the model in any particular programming language. We use a programming language independent object example notation to describe objects in any application domain.

The objects in the application domain are naturally grouped into classes of objects with similar subobjects. For our object example notation it is important that the designer names those classes consistently. Each object in the application domain has either explicitly named or numbered subobjects. It is again important for our object example notation that the explicitly named parts are named consistently. This consistency in naming classes and subparts is not difficult since it is naturally implied by the application domain.

An object is described by giving its class name, followed by the named parts. The parts are either physical parts of the object (e.g., legs of the table) or attributes or properties (e.g., owner or color). An object example is in Fig. 3 which defines a table object with 6 parts: 4 physical parts (legs) and two attributes: color and owner. The object example also indicates that the

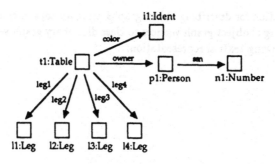

Figure 3: Table object

four legs have no parts and that the owner is a Person object with one part called ssn which is a Number.

Definition 5 *An* **object example graph with respect to a set of classes, S,** *is a graph* $H = (W, S, \Lambda_H; E, \lambda)$ *with vertex set* W. Λ_H *is a set of edge labels.* E *is a ternary relation on* $W \times W \times \Lambda_H$. *If* $(v, w, l) \in E$, *we call* l *the label of the labeled edge* (v, w, l), *from* v *to* w. *The function* $\lambda : W \to S$ *labels each vertex of* H *with an element of* S. *The following axioms must hold for* H:

(1) No vertex of H *may have two outgoing edges with the same label. (2) All vertices which have the same element* $s \in S$ *as label (under* λ*) must have either outgoing edges with the same labels or no outgoing edges at all.*

Definition 6 *An* **object graph with respect to a class dictionary graph,** ϕ
is an object example graph, $H = (W, S, \Lambda_H; E, \lambda)$ *with respect to set* S, *where* $S = VC_\phi$ *and* $\Lambda_H \subseteq \Lambda_\phi$.

Not every object graph with respect to a class dictionary graph is legal; intuitively, the object structure has to be consistent with the class definitions. For a formal definition of legality see [LBS91].

The set of all legal object graphs defined by a class dictionary graph ϕ is called $Objects(\phi)$.

When we optimize a class dictionary graph, we must insure that the optimized version defines the same set of objects. The following definition formalizes the concept that two sets of class definitions define the same set of objects.

Definition 7 *A class dictionary graph* $G1$ *is* **object-equivalent** *to a class dictionary graph* $G2$ *if* $Objects(G1) = Objects(G2)$.

We use a textual notation for describing object graphs using an adjacency representation which also shows the mapping of object graph vertices to class dictionary graph vertices. The example of Fig. 3 has the following textual representation:

```
t1:Table(
  <leg1> l1:Leg()
  <leg2> l2:Leg()
  <leg3> l3:Leg()
  <leg4> l4:Leg()
  <color> i1:Ident()
  <owner> p1:Person(
    <ssn> n1:Number())))
```

The vertices correspond to the instance names. The name after the instance name is preceded by a ":" and gives the label assigned by λ. The edge labels are between the < and > signs.

1.3   A simple example of incremental class dictionary learning

Example 1 *Consider the two object graphs which represent a basket containing two apples and a basket with an orange:*

```
b1:Basket(
  <contents> o1:OneOrMore(
                <one> a1:Apple( <weight> n1:Number())
                <more> o2:OneOrMore(
                            <one> a2:Apple( <weight> n2:Number())
                            <more> no1:None()))))

b1:Basket(
  <contents> o1:OneOrMore(
                <one> or1:Orange( <weight> n1:Number())
                <more> no1:None()))
```

After seeing the first object example graph, the learning algorithm generates the class dictionary graph in Fig. 4a. Now when the second object example is presented, the algorithm will learn the class dictionary graph in Fig. 4b.

Notice that the algorithm "invents" two abstract classes, *SeveralFruit* and *Fruit*. Since both subclasses of *Fruit* have a *weight* part, that part is attached to the *Fruit* class and is inherited in the *Apple* and *Orange* classes.

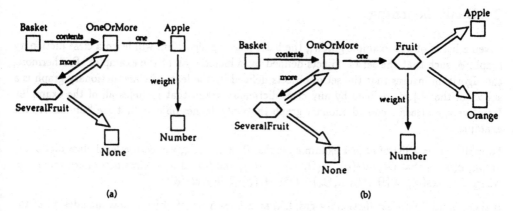

Figure 4: Fruit basket class dictionary graphs

A sample program to calculate the weight of a fruit basket is given below. All of the user written code is shown. The class definitions and remaining code are generated automatically from the class dictionary by the Demeter System CASE tool.

```
// Basket = <contents> SeveralFruit.
Number Basket::get_weight()
{ return contents->get_weight(); }

// SeveralFruit : None | OneOrMore.
virtual Number SeveralFruit::get_weight()
{}

// OneOrMore = <one> Fruit <more> SeveralFruit.
Number OneOrMore::get_weight()
{ return (one->get_weight() + more->get_weight()); }

// None = .
Number None::get_weight()
{ return Number(0); }

// Fruit : Apple | Orange *common* <weight> Number.
Number Fruit::get_weight()
{ return *weight; }
```

2   Basic Learning

Given a list of object example graphs, the basic learning algorithm will learn a class dictionary graph, ϕ, such that the set of objects defined by ϕ includes all of the examples. Furthermore, the algorithm insures that the set of objects defined by the learned class dictionary graph is a subset of the objects defined by any class dictionary graph that includes all of the examples. Intuitively, we learn a class dictionary graph that only defines objects that are "similar" to the examples.

Formally, given a list of object example graphs, $\Omega_1, \Omega_2, ..., \Omega_n$, we learn a legal class dictionary graph, ϕ, such that $Objects(\phi) \supseteq \{\Omega_1, \Omega_2, ..., \Omega_n\}$, and for all legal class dictionary graphs, ϕ' where $Objects(\phi') \supseteq \{\Omega_1, \Omega_2, ..., \Omega_n\} : Objects(\phi) \subseteq Objects(\phi')$.

If there is no legal class dictionary graph that defines a set of objects that includes all of the examples, we say that the list of object example graphs is not legal. The following definition gives the conditions under which a list of object example graphs is legal.

Definition 8 *A list of object example graphs $\Omega_1, ..., \Omega_n$ is legal if all vertices which have the same element $s \in S$ as label (under λ_{Ω_i} for some $i, 1 \leq i \leq n$) have either outgoing edges with the same labels (under E for Ω_i) or no outgoing edges at all.*

A legal list of object example graphs $\Omega_1, ..., \Omega_n$ of the form $\Omega = (W_\Omega, S_\Omega, \Lambda_\Omega; E_\Omega, \lambda_\Omega)$ is translated into a class dictionary graph $\phi = (V, \Lambda; EC, EA)$ as follows:

1. $\Lambda = \bigcup_{1 \leq i \leq n} \Lambda_{\Omega_i}$

   The construction edges of the class dictionary graph are given the same labels as the edges in the object example graph.

2. $VC = \{r \mid r = \lambda_{\Omega_i}(v) \text{ and } v \in W_{\Omega_i} \text{ where } 1 \leq i \leq n\}$

   We interpret λ as a function that maps objects to their classes. For each class that appears in an object example, we generate a construction class which is represented as a construction vertex in the class dictionary graph.

3. $VA = \{(r, l) \mid r \in VC, l \in \Lambda, \exists i, j, v1, v2, w1, w2 : (v1, w1, l) \in E_{\Omega_i}, (v2, w2, l) \in E_{\Omega_j},$
   $\lambda_{\Omega_i}(v1) = \lambda_{\Omega_j}(v2) = r, \lambda_{\Omega_i}(w1) \neq \lambda_{\Omega_j}(w2)\}$

   When we learn that objects of class r have a part labeled l that is not always of the same class, we create an abstract class represented in the class dictionary graph as an alternation vertex (r, l). In step 6, we will make each of the part's possible classes a subclass of the new abstract class.

4. $V = VC \cup VA$

   The vertices of the class dictionary graph are given by the union of the construction vertices and alternation vertices.

5. $EC = \{(r, s, l) \mid r, s \in V, \exists i, v, w : (v, w, l) \in E_{\Omega_i}, \lambda_{\Omega_i}(v) = r, \lambda_{\Omega_i}(w) = s, (r, l) \notin VA\}$
$\cup \{(r, (r, l), l) \mid r \in V, (r, l) \in VA\}$

If an object of class r has a part of class s with label l, then we create a construction edge from the construction vertex representing r to the construction vertex representing s with label l. But if the part can have more than one class, in which case an alternation vertex representing all of the possible classes was created in step 3, we instead create a construction edge to that alternation vertex.

6. $EA = \{((r, l), s) \mid (r, l) \in VA, s \in V, \exists i, v, w : (v, w, l) \in E_{\Omega_i}, \lambda_{\Omega_i}(v) = r, \lambda_{\Omega_i}(w) = s\}$

Finally, we create a alternation edge from each alternation vertex (representing an abstract class) to each vertex which represents a subclass.

The following example serves to illustrate the operation of the algorithm:

Example 2 .
Ω_1: $a1:A(\langle x\rangle\ b1:B(\langle y\rangle\ a2:A))$

- $W = \{a1, a2, b1\}$
- $S = \{A, B\}$
- $\Lambda = \{x, y\}$
- $E = \{(a1, b1, x), (b1, a2, y)\}$
- $\lambda_W = \{a1 \to A, a2 \to A, b1 \to B\}$

Ω_2: $a1:A(\langle x\rangle\ c1:C())$

- $W = \{a1, c1\}$
- $S = \{A, C\}$
- $\Lambda = \{x\}$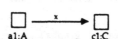
- $E = \{(a1, c1, x)\}$
- $\lambda_W = \{a1 \to A, c1 \to C\}$

ϕ :

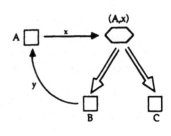

- $\Lambda = \{x, y\}$

- $VC = \{A, B, C\}$

- $VA = \{(A, x)\}$

- $V = \{A, B, C, (A, x)\}$

- $EC = \{(B, A, y), (A, (A, x), x)\}$

- $EA = \{((A, x), B), ((A, x), C)\}$

3 Incremental Learning

Given a class dictionary graph, ϕ, and an object example graph, Ω, the incremental learning algorithm will learn a class dictionary graph, ϕ', such that the set of objects defined by ϕ' includes Ω and all of the objects defined by ϕ. Furthermore, the algorithm insures that the set of objects defined by ϕ' is a subset of the objects defined by any class dictionary graph that includes Ω and all of the objects defined by ϕ. Intuitively, we extend the set of objects defined by ϕ only enough to include objects "similar" to Ω.

Formally, given a class dictionary graph, ϕ_1, and an object example graph, Ω, we learn a legal class dictionary graph, ϕ_2, such that $Objects(\phi_2) \supseteq Objects(\phi_1) \cup \Omega$, and for all legal class dictionary graphs, ϕ_3 where $Objects(\phi_3) \supseteq Objects(\phi_1) \cup \Omega$: $Objects(\phi_2) \subseteq Objects(\phi_3)$.

If there is no legal class dictionary graph that defines a set of objects that includes Ω and all of the objects defined by ϕ, we say that the object example graph Ω is not incrementally legal with respect to ϕ.

Definition 9 *An object example graph Ω is* incrementally legal *with respect to a class dictionary graph ϕ if there exists a legal class dictionary ϕ' such that $Objects(\phi') \supseteq Objects(\phi) \cup \Omega$.*

If a list of object example graphs $\Omega_1, ..., \Omega_n$ is legal, then each Ω_i in the list must be incrementally legal with respect to the class dictionary graph learned from $\Omega_1, ..., \Omega_{i-1}$. Therefore a class dictionary graph can be learned incrementally from a legal list of object example graphs.

Denote the intermediate class dictionary learned from $\Omega_1, \Omega_2, ..., \Omega_m$ by ϕ_m, and let $\phi_0 = (\emptyset, \emptyset; \emptyset, \emptyset)$. Then ϕ_m is learned from ϕ_{m-1} and Ω_m, where $1 \leq m \leq n$, as follows:

1. $\Lambda = \Lambda_{\phi_{m-1}} \cup \Lambda_{\Omega_m}$

   For each edge in the object example graph there is a construction edge in the class dictionary graph with the same label.

2. $VC = VC_{\phi_{m-1}} \cup \{r \mid \exists v \in W_{\Omega_m} : \lambda_W^{\Omega_m}(v) = r\}$

We interpret λ as a function that maps objects to their classes. For each new class that appears in the object example graph, we add a construction class which is represented as a construction vertex in the class dictionary graph.

3. $VA = VA_{\phi_{m-1}}$
$\cup \{(r,l) \mid r \in VC, l \in \Lambda, \exists v1, v2, w1, w2 \in W_{\Omega_m} :$
$\lambda_W^{\Omega_m}(v1) = \lambda_W^{\Omega_m}(v2) = r, \lambda_W^{\Omega_m}(w1) \neq \lambda_W^{\Omega_m}(w2), (v1, w1, l), (v2, w2, l) \in E_{\Omega_m}\}$
$\cup \{(r,l) \mid r \in VC, l \in \Lambda, \exists v, w \in W_{\Omega_m}, s \in VC :$
$\lambda_W^{\Omega_m}(v) = r, \lambda_W^{\Omega_m}(w) \neq s, (v, w, l) \in E_{\Omega_m}, (r, s, l) \in EC_{\phi_{m-1}}\}$

The first term represents the alternation vertices already learned in ϕ_{m-1}. The second term adds the alternations we learn from Ω_m alone (this is the same term as in the Basic Algorithm, where $\Omega_i = \Omega_j = \Omega_m$). The last term adds alternations that are learned in the Basic Algorithm when $\Omega_i \neq \Omega_j$. In the case of incremental learning we rely on the fact that the edges of $\Omega_1, ..., \Omega_{m-1}$ are recorded in ϕ_{m-1} as construction edges.

4. $V = VC \cup VA$

The vertices of the class dictionary graph are given by the union of the construction vertices and alternation vertices.

5. $EC = (EC_{\phi_{m-1}} - \{(r, s, l) \mid (r, l) \in (VA - VA_{\phi_{m-1}})\})$
$\cup \{(r, (r, l), l) \mid (r, l) \in (VA - VA_{\phi_{m-1}})\}$
$\cup \{(r, s, l) \mid r, s \in V, \exists v, w \in W_{\Omega_m} : \lambda_W^{\Omega_m}(v) = r, \lambda_W^{\Omega_m}(w) = s, (v, w, l) \in E_{\Omega_m}, (r, l) \notin VA\}$

We start with the construction edges in ϕ_{m-1}, but if we learned a new abstract class, represented by (r,l), we remove any construction edges to vertices representing subclasses of the new abstract class (first term) and replace them with construction edges to (r,l) (second term). Finally, the third term adds new construction edges learned from Ω_m.

6. $EA = EA_{\phi_{m-1}}$
$\cup \{((r, l), s)(r, l) \in VA, s \in V, \exists v, w \in W_{\Omega_m} : \lambda_W^{\Omega_m}(v) = r, \lambda_W^{\Omega_m}(w) = s, (v, w, l) \in E_{\Omega_m}\}$
$\cup \{((r, l), s)(r, l) \in VA, s \in V, (r, l, s) \in EC_{\phi_{m-1}}\}$

Here we start with the alternation edges from the previous class dictionary graph and add edges learned from Ω_m alone, and from Ω_m and ϕ_{m-1}. The three terms correspond to the three terms used to learn the alternation vertices in step 3.

The following theorem can be easily proven by induction on the length of the object example graph list:

Theorem 1 *A class dictionary graph learned incrementally is identical to the class dictionary graph learned using the basic learning algorithm.*

4 Incremental Optimization

In this section, we develop an algorithm for incrementally learning minimum single-inheritance class dictionary graphs. We measure class dictionary graphs by counting the number of edges, except that we consider construction edges to be at least twice as expensive as alternation edges. Consideration of this problem leads to some important observations regarding class dictionary design.

Informally, we say that a class dictionary graph is in common normal form (CNF) if it has no redundant parts. If a vertex, v, in a class dictionary graph has two incoming construction edges with the same label, l, the part (l, v) is redundant.

We observe that we can always avoid redundant parts by introducing multiple inheritance. Sometimes, we can avoid multiple inheritance by introducing redundant parts, but other times we can not eliminate multiple inheritance while maintaining object equivalence. When faced with a choice, multiple inheritance always produces the smaller class dictionary, since construction edges are at least twice as expensive as alternation edges.

In [LBS91] an efficient algorithm is presented for abstracting minimum single-inheritance class dictionary graphs from class dictionary graphs learned using the basic learning algorithm (section 2). It is shown that a class dictionary graph with no redundant parts (i.e., it is in class dictionary common normal form, or CNF), no useless alternation vertices, and with a single-inheritance hierarchy is guaranteed minimal. An alternation vertex is "useless" if it does not have at least two outgoing alternation edges.

Clearly, an incremental learning algorithm will produce a minimum single-inheritance class dictionary graph if with each new example the algorithm maintains a class dictionary graph that has a single-inheritance hierarchy and no redundant parts. We define the Incremental Single-Inheritance Minimum Class Dictionary Learning problem as follows:

Instance:
A minimum single-inheritance class dictionary graph, ϕ, and an object example graph, Ω, where Ω is incrementally·legal with respect to ϕ.

Problem:
Find a minimum single-inheritance class dictionary graph, ϕ', such that
$Objects(\phi') \supseteq Objects(\phi) \cup \Omega$.

In order to maintain the desired conditions in the intermediate class dictionary graphs, each new object example graph must meet two criteria:

1. If we learn from an object example graph, $H = (W, S, \Lambda_H; E, \lambda)$, that a class occurring in H (under λ) has a part in common with some other class, C, in the class dictionary it must have all the parts inherited by C.

2. If an object has a class with parts in common with two or more classes in the class dictionary, all of the classes with which it has parts in common must lie on a single alternation path.

It is easy to see how the incremental learning algorithm presented in section 3 can be extended to produce minimum single-inheritance class dictionaries.

5 Practical Relevance

In this paper we propose a metric (minimizing the number of edges) for measuring class hierarchies. We propose to minimize the number of construction and alternation edges of a class dictionary graph while keeping the set of objects invariant. Our technique is as good as the input which it gets: If the input does not contain the structural key abstractions of the application domain then the optimized hierarchy will not be useful either, following the maxim: garbage in – garbage out.

However if the input uses names consistently to describe either example objects or a class dictionary then our metric is useful in finding "good" hierarchies. However, we don't intend that our algorithms be used to restructure class hierarchies without human control. We believe that the output of our algorithms makes valuable proposals to the human designer who then makes a final decision.

Our current metric is quite rough: we just minimize the number of edges. We also minimize the amount of multiple inheritance (since this is consistent with minimizing edge size), but ignore other criteria such as the amount of repeated inheritance. This is left for future research.

We motivate now why our metric produces class hierarchies which are good from a software engineering point of view.

5.1 Minimizing the number of construction edges: CNF

We minimize the number of construction edges by eliminating redundant parts. We say a class dictionary with no redundant parts is in class dictionary common normal form (CNF).

Even simple functions cannot be implemented properly if a class dictionary is not in CNF. By properly we mean with resilience to change. Consider the class dictionary in Figure 5 which is not in CNF. Suppose we implement a print function for Coin and Brick. Now assume that several hundred years have passed and we find ourselves on the moon where the weight has a different composition: a gravity and a mass. We then have to rewrite our print function for both Coin and Brick.

After transformation to CNF we get the class dictionary in Figure 6. Now we implement the print function for Coin:

```
void Coin::print() { radius->print(); Weight_related::print(); }
```

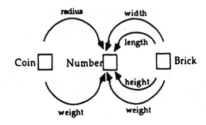

Figure 5: A class dictionary not in CNF

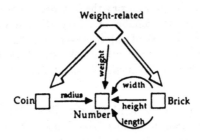

Figure 6: After transforming to CNF

After the change of the weight composition, we get the class dictionary in Figure 7. We reimplement the print function for this new class and no change is necessary for classes Brick and Coin.

In summary: if the class dictionary is in CNF and the functions are written following the strong Law of Demeter [LHR88], the software is more resilient to change. The strong Law of Demeter says that a function f attached to class C should only call functions of the *immediate* part classes of C, of argument classes of f, including C, and of classes which are instantiated in f.

Transformation to CNF can be more complicated, but not less beneficial, than the above example suggests.

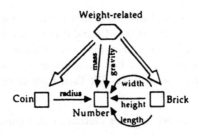

Figure 7: After change of weight composition

5.2 Minimizing the number of alternation edges

Consider the non-minimal class dictionary in Figure 8. By changing the class definitions for Occupation and Univ-employee we get the class dictionary in Figure 9. We have now reduced the number of alternation edges by 5 and have also reduced the amount of multiple inheritance, which we propose as another metric to produce "good" schemas from the software engineering point of view.

Another indication that our class dictionary optimization algorithm is useful is that it succeeds in finding single-inheritance solutions. We can prove the following statement: If we give a class dictionary which is object-equivalent to a single-inheritance class dictionary to the optimization algorithm, it will return such a single-inheritance class dictionary. From a software engineering standpoint, a single inheritance hierarchy is simpler than a multiple-inheritance hierarchy and our optimization algorithm will find such a hierarchy, if there is one.

6 Related work

Our work is a continuation of earlier work on inductive inference [CF82, Chapter XIV: Learning and inductive inference], [AS83]. Our contribution is an efficient algorithm for inductive inference of high-level class descriptions from examples. Related work has been done in the area of learning context-free grammars from examples and syntax trees [AS83]. The key difference to our work is that our approach learns grammars with a richer structure, namely the class dictionary graphs we learn, define both classes and languages.

In [Cas89,Cas90] and in his upcoming dissertation, Eduardo Casais introduces incremental class hierarchy reorganization algorithms. Those algorithms differ from our work in a number of ways:

- The models used are different. Casais uses general graphs while we use graphs with a special structure which has to satisfy two axioms needed for data modeling. For example, we distinguish between abstract and concrete classes.

- A step in Casais' incremental algorithm consists of adding a new subclass with potentially rejected attributes. In our work, an incremental step is adding a new object to a class hierarchy and to restructure the hierarchy so that it is optimal and at the same time describes the newly added object.

- The goal of Casais' algorithms is to restructure class hierarchies to avoid explicit rejection of inherited properties. In our work we avoid rejected properties.

- Casais' algorithms deal with operation signatures. In our work we have not added operation signatures yet. However, an operation of a class can be easily represented as a part by encoding the signature into the part's class name.

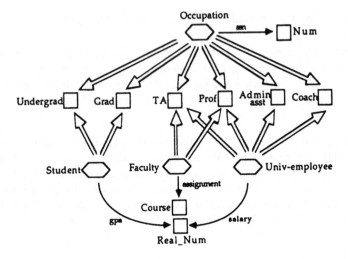

Figure 8: Before minimizing alternation edges

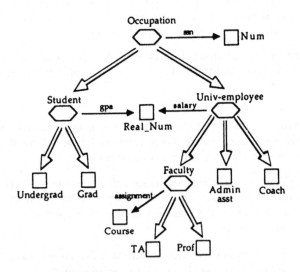

Figure 9: After alternation edge minimization

In [LM91] several ways in which conceptual database evolution can occur through learning are discussed. One of these, the generalization of types to form supertypes, is a special case of our abstraction of common parts, where there are only two objects from which the common parts are abstracted. Another, the expansion of a type into subtypes, is similar to the introduction of alternation vertices which occurs during the basic learning phase of our algorithm.

A major difference in our work is that we focus on learning from *examples*, while in [LM91] the emphasis is on learning from observation of *instances* (e.g., noticing that some of the instances of a type object have null values for a given attribute). Our examples are more general than instances since we don't supply values for attributes.

7 Conclusion

We have presented novel algorithms for incremental learning and optimization of class dictionaries. Earlier we have studied global class reorganization algorithms [LBS90], [LBS91]. Incremental algorithms are useful for at least two reasons:

First, incremental algorithms are much more efficient than global reorganization algorithms. If we have a class library with several hundred classes, we don't want to globally restructure all those classes if there is a small evolution of some class definition.

Second, incremental algorithms give further insight into the design process. They serve as a tool to understand change propagation when there is a change in the class structure.

Our algorithms are a useful ingredient to a tool suite for object-oriented design and programming and we have implemented them in the Demeter System.

Acknowledgments: We would like to thank Ignacio Silva-Lepe for the university example given in section 6.2.

References

[AS83]   Dana Angluin and Carl Smith. Inductive inference: theory. *ACM Computing Surveys*, 15(3):237–269, September 1983.

[BDG*88] D.G. Bobrow, L.G. DeMichiel, R.P. Gabriel, S.E. Keene, G. Kiczales, and D.A. Moon. Common Lisp Object System Specification. *SIGPLAN Notices*, 23, September 1988.

[Cas89]   Eduardo Casais. Reorganizing an object system. In Dennis Tsichritzis, editor, *Object Oriented Development*, pages 161–189, Centre Universitaire D'Informatique, Genève, 1989.

[Cas90]   Eduardo Casais. Managing class evolution in object-oriented systems. In Dennis Tsichritzis, editor, *Object Management*, pages 133–195, Centre Universitaire D'Informatique, Genève, 1990.

[CF82] Paul R. Cohen and Edward A. Feigenbaum. *The Handbook of Artificial Intelligence.* Volume 3, William Kaufmann, Inc., 1982.

[GR83] A. Goldberg and D. Robson. *Smalltalk-80: The Language and its Implementation.* Addison Wesley, 1983.

[LBS90] Karl J. Lieberherr, Paul Bergstein, and Ignacio Silva-Lepe. Abstraction of object-oriented data models. In Hannu Kangassalo, editor, *Proceedings of International Conference on Entity-Relationship*, pages 81–94, Elsevier, Lausanne, Switzerland, 1990.

[LBS91] Karl J. Lieberherr, Paul Bergstein, and Ignacio Silva-Lepe. From objects to classes: algorithms for optimal object-oriented design. *Software Engineering Journal*, 1991. Accepted for publication.

[LHR88] Karl J. Lieberherr, Ian Holland, and Arthur J. Riel. Object-oriented programming: an objective sense of style. In *Object-Oriented Programming Systems, Languages and Applications Conference, in Special Issue of SIGPLAN Notices*, pages 323–334, San Diego, CA., September 1988. A short version of this paper appears in IEEE Computer, June 88, Open Channel section, pages 78-79.

[Lie88] Karl Lieberherr. Object-oriented programming with class dictionaries. *Journal on Lisp and Symbolic Computation*, 1(2):185–212, 1988.

[LM91] Qing Li and Dennis McLeod. Conceptual database evolution through learning. In Rajiv Gupta and Ellis Horowitz, editors, *Object-oriented Databases with applications to CASE, networks and VLSI CAD*, pages 62–74, Prentice Hall Series in Data and Knowledge Base Systems, 1991.

[LR88] Karl J. Lieberherr and Arthur J. Riel. Demeter: a CASE study of software growth through parameterized classes. *Journal of Object-Oriented Programming*, 1(3):8–22, August, September 1988. A shorter version of this paper was presented at the *10th International Conference on Software Engineering, Singapore, April 1988, IEEE Press*, pages 254-264.

[Mey88] Bertrand Meyer. *Object-Oriented Software Construction. Series in Computer Science*, Prentice Hall International, 1988.

[MM88] Ole Lehrmann Madsen and Birger Møller-Pedersen. What object-oriented programming may be - and what it does not have to be. In S.Gjessing and K. Nygaard, editors, *European Conference on Object-Oriented Programming*, pages 1–20, Springer Verlag, Oslo, Norway, 1988.

[PBF*89] B. Pernici, F. Barbic, M.G. Fugini, R. Maiocchi, J.R. Rames, and C. Rolland. C-TODOS: an automatic tool for office system conceptual design. *ACM Transactions on Office Information Systems*, 7(4):378–419, October 1989.

[Sno89]   Richard Snodgrass. *The interface description language*. Computer Science Press, 1989.

[Str86]   B. Stroustrup. *The C++ Programming Language*. Addison Wesley, 1986.

[TYF86]   T.J. Teorey, D. Yang, and J.P. Fry. A logical design methodology for relational data bases. *ACM Computing Surveys*, 18(2):197–222, June 1986.

[WJ90]   Rebecca J. Wirfs-Brock and Ralph E. Johnson. A survey of current research in object-oriented design. *Communications of the ACM*, 33(9):104–124, September 1990. The description of the Demeter project starts on page 120.

Lecture Notes in Computer Science

For information about Vols. 1–420
please contact your bookseller or Springer-Verlag

Vol. 464: J. Dassow, J. Kelemen (Eds.), Aspects and Prospects of Theoretical Computer Science. Proceedings, 1990. VI, 298 pages. 1990.

Vol. 465: A. Fuhrmann, M. Morreau (Eds.), The Logic of Theory Change. Proceedings, 1989. X, 334 pages. 1991. (Subseries LNAI).

Vol. 466: A. Blaser (Ed.), Database Systems of the 90s. Proceedings, 1990. VIII, 334 pages. 1990.

Vol. 467: F. Long (Ed.), Software Engineering Environments. Proceedings, 1969. VI, 313 pages. 1990.

Vol. 468: S.G. Akl, F. Fiala, W.W. Koczkodaj (Eds.), Advances in Computing and Information – ICCI '90. Proceedings, 1990. VII, 529 pages. 1990.

Vol. 469: I. Guessarian (Ed.), Semantics of Systeme of Concurrent Processes. Proceedings, 1990. V, 456 pages. 1990.

Vol. 470: S. Abiteboul, P.C. Kanellakis (Eds.), ICDT '90. Proceedings, 1990. VII, 528 pages. 1990.

Vol. 471: B.C. Ooi, Efficient Query Processing in Geographic Information Systems. VIII, 208 pages. 1990.

Vol. 472: K.V. Nori, C.E. Veni Madhavan (Eds.), Foundations of Software Technology and Theoretical Computer Science. Proceedings, 1990. X, 420 pages. 1990.

Vol. 473: I.B. Damgård (Ed.), Advances in Cryptology – EUROCRYPT '90. Proceedings, 1990. VIII, 500 pages. 1991.

Vol. 474: D. Karagiannis (Ed.), Information Syetems and Artificial Intelligence: Integration Aspects. Proceedings, 1990. X, 293 pages. 1991. (Subseries LNAI).

Vol. 475: P. Schroeder-Heister (Ed.), Extensions of Logic Programming. Proceedings, 1989. VIII, 364 pages. 1991. (Subseries LNAI).

Vol. 476: M. Filgueiras, L. Damas, N. Moreira, A.P. Tomás (Eds.), Natural Language Processing. Proceedings, 1990. VII, 253 pages. 1991. (Subseries LNAI).

Vol. 477: D. Hammer (Ed.), Compiler Compilers. Proceedings, 1990. VI, 227 pages. 1991.

Vol. 478: J. van Eijck (Ed.), Logics in AI. Proceedings, 1990. IX, 562 pages. 1991. (Subseries in LNAI).

Vol. 480: C. Choffrut, M. Jantzen (Eds.), STACS 91. Proceedings, 1991. X, 549 pages. 1991.

Vol. 481: E. Lang, K.-U. Carstensen, G. Simmons, Modelling Spatial Knowledge on a Linguistic Basis. IX, 138 pages. 1991. (Subseries LNAI).

Vol. 482: Y. Kodratoff (Ed.), Machine Learning – EWSL-91. Proceedings, 1991. XI, 537 pages. 1991. (Subseries LNAI).

Vol. 483: G. Rozenberg (Ed.), Advances In Petri Nets 1990. VI, 515 pages. 1991.

Vol. 484: R. H. Möhring (Ed.), Graph-Theoretic Concepts In Computer Science. Proceedings, 1990. IX, 360 pages. 1991.

Vol. 485: K. Furukawa, H. Tanaka, T. Fullsaki (Eds.), Logic Programming '89. Proceedings, 1989. IX, 183 pages. 1991. (Subseries LNAI).

Vol. 486: J. van Leeuwen, N. Santoro (Eds.), Distributed Algorithms. Proceedings, 1990. VI, 433 pages. 1991.

Vol. 487: A. Bode (Ed.), Distributed Memory Computing. Proceedings, 1991. XI, 506 pages. 1991.

Vol. 488: R. V. Book (Ed.), Rewriting Techniques and Applications. Proceedings, 1991. VII, 458 pages. 1991.

Vol. 489: J. W. de Bakker, W. P. de Roever, G. Rozenberg (Eds.), Foundations of Object-Oriented Languages. Proceedings, 1990. VIII, 442 pages. 1991.

Vol. 490: J. A. Bergstra, L. M. G. Feljs (Eds.), Algebraic Methods II: Theory, Tools and Applications. VI, 434 pages. 1991.

Vol. 491: A. Yonezawa, T. Ito (Eds.), Concurrency: Theory, Language, and Architecture. Proceedings, 1989. VIII, 339 pages. 1991.

Vol. 492: D. Sriram, R. Logcher, S. Fukuda (Eds.), Computer-Aided Cooperative Product Development. Proceedings, 1989 VII, 630 pages. 1991.

Vol. 493: S. Abramsky, T. S. E. Maibaum (Eds.), TAPSOFT '91. Volume 1. Proceedings, 1991. VIII, 455 pages. 1991.

Vol. 494: S. Abramsky, T. S. E. Maibaum (Eds.), TAPSOFT '91. Volume 2. Proceedings, 1991. VIII, 482 pages. 1991.

Vol. 495: 9. Thalheim, J. Demetrovics, H.-D. Gerhardt (Eds.), MFDBS '91. Proceedings, 1991. VI, 395 pages. 1991.

Vol. 496: H.-P. Schwefel, R. Männer (Eds.), Parallel Problem Solving from Nature. Proceedings, 1991. XI, 485 pages. 1991.

Vol. 497: F. Dehne, F. Fiala. W.W. Koczkodaj (Eds.), Advances in Computing and Intormation - ICCI '91 Proceedings, 1991. VIII, 745 pages. 1991.

Vol. 498: R. Andersen, J. A. Bubenko jr., A. Sølvberg (Eds.), Advanced Information Systems Engineering. Proceedings, 1991. VI, 579 pages. 1991.

Vol. 499: D. Christodoulakis (Ed.), Ada: The Choice for '92. Proceedings, 1991. VI, 411 pages. 1991.

Vol. 500: M. Held, On the Computational Geometry of Pocket Machining. XII, 179 pages. 1991.

Vol. 501: M. Bidoit, H.-J. Kreowski, P. Lescanne, F. Orejas, D. Sannella (Eds.), Algebraic System Specification and Development. VIII, 98 pages. 1991.

Vol. 502: J. Bārzdiņš, D. Bjørner (Eds.), Baltic Computer Science. X, 619 pages. 1991.

Vol. 503: P. America (Ed.), Parallel Database Systems. Proceedings, 1990. VIII, 433 pages. 1991.

Vol. 504: J. W. Schmidt, A. A. Stogny (Eds.), Next Generation Information System Technology. Proceedings, 1990. IX, 450 pages. 1991.

Vol. 505: E. H. L. Aarts, J. van Leeuwen, M. Rem (Eds.), PARLE '91. Parallel Architectures and Languages Europe, Volume I. Proceedings, 1991. XV, 423 pages. 1991.

Vol. 506: E. H. L. Aarts, J. van Leeuwen, M. Rem (Eds.), PARLE '91. Parallel Architectures and Languages Europe, Volume II. Proceedings, 1991. XV, 489 pages. 1991.

Vol. 507: N. A. Sherwani, E. de Doncker, J. A. Kapenga (Eds.), Computing in the 90's. Proceedings, 1989. XIII, 441 pages. 1991.

Vol. 508: S. Sakata (Ed.), Applied Algebra, Algebraic Algorithms and Error-Correcting Codes. Proceedings, 1990. IX, 390 pages. 1991.

Vol. 509: A. Endres, H. Weber (Eds.), Software Development Environments and CASE Technology. Proceedings, 1991. VIII, 286 pages. 1991.

Vol. 510: J. Leach Albert, B. Monien, M. Rodríguez (Eds.), Automata, Languages and Programming. Proceedings, 1991. XII, 763 pages. 1991.

Vol. 511: A. C. F. Colchester, D.J. Hawkes (Eds.), Information Processing in Medical Imaging. Proceedings, 1991. XI, 512 pages. 1991.

Vol. 512: P. America (Ed.), ECOOP '91. European Conference on Object-Oriented Programming. Proceedings, 1991. X, 396 pages. 1991.